T0270907

Econometric Analysis of Stochastic Dominance

This book offers an up-to-date, comprehensive coverage of stochastic dominance and its related concepts in a unified framework. A method for ordering probability distributions, stochastic dominance has grown in importance recently as a way to measure comparisons in welfare economics, inequality studies, health economics, insurance wages, and trade patterns. Whang pays particular attention to inferential methods and applications, citing and summarizing various empirical studies in order to relate the econometric methods with real applications and using computer codes to enable the practical implementation of these methods. Intuitive explanations throughout the book ensure that readers understand the basic technical tools of stochastic dominance.

Yoon-Jae Whang is Professor of Economics at Seoul National University. He is an elected fellow of the Econometric Society and the *Journal of Econometrics* and is Co-Director of the Center for Econometrics at Seoul National University.

Themes in Modern Econometrics

Series Editor
PETER C. B. PHILLIPS, *Sterling Professor of Economics, Yale University*

Themes in Modern Econometrics provides an organized sequence of advanced textbooks in econometrics aimed directly at the student population and is the first series in the discipline to have this as its express aim. Written at a level accessible to those who have completed an introductory course in econometrics, each book addresses topics and themes that students and researchers encounter daily. All areas of econometrics are covered within the series. Particular emphasis is given to theory fundamentals and practical implementation in breaking research areas that are relevant to empirical applications. Each book stands alone as an authoritative survey in its own right. The distinct emphasis throughout is on pedagogic excellence and accessibility.

Books in the Series
Structural Vector Autoregressive Analysis (2017) LUTZ KILIAN *and* HELMUT LÜTKEPOHL
Almost All About Unit Roots (2015) IN CHOI
Granularity Theory with Applications to Finance and Insurance (2014) PATRICK GAGLIARDINI *and* CHRISTIAN GOURIÉROUX,
Econometric Modeling with Time Series (2012) VANCE MARTIN, STAN HURN, *and* DAVID HARRIS
Economic Modeling and Inference (2007) JEAN-PIERRE FLORENSE, VELAYOUDOM MARIMOUTOU, *and* ANNE PEGUIN-FEISSOLLE *Translated by* JOSEF PERKTOLD *and* MARINE CARRASCO
Introduction to the Mathematical and Statistical Foundations of Econometrics (2004) HERMAN J. BIERENS
Applied Time Series Econometrics (2004) HELMUT LÜTKEPOHL *and* MARKUS KRÄTZIG
Semiparametric Regression for the Applied Econometrician (2003) ADONIS YATCHEW
The Econometric Analysis of Seasonal Time Series (2001) ERIC GHYSELS *and* DENISE R. OSBORN
Econometrics of Qualitative Dependent Variables (2000) CHRISTIAN GOURIEROUX *Translated by* PAUL B. KLASSEN
Nonparametric Econometrics (1999) ADRIAN PAGAN *and* AMAN ULLAH
Generalized Method of Moments Estimation (1999) *Edited by* LÁSZLÓ MÁTYÁS
Unit Roots, Cointegration, and Structural Change (1999) G.S. MADDALA *and* IN-MOO KIM
Time Series and Dynamic Models (1997) CHRISTIAN GOURIEROUX *and* ALAIN MONFORT *Translated and edited by* GIAMPIERO GALLO
Statistics and Econometric Models: Volumes 1 and 2 (1995) CHRISTIAN GOURIEROUX *and* ALAIN MONFORT *Translated by* QUANG VUONG

ECONOMETRIC ANALYSIS OF STOCHASTIC DOMINANCE

Concepts, Methods, Tools, and Applications

YOON-JAE WHANG
Seoul National University

CAMBRIDGE
UNIVERSITY PRESS

CAMBRIDGE
UNIVERSITY PRESS

Shaftesbury Road, Cambridge CB2 8EA, United Kingdom

One Liberty Plaza, 20th Floor, New York, NY 10006, USA

477 Williamstown Road, Port Melbourne, VIC 3207, Australia

314–321, 3rd Floor, Plot 3, Splendor Forum, Jasola District Centre, New Delhi – 110025, India

103 Penang Road, #05–06/07, Visioncrest Commercial, Singapore 238467

Cambridge University Press is part of Cambridge University Press & Assessment, a department of the University of Cambridge.

We share the University's mission to contribute to society through the pursuit of education, learning and research at the highest international levels of excellence.

www.cambridge.org
Information on this title: www.cambridge.org/9781108472791

DOI: 10.1017/9781108602204

Yoon-Jae Whang © 2019

First published 2019

A catalogue record for this publication is available from the British Library

Library of Congress Cataloging-in-Publication data
Names: Whang, Yoon-Jae, author.
Title: Econometric analysis of stochastic dominance: concepts, methods, tools, and applications / Yoon-Jae Whang, Seoul National University.
Description: New York : Cambridge University Press, [2018] |
    Includes bibliographical references and index.
Identifiers: LCCN 2018012045 | ISBN 9781108472791 (alk. paper)
Subjects: LCSH: Economics, Mathematical. | Stochastic processes. |
    Mathematical statistics.
Classification: LCC HB135 .W464 2018 | DDC 330.01/51923–dc23
LC record available at https://lccn.loc.gov/2018012045

ISBN   978-1-108-47279-1   Hardback

To my parents
and
Mi Kyung, Sun Young, and Soo Young

Contents

x　　　**Contents**

Figures

Tables

Preface

Stochastic dominance (SD) is an ordering rule of distribution functions. Since the work of Hadar and Russell (1969), Hanoch and Levy (1969), and Rothschild and Stiglitz (1970), the concept has been theoretically explored and empirically implemented in various areas including economics, finance, insurance, medicine, and statistics. The stochastic dominance rule is based on the expected utility paradigm and gives a uniform ordering of prospects that does not depend on specific utility (or social welfare) functions. For example, it can produce a majority assessment (valid over a large class of utility functions) on investment strategies, welfare outcomes (income distributions or poverty levels), and program evaluation exercises. In contrast, the traditional strong orders, based on specific indices of inequality or poverty in welfare, mean-variance analysis in finance, or performance indices in program evaluation, do not achieve consensus. In addition, the stochastic dominance rule does not require restrictive parametric assumptions on the distributions of the prospects.

Since the early work of McFadden (1989), a substantial body of literature has been developed on nonparametric inference on stochastic dominance and its related concepts. The stochastic dominance relation corresponds to an inequality restriction between (functionals of) nonparametric distribution functions. Not only is its statistical inference complicated, but it is also multifarious; since the concept of stochastic dominance itself has many variants in different contexts, it calls for separate inference procedures.

The purpose of this book is to provide an overview of the literature in a unified framework, with a focus on recent developments. There are excellent books on stochastic dominance, including Levy (2016) and Sriboonchita, Wong, Dhompongsa, and Nguyen (2010). There are also several surveys: Levy (1992), Maasoumi (2001), Davidson (2010), and Guo (2013). However, the main focus of the two books mentioned is on the theoretical aspects of stochastic dominance rules in finance, rather than on statistical inference for the rules. Also, the coverage of the surveys is somewhat limited. In contrast, this book provides up-to-date and comprehensive coverage of the inference methods proposed in the literature. This book also cites and summarizes several empirical studies that employ the inference methods, so that the reader can relate the econometric methods to real applications.

This book is intended for graduate students and researchers in economics and other sciences who are interested in applications of the stochastic dominance rules. It is also useful to theoretical econometricians as a reference, because it shows several examples of using modern econometric tools to compare functional variables and suggests some open questions. It is expected that the reader has a good background in econometrics at the level of, for example, Greene (2012) or Hayashi (2000). Some knowledge of nonparametric inference methods and probability theory would be desirable but is not essential.

I am grateful to many people who helped me in the writing of this book in one way or another. First of all, I would like to thank my advisors, Professors Don Andrews and Peter Phillips at Yale, for their encouragement and support in the early 1990s. My special thanks also go to Oliver Linton, who introduced me to the fascinating topic of stochastic dominance, and who has been working together with me on various subjects over the past decades. I am also grateful to Gordon Anderson and Kyungchul Song, who read an earlier version of the entire manuscript and gave me very useful comments. I also owe a great intellectual debt to Xiaohong Chen, Doo-Bong Han, Yuichi Kitamura, Sokbae Lee, Haim Levy, Essie Maasoumi, Taisuke Otsu, Joon Park, Thierry Post, and Myung Hwan Seo. Parts of this book were written while I was visiting the Cowles Foundation at Yale, whose hospitality is gratefully acknowledged. Deborah Kim (now a graduate student at Northwestern) wrote the MATLAB code in Appendix B, which I deeply appreciate. I also thank Yeongmi Jeong, MinKyung Kim, Sue-Youl Kim, and Jaewon Lee (now a graduate student at Yale) for their excellent research assistance. Thanks also go to Jooyoung Cha, Danbi Chung, Jae Yu Jung, Eunsun Kim, Hyunkyeong Lim, and Siwon Ryu for their careful proofreading. This book was financially supported by the Korea Research Foundation Grant funded by the Korean Government (NRF-2011-342-B00004).

Last, but not least, my warmest thanks go to my parents, my wife Mi Kyung, and my daughters Sun Young and Soo Young, for their love and support. They have been the most important source of my personal strength throughout my academic life.

Abbreviations and Notation

CDF	cumulative distribution function
CDTE	conditional distributional treatment effect
CLT	central limit theorem
EL	empirical likelihood
FSD	first-order stochastic dominance
i.i.d.	independent and identically distributed
LCM	least concave majorant
LFC	least favorable case
PDF	probability density function
QTE	quantile treatment effect
SD	stochastic dominance
SDE	stochastic dominance efficiency
SM	stochastic monotonicity
SMM	studentized maximum modulus
SSD	second-order stochastic dominance
TSD	third-order stochastic dominance
WLLN	weak law of large numbers
$\succeq_s$	stochastic dominance at order s
$F^{(s)}(x)$	integrated CDF at order s
$\bar{F}^{(s)}(x)$	integrated empirical CDF at order s
$D_{1,2}^{(s)}(x)$	difference $F_1^{(s)}(x) - F_2^{(s)}(x)$ between integrated CDFs
$\bar{D}_{1,2}^{(s)}(x)$	difference $\bar{F}_1^{(s)}(x) - \bar{F}_2^{(s)}(x)$ between integrated empirical CDFs
$Q^{(s)}(x)$	integrated quantile function at order s
$[x]_+$	$\max\{x, 0\}$ (i.e., maximum of x and 0)
$[x]_-$	$\min\{x, 0\}$ (i.e., minimum of x and 0)
$a \vee b$	$\max\{a, b\}$ (i.e., maximum of a and b)
$a \wedge b$	$\min\{a, b\}$ (i.e., minimum of a and b)
$sgn(x)$	sign of x
$\to_p$	convergence in probability

$\Rightarrow$	convergence in distribution or weak convergence
$x := y$	equality by definition (i.e., x and y are equal by definition)
$X \stackrel{d}{=} Y$	equality in distributions (i.e., X and Y have the same distribution)
A^{T}	transpose of matrix A
$f'(x)$	first-derivative of f with respect to x
$f''(x)$	second-derivative of f with respect to x
$\mathbb{Z}$	standard normal random variable, $N(0, 1)$
$U(a, b)$	uniform distribution on (a, b)

1 Introduction

This chapter begins with the basic concepts and properties of stochastic dominance. It then gives examples of applications of stochastic dominance to various fields in economics: welfare analysis, finance, industrial organization, labor, international, health, and agricultural economics. The final subsection gives an overview of the subsequent chapters.

1.1 Concepts of Stochastic Dominance

1.1.1 Definitions

First-Order Stochastic Dominance (FSD) Let X_1 and X_2 be two (continuous) random variables with the cumulative distribution functions (CDFs) given by F_1 and F_2, respectively.[1] In economic applications, they typically correspond to incomes or financial returns of two different populations, which may vary regarding time, geographical regions or countries, or treatments. For $k = 1, 2$, let $Q_k(\tau) = \inf\{x : F_k(x) \geq \tau\}$ denote the quantile function of X_k, respectively, and let $\mathcal{U}_1$ denote the class of all monotone increasing (utility or social welfare) functions. If the functions are assumed to be differentiable, then we may write

$$\mathcal{U}_1 = \{u(\cdot) : u' \geq 0\}.$$

Definition 1.1.1 *The random variable X_1 is said to first-order stochastically dominate the random variable X_2, denoted by $F_1 \succeq_1 F_2$ (or X_1 FSD X_2),[2] if*

---

[1] Stochastic dominance can be defined for discrete or mixed continuous–discrete distributions. However, for the purpose of explanation, we shall mainly focus on continuous random variables, unless it is stated otherwise.

[2] To denote stochastic dominance relations, it is a convention to freely exchange the random variables with their respective distribution functions. For example, for first-order stochastic dominance, we may write $X_1 \succeq_1 X_2$ or F_1 FSD F_2. The same rule applies to the other concepts of stochastic dominance defined later.

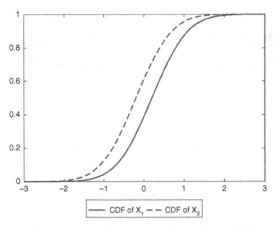

Figure 1.1 X_1 first-order stochastically dominates X_2

any of the following equivalent conditions holds: (1) $F_1(x) \leq F_2(x)$ for all $x \in \mathbb{R}$; *(2) $E[u(X_1)] \geq E[u(X_2)]$ for all $u \in \mathcal{U}_1$; and (3) $Q_1(\tau) \geq Q_2(\tau)$ for all $\tau \in [0, 1]$.*

This is the definition of *weak* stochastic dominance. If the inequalities hold with strict inequality for some $x \in \mathbb{R}$, some $u \in \mathcal{U}_1$, and some $\tau \in [0, 1]$, then the above serves as the definition of *strong* stochastic dominance, while one has *strict* stochastic dominance if the inequalities hold with strict inequality for all $x \in \mathbb{R}$, all $u \in \mathcal{U}_1$, and all $\tau \in [0, 1]$.[3] The equivalence of the three definitions will be discussed below.

Figure 1.1 illustrates two distributions with a first-order stochastic dominance relation. It shows that, when X_1 FSD X_2, the CDF of X_1 lies below that of X_2. To interpret the FSD relation, suppose that the random variables correspond to incomes of two different populations. Then, the inequality $F_1(x) \leq F_2(x)$ implies that the proportion of individuals in population 1 with incomes less than or equal to an income level x is not larger than the proportion of such individuals in population 2. If we measure poverty by the proportion of individuals earning less than a predetermined level of income (poverty line) x, then this implies that, whatever poverty line we choose, we have less poverty in F_1 than in F_2.[4] Therefore, the distribution F_1 would be preferred by any social planner having a welfare function that respects monotonicity ($u \in \mathcal{U}_1$),

---

[3] This classification is adopted from McFadden (1989, p. 115). The distinction among weak, strong, and strict dominance could be important in theoretical arguments. However, from a statistical point of view, the theoretically distinct hypotheses often induce the same test statistic and critical region, and hence the distinction is not very important; see McFadden (1989) and Davidson and Duclos (2000) for this point.

[4] See Section 5.2 for a general discussion about the relationship between poverty and SD concepts.

explaining the fact that we say that F_1 first-order stochastically dominates F_2 when the dominance of the CDFs as functions is the other way around.

To explain the FSD relation in an alternative perspective, write the (weak) first-order stochastic dominance relation $F_1 \succeq_1 F_2$ as

$$P(X_1 > x) \geq P(X_2 > x) \text{ for all } x \in \mathbb{R}. \tag{1.1.1}$$

Consider a portfolio choice problem of an investor and suppose that the random variables denote returns of some financial assets. Then, (1.1.1) implies that, for all values of x, the probability of obtaining returns not less than x is larger under F_1 than under F_2. Such a probability would be desired by every investor who prefers higher returns, explaining again the first-order stochastic dominance of F_1 over F_2. Conversely, if the two CDFs intersect, then (1.1.1) does not hold. In this case, one could find an investor with utility function $u \in \mathcal{U}_1$ such that $E[u(X_1)] > E[u(X_2)]$, and another investor with utility function $v \in \mathcal{U}_1$ such that $E[v(X_1)] < E[v(X_2)]$, violating the FSD of F_1 over F_2.

Second-Order Stochastic Dominance (SSD) To define the second-order stochastic dominance, let $\mathcal{U}_2$ denote the class of all monotone increasing and concave (utility or social welfare) functions. If the functions are assumed to be twice differentiable, then we may write

$$\mathcal{U}_2 = \{u(\cdot) : u' \geq 0, \ u'' \leq 0\}.$$

Definition 1.1.2 *The random variable X_1 is said to second-order stochastically dominate the random variable X_2, denoted by $F_1 \succeq_2 F_2$ (or X_1 SSD X_2), if any of the following equivalent conditions holds: (1) $\int_{-\infty}^{x} F_1(t)dt \leq \int_{-\infty}^{x} F_2(t)dt$ for all $x \in \mathbb{R}$; (2) $E[u(X_1)] \geq E[u(X_2)]$ for all $u \in \mathcal{U}_2$; and (3) $\int_0^{\tau} Q_1(p)dp \geq \int_0^{\tau} Q_2(p)dp$ for all $\tau \in [0, 1]$.*

For SSD, the accumulated area under F_1 must be smaller than the counterpart under F_2 below any value of x. If X_1 first-order dominates X_2, or equivalently, if $F_1(x)$ is smaller than $F_2(x)$ for all x, then it is easy to see that X_1 second-order dominates X_2, but the converse is not true.

Figure 1.2 illustrates that, even when there is no first-order stochastic dominance between them (i.e., when the two CDFs intersect), X_1 may second-order stochastically dominate X_2.

To have second-order stochastic dominance $F_1 \succeq_2 F_2$, for any negative area ($F_2 < F_1$) there should be a positive area ($F_1 < F_2$) which is greater than or equal to the negative area and which is located before the negative area. To relate this to the second definition (2) of SSD, consider the expression

$$E[u(X_1)] - E[u(X_2)] = \int_{-\infty}^{\infty} [F_2(x) - F_1(x)] \, u'(x)dx,$$

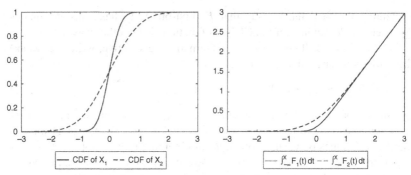

Figure 1.2 X_1 does not first-order stochastically dominate X_2, but X_1 second-order stochastically dominates X_2

which follows from integration by parts under regularity conditions (lemma 1 of Hanoch and Levy 1969; see also Equation 1.1.6). Whenever u' is a decreasing function (i.e., $u'' < 0$), the positive area is multiplied by a larger number $u'(x) > 0$ than the negative area which comes later on, so that the total integral becomes non-negative, establishing the second-order stochastic dominance of X_1 over X_2 under Definition 1.1.2 (2).

In the analysis of income distributions, the concavity assumption $u'' \leq 0$ implies that a transfer of income from a richer to a poorer individual always increases social welfare, which is a weaker form of the transfer principle (Dalton 1920). In the portfolio choice problem, on the other hand, the concavity assumption reflects risk aversion of an investor. That is, a risk-averse investor would prefer a portfolio with a guaranteed payoff to a portfolio without the guarantee, provided they have the same expected return. Therefore, the definition implies that any risk-averse investor would prefer a portfolio which dominates the other in the sense of SSD, because it yields a higher expected utility.

Higher-Order Stochastic Dominance The concept of stochastic dominance can be extended to higher orders. Higher-order SD relations correspond to increasingly smaller subsets of utility functions. Davidson and Duclos (2000) offer a very useful characterization of stochastic dominance of any order.

For $k = 1, 2$, define the *integrated CDF* and the *integrated quantile function* to be

$$F_k^{(s)}(x) = \begin{cases} F_k(x) & \text{for } s = 1 \\ \int_{-\infty}^x F_k^{(s-1)}(t)dt & \text{for } s \geq 2 \end{cases} \tag{1.1.2}$$

and

$$Q_k^{(s)}(x) = \begin{cases} Q_k(x) & \text{for } s = 1 \\ \int_0^x Q_k^{(s-1)}(t)dt & \text{for } s \geq 2. \end{cases} \tag{1.1.3}$$

respectively. For $s \geq 1$, let

$$\mathcal{U}_s = \{u(\cdot) : u' \geq 0, u'' \leq 0, \ldots, (-1)^{s+1} u^{(s)} \geq 0\}$$

denote a class of (utility or social welfare) functions, where $u^{(s)}$ denotes the sth-order derivative of u (assuming that it exists).

Definition 1.1.3 *The random variable X_1 is said to stochastically dominate the random variable X_2 at order s, denoted by $F_1 \succeq_s F_2$, if any of the following equivalent conditions holds: (1) $F_1^{(s)}(x) \leq F_2^{(s)}(x)$ for all $x \in \mathbb{R}$ and $F_1^{(r)}(\infty) \leq F_2^{(r)}(\infty)$ for all $r = 1, \ldots, s - 1$; (2) $E[u(X_1)] \geq E[u(X_2)]$ for all $u \in \mathcal{U}_s$; and (3) $Q_1^{(s)}(\tau) \geq Q_2^{(s)}(\tau)$ for all $\tau \in [0, 1]$ and $Q_1^{(r)}(1) \geq Q_2^{(r)}(1)$ for all $r = 1, \ldots, s - 1$.*

Whitmore (1970) introduces the concept of third-order stochastic dominance ($s = 3$, TSD) in finance; see also Whitmore and Findlay (1978). Levy (2016, section 3.8) relates the additional requirement $u''' \geq 0$ to the skewness of distributions and shows that TSD may reflect the preference for "positive skewness," i.e., investors dislike negative skewness but like positive skewness. Shorrocks and Foster (1987) show that the addition of a "transfer sensitivity" requirement leads to TSD ranking of income distributions. This requirement is stronger than the Pigou–Dalton principle of transfers since it makes regressive transfers less desirable at lower income levels.

If we let $s \to \infty$, then the class $\mathcal{U}_\infty$ of utility functions has marginal utilities that are completely monotone. This leads to the concept of infinite-order stochastic dominance, which is the weakest notion of stochastic dominance; see Section 5.4.3 for details.

Equivalence of the Definitions We now show the equivalence of the conditions that appear in the definitions of SD. For simplicity, we discuss the case of FSD and SSD, and assume that X_1 and X_2 have a common compact support, say $\mathcal{X} = [0, 1]$.[5]
We first establish the following lemma:

Lemma 1.1.1 *If $F_1(x) \leq F_2(x)$ for all $x \in \mathbb{R}$, then $EX_1 \geq EX_2$.*

Proof: Recall that, for any nonnegative random variable X with CDF F,

$$EX = \int_0^\infty P(X > t)\, dt = \int_0^\infty [1 - F(t)]\, dt; \tag{1.1.4}$$

---

[5] The equivalence results can be extended to general random variables, possibly with unbounded supports; see Hanoch and Levy (1969) and Tesfatsion (1976). The proofs in this subsection are based on Wolfstetter (1999, chapter 4) and Ross (1996, chapter 9). For a proof of strong stochastic dominance, see Levy (2016, section 3).

see, e.g., Billingsley (1995, equation 21.9). Therefore,

$$EX_1 - EX_2 = \int_0^\infty [P(X_1 > t) - P(X_2 > t)] \, dt$$

$$= \int_0^\infty [F_2(t) - F_1(t)] \, dt \geq 0. \tag{1.1.5}$$

$\square$

The following theorem establishes the equivalence of (1) and (2) in Definition 1.1.1:[6]

Theorem 1.1.2 $F_1(x) \leq F_2(x)$ *for all* $x \in \mathbb{R}$ *if and only if* $E[u(X_1)] \geq E[u(X_2)]$ *for all* $u \in \mathcal{U}_1$.

Proof: Suppose that $F_1(x) \leq F_2(x)$ for all $x \in \mathbb{R}$ and let $u \in \mathcal{U}_1$ be an increasing function. Let $u^{-1}(z) = \inf\{x : u(x) > z\}$. For any $z \in \mathbb{R}$, we have

$$P(u(X_1) > z) = P\left(X_1 > u^{-1}(z)\right)$$

$$= 1 - F_1\left(u^{-1}(z)\right)$$

$$\geq 1 - F_2\left(u^{-1}(z)\right)$$

$$= P\left(X_2 > u^{-1}(z)\right)$$

$$= P(u(X_2) > z).$$

Therefore, by Lemma 1.1.1, we have $E[u(X_1)] \geq E[u(X_2)]$ for any $u \in \mathcal{U}_1$. Conversely, suppose that $E[u(X_1)] \geq E[u(X_2)]$ for all $u \in \mathcal{U}_1$. Let

$$u_x(z) = \begin{cases} 1 & \text{if } z > x \\ 0 & \text{if } z \leq x \end{cases}.$$

Clearly, $u_x(\cdot) \in \mathcal{U}_1$ for each x. Therefore, for each $x \in \mathbb{R}$,

$$P(X_1 > x) = E[u_x(X_1)]$$

$$\geq E[u_x(X_2)]$$

$$= P(X_2 > x).$$

$\square$

For SSD, the following theorem establishes the equivalence of (1) and (2) in Definition 1.1.2:[7]

Theorem 1.1.3 $\int_0^x F_1(t)dt \leq \int_0^x F_2(t)dt$ *for all* $x \in \mathcal{X}$ *if and only if* $E[u(X_1)] \geq E[u(X_2)]$ *for all* $u \in \mathcal{U}_2$.

---

[6] The equivalence of the conditions (1) and (3) easily follows from monotonicity of the CDFs.
[7] For a proof of the equivalence of the conditions (1) and (3), see Thistle (1989, proposition 4).

Proof: Suppose that $E[u(X_1)] \geq E[u(X_2)]$ for all $u \in \mathcal{U}_2$. Consider the following function:

$$u_x(z) = \begin{cases} z & \text{if } z \leq x \\ x & \text{if } z > x \end{cases}.$$

Obviously, for each $x \in \mathcal{X}$, $u_x(\cdot) \in \mathcal{U}_2$ so that

$$0 \leq E[u_x(X_1)] - E[u_x(X_2)]$$
$$= \int_0^x [1 - F_1(t)]\,dt - \int_0^x [1 - F_2(t)]\,dt$$
$$= \int_0^x [F_2(t) - F_1(t)]\,dt.$$

Conversely, suppose that $\int_0^x F_1(t)dt \leq \int_0^x F_2(t)dt$ for all $x \in \mathcal{X}$. Since monotonicity implies differentiability almost everywhere (a.e.), we have $u' > 0$ and $u'' \leq 0$ a.e. for each $u \in \mathcal{U}_2$. Therefore, by integration by parts, we have

$$\Delta u := E[u(X_1)] - E[u(X_2)]$$
$$= -\int_0^1 u(x)d[F_2(x) - F_1(x)]$$
$$= \int_0^1 u'(x)[F_2(x) - F_1(x)]\,dx \qquad (1.1.6)$$
$$= u'(1)\int_0^1 [F_2(t) - F_1(t)]\,dt \qquad (1.1.7)$$
$$- \int_0^1 u''(t)\int_0^t [F_2(s) - F_1(s)]\,ds\,dt.$$

Since $u' > 0$ and $u'' \leq 0$, the assumed condition $\int_0^x [F_2(t) - F_1(t)]\,dt \geq 0$ for all $x \in \mathcal{X}$ implies immediately $\Delta u \geq 0$. This establishes Theorem 1.1.3. $\square$

1.1.2 Basic Properties of Stochastic Dominance

While stochastic dominance relations compare *whole* distribution functions, they are also related to the moments and other aspects of distributions.

Let $supp(F)$ denote the support of distribution F. The following theorem gives sufficient and necessary conditions for the first-order stochastic dominance.

Theorem 1.1.4 *Let X_1 and X_2 be random variables with distribution functions F_1 and F_2, respectively. (1) If $P(X_2 \leq X_1) = 1$, then X_1 FSD X_2; (2) If $\min\{supp(F_1)\} \geq \max\{supp(F_2)\}$, then X_1 FSD X_2; (3) If X_1 FSD X_2, then $EX_1 \geq EX_2$ and $\min\{supp(F_1)\} \geq \min\{supp(F_2)\}$.*

(1) and (2) in the above theorem give sufficient conditions for the FSD. (1) holds because, if X_1 is not smaller than X_2 (with probability 1), then

$$X_1 \leq x \text{ implies } X_2 \leq x \text{ for all } x$$
$$\Longrightarrow \{X_1 \leq x\} \subseteq \{X_2 \leq x\} \text{ for all } x$$
$$\Longrightarrow P(X_1 \leq x) \leq P(X_2 \leq x) \text{ for all } x$$
$$\Longrightarrow F_1(x) \leq F_2(x) \text{ for all } x.[8]$$

For example, if $X_1 = X_2 + a$ for a constant $a > 0$, then (1) implies that X_1 FSD X_2. (2) says that if the minimum of the support of F_1 is not less than the maximum of the support of F_2, then we have first-order stochastic dominance of X_1 over X_2. This follows directly from (1).

On the other hand, (3) gives necessary conditions for FSD. That is, if X_1 FSD X_2, then the mean of X_1 is not smaller than the mean of X_2. This follows from the expression[9]

$$EX_1 - EX_2 = \int_{-\infty}^{\infty} [F_2(x) - F_1(x)] \, dx, \tag{1.1.8}$$

which is nonnegative, provided the integral exists; see also Lemma 1.1.1. Also, if X_1 FSD X_2, then the minimum of the support of F_1 is not smaller than that of F_2. This is called the "left tail" condition because it implies that F_2 has a thicker left tail than F_1. This result holds because, otherwise, there would exist a value x_0 such that $F_1(x_0) > F_2(x_0)$, and hence X_1 could not first-order stochastically dominate X_2.

For second-order stochastic dominance, analogous conditions can be established (the proofs are also similar):

Theorem 1.1.5 *Let X_1 and X_2 be random variables with distribution functions F_1 and F_2, respectively. (1) If X_1 FSD X_2, then X_1 SSD X_2; (2) If $\min\{supp(F_1)\} \geq \max\{supp(F_2)\}$, then X_1 SSD X_2; (3) If X_1 SSD X_2, then $EX_1 \geq EX_2$ and $\min\{supp(F_1)\} \geq \min\{supp(F_2)\}$.*

In the above theorem, (3) shows that $EX_1 \geq EX_2$ is a necessary condition for the SSD. Is there any general condition on variances which is also a necessary condition for the SSD? In general, the answer is no. However, for distributions with an equal mean, we can state a necessary condition for the SSD using their variances.

---

[8] Here, the notation '$A \Longrightarrow B$' means 'A implies B'.

[9] This holds because, for any random variable X with CDF F,

$$EX = \int_0^{\infty} [1 - F(x) - F(-x)] \, dx,$$

provided the integral exists.

Theorem 1.1.6 *Let X_1 and X_2 be random variables with $EX_1 = EX_2$. If X_1 SSD X_2, then $Var(X_1) \leq Var(X_2)$.*

To see this, take, for example, a quadratic utility function $u(x) = x + \beta x^2$ for $\beta < 0$, which certainly lies in $\mathcal{U}_2$. Then, $Eu(X_1) \geq Eu(X_2)$ and $EX_1 = EX_2$ together immediately imply that $Var(X_1) \leq Var(X_2)$. The mean-variance approach in the portfolio choice problem compares only the first two moments of distributions. A natural question would be whether F_1 second-order stochastically dominates F_2, if F_1 has larger mean and smaller variance than F_2. The answer is no, in general. This can be illustrated using the following counterexample (Levy, 1992, p. 567):

x	$P(X_1 = x)$	x	$P(X_2 = x)$
1	0.80	10	0.99
100	0.20	1000	0.01

Note that $EX_1 = 20.8 > EX_2 = 19.9$ and $Var(X_1) = 1468 < Var(X_2) = 9703$. Hence, X_1 dominates X_2 by the mean-variance criterion. However, X_1 does not second-order stochastically dominate X_2 because a risk-averse investor with utility function $u(x) = \log(x)$ would prefer X_2 over X_1, since $Eu(X_1) = 0.4 < Eu(X_2) = 1.02$; see the next subsection for another example with continuously distributed random variables.

The foregoing discussion implies that there is no direct relationship between the mean-variance approach and the stochastic dominance approach in general. However, in the special case of normal distributions, stochastic dominance can be related to mean-variance in the following sense:

Theorem 1.1.7 *Let X_1 and X_2 be random variables with normal distributions. Then, (1) $EX_1 > EX_2$ and $Var(X_1) = Var(X_2)$ if and only if X_1 FSD X_2; (2) if $EX_1 > EX_2$ or $Var(X_1) < Var(X_2)$, then X_1 SSD X_2.*

For more complete discussions on the properties of stochastic dominance, the reader may refer to Levy (2016) and Wolfstetter (1999, chapters 4–5).

1.1.3 A Numerical Example

The mean-variance criterion has been widely adopted in portfolio choice problems. It is a simple performance indicator comparing only the first two moments of distributions; whenever the mean is higher and the variance is lower for one distribution than for the other, the former distribution is preferred. However, it is well known that the criterion is valid only in certain cases: (1) when the utility function is quadratic, and (2) when the distributions of the portfolios are all members of a two-parameter family; see Hanoch and Levy (1969). In reality, however, the assumptions are restrictive and the stochastic dominance approach provides an ordering of prospects under much less restrictive conditions.

To illustrate how the two approaches yield different results, we present a simple numerical example using two prospects, X and Y, with probability density functions (PDFs) and cumulative distribution functions (CDFs) given by

$$f_X(x) = 0.1 \cdot 1(0 \le x < 1 \text{ or } 2 \le x \le 3) + 0.8 \cdot 1(1 \le x < 2),$$
$$f_Y(x) = 0.5 \cdot 1(0.5 \le x \le 2.5)$$

and

$$F_X(x) = 0.1x \cdot 1(0 \le x < 1) + (0.8x - 0.7) \cdot 1(1 \le x < 2)$$
$$+ (0.1x + 0.7) \cdot 1(2 \le x \le 3) + 1(x > 3),$$
$$F_Y(x) = 0.5(x - 0.5) \cdot 1(0.5 \le x \le 2.5) + 1(x > 2.5),$$

respectively, where $1(\cdot)$ denotes the indicator function. Figure 1.3 depicts the PDFs and the CDFs of the prospects. Their expected values and variances are given by $E(X) = 3/2$, $Var(X) = 17/60$, $E(Y) = 3/2$, and $Var(Y) = 1/3$.

In terms of the mean-variance criterion, the prospect X is more efficient than the prospect Y. However, X does not second-order stochastically dominate Y, which can easily be observed from Figure 1.3. Since the value of the CDF of X is greater than that of Y over the region $[0, 0.5]$, the integrated area of the distribution of X is greater than that of the distribution of Y. This violates the second-order stochastic dominance of X over Y.

In reality, we do not observe the population distributions F_X and F_Y, but rather a sample randomly drawn from the distributions. This motivates us

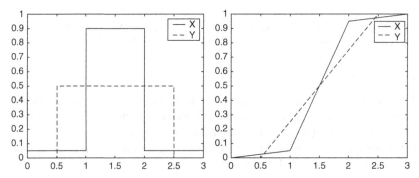

Figure 1.3 PDFs (left) and CDFs (right) for the simulation design

Table 1.1 *Mean-variance and SSD criteria*

	Mean-Variance Criterion	
	Sample Mean	Sample Variance
X	1.5002	0.2831
Y	1.4997	0.3329
	SSD Test	
Rejection rate	0.186	

to consider a statistical inference method: a scientific procedure to make a conjecture, based on samples, on the population distribution.

To give an early idea of SD tests, we draw a sample of size 500 from each distribution, then test the null hypothesis that "X second-order stochastically dominates Y" using a standard SD test (Barrett and Donald [BD] Test; see Section 2.2.2) at the significance level 0.10. We repeat this procedure 1,000 times. Table 1.1 summarizes the simulation results.

Sample means and sample variances are very close to their population values, implying that prospect X dominates prospect Y in the sample in terms of the mean-variance efficiency criterion.[10] On the other hand, the estimated rejection rate of the BD test in the simulation experiment is about 0.186. This means that the null hypothesis is rejected 186 out of 1,000 times. We may interpret this result as statistical evidence against second-order stochastic dominance of X over Y, which is consistent with the population relationship. This implies that SD tests can yield rankings of prospects that are fundamentally different from those based on the traditional mean-variance criterion.

1.1.4 Extensions and Some Related Concepts

In this subsection, we present a brief overview of some of the extensions and related concepts of stochastic dominance, which will be discussed in detail in the subsequent chapters.

Suppose that $F_1(y|x)$ and $F_2(y|x)$ denote the conditional CDFs of random variables Y_1 and Y_2 given $X = x$, respectively. We say that *the distribution of Y_1 (first-order) stochastically dominates the distribution of Y_2, conditional on X*, if

$$F_1(y|x) \leq F_2(y|x) \text{ for all } y, x.$$

---

[10] More formally, we cannot reject the null hypothesis of "$E(X) = E(Y)$ and $Var(X) \leq Var(Y)$."

This concept of *conditional stochastic dominance* is useful when one wishes to compare distributions of two population subgroups defined by some observed covariates X.

Stochastic monotonicity is a continuum version of the stochastic dominance hypothesis for conditional distributions. Let Y and X denote two random variables whose joint distribution is absolutely continuous with respect to a Lebesgue measure on $\mathbb{R}^2$. Let $F_{Y|X}(\cdot|x)$ denote the distribution of Y conditional on $X = x$. The hypothesis of stochastic monotonicity is defined to be

$$F_{Y|X}(y|x) \leq F_{Y|X}\left(y|x'\right) \text{ for all } y \text{ and } x \geq x'.$$

For example, if X is some policy or other input variable, it amounts to the hypothesis that its effect on the distribution of Y is increasing.

The *Lorenz curve (LC)* plots the percentage of total income earned by various portions of the population when the population is ordered by their incomes, i.e., from the poorest to the richest. It is a fundamental tool for the analysis of economic inequality. The Lorenz curve is defined to be

$$L_k(p) = \frac{\int_0^p Q_k(t)dt}{\mu_k},$$

for $p \in [0, 1]$, where $Q_k(p)$ and μ_k denote the quantile function and the mean of F_k, respectively, for the population $k = 1, 2$. *Lorenz dominance of L_1 over L_2* is defined by

$$L_2(p) \leq L_1(p) \text{ for all } p \in [0, 1].$$

Kahneman and Tversky (1979) criticize the expected utility theory and introduce an alternative theory, called prospect theory. They argue that individuals would rank prospects according to the expected value of S-shaped utility functions $u \in \mathcal{U}_P \subseteq \mathcal{U}_1$ for which $u''(x) \leq 0$ for all $x > 0$ but $u''(x) \geq 0$ for all $x < 0$. We say that X_1 *prospect stochastically dominates* X_2 if

$$\int_y^x F_1(t)dt \leq \int_y^x F_2(t)dt$$

for all pairs (x, y) with $x > 0$ and $y < 0$.

On the other hand, Levy and Levy (2002) discuss the concept of *Markowitz stochastic dominance*. In this case, individuals rank outcomes according to the expected value of reverse S-shaped utility functions $u \in \mathcal{U}_M \subseteq \mathcal{U}_1$ for which $u''(x) \geq 0$ for all $x > 0$ but $u''(x) \leq 0$ for all $x < 0$. We say that X_1 *Markowitz stochastically dominates* X_2 if

$$\left(\int_{-\infty}^y + \int_x^\infty\right) F_1(t)dt \leq \left(\int_{-\infty}^y + \int_x^\infty\right) F_2(t)dt$$

for all pairs (x, y) with $x > 0$ and $y < 0$.

Let F_1 and F_2 denote two CDFs, both continuous and with supports on $[0, \infty)$. We say that F_1 *initially dominates* F_2 up to an (unknown) point x_1, if

$$F_1(x) \leq F_2(x) \text{ for all } x \in [0, x_1)$$

with strict inequality for some $x \in (0, x_1)$. x_1 is called the "maximal point of initial dominance," when F_1 initially dominates F_2 up to x_1 and $F_1(x) > F_2(x)$ for all $x \in (x_1, x_1 + \varepsilon)$ for some sufficiently small $\varepsilon > 0$. This concept is useful to determine whether a stochastic dominance restriction holds over some unknown subset of the supports.

Let $X = (X_1, \ldots, X_K)^\mathsf{T}$ be a vector of K prospects (e.g., asset returns), and let Y be a benchmark portfolio. We say that Y is *stochastic dominance efficient* if there does not exist any portfolio $\{X^\mathsf{T}\lambda \: : \: \lambda \in \Lambda_0\}$ that stochastically dominates Y, where Λ_0 is a set of portfolio weights. This concept allows for full diversification of portfolios and provides a method of inference based on the first-order optimality condition of an investor's expected utility maximization problem.

Convex stochastic dominance, suggested by Fishburn (1974), is an extension of stochastic dominance to mixtures or convex combinations of distributions. If there are multiple choices available, a decision-maker can make pairwise comparisons with all prospects and establish whether a given choice is "SD admissible" in the sense that it is not dominated by any of the other alternatives. However, it is possible that some members of the SD admissible set may never be chosen by any individual with utility function in the hypothesized class. Instead, there may exist an "SD optimal" set, which is a subset of the SD admissible set that consists of the elements that *will* be chosen by some individuals with a utility function in the hypothesized class. The concept of convex stochastic dominance is useful to identify the SD optimal set.

The SD rule provides rankings of distributions based on *all* utility functions in a certain class. However, this can be restrictive in practice, because a small violation of the SD rule can make the ranking invalid. *Almost stochastic dominance,* suggested by Leshno and Levy (2002), is a weaker concept than the standard stochastic dominance. It applies to *most* rather than *all* decision-makers by eliminating economically pathological preferences. For example, let $\mathcal{U}_2^*(\varepsilon)$ denote the class of all increasing and concave functions with second derivatives satisfying some restrictions for some $\varepsilon > 0$. We say that X_1 ε-*almost second-order stochastically dominates* X_2, if $E[u(X_1)] \geq E[u(X_2)]$ for all $u \in \mathcal{U}_2^*(\varepsilon)$, or, equivalently,

$$\int \left[F_1^{(2)}(x) - F_2^{(2)}(x) \right]_+ dx \leq \varepsilon \int \left| F_1^{(2)}(x) - F_2^{(2)}(x) \right| dx,$$

where $[x]_+ = \max\{x, 0\}$. This concept also allows us to construct a measure of disagreement with stochastic dominance.

Approximate stochastic dominance, introduced by Álvarez-Esteban, del Barrio, Cuesta-Albertos, and Matrán (2016), is another weaker concept of the stochastic dominance relationship based on contaminated models. This concept is useful for determining whether one can establish stochastic dominance after trimming away some fraction of the (possibly contaminated) observations at the tails. The minimum level of contamination needed to establish SD can also serve as an alternative measure of disagreement with stochastic dominance.

Infinite-order stochastic dominance, characterized by Thistle (1993), is the weakest notion of stochastic dominance. It is defined by letting $s \to \infty$ in the definition of the sth-order stochastic dominance. Since the SD efficient set or the SD optimal sets are monotonically decreasing in s, the choice based on infinite-order stochastic dominance yields the smallest SD efficient or optimal set, which is a useful property for the portfolio choice problem.

There are many related concepts of stochastic dominance, other than the aforementioned ones. Let X_1 and X_2 be random variables with the absolute continuous distributions F_1 and F_2 with the densities f_1 and f_2, respectively. Then, we say that X_1 *density ratio dominates* X_2 if

$$\frac{f_2(t)}{f_1(t)} \text{ is nonincreasing over } t.$$

It can be shown that this holds if and only if

$$X_1 | (a \leq X_2 \leq b) \text{ first-order stochastically dominates } X_2 | (a \leq X_1 \leq b)$$

whenever $a \leq b$, where $X|A$ denotes the conditional distribution of X given A. This concept of density ratio (or likelihood ratio) ordering has been frequently applied in portfolio choice, insurance, mechanism design, and auction theory.

We say that X_1 *uniformly stochastically dominates* X_2, if

$$\frac{1 - F_2(t)}{1 - F_1(t)} \text{ is nonincreasing in } t \in [0, b_{F_2}),$$

where $1 - F_k$ denotes the survival function for $k = 1, 2$ and $b_{F_2} = \inf\{x : F_2(x) = 1\}$. Uniform stochastic ordering is useful in many applications in which risks change dynamically over time. For example, in choosing medical treatments, the survival time of treatment A might stochastically dominate that of treatment B at the initial stage, but it may not be true when patients are examined at later stages. Also, the concept is used to compare distributions in the upper tails of financial returns. It is a stronger concept than the FSD.

The concept of SD is also closely related to various concepts of dependence among random variables. Let X and Y be two random variables with the CDFs F and G, respectively. We say that Y *is positive quadrant dependent on X*, if

$$P(X \leq x, Y \leq y) \geq P(X \leq x) P(Y \leq y) \text{ for all } (x, y).$$

We also say that Y *is positive expectation dependent on* X, if

$$E(Y) - E(Y|X \leq x) \geq 0 \text{ for all } x.$$

These concepts have been applied extensively in the literature of finance, insurance, and risk management. Expectation dependence (Wright, 1987) is a weaker concept than quadrant dependence, but is a stronger concept than correlation. Expectation dependence also plays an important role in portfolio theory, because it is used to determine the necessary and sufficient conditions for portfolio diversification.

Central dominance (Gollier, 1995) provides the conditions under which a change in distribution increases the optimal value of a decision variable for all risk-averse agents. It implies a deterministic change in optimal decision variables, such as demand for risky assets or a social welfare policy, when the distribution changes. It is shown that stochastic dominance is neither sufficient nor necessary for central dominance.

Spatial dominance (Park, 2005) is a generalization of stochastic dominance from the frequency domain to the spatial domain. It allows us to compare, for example, performances of two assets over a given time interval. It has important implications for optimal investment strategies that may be horizon-dependent.

1.2 Applications of Stochastic Dominance

The concept of stochastic dominance and related concepts have been applied to real data in many areas of social and natural sciences. The literature has been expanding quite rapidly and it is beyond the scope of this book to cover all of the applications; see Mosler and Scarsini (1993) for an extensive bibliography on the literature up to the early 1990s. See also Wolfstetter (1999, chapter 5) for an overview of theoretical developments of SD in economics.

In this section, we briefly summarize some recent empirical applications of stochastic dominance, mainly to economics. They are chosen to illustrate the wide applicability of SD concepts and are not meant to be comprehensive. Some of them will be discussed in more detail in subsequent chapters.

1.2.1 Welfare Analysis

One of the main applications of stochastic dominance is welfare analysis. In particular, the issues of inequality, poverty, and polarization have frequently been analyzed using the concept of SD. For an excellent overview of the literature, see Cowell and Flachaire (2015).

Anderson (2003) uses SD criteria to examine improvements to poverty alleviation in the United States in the 1980s using the PSID data. Anderson (2004a), on the other hand, examines enhancements to polarization, welfare, and poverty based on per-capita Gross National Products (GNP) of different countries. Anderson and Leo (2009) study changes in child poverty, investment in children, and generational mobility since the introduction of China's One Child Policy (OCP) in 1979. They compare child poverty in China (1987, 2001) with that in other countries such as Canada (1997, 2004), the United Kingdom (1996, 2002), and India (1994, 2004) by utilizing SD methods. Evolution of poverty is also studied by Contreras (2001) using Chilean data from 1990 to 1996 (a period of rapid growth in Chile).

Amin, Rai, and Topa (2003) use SD methods to evaluate whether microcredit programs in Bangladesh reach relatively poorer and more vulnerable people. They test the hypothesis that distributions of consumption and vulnerability of program participants stochastically dominate those of nonparticipants. They find that the microcredit program effectively reaches the poor, but it is not very successful at reaching the vulnerable. On the other hand, Skoufias and Di Maro (2008) investigate the effect of Progressa, which is a conditional cash transfer program implemented in Mexico, on poverty. They find that the income distribution of treated households first-order stochastically dominates that of controlled households, strengthening robustness of the other results obtained using different methods.

There are also several empirical studies that try to compare distributions of income and/or other socioeconomic variables using various SD tests. Heshmati and Rudolf (2014) examine inequality and poverty in Korea using distributions of income and consumption. Valenzuela, Lean, and Athanasopoulos (2014) study inequality in income and expenditure distributions in Australia from 1983 to 2010. Maasoumi and Heshmati (2000) consider multivariate generalizations of a univariate SD test to examine Sweden's income distributions for the whole population and its subgroups.

Maasoumi, Su, and Heshmati (2013) examine inequality and relative welfare levels over time and among population subgroups using the Chinese Household Nutrition Survey (CHNS) data. Chen (2008) employs SD methods to study regional income disparities in Canada. Zarco, Pérez, and Alaiz (2007) also use an SD method to investigate the effect of the European Union (EU)'s structural funds on convergence of the income distributions in Spanish regions for the time period from 1990 to 2003; see also Carrington (2006) and Liontakis, Papadas, and Tzouramani (2010) for related results about the regional income convergence.

Pinar, Stengos, and Topaloglou (2013) emphasize joint dependence among various attributes of welfare such as income, health, and education (see, e.g., Maasoumi 1999 or Fleurbaey 2009 for an overview). Using the concept of stochastic dominance efficiency (see Section 5.3.2), they propose an optimal weighting scheme for measuring human development. Compared to the traditional United Nation's Development Program's Human Development Index (HDI) which puts equal weights to three basic components (life expectancy, education, and GNI), the optimal index leads to a marked improvement of measured development. Based on the panel data of different countries for the period 1975 to 2000, they present new country rankings that are quite different from those based on the HDI.

1.2.2 Finance

Another major area of applications of stochastic dominance is financial economics. There are numerous applications of SD in the finance literature; see Levy (2016) and Sriboonchita, Wong, Dhompongsa, and Nguyen (2010) for extensive surveys. Below we mention just a few recent applications.

SD tests have been implemented to track down evidence of financial market inefficiency. One of the representative phenomena demonstrating market inefficiency is the calendar effect, i.e., investment strategies linked to particular times may earn more profits. Seyhun (1993) examines the *January Effect*, which refers to the unusually large, positive average stock returns during the last few days of December and the first week of January. Cho, Linton, and Whang (2007) find empirical evidence for the *Monday Effect*, the phenomenon that Monday stock returns are systematically smaller than returns on any other day of the week (Section 2.5.2).

SD methods have also been used to evaluate the profitability of investment strategies. Bali, Demirtas, Levy, and Wolf (2009), using the concept of almost stochastic dominance (see Section 5.4.1), find empirical evidence in favor of the popular practice of primarily allocating a greater proportion to stocks and then gradually relocating funds to bonds as the investment horizon shortens. Ibarra (2013) also finds evidence that bonds dominate stocks at short horizons, while stocks dominate bonds at long horizons, based on spatial dominance (see Section 5.5.6). Meanwhile, Abhyankar, Ho, and Zhao (2009) focus on investors' preference of value stocks to growth stocks, and demonstrate that the value premium is country- and sample-specific. Fong, Wong, and Lean (2005) test the hypothesis that there exist general asset pricing models that explain the *Momentum Effect*, which is a tendency for portfolios of stocks that have performed well in recent months to continue to earn positive returns over the next year. Fong (2010) examines profitability of the investment strategy of yen carry trade over the period 2001–09. Chan, de Peretti, Qiao, and Wong (2012) show the efficiency of the UK covered warrants market by comparing the returns of covered warrants and their underlying shares.

Post (2003) develops a statistical test of stochastic dominance efficiency (see Section 5.3.2) to test superior profitability of a given portfolio over other possible combinations of assets. He shows the inefficiency of the Fama and French market portfolio relative to the benchmark portfolios formed on market capitalization and book-to-market equity ratio; see also Post and van Vliet (2006) for related results. Li and Linton (2010) propose a method to construct a portfolio based on SD and demonstrate that the hedge fund portfolios constructed by stochastic dominance criteria outperform other randomly selected hedge fund portfolios and a mean-variance efficient hedge fund portfolio. Using the concept of stochastic dominance efficiency, Agliardi et al. (2012) construct a sovereign risk index in emerging markets by aggregating various risk factors such as economic, political, and financial risks; see also Agliardi, Pinar, and Stengos (2014) and Pinar, Stengos, and Yazgan (2012) for related applications.

1.2.3 Industrial Organization

Guerre, Perrigne, and Vuong (2009, GPV) investigate nonparametric identification of the first-price auction model with risk-averse bidders. They show that quantiles of the observed equilibrium bid distributions with different numbers of bidders should satisfy a set of inequality restrictions, which in turn implies a stochastic dominance relationship between the distributions.

Specifically, let $I_2 > I_1 \geq 2$ denote the two different numbers of bidders. For each τ such that $0 < \tau < 1$, let $Q_k(\tau)$ denote the τ quantile of the observed equilibrium bid distribution G_k when the number of bidders is I_k for $k \in \{1, 2\}$. If the auctions are homogeneous and the private values are independent of the number of bidders, then GPV (equation 5, p. 1201) show that, under some additional assumptions, the quantiles should satisfy:

$$\frac{I_1 - 1}{I_2 - 1} Q_2(\tau) + \frac{I_2 - I_1}{I_2 - 1}\underline{b} < Q_1(\tau) < Q_2(\tau) \qquad (1.2.1)$$
$$< \frac{I_2 - 1}{I_1 - 1} Q_1(\tau) + \frac{I_1 - I_2}{I_1 - 1}\underline{b}$$

for any $\tau \in (0, 1]$, where $\underline{b}$ is the left endpoint of the support of the observed bid distributions. The inequality (1.2.1) offers a testable implication: the observed bid distribution with I_2 bidders first-order stochastically dominates the distribution with I_1 bidders, i.e., $G_2 \succeq_1 G_1$. On the other hand, if the auctions are heterogeneous so that the private values are affected by (observed) characteristics, then one may consider conditionally exogenous participation with the conditional version of the restrictions:

$$\frac{I_1 - 1}{I_2 - 1} Q_2(\tau|x) + \frac{I_2 - I_1}{I_2 - 1}\underline{b} < Q_1(\tau|x) < Q_2(\tau|x)$$
$$< \frac{I_2 - 1}{I_1 - 1} Q_1(\tau|x) + \frac{I_1 - I_2}{I_1 - 1}\underline{b} \qquad (1.2.2)$$

for any $\tau \in (0, 1]$ and $x \in \mathcal{X}$, where $\mathcal{X}$ is the support of X, $Q_k(\tau|x)$ is the τth conditional quantile (given $X = x$) of the observed equilibrium bid distribution when the number of bidders is I_k, and X denotes the observed auction characteristics such as appraisal values (see section 3.2 of GPV). In this case, the testable implication is stochastic dominance between the conditional distributions, i.e., $G_2(\cdot|\cdot) \succeq_1 G_1(\cdot|\cdot)$. Using a timber auction data, Lee, Song, and Whang (2017) test the latter hypothesis and find no empirical evidence against (1.2.2); see Section 6.2 for details.

De Silva, Dunne, and Kosmopoulou (2003) compare the bidding patterns of entrants and incumbents in road construction auctions, using data from the Oklahoma Department of Transportation. They find that entrants bid more aggressively (in the sense of lower bids relative to engineering costs) and win auctions with much lower bids than incumbents. They also find that the difference is more prominent in the lower tail of the bid distribution. They justify this phenomenon theoretically by using an auction model with information asymmetries due to varying levels of experience and efficiency of the auction participants. In particular, they show that if the distribution of cost estimates of entrants first-order stochastically dominates that of incumbents, then the entrants will bid more aggressively relative to their cost estimates than the incumbents will. Based on quantile regressions controlling for auction heterogeneity, they find no evidence against the implication of their asymmetric auction model (see Section 2.2.4 for the relationship between SD tests and quantile regressions).

Pesendorfer (2000) studies collusive behaviors in first-price auctions, focusing on the Florida and Texas school milk cartels in the 1980s. He considers a theoretical model of cartel behavior and shows that if cartel firms and non-cartel firms are identical, and the cartel is efficient (in the sense that it selects the lowest-cost cartel firm), then there will be an induced asymmetry between selected cartel bidders and non-cartel firms. One of the testable implications of the bidding equilibrium is that the ex ante bid distribution of the cartel is first-order stochastically dominated by that of non-cartel bidders. Based on the data of 4,077 contracts, he tests the equality of the distributions of the residuals from the OLS regressions of cartel bids and non-cartel bids on covariates that represent auction heterogeneity. Figures 3 and 4 of the latter paper suggest that the distribution of cartel residuals is first-order stochastically dominated by that of non-cartel residuals. He does not perform a formal SD test, but employs a Chow test and a rank test and concludes that there is empirical evidence consistent with the implication of his theoretical model.

Aryal and Gabrielli (2013) provide a method to detect collusion in asymmetric first-price auctions. The basic idea is that, if the same bid data are used to recover the underlying latent cost, the cost under competition must stochastically dominate the cost under collusion, because collusion tends to increase the markup. This suggests that detecting collusion can boil down to testing for the first-order stochastic dominance. They implement the standard Kolmogorov–Smirnov and Mann–Whitney–Wilcoxon tests to the highway procurement data and find no evidence of collusion in the data.

1.2.4 Labor Economics

Maasoumi, Millimet, and Rangaprasad (2005) analyze the effect of class sizes on student achievements with a US data set using the SD approach. In their study, the actual class sizes and the distributions of test scores of the 8th and 10th grades are utilized as the indicators for school quality and measures of student achievements, respectively. The dominance relation of the test score distributions are tested by actual class sizes: small, medium, and large. Eren and Henderson (2008) and Eren and Millimet (2008) also employ SD methods to examine the factors that impact on student achievements (such as homework) and organizational structures of schools, respectively.

Millimet and Wang (2006) examine the gender earnings gap in China based on the generalized Kolmogorov–Smirnov test proposed by Linton, Maasoumi, and Whang (2005) (see Section 2.2.2) and Maasoumi and Heshmati (2000). The dominance relation for the distributions of annual earnings and hourly wages for male and female workers is investigated for the years 1988 and 1995. See also Maasoumi and Wang (2018) for a related study of the gender earnings gap for the US labor market over the last several decades.

Maasoumi, Millimet, and Sarkar (2009) investigate the marriage premium, which is a phenomenon that the average earnings of married men are higher than those of unmarried men, by employing the SD approach to examine whether the phenomenon appears for the whole wage distribution. They find that the marriage premium is confined primarily to the lower tails of the wage distribution and the majority of the premium can be explained by self-selection.

1.2.5 International Economics

Delgado, Farinas, and Ruano (2002) adopt the SD approach to examine the total factor productivity difference between exporting and non-exporting firms based on a sample of Spanish manufacturing firms from 1991 to 1996. The productivity of four groups (exporters, non-exporters, entering exporters, and exiting exporters) is compared in the paper. They find that the productivity distribution of small exporting firms stochastically dominates that of small non-exporting firms, but, in the case of large firms, no dominance relation seems to exist. A related research is conducted by Girma, Görg, and Strobl (2004) and Elliott and Zhou (2013).

Helpman, Melitz, and Yeaple (2004) provide a theoretical framework for the *Market Selection Hypothesis* that firms determine the types of markets in which they run their business depending on their own profitability (that is, high profitability = foreign direct investment, medium profitability = foreign markets through exporting, and low profitability = domestic markets). Girma, Kneller, and Pisu (2005) test the hypothesis using the SD approach. They find that the productivity distribution of multinational firms dominates that of export firms, which in turn dominates that of non-exporters. Wagner (2006) also compares the productivity distributions using a German data set and finds that the productivity distribution of foreign direct investors dominates that of exporters, which in turn dominates that of national market suppliers; see also Arnold and Hussinger (2010) for a related result.

1.2.6 Health Economics

Bishop, Formby, and Zeager (2000) examine the impact of food stamp cashout on undernutrition using a household data from cashout experiments in Alabama and San Diego. They compare the CDFs of nutrients for two population subgroups (cash recipients and food coupon recipients), truncated in the neighborhood of the RDA (Recommended Dietary Allowances). They apply the FSD test of Bishop, Formby, and Thistle (1989) to the data and find that a substantial proportion of household participants falls short of the recommended levels of food energy and a variety of nutrients. Furthermore, in Alabama, the cash recipients show higher deficiency of Vitamin E and B than the coupon recipients.

Pak, Ferreira, and Colson (2016) investigate the obesity inequality among US adults over time using an SD test. Because people care about their weights relative to their peers, obesity inequality plays an important role in subjective well-being. Using the National Health and Nutritional Examination Survey (NHANES) data, they find that the BMI (Body Mass Index) distribution of each NHANES study first-order stochastically dominates that of the previous wave from 1971–74 to 2003–06, while more recent comparisons fail to reject the null hypothesis of nondominance. Madden (2012) and Sahn (2009) also investigate the obesity issue using SD methods.

1.2.7 Agricultural Economics

Langyintuo et al. (2005) use the SD approach to assess risk efficiency of yields and returns to farmers' household resources in rice production across different production systems. An improved (short-duration cover crop) fallow system is compared with two alternative fallow systems (the traditional natural bush fallow and continuous rice-cropping systems). The analysis assumes that farmers try to maximize both food self-sufficiency (rice grain yield) and cash income (monetary returns to farm household resources). Using agronomic data from Northern Ghana and employing the two-sample Kolmogorov–Smirnov test, they conclude that the yield and income distributions of the improved fallow system stochastically dominate those of the alternative systems. See Mahoney et al. (2004), Smith, Clapperton, and Blackshaw (2004), Ribera, Hons, and Richardson (2004), and Lien et al. (2006) for related studies.

It is important to prevent land degradation in the form of soil erosion and nutrient depletion in order to ensure food security and sustainability of agricultural production in many developing countries. Kassie et al. (2008) examine the impact of stone bunds on the value of crop production in the areas of the Ethiopian highlands using cross-sectional data. They find that, in the regions with low rainfall, the yield distributions with conservation first-order stochastically dominate those without conservation, while the relation is reversed and is not significant in the regions with heavy precipitation. For related studies, see Kassie et al. (2009) and Bekele (2005).

1.3 Outline of Subsequent Chapters

Chapter 2 introduces the basic ideas of standard tests of stochastic dominance, frequently used in the literature. The tests are classified into different categories depending on hypotheses of interest and types of test statistics. Various types of test statistics are discussed and compared. Two empirical examples are also given to illustrate how the tests can be used in practical applications.

Chapter 3 introduces methods to improve power performance of some SD tests. Many of the existing tests of stochastic dominance consider the least favorable case (LFC) of the null hypothesis to compute critical values. However, they may be too conservative in practice, because their asymptotic distributions depend only on the binding part (or so-called "contact set") of the inequality restrictions. This chapter discusses various approaches to improve power performance by utilizing information about the binding restrictions. This chapter also introduces applications of stochastic dominance to program evaluations. In particular, inference methods for distributional treatment effects and counterfactual policy effects are discussed. Some other issues of stochastic dominance tests, such as the problem of unbounded supports, classification rules for SD relations, and large deviation approximation of the distribution of the SD test statistics, are also discussed. This chapter provides empirical examples to evaluate distributional treatment effects and returns to schooling.

Chapter 4 provides the main ideas of how to test stochastic dominance when there are covariates. Consideration of the covariates is important in many economic applications because stochastic dominance relations might hold only for subpopulations defined by observed covariates. In particular, this chapter introduces the notions of stochastic monotonicity and conditional stochastic dominance. It also illustrates empirical applications to evaluate distributional conditional treatment effects using a real data set on academic achievements and to test a strong leverage hypothesis in financial markets.

Chapter 5 introduces nonparametric testing procedures for various extensions of stochastic dominance, including multivariate stochastic dominance, Lorenz dominance, poverty dominance, initial dominance, marginal conditional stochastic dominance, stochastic dominance efficiency, convex stochastic dominance, almost stochastic dominance, approximate stochastic dominance, and infinite-order stochastic dominance, as well as some related concepts such as density ratio ordering, uniform stochastic ordering, positive quadrant dependence, expectation dependence dominance, central dominance, and spatial dominance.

Chapter 6 discusses some further topics recently studied in the literature. They include inference on a distributional overlap measure, testing for generalized functional inequalities, SD tests under measurement errors, conditional SD tests with many covariates, and robust forecasting comparisons.

Chapter 7 concludes the book and suggests some future directions for econometric research on stochastic dominance.

Finally, the appendices provide the basic technical tools and the MATLAB code for some of the SD tests discussed in the main text.

2 Tests of Stochastic Dominance: Basic Results

This chapter discusses several tests of stochastic dominance hypotheses. The tests are classified first into different categories, depending on (i) types of hypotheses of interest and (ii) types of test statistics. Section 2.1 presents three types of hypotheses mainly considered in the literature. Sections 2.2–2.4 discuss various test statistics for each type of the hypothesis. The final section presents two empirical examples to show how some of the aforementioned tests can be used in practical applications.

2.1 Introduction

There are three types of hypotheses mainly considered in the literature:

(A) $H_0 : F_1(x) \le F_2(x)$ for all x vs. $H_1 : F_1(x) > F_2(x)$ for some x.
(B) $H_0 : F_1(x) \ge F_2(x)$ for some x vs. $H_1 : F_1(x) < F_2(x)$ for all x.
(C) $H_0 : F_1(x) = F_2(x)$ for all x vs. $H_1 : F_1(x) < F_2(x)$ for all x.

(For higher-order dominance, the hypotheses can be stated with F_k replaced by $F_k^{(s)}$ for $k = 1, 2$.)

Type (A) has been the most popular in the literature. It considers the null hypothesis of dominance against the alternative hypothesis of non-dominance, following the usual convention of taking the theory of interest as the null hypothesis and trying to find evidence against it. The null hypothesis is composite and consists of a set of (a possibly infinite number of) inequality restrictions. It is an intersection-union-type test because the null is an intersection of individual hypotheses (for different grid points) and the alternative is a union of the hypotheses. If the null is rejected, then one can infer non-dominance. Of course, non-rejection of the null may be due to a lack of power and hence does not necessarily imply dominance. This testing problem is similar in spirit to the goodness of fit test problem, in the sense that it looks for evidence against stochastic dominance as a minimal requirement to pursue an analysis under stochastic dominance.

Type (B) considers the null hypothesis of non-dominance against the alternative hypothesis of (strict) stochastic dominance. This approach has an advantage in that if the null is rejected then one can infer stochastic dominance. However, it also has a limitation because it is impossible to reject non-dominance in favor of dominance over the entire supports of the distributions when the distributions are continuous. To test the null of non-dominance, it is necessary to put a restriction on the range over which the dominance relationship is investigated; see Section 2.3.2. It is a union-intersection-type test because the null is the union of individual hypotheses (for different grid points) and the alternative is the intersection of the hypotheses.

Finally, type (C) considers the null hypothesis of equal distributions against the alternative hypothesis of (strict) stochastic dominance. This is a one-sided testing problem for infinite-dimensional parameters, i.e., real-valued functions F_1 and F_2. It implicitly assumes that stochastic dominance holds as a maintained hypothesis and tries to find statistical evidence for strict dominance. In many situations, however, this assumption is hard to justify and the dominance itself needs to be verified. In fact, the main difficulty with this approach is that the alternative hypothesis is not the negation of the null hypothesis. Therefore, there may exist F_1 and F_2 such that both H_0 and H_1 are false, which makes the test results hard to interpret.

2.2 Null of Dominance against Non-Dominance

The majority of the existing tests in the literature consider the null hypothesis of dominance against the alternative hypothesis of non-dominance, i.e., type (A) above. The tests can be classified into two categories: (I) tests based on comparing two CDFs at *finite* number of grid points and (II) tests based on comparing two CDFs at *all* points in an interval (possibly a subset of the supports). At each category, several different types of tests have been suggested.

Examples of the tests based on finite multiple comparisons of CDFs (Category I) include, among others, Anderson (1996) and Davidson and Duclos (2000); see also Zheng, Formby, Smith, and Chow (2000) and the references cited therein. The tests are extensions of Pearson's goodness of fit (Anderson, 1996), Wald, and maximum-t tests (Davidson and Duclos, 2000) to the setting of a finite number of inequalities. The tests are relatively easy to implement because the critical values are usually tabulated and hence readily available. They are also informative in highlighting where the discrepancies in the distributions occur. However, they are not consistent against all alternatives (of non-dominance).[1]

---

[1] See Rao (1973) for a general discussion about tests based on finite multiple comparisons and those based on a full comparison of functions.

The tests based on a full comparison of CDFs (Category II), by construction, are consistent against all alternatives. Examples include (one-sided) Kolmogorov–Smirnov or Supremum-type tests (McFadden, 1989; Klecan, McFadden, and McFadden, 1991; Barrett and Donald, 2003; and Linton, Maasoumi, and Whang, 2005), Cramér–von Mises-type tests (Hall and Yatchew, 2005), Anderson–Darling-type tests (Bennett, 2008), Neyman's smooth tests (Ledwina and Wyłupek, 2012a), and Quantile-based tests (Koenker and Xiao, 2002; Ng, Wong, and Xiao, 2017; Chernozhukov and Fernández-Val, 2005), among others.

In the statistics literature, there are also numerous results available, other than the aforementioned tests. Important examples include Robertson and Wright (1981), who consider a *likelihood ratio test* for the null of dominance when the distributions are discrete, and Dykstara, Madsen, and Fairbanks (1983), who extend the latter results to continuous distributions. Schmid and Trede (1996) consider a *one-sided Mann–Whitney–Wilcoxon-type test* for first-order stochastic dominance. Their test is based on the population quantity

$$d_{ST} := \int_0^1 \left[F_1 \left\{ F_2^{-1}(p) - 0 \right\} - p \right]_+ dp$$
$$= \int_{-\infty}^\infty [F_1(x) - F_2(x)]_+ \, dF_2(x),$$

where $[\cdot]_+ = \max\{\cdot, 0\}$, which is non-positive under the null but is positive under the alternative. The test statistic is an empirical analogue of d_{ST} and is shown to be asymptotically pivotal. Schmid and Trede (1998) also consider a one-sided Kolmogorov–Smirnov-type test for second-order stochastic dominance, though it is applicable only to one-sample settings in which one of the distributions is known (uniform).

Below, we shall discuss some of the SD tests that have been applied frequently in econometric applications.

2.2.1 Tests Based on Multiple Comparisons

(1) Anderson Test Anderson (1996) proposes a test of stochastic dominance by comparing CDFs at finite numbers of grid points. The test is an extension of the Pearson's goodness of fit test to a setting of multiple inequalities.

Let $\mathcal{X}_J = \{x_0, \ldots, x_J\}$ be a set of grid points chosen by an investigator for $J < \infty$. (In practice, Anderson, 1996, suggests choosing the grid points to be the deciles of the pooled sample from the two distributions to be compared.) He considers the hypotheses of sth-order stochastic dominance for $s = 1, 2, 3$:

$$H_0 : F_1^{(s)}(x) \le F_2^{(s)}(x) \text{ for all } x \in \mathcal{X}_J, \tag{2.2.1}$$
$$H_1 : F_1^{(s)}(x) > F_2^{(s)}(x) \text{ for some } x \in \mathcal{X}_J, \tag{2.2.2}$$

where $F_k^{(s)}(x)$, $k = 1, 2$ denotes the *integrated CDF* (defined in Equation 1.1.2).

Let $\{X_{1,i} : i = 1, \ldots, N_1\}$ and $\{X_{2,i} : i = 1, \ldots, N_2\}$ be random samples independently drawn from F_1 and F_2, respectively. Given $\mathcal{X}_J$, let

$$p_{kj} := P(x_{j-1} < X_k \leq x_j) = F_k(x_j) - F_k(x_{j-1}), \quad j = 1, \ldots, J, \tag{2.2.3}$$

$$\mathbf{p}_k := (p_{k1}, \ldots, p_{kJ})^\mathsf{T} \in \mathbb{R}^J$$

denote the probabilities of X_k falling in the J subintervals for $k = 1, 2$. Define the $J \times J$ matrices

$$I_1 = \begin{bmatrix} 1 & 0 & \cdots & 0 \\ 1 & 1 & \cdots & 0 \\ \vdots & \vdots & \ddots & \vdots \\ 1 & 1 & \cdots & 1 \end{bmatrix},$$

$$I_2 = 0.5 \begin{bmatrix} x_1 - x_0 & 0 & 0 & \cdots & 0 \\ x_2 - x_0 & x_2 - x_1 & 0 & \cdots & 0 \\ x_2 - x_0 & x_3 - x_1 & x_3 - x_2 & \cdots & 0 \\ \vdots & \vdots & \vdots & \ddots & \vdots \\ x_2 - x_0 & x_3 - x_1 & x_4 - x_2 & \cdots & x_J - x_{J-1} \end{bmatrix}.$$

To approximate the sth-order integral $F_k^{(s)}$ in (2.2.1), Anderson suggests using a trapezoidal rule, which yields the hypotheses

$$\tilde{H}_0 : I_2^{s-1} I_1 (\mathbf{p}_1 - \mathbf{p}_2) \leq 0, \tag{2.2.4}$$

$$\tilde{H}_1 : I_2^{s-1} I_1 (\mathbf{p}_1 - \mathbf{p}_2) \nleq 0. \tag{2.2.5}$$

The hypothesis $\tilde{H}_0$ (or $\tilde{H}_1$) is approximately equivalent to H_0 (or H_1) because, for any $\mathbf{p}_k$,

$$I_1 \mathbf{p}_k = (p_{k1}, (p_{k1} + p_{k2}), \ldots, (p_{k1} + \cdots + p_{kJ}))^\mathsf{T}$$
$$= (F_k(x_1), F_k(x_2), \ldots, F_k(x_J))^\mathsf{T},$$
$$I_2 I_1 \mathbf{p}_k \approx (F_k^{(2)}(x_1), F_k^{(2)}(x_2), \ldots, F_k^{(2)}(x_J))^\mathsf{T} \tag{2.2.6}$$

and so on.[2]

Define

$$\hat{p}_{k,j} = \frac{1}{N_k} \sum_{i=1}^{N_k} 1\left(x_{j-1} < X_{k,i} \leq x_j\right), \quad j = 1, \ldots, J, \tag{2.2.7}$$

$$\hat{\mathbf{p}}_k = (\hat{p}_{k1}, \ldots, \hat{p}_{kJ})^\mathsf{T} \in \mathbb{R}^J$$

to be the empirical cell frequencies.

---

[2] The notation $\approx$ is used to represent the trapezoidal rule for approximating integrals; see Goodman (1967).

Under the *least favorable case (LFC)* of the (approximate) null hypothesis $\tilde{H}_0$ (i.e., $\mathbf{p}_1 = \mathbf{p}_2 = \mathbf{p}$),[3] provided that $N_1/(N_1 + N_2)$ converges to a positive constant as $N_1, N_2 \to \infty$, a central limit theorem (CLT) for i.i.d. observations yields

$$\hat{\Lambda}_s := \sqrt{\frac{N_1 N_2}{N_1 + N_2}} I_2^{s-1} I_1 (\hat{\mathbf{p}}_1 - \hat{\mathbf{p}}_2) \Rightarrow N(0, V_s),$$

where

$$V_s = I_2^{s-1} I_1 \Omega (I_2^{s-1} I_1)^{\mathsf{T}}, \tag{2.2.8}$$

$$\Omega = \begin{bmatrix} p_1(1 - p_1) & -p_1 p_2 & \cdots & -p_1 p_J \\ -p_2 p_1 & p_2(1 - p_2) & \cdots & -p_2 p_J \\ \vdots & \vdots & \ddots & \vdots \\ -p_J p_1 & -p_J p_2 & \cdots & p_J(1 - p_J) \end{bmatrix}.$$

Let $\hat{\Lambda}_s = \left(\hat{\Lambda}_{s,1}, \ldots, \hat{\Lambda}_{s,J} \right)^{\mathsf{T}}$ and define $\hat{V}_s = (\hat{V}_{s,ij})$ to be the sample analogue of V_s that estimates p_j by the empirical frequency from the pooled sample in the cell $(x_{j-1}, x_j]$ for $j = 1, \ldots, J$.

Consider the test statistic:

$$AD_N = \max_{j=1,\ldots,J} \frac{\hat{\Lambda}_{s,j}}{\sqrt{\hat{V}_{s,jj}}}. \tag{2.2.9}$$

Anderson (1996) suggests to reject the hypothesis $\tilde{H}_0$ if AD_N takes a value larger than a critical value from the *Studentized Maximum Modulus (SMM)* distribution (defined below).

The following theorem shows that the test has an asymptotically correct size under the null hypothesis $\tilde{H}_0$ and is consistent against the fixed alternative $\tilde{H}_1$:

Theorem 2.2.1 *(a) Under the hypothesis $\tilde{H}_0$,*

$$\limsup_{N \to \infty} P\left[AD_N \geq c_{1-\alpha, J, \infty}^{SMM} \right] \leq \alpha,$$

where $c_{1-\alpha, J, \infty}^{SMM}$ denotes the $(1 - \alpha)$ quantile of the SMM distribution with parameter J and ∞ degrees of freedom. (b) Under the hypothesis $\tilde{H}_1$,

$$\lim_{N \to \infty} P\left[AD_N \geq c_{1-\alpha, J, \infty}^{SMM} \right] = 1.$$

---

[3] Under a composite null hypothesis, the least favorable case is the distribution for which the null holds, but which is most difficult to distinguish (in the sense of having the highest rejection probability) from any distribution in the alternative hypothesis; see, e.g., Lehmann and Romano (2005, section 3).

In general, the SMM distribution with parameter r and v degrees of freedom is the distribution of

$$M(r, v) := \max_{j=1,\ldots,r} |Z_j| / \hat{\sigma},$$

where $\mathbf{Z} = (Z_1, \ldots, Z_r)^\mathsf{T}$ has a $N(0, \sigma^2 I_r)$ distribution and $\hat{\sigma}^2$ is an estimator of σ^2 which is distributed as $\sigma^2 \chi^2(v)/v$ and is independent of $\mathbf{Z}$. Let $c_{1-\alpha,r,v}^{SMM}$ be the $(1 - \alpha)$ quantile of $M(r, v)$,[4] that is

$$P\left[M(r, v) \geq c_{1-\alpha,r,v}^{SMM} \mid \mathbf{Z} \text{ is } N(0, \sigma^2 I_r) \right] = \alpha. \tag{2.2.10}$$

If $\mathbf{Z} = (Z_1, \ldots, Z_r)^\mathsf{T}$ has an arbitrary covariance structure Σ, however, the probability statement (2.2.10) is conservative in the sense that

$$P\left[M(r, v) \geq c_{1-\alpha,r,v}^{SMM} \mid \mathbf{Z} \text{ is } N(0, \Sigma) \right] \leq \alpha; \tag{2.2.11}$$

see Stoline and Ury (1979). Given that V_s in (2.2.8) is not diagonal, this implies that the test AD_N based on the SMM critical value $c_{1-\alpha,J,\infty}^{SMM}$ is conservative.[5]

Anderson (1996)'s test is relatively easy to use and has an advantage of highlighting the exact points in the distribution where discrepancies occur. However, it also has some limitations. First, since the test compares distributions only at finite points, it may be inconsistent against general alternatives. The reason is that the two distributions might coincide at the chosen (finite number of) points, but violate the null hypothesis at the other (possibly uncountably many) points in the supports. Furthermore, the choice of the grid points can be arbitrary and test results might depend sensitively on the choice. Second, as seen from (2.2.11), the test is conservative because the SMM critical values are upper bounds of the exact asymptotic critical values. Third, for $s \geq 2$, the errors in approximating the integral by (2.2.6) may induce biases in estimating the true cell probabilities. These biases may have negative effects on the power of the test when $s \geq 2$; see Barrett and Donald (2003, p. 84) for this point.

(2) Davidson and Duclos Test Davidson and Duclos (2000, hereafter DD) also suggest tests of stochastic dominance based on finite grid points. Let $\mathcal{X}_J = \{x_1, \ldots, x_J\}$ be a set of grid points. DD consider the null hypothesis of sth-order stochastic dominance for $1 \leq s < \infty$ (Strictly speaking, when $s \geq 3$, the hypothesis is necessary for SD; see Definition 1.1.3.):

---

[4] The quantiles of the SMM distribution are tabulated; see Stoline and Ury (1979). For example, the 1% critical value ($\alpha = 0.01$) of the SMM distribution with parameter $(10, \infty)$ is 3.289.

[5] For one-sided hypotheses, including the SD hypothesis, it may be less conservative to use the critical values from $\max_{j=1,\ldots,J} \mathbb{Z}_j$, where $\mathbb{Z}_j$s are standard normal random variables, provided the sample size is sufficiently large so that s is close to σ; see Tong (1990) and Barrett and Donald (2003, footnote 18). The latter critical values can be calculated using $c_\alpha = \Phi^{-1}\left((1 - \alpha)^{1/J}\right)$ for a test with significance level α.

$$H_0 : F_1^{(s)}(x) \leq F_2^{(s)}(x) \text{ for all } x \in \mathcal{X}_J, \tag{2.2.12}$$

$$H_1 : F_1^{(s)}(x) > F_2^{(s)}(x) \text{ for some } x \in \mathcal{X}_J. \tag{2.2.13}$$

Let $\{X_{1,i} : i = 1, \ldots, N\}$ and $\{X_{2,i} : i = 1, \ldots, N\}$ be (possibly mutually dependent) random samples from F_1 and F_2, respectively, with the supports contained in the nonnegative real line. By integration by parts, the integrated CDF $F_k^{(s)}$ can be expressed as

$$F_k^{(s)}(x) = \frac{1}{(s-1)!} \int_0^x (x-t)^{s-1} dF_k(t)$$

$$= \frac{1}{(s-1)!} E\left[x - X_k\right]_+^{s-1}, \tag{2.2.14}$$

where $[\cdot]_+ := \max\{\cdot, 0\}$. A natural estimator of (2.2.14) is given by its sample analogue:

$$\bar{F}_k^{(s)}(x) = \frac{1}{N(s-1)!} \sum_{i=1}^N \left[x - X_{k,i}\right]_+^{s-1}. \tag{2.2.15}$$

When $s = 1$, $\bar{F}_k^{(s)}$ is called the *empirical CDF*:

$$\bar{F}_k(x) := \bar{F}_k^{(1)}(x) = \frac{1}{N} \sum_{i=1}^N \mathbf{1}\left(X_{k,i} \leq x\right), \tag{2.2.16}$$

which is a nonparametric estimator of the true CDF F_k.[6] For $k \neq l$, define the differences between integrated CDFs and empirical integrated CDFs:

$$D_{k,l}^{(s)}(x) = F_k^{(s)}(x) - F_l^{(s)}(x), \tag{2.2.17}$$

$$\bar{D}_{k,l}^{(s)}(x) = \bar{F}_k^{(s)}(x) - \bar{F}_l^{(s)}(x). \tag{2.2.18}$$

(We shall maintain the notation (2.2.15)–(2.2.18) throughout this book.)

Let

$$\Delta_s = \left(D_{1,2}^{(s)}(x_1), \ldots, D_{1,2}^{(s)}(x_J)\right)^{\mathsf{T}}$$

and

$$\hat{\Delta}_s = \left(\bar{D}_{1,2}^{(s)}(x_1), \ldots, \bar{D}_{1,2}^{(s)}(x_J)\right)^{\mathsf{T}}$$

$$:= \left(\hat{\Delta}_{s,1}, \ldots, \hat{\Delta}_{s,J}\right)^{\mathsf{T}}.$$

A multivariate CLT yields that $\hat{\Delta}_s$ is asymptotically normally distributed (theorem 1 of DD):

---

[6] Under weak assumptions, the empirical CDF is a (uniformly) consistent estimator of the true CDF. See Appendix A for its asymptotic properties.

Theorem 2.2.2 *Suppose $E |X_k|^{2(s-1)} < \infty$ for $k = 1, 2$. Then,*

$$\sqrt{N} \left(\hat{\Delta}_s - \Delta_s \right) \Rightarrow N(0, \Omega_s),$$

where $\Omega_s = \left(\Omega_{s,m,n} \right) := \left(\Omega_{s,m,n}^{1,1} - \Omega_{s,m,n}^{1,2} - \Omega_{s,m,n}^{2,1} + \Omega_{s,m,n}^{2,2} \right)$ is a $J \times J$ covariance matrix with

$$\Omega_{s,m,n}^{k,l} = \frac{1}{((s-1)!)^2} E\{[x_m - X_k]_+^{s-1} [x_n - X_l]_+^{s-1}\} - F_k^{(s)}(x_m) F_l^{(s)}(x_n)$$

for $k, l \in \{1, 2\}$ and $m, n \in \{1, \ldots, J\}$.

Let $\hat{\Omega}_s = \left(\hat{\Omega}_{s,m,n} \right)$ be the sample analogue estimator of Ω_s with

$$\hat{\Omega}_{s,m,n}^{k,l} = \frac{1}{N \left((s-1)!\right)^2} \sum_{i=1}^{N} [x_m - X_{k,i}]_+^{s-1} [x_n - X_{l,i}]_+^{s-1} - \bar{F}_k^{(s)}(x_m) \bar{F}_l^{(s)}(x_n).$$

Two types of test statistics are considered by DD:

$$W_N = \min_{\Delta \in \mathbb{R}_-^J} \left(\hat{\Delta}_s - \Delta \right)^{\mathsf{T}} \hat{\Omega}_s^{-1} \left(\hat{\Delta}_s - \Delta \right), \tag{2.2.19}$$

$$DD_N = \max_{j=1,\ldots,J} \frac{\hat{\Delta}_{s,j}}{\sqrt{\hat{\Omega}_{s,jj}}}. \tag{2.2.20}$$

W_N is a *Wald statistic* for multiple inequality restrictions and, under the least favorable case (LFC) ($\Delta_s = 0$), its asymptotic distribution is given by a mixture of chi-squared distributions. On the other hand, DD_N is a *maximum t-statistic* and its asymptotic distribution under the LFC is stochastically bounded by a Studentized Maximum Modulus (SMM) distribution.

The asymptotic properties of the tests are summarized as follows:

Theorem 2.2.3 *Suppose the conditions of Theorem 2.2.2 hold. Then, (a) under the null hypothesis (2.2.12),*

$$\limsup_{N \to \infty} P \left[W_N > c_{1-\alpha, J}^M \right] \leq \alpha,$$

$$\limsup_{N \to \infty} P \left[DD_N > c_{1-\alpha, J, \infty}^{SMM} \right] \leq \alpha,$$

where $c_{1-\alpha, J}^M$ and $c_{1-\alpha, J, \infty}^{SMM}$ denote the $(1 - \alpha)$ quantiles of the mixture of chi-squared distributions $\sum_{v=0}^{J} P(\chi^2(v) \leq c) w(J, J - v, \Omega_s)$ for $c > 0$ and the SMM distribution $M(J, \infty)$, respectively; (b) under the alternative hypothesis (2.2.13),

$$\lim_{N \to \infty} P\left[W_N > c^M_{1-\alpha, J} \right] = 1,$$

$$\lim_{N \to \infty} P\left[DD_N > c^{SMM}_{1-\alpha, J, \infty} \right] = 1.$$

Although closed-form solutions for the weights ($w(\cdot, \cdot, \cdot)$) of mixtures of chi-squared distributions are available for small J (say $J \leq 4$; see Kudo, 1963), the test requires Monte Carlo simulations to compute the weights when J is large; see Perlman (1969), Kodde and Palm (1986), and Wolak (1987, 1989, 1991) for general order-restricted inference methods. To compute the critical values of DD_N, one can either use the SMM distribution tables (Stoline and Ury, 1979) or do Monte Carlo simulations.

The pros and cons of the DD tests (W_N and DD_N) are similar to those of Anderson's test since both are based on comparisons of CDFs at finite numbers of points. The main differences are that DD use an exact unbiased estimator of $F_k^{(s)}$, while Anderson (1996) uses a trapezoidal rule to approximate the integrals. Also, DD allow dependence between the two samples, which can be useful in some applications, e.g., comparing before-tax and after-tax incomes for the same individual. Both tests have been used quite extensively in empirical applications.

2.2.2 Supremum-Type Tests

(1) McFadden Test McFadden (1989) proposes nonparametric tests of FSD and SSD hypotheses.[7]

For $k = 1, 2$, let $\{X_{k,i} : i = 1, \ldots, N\}$ be a random sample of size N from the distribution F_k supported on $\mathcal{X} = [0, 1]$. (The two samples are assumed to be drawn independently.) For $s = 1, 2$, consider the SD hypothesis over the full support:

$$H_0 : F_1^{(s)}(x) \leq F_2^{(s)}(x) \text{ for all } x \in \mathcal{X}, \tag{2.2.21}$$

$$H_1 : F_1^{(s)}(x) > F_2^{(s)}(x) \text{ for some } x \in \mathcal{X}. \tag{2.2.22}$$

To test the hypothesis, a supremum-type test statistic is considered:

$$MF_{s,N} = \sup_{x \in \mathcal{X}} \sqrt{N} \left(\bar{D}_{1,2}^{(s)}(x) \right), \tag{2.2.23}$$

where $\bar{D}_{1,2}^{(s)}(x)$ denotes the difference between the two empirical (integrated) CDFs; see (2.2.18) for the definition.

---

[7] There are some early results on parametric tests of the utility maximization hypotheses assuming knowledge of distribution of the prospects; examples include Green, Lau, and Polemarchakis (1978), Varian (1983), and Green and Srivastava (1986).

The asymptotic null distributions of the test statistic for $s = 1, 2$ are given by the following theorem.

Theorem 2.2.4 *Under the least favorable case (LFC)* $(F := F_1 = F_2)$ *of* H_0,

$$MF_{1,N} \Rightarrow \sup_{x \in \mathcal{X}} \mathcal{B}(x), \tag{2.2.24}$$

$$MF_{2,N} \Rightarrow \sup_{x \in \mathcal{X}} \int_0^x \mathcal{B}(F(t))dt, \tag{2.2.25}$$

where $\mathcal{B}$ *denotes a standard Brownian bridge.*

When $s = 1$, the test statistic is the well-known one-sided Kolmogorov–Smirnov statistic and the result of Theorem 2.2.4 follows from a standard argument (Billingsley, 1968, p. 85).[8] The limit distribution in (2.2.24) satisfies

$$P\left(\sup_{x \in [0,1]} \mathcal{B}(x) \leq c \right) = 1 - e^{-2c^2}, \quad c \in \mathbb{R}_+, \tag{2.2.26}$$

so that one can compute a p-value by $\exp\left(-2 \left(MF_{1,N} \right)^2 \right)$ or use the critical values 1.073, 1.2239, and 1.5274 for the significance levels 10%, 5%, and 1%, respectively.

On the other hand, when $s = 2$, the limit distribution in (2.2.25) is the supremum of a Gaussian process $\int_0^x \mathcal{B}(F(t))dt := \nu_F(x)$ whose covariance function is given by

$$
\begin{aligned}
C(x_1, x_2; F) &= E\nu_F(x_1)\nu_F(x_2) \\
&= 2\{\lambda_F (x_1 \wedge x_2) + |x_1 - x_2| \psi_F(x_1 \wedge x_2) \\
&\quad -\psi_F(x_1)\psi_F(x_2)\}
\end{aligned}
$$

for $\psi_F(s) = \int_0^s (s - u)dF(u)$ and $\lambda_F(s) = \int_0^s (s - u)^2 dF(u)$. We can see that, in contrast to (2.2.26), the limit distribution in (2.2.25) depends on the true distribution F and hence cannot be tabulated once and for all. In view of this, McFadden (1989) suggests a permutation procedure based on the pooled sample to compute critical values.

McFadden (1989)'s test is consistent against the alternative H_1 in (2.2.22), which is obviously more general than H_1 in (2.2.13) since $\mathcal{X}_J$ is a strict subset of $\mathcal{X}$. However, it is conservative because the critical values are based on the LFC of the null hypothesis. It also requires independence both across and within the samples.

Klecan, McFadden, and McFadden (1991) extend this result to time series observations. They require "generalized exchangeability" among prospects at

---

[8] This result follows from the functional CLT and continuous mapping theorem; see Appendix A for the basic technical tools.

a given time, but it can be restrictive in some applications.[9] Also, the critical values proposed are not applicable to general time-series settings because they require independence over time. A subsequent work by Linton, Maasoumi, and Whang (2005) relaxes the requirement using a subsampling approach; see Section 2.2.2.

(2) Barrett and Donald Test Barrett and Donald (2003, BD) propose a Kolmogorov–Smirnov-type test of (possibly higher-order) stochastic dominance. Their hypotheses of interest are

$$H_0 : F_1^{(s)}(x) \le F_2^{(s)}(x) \; \forall x \in \mathcal{X}, \tag{2.2.27}$$

$$H_1 : F_1^{(s)}(x) > F_2^{(s)}(x) \; \text{for some } x \in \mathcal{X}, \tag{2.2.28}$$

where $\mathcal{X}$ is a compact set satisfying Assumption 2.2.1 below.[10] The test is applicable to independent samples from two populations. (BD allow the sample sizes to be different, but for simplicity we discuss the case of equal sample sizes below.) They suggest several bootstrap procedures to compute critical values.

Assumption 2.2.1 *(a) F_1 and F_2 have common support $[0, \bar{x}] = \mathcal{X}$, where $\bar{x} < \infty$, and are continuous functions on $\mathcal{X}$. (b) $\{X_{1,i} : i = 1, \dots, N\}$ and $\{X_{2,i} : i = 1, \dots, N\}$ are independent random samples from F_1 and F_2, respectively.*

The test statistic is given by

$$BD_N = \sqrt{N} \sup_{x \in \mathcal{X}} \left(\bar{D}_{1,2}^{(s)}(x) \right), \tag{2.2.29}$$

where $\bar{D}_{1,2}^{(s)}(x)$ is defined in (2.2.18) as before.

Write the higher-order integral $F^{(s)}$ as a functional of F:

$$\mathcal{J}_s(x, F) := F^{(s)}(x) = \frac{1}{(s-1)!} \int_0^x (x-t)^{s-1} dF(t). \tag{2.2.30}$$

Notice that $\mathcal{J}_s$ is a linear (and hence continuous) operator. The asymptotic null distribution of BD_N can be characterized using the following result:

---

[9] The random variables $X_1, \dots, X_K$ are said to be *generalized exchangeable* if $Y_1 = F_1(X_1)$, $\dots, Y_K = F_K(X_K)$ are exchangeable (i.e., the joint distribution of any permuted sequence of random variables is the same as that of the original sequence of random variables).

[10] Horváth, Kokoszka, and Zitikis (2006) show that, if $\mathcal{X}$ is an unbounded set, the supremum test statistic for higher-order SD hypotheses may not be always well defined, and suggest introducing a weight function to the test statistic; see Section 3.3.1.

Theorem 2.2.5 *Suppose Assumption 2.2.1 holds. Then, for $k = 1, 2$,*

$$\sqrt{N}\left(\bar{F}_k^{(s)}(\cdot) - F_k^{(s)}(\cdot)\right) \Rightarrow \mathcal{J}_s(\cdot, \mathcal{B}_k \circ F_k),$$

where $\mathcal{B}_1$ and $\mathcal{B}_2$ are independent standard Brownian bridges.

The result of Theorem 2.2.5 follows from a standard argument in the empirical process literature.[11] That is, by the Donsker theorem, the empirical CDF converges weakly to an F_k-Brownian bridge, i.e.,

$$\sqrt{N}\left(\bar{F}_k(\cdot) - F_k(\cdot)\right) \Rightarrow \mathcal{B}_k(F_k(\cdot)) = \mathcal{B}_k \circ F_k(\cdot).$$

Then, by the continuous mapping theorem, we have

$$\begin{aligned}
\sqrt{N}\left(\bar{F}_k^{(s)}(\cdot) - F_k^{(s)}(\cdot)\right) &= \sqrt{N}\left[\mathcal{J}_s(\cdot, \bar{F}_k) - \mathcal{J}_s(\cdot, F_k)\right] \\
&= \mathcal{J}_s(\cdot, \sqrt{N}\left(\bar{F}_k - F_k\right)) \\
&\Rightarrow \mathcal{J}_s(\cdot, \mathcal{B}_k \circ F_k). \quad (2.2.31)
\end{aligned}$$

The limiting process $\mathcal{J}_s(\cdot, \mathcal{B}_k \circ F_k)$ in the above Theorem is a Gaussian process with mean zero and covariance function given by

$$C_s(x_1, x_2; F_k) = E\mathcal{J}_s(x_1, \mathcal{B}_k \circ F_k)\mathcal{J}_s(x_2, \mathcal{B}_k \circ F_k).$$

For example, for $x_2 > x_1$ and $s = 2$, the covariance function can be written as

$$\begin{aligned}
C_2(x_1, x_2; F_k) = &E\left[(x_1 - X_k)^2 1(X_k \leq x_1)\right] \\
&+ (x_2 - x_1)E\left[(x_1 - X_k)1(X_k \leq x_1)\right].^{12}
\end{aligned}$$

Define

$$\nu_s(\cdot) = \mathcal{J}_s(\cdot, \mathcal{B}_1 \circ F_1) - \mathcal{J}_s(\cdot, \mathcal{B}_2 \circ F_2).$$

Let $c_{1-\alpha}^{BD}$ be the $(1 - \alpha)$ quantile of $\sup_{x \in \mathcal{X}} \nu_s(x)$. BD establish the following results:

Theorem 2.2.6 *Suppose Assumption 2.2.1 holds. Then, (a) under the null hypothesis H_0,*

$$\limsup_{N \to \infty} P\left[BD_N \geq c_{1-\alpha}^{BD}\right] \leq \alpha,$$

where the equality holds when $F_1(x) = F_2(x)$ for all $x \in \mathcal{X}$; (b) under the alternative hypothesis H_1,

$$\lim_{N \to \infty} P\left[BD_N \geq c_{1-\alpha}^{BD}\right] = 1.$$

We now explain the asymptotic behavior of BD_N under the null hypothesis. Theorem 2.2.5 and Assumption 2.2.1 (b) imply that

---

[11] See Appendix A for the basic concepts and technical tools.
[12] See lemma 1 of BD for a general expression.

$$\hat{T}_s(\cdot) := \sqrt{N} \left\{ \left(\bar{F}_1^{(s)}(\cdot) - F_1^{(s)}(\cdot) \right) - \left(\bar{F}_2^{(s)}(\cdot) - F_2^{(s)}(\cdot) \right) \right\}$$

$$\Rightarrow v_s(\cdot). \tag{2.2.32}$$

Therefore,

$$BD_N = \sup_{x \in \mathcal{X}} \left\{ \hat{T}_s(x) + \sqrt{N} \left[D_{1,2}^{(s)}(x) \right] \right\} \tag{2.2.33}$$

$$\leq \sup_{x \in \mathcal{X}} \hat{T}_s(x) \tag{2.2.34}$$

$$\Rightarrow \sup_{x \in \mathcal{X}} v_s(x), \tag{2.2.35}$$

where the inequality (2.2.34) holds under the null hypothesis H_0, and (2.2.35) follows from (2.2.32) and the continuous mapping theorem. The equality in (2.2.34) holds when the two distribution functions are equal over all $\mathcal{X}$, which corresponds to the LFC of the null hypothesis. This establishes Theorem 2.2.6 (a) since

$$\limsup_{N \to \infty} P \left[BD_N \geq c_{1-\alpha}^{BD} \right] \leq P \left[\sup_{x \in \mathcal{X}} v_s(x) \geq c_{1-\alpha}^{BD} \right] = \alpha.$$

In practice, the distribution $\sup_{x \in \mathcal{X}} v_s(x)$ is non-pivotal (i.e., it depends on the true CDFs) and hence critical values cannot be tabulated. In view of this, BD propose Monte Carlo simulation and bootstrap methods to approximate the distribution of $\sup_{x \in \mathcal{X}} v_s(x)$.

1. *Multiplier Method:* Let $\{U_{1,i} : i = 1, .., N\}$ and $\{U_{2,i} : i = 1, .., N\}$ be two independent sequences of i.i.d. $N(0, 1)$ random variables that are independent of the sample. Define the simulated process

$$\mathcal{B}_k^* \circ \bar{F}_k(x) = \frac{1}{\sqrt{N}} \sum_{i=1}^{N} \left[1(X_{k,i} \leq x) - \bar{F}_k(x) \right]$$

$$\times U_{k,i} \text{ for } k = 1, 2. \tag{2.2.36}$$

This process mimics paths of the F_k-Brownian bridge $\mathcal{B}_k \circ F_k(x)$. Then, for $k = 1, 2$,

$$\mathcal{J}_s(x, \mathcal{B}_1^* \circ \bar{F}_k) = \frac{1}{\sqrt{N}(s-1)!} \sum_{i=1}^{N} Z_{k,i} U_{k,i}, \text{ where}$$

$$\tag{2.2.37}$$

$$Z_{k,i} = \left(x - X_{k,i} \right)^{s-1} 1 \left[X_{k,i} \leq x \right]$$

$$- \frac{1}{N} \sum_{j=1}^{N} \left(x - X_{k,j} \right)^{s-1} 1 \left[X_{k,j} \leq x \right].$$

The α-level multiplier method critical values are defined to be the $(1 - \alpha)$ quantiles of the simulated distribution of

$$KS2^* = \sup_{x \in \mathcal{X}} \left\{ \mathcal{J}_s(x, \mathcal{B}_1^* \circ \bar{F}_1) - \mathcal{J}_s(\cdot, \mathcal{B}_2^* \circ \bar{F}_2) \right\}. \quad (2.2.38)$$

It can be shown that (2.2.38) mimics the limit distribution $\sup_{x \in \mathcal{X}} v_s(x)$, conditional on the original sample.

2. *Bootstrap Methods:*

(a) *Pooled Sample Bootstrap*: Draw bootstrap samples $\mathcal{S}_k^* = \{X_{k,i}^* : i = 1, \ldots, N\}$, $k = 1, 2$ independently from the pooled sample

$$\{X_{1,1}, \ldots, X_{1,N}, X_{2,1}, \ldots, X_{2,N}\}$$

and compute the empirical CDFs using the bootstrap samples:

$$\bar{F}_k^*(x) = \frac{1}{N} \sum_{i=1}^{N} 1(X_{k,i}^* \leq x), \ k = 1, 2.$$

Then, the α-level *pooled sample bootstrap* critical values are defined to be the $(1 - \alpha)$ quantiles of the distribution of the bootstrap statistic

$$KSB2^* = \sup_{x \in \mathcal{X}} \left\{ \mathcal{J}_s(x, \bar{F}_1^*) - \mathcal{J}_s(x, \bar{F}_2^*) \right\}. \quad (2.2.39)$$

(b) *Recentered Bootstrap*: Draw bootstrap samples $\mathcal{S}_1^*$ and $\mathcal{S}_2^*$ independently from the original samples

$$\{X_{1,1}, \ldots, X_{1,N}\} \text{ and } \{X_{2,1}, \ldots, X_{2,N}\},$$

respectively, then compute the empirical CDF $\bar{F}_k^*$, $k = 1, 2$ using each bootstrap sample. Then, the α-level *recentered bootstrap* critical values are defined to be the $(1 - \alpha)$ quantiles of the distribution of the bootstrap statistic

$$KSB3^* \quad (2.2.40)$$
$$= \sup_{x \in \mathcal{X}} \left\{ \left[\mathcal{J}_s(x, \bar{F}_1^*) - \mathcal{J}_s(x, \bar{F}_1) \right] \right.$$
$$\left. - \left[\mathcal{J}_s(x, \bar{F}_2^*) - \mathcal{J}_s(x, \bar{F}_2) \right] \right\}.$$

All of the above procedures impose the restriction of the LFC of the null hypothesis.[13] That is, the multiplier method directly approximates the LFC distribution $\sup_{x \in \mathcal{X}} v_s(x)$. On the other hand, the pooled bootstrap (2.2.39) generates bootstrap samples from the same (pooled) distribution F ($:= F_1 = F_2$). Also, the recentered bootstrap (2.2.40) imposes the LFC restriction by

---

[13] BD also propose one-sample versions of the multiplier method ($KS1^*$) and the bootstrap method ($KSB1^*$). For simplicity, however, we do not discuss them.

recentering, which effectively removes a bootstrap analog of the second term inside the supremum in (2.2.33).

It can be shown that Theorem 2.2.6 holds with $c_{1-\alpha}^{BD}$ replaced by any of the critical values described above (proposition 2 of BD). This implies that the BD test based on the above critical values has asymptotically correct size and is consistent against all nonparametric alternatives.

Since the critical values are based on the LFC of the null hypothesis, however, the BD test can be conservative in practice. In fact, using a more refined argument (given below), it can be shown that the limiting null distribution of BD_N is generally stochastically smaller than $\sup_{x \in \mathcal{X}} v_s(x)$.

Theorem 2.2.7 *Suppose Assumption 2.2.1 holds. Then, under the null hypothesis H_0,*

$$BD_N \Rightarrow \sup_{x \in \mathcal{C}_0} \{v_s(x)\}, \tag{2.2.41}$$

where

$$\mathcal{C}_0 = \{x \in \mathcal{X} : D_{1,2}^{(s)}(x) = 0\}. \tag{2.2.42}$$

Here, $\mathcal{C}_0$ denotes the "contact set" where the two distributions coincide (Linton, Song, and Whang, 2010, section 3.1.1). Since $\mathcal{C}_0 \subseteq \mathcal{X}$, the distribution of $\sup_{x \in \mathcal{X}} v_s(x)$ stochastically dominates the distribution of $\sup_{x \in \mathcal{C}_0} \{v_s(x)\}$. Therefore, unless $D_{1,2}^{(s)}(x) = 0$ for all $x \in \mathcal{X}$ (i.e., $\mathcal{C}_0 = \mathcal{X}$), the size of the α-level BD test would be strictly less than α. One way of improving the power performance is to directly approximate the limit distribution $\sup_{x \in \mathcal{C}_0} \{v_s(x)\}$; see Sections 2.2.2 and 3.1 for various approaches.

We now explain why (2.2.41) is true. Heuristically, this holds because $\hat{T}_s(x)$ is $O_p(1)$ for all x in $\mathcal{X}$, but $\sqrt{N}\left[D_{1,2}^{(s)}(x)\right]$ diverges to $-\infty$ at $x \in \mathcal{X} \backslash \mathcal{C}_0$ under the null hypothesis, so that the supremum of the sum of two terms is achieved at x in the contact set $\mathcal{C}_0$. More specifically, notice that

$$BD_N \geq \sqrt{N} \sup_{x \in \mathcal{C}_0} \left(\bar{D}_{1,2}^{(s)}(x)\right) = \sup_{x \in \mathcal{C}_0} \hat{T}_s(x), \tag{2.2.43}$$

where the inequality holds because $\mathcal{C}_0 \subseteq \mathcal{X}$. On the other hand, the weak convergence in (2.2.32) implies stochastic equicontinuity of $\hat{T}_s(\cdot)$;[14] i.e., for any $\varepsilon, \gamma > 0$, there exists $\delta > 0$ such that

$$\limsup_{N \to \infty} P\left(\sup_{|x_1 - x_2| < \delta} \left|\hat{T}_s(x_1) - \hat{T}_s(x_2)\right| > \varepsilon\right) < \gamma. \tag{2.2.44}$$

---

[14] See Theorems A.2.3 and A.2.4 in Appendix A.

Let $\hat{x} \in \mathcal{X}$ be the value of x that achieves the supremum in (2.2.29). Define $\mathcal{C}_0^+ := \{x \in \mathcal{C}_0 : |x - \hat{x}| < \delta\}$ to be the δ-neighborhood of $\hat{x}$ in $\mathcal{C}_0$.[15] Then, we have

$$
\begin{aligned}
BD_N &= \sqrt{N} \left(\bar{D}_{1,2}^{(s)}(\hat{x}) \right) \\
&= \hat{T}_s(\hat{x}) + \sqrt{N} \left[D_{1,2}^{(s)}(\hat{x}) \right] \\
&\leq \sup_{x \in \mathcal{C}_0} \hat{T}_s(x) + \left\{ \hat{T}_s(\hat{x}) - \inf_{x \in \mathcal{C}_0^+} \hat{T}_s(x) \right\} + \sqrt{N} \left[D_{1,2}^{(s)}(\hat{x}) \right] \\
&\leq \sup_{x \in \mathcal{C}_0} \hat{T}_s(x) + \sup_{x \in \mathcal{C}_0^+} \left\{ \hat{T}_s(\hat{x}) - \hat{T}_s(x) \right\} \\
&\leq \sup_{x \in \mathcal{C}_0} \hat{T}_s(x) + \sup_{|x_1 - x_2| < \delta} \left| \hat{T}_s(x_1) - \hat{T}_s(x_2) \right|,
\end{aligned}
\tag{2.2.45}
$$

where the third line follows from the fact $\sup_{x \in \mathcal{C}_0} \hat{T}_s(x) \geq \inf_{x \in \mathcal{C}_0^+} \hat{T}_s(x)$, the fourth line holds under the null hypothesis and the last line follows from the definition of $\mathcal{C}_0^+$. Now the second term on the right-hand side of (2.2.45) can be made asymptotically negligible by the stochastic equicontinuity (2.2.44). Combining (2.2.43) and (2.2.45), we can establish (2.2.41).

(3) Linton, Maasoumi, and Whang Test Linton, Maasoumi, and Whang (2005, LMW) propose a Kolmogorov–Smirnov-type test of stochastic dominance of arbitrary order in the general K-prospect case ($K \geq 2$), allowing for general sampling schemes. They consider the following hypotheses:

$$
H_0 : \min_{k \neq l} \left\{ D_{k,l}^{(s)}(x) \right\} \leq 0 \text{ for all } x \in \mathcal{X},
\tag{2.2.46}
$$

$$
H_1 : \min_{k \neq l} \left\{ D_{k,l}^{(s)}(x) \right\} > 0 \text{ for some } x \in \mathcal{X},
\tag{2.2.47}
$$

where $D_{k,l}^{(s)}(x)$ is defined as in (2.2.17), $\mathcal{X}$ is a set contained in the union of the supports of X_k for $k = 1, \ldots, K$, and the minimum is taken over all $k, l \in \{1, \ldots, K\}$ with $k \neq l$.

The null hypothesis (2.2.46) is that of *stochastic maximality* (Klecan, McFadden, and McFadden (1991)), i.e., there exists at least one prospect in the set of K-prospects which sth-order stochastically dominates some of the others. The alternative hypothesis is its negation, i.e., there is no prospect which sth-order dominates any of the others.

---

[15] It can be shown that $\mathcal{C}_0^+$ is nonempty with probability that goes to 1, which implies that the supremum is achieved at the neighborhood of the contact set. This makes intuitive sense because outside the neighborhood (which is at the interior of the null hypothesis), $\hat{T}_s(x)$ will take very small negative values when N is large, while the mean of $\hat{T}_s(x)$ remains constant (zero) for all x in the contact set.

When $K = 2$, the null hypothesis H_0 corresponds to the two-sided version of the stochastic dominance hypothesis, i.e., either F_1 SD F_2 or F_2 SD F_1 at order s. Therefore, it is straightforward to see that the results of LMW can be applied to test the conventional one-sided version of the stochastic dominance hypothesis by removing $\min_{k \neq l}$.

The main features of LMW are as follows: (i) SD of arbitrary order;[16] (ii) serially dependent observations with general dependence among the prospects; (iii) prospects from parametric models, opening a way for conditional ranking; (iv) subsampling critical values.

One of the main advantages of the LMW test is that it allows for general sampling schemes. Specifically, they allow the observations to be strictly stationary and α-mixing, so that the test can be used in time series contexts.[17] Also, they allow arbitrary dependence among prospects at a given time, which is also useful in many examples.

Another feature of LMW is that they consider the case of "residual" dominance, which assumes that $X_{k,i} := X_{k,i}(\theta_{k0})$ might depend on an unknown finite dimensional parameter θ_{k0}. For example, one may consider a linear model $X_{k,i}(\theta) = Y_{k,i} - Z_{k,i}^{\mathsf{T}} \theta$ and compare the distributions of the estimated prospects $\widehat{X}_{k,i} = X_{k,i}(\widehat{\theta}_k)$, where $\widehat{\theta}_k$ is an estimator of θ_{k0}. They require $\widehat{\theta}_k$ to satisfy the linear representation

$$\sqrt{N}(\widehat{\theta}_k - \theta_{k0}) = \frac{1}{\sqrt{N}} \sum_{i=1}^{N} \Gamma_{k0} \psi_k(Y_{ki}, Z_{ki}, \theta_{k0}) + o_p(1),$$

where Γ_{k0} is a non-stochastic matrix and $E\psi_k(Y_{ki}, Z_{ki}, \theta_{k0}) = 0$. This requirement is weak and is satisfied by many parametric and semiparametric estimators such as the OLS and MLE.

The motivation for considering estimated prospects is that, when data is limited, one may want to use a model to adjust for systematic differences. Common practice is to group the data into subsets (say, of families with different sizes, or by educational attainment, or subgroups of funds by investment goals), and then make comparisons across homogenous subpopulations. When we have limited data, however, this can be difficult. In addition, the preliminary regressions may identify "causes" of different outcomes which may be of substantive interest and useful to control for.[18]

---

[16] LMW also discuss tests of Prospect and Markowitz Stochastic Dominance, but for simplicity we shall not discuss them in this section.

[17] See Appendix A for the concepts of stationarity and mixing.

[18] Linton, Song, and Whang (2010, LSW) extend this idea to semiparametric and nonparametric models. The idea of controlling for systematic differences is closely related to that of conditional stochastic dominance (discussed in Chapter 4). However, the two approaches differ in that the modeling approach (LMW or LSW) controls for the effect of covariates only on the mean of a prospect, whereas the conditional stochastic dominance approach controls for their effect on the whole (conditional) distribution of the prospect. If the dimension of the covariates

As an example of the residual-based testing, one can consider a test of stochastic dominance of different residuals from a *style regression*. Return-based style analysis (originally proposed by Sharpe, 1992) is a popular practitioner's tool to study the performances of fund managers. The style regression for returns R_k of a given fund $k \in \{1, \ldots, K\}$ is

$$R_{k,i} = \alpha_k + \sum_{j=1}^{J} \beta_{jk} F_{j,i} + \varepsilon_{k,i}, \ i = 1, \ldots, N,$$

where $F_{j,i}$ is the (observed) return of asset class $j = 1, \ldots, J$ and the β_{jk}s are the factor loadings, while $\varepsilon_{k,i}$ is an idiosyncratic disturbance term that contains the unexplained part of the funds' performances. The term $u_{k,i} = \alpha_k + \varepsilon_{k,i}$ represents the own choice of the fund manager and is called the "selectivity of the fund." It may be of interest to compare $u_{k,i}$s from different funds and to rank them according to some criteria. For $u_{k,i}$s, it is a common practice to interpret α_k of each fund as a measure of its success in selection. Given considerable evidence on non-normality of stock returns, relying purely on a location measure to evaluate performances may not be appropriate.

For $k = 1, \ldots, K$, define

$$F_k^{(1)}(x, \theta) := F_k(x, \theta) = P\left(X_{k,i}(\theta) \le x\right),$$

$$F_k^{(s)}(x, \theta) = \int_{-\infty}^{x} F_k^{(s-1)}(t, \theta) dt \text{ for } s \ge 2.$$

Let $\overline{F}_k^{(s)}(x, \theta)$ denote the sample analogue of $F_k^{(s)}(x, \theta)$ for $s \ge 1$. We shall denote $F_k^{(s)}(x) := F_k^{(s)}(x, \theta_{k0})$ and $\overline{F}_k^{(s)}(x) := \overline{F}_k^{(s)}(x, \theta_{k0})$.

Consider the population functional:

$$d_s := \min_{k \ne l} \sup_{x \in \mathcal{X}} \left[D_{k,l}^{(s)}(x) \right]. \tag{2.2.48}$$

Then, it is easy to see that the hypotheses (2.2.46) can be equivalently written as

$$H_0 : d_s \le 0 \text{ vs. } H_1 : d_s > 0.$$

The test statistic of LMW is given by the sample analogue of d_s:

$$LMW_N = \sqrt{N} \min_{k \ne l} \sup_{x \in \mathcal{X}} \left[\overline{F}_k^{(s)}(x, \hat{\theta}_k) - \overline{F}_l^{(s)}(x, \hat{\theta}_l) \right]. \tag{2.2.49}$$

Under some regularity conditions, LMW (theorem 1) show that the asymptotic null distribution of LMW_N is a functional of a mean zero Gaussian

---

is large, then the modeling approach has an advantage over the conditional stochastic dominance approach because it is less subject to the curse of dimensionality problem; see Section 4.1 for further discussion.

process in the "boundary" of the null hypothesis in which $d_s = 0$. In the interior case $d_s < 0$, however, the test statistic may degenerate to $-\infty$.

To illustrate the asymptotic distribution heuristically in a simple setting, assume that $K = 2$ and there are no estimated parameters. Then, LMW_N can be written as

$$LMW_N^0 = \sqrt{N} \min \left\{ \sup_{x \in \mathcal{X}} [\bar{D}_{1,2}^{(s)}(x)], \sup_{x \in \mathcal{X}} [\bar{D}_{2,1}^{(s)}(x)] \right\}.$$

The asymptotic behavior of LMW_N^0 is given by the following theorem.

Theorem 2.2.8 *Suppose that Assumption 1 (or 1*) of LMW hold. Then, (a) under the null hypothesis H_0, we have*

$$LMW_N^0$$
$$\Rightarrow \begin{cases} \min \left\{ \sup_{x \in \mathcal{C}_0} \left[v_{1,2}^{(s)}(x) \right], \sup_{x \in \mathcal{C}_0} \left[v_{2,1}^{(s)}(x) \right] \right\} & \text{if } d_s = 0 \\ -\infty & \text{if } d_s < 0, \end{cases}$$

where $\mathcal{C}_0 = \{ x \in \mathcal{X} : D_{1,2}^{(s)}(x) = 0 \}$ and $v_{k,l}^{(s)}(\cdot)$ is a mean zero Gaussian process for $(k, l) = (1, 2)$ and $(2, 1)$; (b) under the alternative hypothesis H_1, $LMW_N^0 \to \infty$ in probability.

To see this, note that, under the null hypothesis H_0, either $F_1 \succeq_s F_2$ or $F_2 \succeq_s F_1$ is true. If the contact set $\mathcal{C}_0$ is nonempty, then $d_s = 0$. In this case, by an argument similar to (2.2.41), it can be shown that

$$\sup_{x \in \mathcal{X}} [\bar{D}_{k,l}^{(s)}(x)] \Rightarrow \sup_{x \in \mathcal{C}_0} \left[v_{k,l}^{(s)}(x) \right].$$

Therefore, by the continuous mapping theorem, we have

$$LMW_N^0 \Rightarrow \min \left\{ \sup_{x \in \mathcal{C}_0} \left[v_{1,2}^{(s)}(x) \right], \sup_{x \in \mathcal{C}_0} \left[v_{2,1}^{(s)}(x) \right] \right\}, \tag{2.2.50}$$

using the fact that $\min\{\cdot, \cdot\}$ is a continuous operator. If $\mathcal{C}_0$ is empty under the null hypothesis, however, we must have strict dominance of either "F_1 over F_2" or "F_2 over F_1" at the sth-order (the "interior" case), so that $d_s < 0$. In this case, one of the terms inside the minimum operator degenerates to $-\infty$ (in probability), and hence $LMW_N^0 \to_p -\infty$. On the other hand, under the alternative hypothesis ($d_s > 0$), both terms inside the minimum diverge to ∞ and hence $LMW_N^0 \to_p \infty$.

As is clear from the above discussion, the asymptotic null distribution of LMW_N depends on the true underlying distributions and therefore its critical values cannot be tabulated. LMW suggest a subsampling procedure to compute critical values.[19] LMW show that the subsampling procedure provides consistent critical values in a very general setting. They also show that the subsampling based test is asymptotically similar on the boundary of the null hypothesis and is more powerful against some alternatives than the full sample recentered bootstrap based on the least favorable case of the null hypothesis.[20]

The subsampling procedure for the test LMW_N is as follows:[21]

Step 1   Calculate $T_{1,N}$ ($= LMW_N$) using the full sample $\mathcal{S}_{1,N} = \{W_1, \ldots, W_N\}$, where $W_i = \{(Y_{k,i}, Z_{k,i}) : k = 1, \ldots, K\}$.

Step 2   Generate subsamples $\mathcal{S}_{i,b}$ for $i = 1, \ldots, N - b + 1$, where $\mathcal{S}_{i,b} = \{W_i, \ldots, W_{i+b-1}\}$ and b is a subsample size such that $b \to \infty$ and $b/N \to 0$ as $N \to \infty$.

Step 3   Compute $\{T_{i,b} : i = 1, \ldots, N - b + 1\}$ using the subsamples.

Step 4   Compute the subsample critical value $g_{N,b}(1 - \alpha)$ as the $(1 - \alpha)$ quantile of the subsampling distribution of $\{T_{i,b} : i = 1, \ldots, N - b + 1\}$.

Step 5   Reject H_0 if $T_{1,N} > g_{N,b}(1 - \alpha)$.

The following theorem shows the asymptotic validity of the subsampling test:

Theorem 2.2.9 *Suppose that Assumptions 1–4 of LMW hold. Then, (a) under the null hypothesis H_0,*

$$\lim_{N \to \infty} P\left[LMW_N \geq g_{N,b}(1 - \alpha)\right] = \begin{cases} \alpha & \text{if } d_s = 0 \\ 0 & \text{if } d_s < 0 \end{cases} ;$$

(b) under the alternative hypothesis H_1,

$$\lim_{N \to \infty} P\left[LMW_N \geq g_{N,b}(1 - \alpha)\right] = 1.$$

To explain why subsampling works in testing environments, consider a simple setting: let $\{X_1, \ldots, X_N\}$ be a random sample from $N(\mu, 1)$ and the null and alternative hypotheses of interest are given by $H_0 : \mu = 0$ and $H_1 : \mu > 0$, respectively. Consider a t-test statistic $T_N = \sqrt{N}\bar{X}_N$, which satisfies $T_N \Rightarrow N(0, 1)$ as $N \to \infty$ under H_0. Let $g_{N,b}(1 - \alpha)$ be the subsample critical value. Clearly, the test (that rejects H_0 if $T_N > g_{N,b}(1 - \alpha)$) has asymptotically correct size α because a *subsample* of size b is indeed a *sample* of size b from the original population. Now, suppose that the alternative

---

[19] The subsampling method has been proposed in Politis and Romano (1994a) and is thoroughly reviewed in Politis, Romano, and Wolf (1999).

[20] See Section 3.1.1 for the concept of asymptotic similarity and a related discussion.

[21] Linton (2005) shows how to modify the original test statistic and the subsampling procedure of LMW to allow unbalanced time series data in which the samples may have different sizes.

hypothesis H_1 is true. Then, both T_N and $g_{N,b}(1 - \alpha)$ diverge (in probability) to ∞ but the latter diverges at a slower rate than the former, so that the test would reject H_0 with high probability for N large. More specifically, note that, under H_1, both $\overline{X}_N$ and $\overline{X}_b$ converge (in probability) to μ (> 0) as $N, b \to \infty$ and hence

$$P\left(T_N > g_{N,b}(1 - \alpha)\right) = P\left(\sqrt{N/b}\,\overline{X}_N > g_{N,b}(1 - \alpha)/\sqrt{b}\right)$$
$$= P\left(\sqrt{N/b}\,\mu > \mu\right) + o(1) \to 1,$$

where the latter convergence holds since $\liminf_{N \to \infty} (N/b) > 1$. This establishes that the subsampling test is consistent against H_1. On the other hand, consider a sequence of local alternatives $H_a : \mu(= \mu_N) = \delta/\sqrt{N}$, where $\delta > 0$. Under H_a, we have $T_N \Rightarrow N(\delta, 1)$, while $T_b = \sqrt{b}(\overline{X}_b - \mu_N) + (b/N)^{1/2}\delta \Rightarrow N(0, 1)$ since $b/N \to 0$. This implies that

$$P\left(T_N > g_{N,b}(1 - \alpha)\right) \to P\left(N(\delta, 1) > z_{1-\alpha}\right) > \alpha,$$

where $z_{1-\alpha}$ denotes the $(1 - \alpha)$ quantile of the standard normal distribution. This establishes that the test has the same first-order nontrivial local power as the test based on Normal critical values, and is asymptotically locally unbiased against some alternatives as desired.

A practical implementation of the subsampling procedure requires a choice of subsample size b, and test results might sensitively depend on the choice. However, it is an open question how to define the optimal choice of b. The main difficulty is that, in testing problems, the objectives of size and power are often in conflict; the choice of b that is good for size might be bad for power and vice versa. Therefore, unless a practitioner is willing to specify a preference function over the two conflicting objectives, there is no unique best choice of b.

LMW instead suggest three data-dependent methods of choosing subsample sizes: *minimum volatility method* (Politis, Romano, and Wolf, 1999), *mean critical value,* and *median critical value.* The methods first consider a set B_N of candidate subsample sizes and choose the one that minimizes the local (in b) variation of critical values (minimum volatility) or use the mean (or median) of the critical values computed using the subsample sizes in B_N. In practice, however, LMW favor computing a plot of p-values against for a range of subsamples. If the p-values are insensitive to subsample sizes within a "reasonable" range, then inferences are likely to be robust, and no matter which automatic method is chosen, the results will be similar.

LMW compare the subsampling method to the full sample recentered bootstrap method, which was used by Barrett and Donald (2003)[22] and others.

---

[22] See Equation 2.2.40 in the previous subsection.

They show that, compared to the subsampling method, the recentered bootstrap method might be too conservative and hence less powerful against some local alternatives.

As an application, LMW apply their test to a dataset of daily returns on the Dow Jones Industrials and the S&P500 stock returns from August 24, 1988 to August 22, 2000, a total of 3,131 observations. The means of these series are 0.00055 and 0.00068 respectively, while the standard deviations are 0.00908 and 0.0223, yielding Sharpe ratios of 6.1% and 3.1%, respectively. The series are mutually dependent and are also dependent over time. They plot p-values of the tests of the null hypotheses $d_1 \leq 0$ and $d_2 \leq 0$ against various subsample sizes, finding strong evidence against $d_1 \leq 0$ but in favor of $d_2 \leq 0$.

2.2.3 Integral-Type Tests

Hall and Yatchew (2005) and Bennett (2008) suggest integral-type tests of stochastic dominance for independent observations.

Let X_1 and X_2 be nonnegative random variables with continuous distribution functions F_1 and F_2, respectively. The hypotheses of interest are given by

$$H_0 : F_1^{(s)}(x) \leq F_2^{(s)}(x) \; \forall x \in \mathcal{X}, \tag{2.2.51}$$

$$H_1 : F_1^{(s)}(x) > F_2^{(s)}(x) \text{ for some } x \in \mathcal{X}, \tag{2.2.52}$$

where $\mathcal{X}$ denotes the common support of X_1 and X_2, which is assumed to be compact.

Consider a population quantity which measures the (squared) area between respective curves over the region for which the null hypothesis is violated:

$$d_s(F_1, F_2) := \int_{\mathcal{X}} \left[D_{1,2}^{(s)}(x) \right]_+^2 \psi(W(x)) dW(x), \tag{2.2.53}$$

where $D_{1,2}^{(s)}(x)$ is defined in (2.2.17), $W : \mathcal{X} \to \mathbb{R}$ is a monotonically increasing bounded differentiable function, and $\psi(\cdot)$ is a continuous nonnegative weight function. We expect $d_s(F_1, F_2)$ to be zero under the null hypothesis H_0, while strictly positive under the alternative hypothesis H_1.

Let $H(x) = \lambda F_1(x) + (1 - \lambda) F_2(x)$ for $\lambda \in (0, 1)$ denote the pooled (mixture) distribution. Hall and Yatchew (2005) consider $W(x) = x$ and $\psi(t) = 1$, so that (2.2.53) reduces to the usual Riemann integral, while Bennett (2008) considers $W(x) = H(x)$ and $\psi(t) = [t(1 - t)]^{-1}$.

Assumption 2.2.2 (a) F_1 and F_2 have common support $[0, \bar{x}] = \mathcal{X}$, where $\bar{x} < \infty$, and are continuous functions on $\mathcal{X}$. (b) $\{X_{1,i} : i = 1, \ldots, N_1\}$ and $\{X_{2,i} : i = 1, \ldots, N_2\}$ are independent random samples from F_1 and F_2, respectively. (c) The sampling scheme is such that as $N_1, N_2 \to \infty$, $N_1/N \to \lambda \in (0, 1)$, where $N = N_1 + N_2$.

Consider the empirical analogue of $d_s(F_1, F_2)$:

$$d_s(\bar{F}_1, \bar{F}_2) = \int_{\mathcal{X}} \left[\bar{D}_{1,2}^{(s)}(x) \right]_+^2 \psi(\bar{H}(x)) d\bar{H}(x),$$

where $\bar{F}_1^{(s)}$ and $\bar{F}_2^{(s)}$ are empirical integrated CDFs (defined in (2.2.15)) based on the first and second samples, respectively, and $\bar{H}(x) = N^{-1}\{N_1\bar{F}_1(x) + N_2\bar{F}_2(x)\}$ is the empirical CDF based on the pooled sample $\{X_{1,1}, \ldots, X_{1,N_1}, X_{2,1}, \ldots, X_{2,N_2}\}$.

As test statistics, Hall and Yatchew (2005) consider

$$HY_N = \frac{N_1 N_2}{N} \int_{\mathcal{X}} \left[\bar{D}_{1,2}^{(s)}(x) \right]_+^2 dx, \tag{2.2.54}$$

while Bennett (2008) considers

$$BN_N = \frac{N_1 N_2}{N} \int_{\mathcal{X}} \frac{\left[\bar{D}_{1,2}^{(s)}(x) \right]_+^2}{\left[\bar{H}(x) \left(1 - \bar{H}(x) \right) \right]} d\bar{H}(x). \tag{2.2.55}$$

HY_N and BN_N correspond to the one-sided *Cramér–von Mises* and *Anderson–Darling*-type test statistics, respectively.

The limiting distributions of the test statistics are functionals of a Gaussian process:

Theorem 2.2.10 *Suppose that Assumption 2.2.2 holds. Under the least favorable case (LFC) ($F := F_1 = F_2$) of H_0,*

$$HY_N \Rightarrow \int_{\mathcal{X}} \left[v_{s,\lambda}(x) \right]_+^2 dx,$$

$$BN_N \Rightarrow \int_{\mathcal{X}} \left[\frac{v_{s,\lambda}(x)}{H(x)(1 - H(x))} \right]_+^2 dH(x),$$

where $v_{s,\lambda}(\cdot) := \sqrt{1 - \lambda} \mathcal{J}_s(\cdot, \mathcal{B}_1 \circ F_1) - \sqrt{\lambda} \mathcal{J}_s(\cdot, \mathcal{B}_2 \circ F_2)$, $\mathcal{J}_s(x, \cdot)$ is the functional defined in (2.2.30), and $\mathcal{B}_1$ and $\mathcal{B}_2$ are independent standard Brownian bridges.

Theorem 2.2.10 holds because, by the Donsker theorem and continuous mapping theorem,

$$\hat{T}_s(\cdot) := \sqrt{\frac{N_1 N_2}{N}} \left\{ \bar{D}_{1,2}^{(s)}(\cdot) - D_{1,2}^{(s)}(\cdot) \right\}$$

$$= \sqrt{\frac{N_2}{N}} \mathcal{J}_s \left(\cdot, \sqrt{N_1} \left(\bar{F}_1 - F_1 \right) \right) - \sqrt{\frac{N_1}{N}} \mathcal{J}_s \left(\cdot, \sqrt{N_2} \left(\bar{F}_2 - F_2 \right) \right)$$

$$\Rightarrow v_{s,\lambda}(\cdot). \tag{2.2.56}$$

Therefore, under the null hypothesis (2.2.51),

$$
\begin{aligned}
HY_N &= \frac{N_1 N_2}{N} \int_{\mathcal{X}} \left[\bar{D}_{1,2}^{(s)}(x) \right]_+^2 dx \\
&= \int_{\mathcal{X}} \left[\hat{T}_s(x) + \sqrt{\frac{N_1 N_2}{N}} D_{1,2}^{(s)}(x) \right]_+^2 dx \\
&\leq \int_{\mathcal{X}} \left[\hat{T}_s(x) \right]_+^2 dx \\
&\Rightarrow \int_{\mathcal{X}} \left[v_{s,\lambda}(x) \right]_+^2 dx,
\end{aligned}
\tag{2.2.57}
$$

where the inequality holds because $D_{1,2}^{(s)}(x) \leq 0$ for all $x \in \mathcal{X}$ under the null. Likewise, the Bennett test satisfies

$$
\begin{aligned}
BN_N &= \frac{N_1 N_2}{N} \int_{\mathcal{X}} \frac{\left[\bar{D}_{1,2}^{(s)}(x) \right]_+^2}{\left[\bar{H}(x) \left(1 - \bar{H}(x) \right) \right]} d\bar{H}(x) \\
&\leq \int_{\mathcal{X}} \left[\frac{\hat{T}_s(x)}{\bar{H}(x) \left(1 - \bar{H}(x) \right)} \right]_+^2 d\bar{H}(x) \\
&\Rightarrow \int_{\mathcal{X}} \left[\frac{v_{s,\lambda}(x)}{H(x) \left(1 - H(x) \right)} \right]_+^2 dH(x).
\end{aligned}
\tag{2.2.58}
$$

When $s = 1$ (FSD), it is notable that the limiting distributions (2.2.57) and (2.2.58) under the least favorable case ($F_1 = F_2$) are pivotal, that is,

$$
HY_N \Rightarrow \int_0^1 [\mathcal{B}(t)]_+^2 dx,
$$

$$
BN_N \Rightarrow \int_0^1 \left[\frac{\mathcal{B}(t)}{t(1 - t)} \right]_+^2 dx,
$$

where $\mathcal{B}$ is a standard Brownian bridge. This follows because, if $F_1 = F_2 := F$, then $v_{1,\lambda} := \sqrt{1 - \lambda}(\mathcal{B}_1 \circ F_1) - \sqrt{\lambda}(\mathcal{B}_2 \circ F_2)$ has the same distribution as $\mathcal{B}(F)$.

In general (especially for $s \geq 2$), however, the asymptotic distributions depend on the true distributions F_1 and F_2, and we can resort to a resampling procedure to compute critical values. Specifically, the following bootstrap procedures can be used:

1. *Pooled Sample Bootstrap* (Two independent samples drawn from pooled observations): Let $\bar{H}_{N_k}^*$ denote the empirical distribution of a bootstrap sample of size N_k generated from $\bar{H}$ for $k = 1, 2$. Then, the bootstrap versions of the statistics are given by

$$HY_N^* = \frac{N_1 N_2}{N} \int_{\mathcal{X}} \left[\bar{D}_s^*(x) \right]_+^2 dx,$$

$$BN_N^* = \frac{N_1 N_2}{N} \int_{\mathcal{X}} \frac{\left[\bar{D}_s^*(x) \right]_+^2}{\bar{H}_N^*(x)(1 - \bar{H}_N^*(x))} d\bar{H}_N^*(x),$$

where

$$\bar{D}_s^*(x) = \bar{H}_{N_1}^*(x) - \bar{H}_{N_2}^*(x).$$

2. *Recentered Bootstrap* (Two independent samples drawn from each distribution): Let $\bar{F}_1^*$ and $\bar{F}_2^*$ denote bootstrap empirical distributions based on random samples of sizes N_1 and N_2 from $\bar{F}_1$ and $\bar{F}_2$, respectively. Then the two-sample bootstrap version of statistics takes the same form as HY_N^* and BN_N^*, with an exception that $\bar{D}_s^*(x)$ is now defined to be the recentered statistic

$$\bar{D}_s^*(x) = (\bar{F}_1^{(s)*}(x) - \bar{F}_2^{(s)*}(x)) - (\bar{F}_1^{(s)}(x) - \bar{F}_2^{(s)}(x))$$

and

$$\bar{H}_N^*(x) = N^{-1}\{N_1 \bar{F}_1^*(x) + N_2 \bar{F}_2^*(x)\}.$$

Using an argument similar to that of Section 2.2.2, it can be shown that the tests based on either of the aforementioned bootstrap critical values have the asymptotically correct size under the null hypothesis (2.2.51) and are consistent against the alternative hypothesis (2.2.52).

Compared to Kolmogorov–Smirnov-type tests, integral-type tests are generally more powerful against the distributions for which the area of non-dominance is relatively large but the maximum deviation from non-dominance is relatively small, and vice versa. On the other hand, among the integral-type tests, the Cramér–von Mises-type test HY_N is known to be less powerful against the alternatives where non-dominance occurs at the tails of the distributions, while the Anderson–Darling-type test BN_N is expected to be powerful against violations evenly over the support. However, both tests are conservative, because the critical values are based on the least favorable case of the null hypothesis.

2.2.4 Quantile-Based Tests

Tests of stochastic dominance hypotheses can equivalently be based on cumulative distribution functions or quantile functions; see Section 1.1.1 for the definitions. Quantile regression (introduced by Koenker and Bassett, 1978) enables a complete statistical analysis of the stochastic relationships among random variables and provides a natural approach to testing for stochastic dominance; see Koenker and Xiao (2002), Ng, Wong, and Xiao (2017), and Linton and Xiao (2017, section 5). In this section, we discuss tests of SD using the quantile regression method.

Consider two random variables Y_1 and Y_2 with distribution functions F_1 and F_2 and quantile functions Q_1 and Q_2, respectively. Recall that F_1 first-order stochastically dominates F_2 if and only if

$$Q_1(\tau) \geq Q_2(\tau) \text{ for all } \tau \in [0, 1]; \tag{2.2.59}$$

see Definition 1.1.1 in Section 1.1.1.

Suppose that the distributions F_1 and F_2 have means α_1 and α_2, respectively and write $Y_1 = \alpha_1 + U_1$ and $Y_2 = \alpha_2 + U_2$, where U_1 and U_2 are mean-zero random variables with distributions F_{U_1} and F_{U_2}, respectively. Let $\{Y_{k,i} : i = 1, \ldots, N_k\}$ be a random sample of size N_k from the distribution F_k for $k = 1, 2$.

We may combine the two samples and define

$$Y_i = \begin{cases} Y_{1,i} & \text{for } i = 1, \ldots, N_1, \\ Y_{2,i-N_1} & \text{for } i = N_1 + 1, \ldots, N, \end{cases} \tag{2.2.60}$$

where $N = N_1 + N_2$. Corresponding to the combined sample $\{Y_i : i = 1, \ldots, N\}$, introduce a dummy variable

$$D_i = \begin{cases} 1 & \text{for } i = 1, \ldots, N_1, \\ 0 & \text{for } i = N_1 + 1, \ldots, N \end{cases} . \tag{2.2.61}$$

Then, we may write

$$Y_i = \alpha + \beta D_i + U_i, \tag{2.2.62}$$

where $\alpha = \alpha_2$, $\beta = \alpha_1 - \alpha_2$, and $U_i = U_{2i} + (U_{1i} - U_{2i})D_i$.

From (2.2.62), the τ conditional quantile function of Y_i given D_i can be written

$$Q_{Y|D}(\tau) = \alpha(\tau) + \beta(\tau)D, \tag{2.2.63}$$

where $\alpha(\tau) = \alpha + Q_{U_2}(\tau)$ and $\beta(\tau) = \beta + Q_{U_1}(\tau) - Q_{U_2}(\tau)$. Notice that

$$\beta(\tau) = Q_{Y|D=1}(\tau) - Q_{Y|D=0}(\tau) = Q_1(\tau) - Q_2(\tau).$$

Hence, the hypothesis of FSD (2.2.59) is equivalent to

$$H_0 : \beta(\tau) \geq 0 \text{ for all } \tau \in [0, 1]. \tag{2.2.64}$$

Koenker and Xiao (2002) and Ng, Wong, and Xiao (2017) suggest a supremum-type test of (2.2.64) based on the difference between two sample quantiles $\hat{\beta}(\tau) = \hat{Q}_1(\tau) - \hat{Q}_2(\tau)$; see below for further results.

On the other hand, Chernozhukov and Fernández-Val (2005, hereafter CF) consider a linear quantile regression model with a general covariate vector $X \in \mathbb{R}^k$ and the dummy variable D as covariates:

$$Q_{Y|X,D}(\tau) = X^\mathsf{T}\alpha(\tau) + \beta(\tau)D. \tag{2.2.65}$$

In the model (2.2.65), $\beta(\tau)$ corresponds to the difference between the conditional quantiles

$$\beta(\tau) = Q_{Y|X,D=1}(\tau) - Q_{Y|X,D=0}(\tau). \tag{2.2.66}$$

In this sense, CF call the hypothesis (2.2.64) for the model (2.2.65) as the *conditional* stochastic dominance hypothesis. This hypothesis is useful to compare two distributions after controlling for the influence of some observed covariates. For example, in a classical randomized medical treatment, one can compare the distributions of survival time of the treatment and control groups with the same ages.[23]

To test the hypothesis (2.2.64) for the model (2.2.63) or (2.2.65), we first need to estimate the process $\beta(\cdot)$. A natural method is the quantile regression (Koenker and Bassett, 1978):

$$\hat{\theta}(\tau) = \arg\min_{\theta} \sum_{i=1}^{N} \rho_\tau \left(Y_i - W_i^{\mathsf{T}} \theta \right), \ \tau \in \mathcal{T},$$

where $W_i = (X_i^{\mathsf{T}}, D_i)^{\mathsf{T}}$, $\theta = (\alpha^{\mathsf{T}}, \beta)^{\mathsf{T}}$, $\rho_\tau(u) = u\,(\tau - 1\,(u < 0))$ is the check function, and $\mathcal{T}$ is a closed subinterval of $(0, 1)$; see Koenker (2005) for a comprehensive treatment of quantile regressions.

Koenker and Xiao (2002, theorem 1) show that the estimated quantile process $\hat{\theta}(\cdot)$ converges weakly to a Gaussian process:

Theorem 2.2.11 *Under regularity conditions,*

$$\sqrt{N}\Omega^{-1/2}(\cdot)\left[\hat{\theta}(\cdot) - \theta(\cdot)\right] \Rightarrow \mathcal{B}_{k+1}(\cdot), \tag{2.2.67}$$

where $\mathcal{B}_{k+1}(\cdot)$ denotes a $(k+1)$-dimensional independent standard Brownian bridge process,

$$\Omega(\tau) = H^{-1}(\tau)J(\tau)H^{-1}(\tau),$$
$$H(\tau) = E\left[f_{Y|W}\left(W^{\mathsf{T}}\theta(\tau)\right)WW^{\mathsf{T}}\right],$$
$$J(\tau) = E\left[WW^{\mathsf{T}}\right],$$

and $f_{Y|W}$ denotes the conditional density of Y given W.

The above theorem implies that

$$\sqrt{N}\left[R\Omega(\tau)R^{\mathsf{T}}\right]^{-1/2}\left[\hat{\beta}(\cdot) - \beta(\cdot)\right] \Rightarrow \mathcal{B}_1(\cdot), \tag{2.2.68}$$

---

[23] However, the concept of conditional stochastic dominance by CF is different from that discussed in Chapter 4, which compares the conditional distributions over the whole support of X or at a specific value of $X = x_0$. It is rather similar in spirit to the concept used by Linton, Maasoumi, and Whang (2005) in the sense that both approaches try to control for covariates by using (parametric) models; see also footnote 18 for a discussion.

where $R = [0, 1]$ or $R = [0_k^T, 1]$ for the quantile regression model (2.2.63) or (2.2.65), respectively.
Let

$$\hat{\Omega}(\tau) = \hat{H}(\tau)^{-1} \hat{J}(\tau) \hat{H}(\tau)^{-1} \qquad (2.2.69)$$

be a consistent estimator of $\Omega(\tau)$, such as

$$\hat{J(\tau)} = \frac{1}{N} \sum_{i=1}^{N} W_i W_i^T,$$

$$\hat{H}(\tau) = \frac{1}{2Nh_N} \sum_{i=1}^{N} 1 \left\{ \left| Y_i - W_i^T \hat{\theta}(\tau) \right| \leq h_N \right\} W_i W_i^T, \qquad (2.2.70)$$

and $h_N \to 0$ as $N \to \infty$ (Powell, 1984, 1986).

To test the hypothesis (2.2.64), Koenker and Xiao (2002), and Ng, Wong, and Xiao (2017) suggest a supremum t-test statistic

$$KX_N = \sqrt{N} \cdot \sup_{\tau \in \mathcal{T}} \left[-\frac{\hat{\beta}(\tau)}{\sqrt{R\hat{\Omega}(\tau)R^T}} \right]. \qquad (2.2.71)$$

Theorem 2.2.12 *Under regularity conditions,*

$$KN_N \Rightarrow \sup_{\tau \in \mathcal{T}} \{\mathcal{B}_1(\tau)\}$$

when $\beta(\tau) = 0$ for all $\tau \in \mathcal{T}$ (the least favorable case of the null hypothesis).

We note that the limiting distribution $\sup_{\tau \in \mathcal{T}} \{\mathcal{B}_1(\tau)\}$ is the supremum of the one-dimensional standard Brownian bridge and is free of nuisance parameters; see (2.2.26).

Chernozhukov and Fernández-Val (2005), on the other hand, give a general inference method for the quantile regression process $\theta(\cdot)$ using subsampling. To test (2.2.64), they also consider a supremum t-test statistic:

$$CF_N = \sqrt{N} \cdot \sup_{\tau \in \mathcal{T}} \left[-\frac{\hat{\beta}(\tau)}{\hat{V}(\tau)} \right], \qquad (2.2.72)$$

where $\hat{V}(\tau)$ is a weight function to be chosen by an investigator. In practice, one may choose $\hat{V}(\tau) = 1$ for simplicity or choose $\hat{V}(\tau)$ to be the subsampling estimator of $V(\tau) = \sqrt{Var(\hat{\beta}(\tau))}$ to increase the test power.

CF allow $\{(Y_i, X_i) : i \geq 1\}$ to be a stationary and α-mixing sequence. They establish the following result:

Theorem 2.2.13 *Under regularity conditions,*

$$CF_N \Rightarrow \sup_{\tau \in \mathcal{T}} \{v_F(\tau)\}, \qquad (2.2.73)$$

where $v_F(\tau)$ is a mean zero Gaussian process, when $\beta(\tau) = 0$ for all $\tau \in \mathcal{T}$ (the least favorable case of the null hypothesis).

The limiting distribution $\sup_{\tau \in \mathcal{T}} \{v_F(\tau)\}$ is not pivotal in general and may depend on the true distributions. To compute critical values, CF suggest a subsampling method, similar to Linton, Maasoumi, and Whang (2005). In contrast to the latter paper, however, CF recommend using a *recentered* statistic for subsampling.

1. Let $\mathcal{S}_{1,N} = \{W_1, \ldots, W_N\}$ denote the full sample, where $W_i = (Y_i, X_i^{\mathsf{T}})^{\mathsf{T}}$.
2. Construct subsamples $\mathcal{S}_{i,b} = \{W_i, \ldots, W_{i+b-1}\}$ for $i = 1, \ldots, N - b + 1$.
3. Compute the recentered test statistic using the subsample $\mathcal{S}_{i,b}$:

$$CF_{i,b} = \sqrt{b} \cdot \sup_{\tau \in \mathcal{T}} \left[-\frac{\hat{\beta}_{i,b}(\tau) - \hat{\beta}(\tau)}{\hat{V}(\tau)} \right],$$
$$i = 1, \ldots, N - b + 1. \qquad (2.2.74)$$

4. Define the subsample critical value $g_{N,b}(1 - \alpha)$ to be the $(1 - \alpha)$ quantile of the subsampling distribution of $\{CF_{i,b} : i = 1, \ldots, N - b + 1\}$.
5. Reject the hypothesis H_0 if $CF_N > g_{N,b}(1 - \alpha)$.

CF show that this test has an asymptotically correct size under the null hypothesis and is consistent against all alternatives.

We now comment on the aforementioned testing procedures. The test KX_N of Koenker and Xiao (2002) and Ng, Wong, and Xiao (2017) is applicable to i.i.d. observations and is computationally easy to use, because it does not require resampling to compute critical values. However, it requires estimating the conditional density $f_{Y|X}$ and it is known that the estimator $\hat{H}(\tau)$ might not perform very well in finite samples and is sensitive to the choice of h_N. In addition, for higher-order stochastic dominance, the test based on the integral of $\hat{\beta}(\tau)$ over τ is no longer asymptotically distribution-free.

On the other hand, the test CF_N of Chernozhukov and Fernández-Val (2005) does not require the estimation of the conditional density $f_{Y|X}$ and is also applicable to time series observations. As reported in the simulation experiments of CF, the recentering of the subsample statistic $CF_{i,b}$ can give better finite sample powers against some alternatives. It is mainly because its limit distribution is $O_p(1)$ under the alternative hypothesis, whereas the standard *non-centered* subsample statistic

$$CF_{i,b}^U = \sqrt{b} \cdot \sup_{\tau \in T} \left[-\frac{\hat{\beta}_{i,b}(\tau)}{\hat{V}(\tau)} \right], \quad i = 1, \ldots, N - b + 1 \qquad (2.2.75)$$

diverges to ∞ under the alternative hypothesis, albeit at a rate slower than the original test statistic CF_N. However, the distribution of the recentered sub-sample statistic (2.2.74) mimics the distribution of the original statistic under the least favorable case of the null hypothesis, i.e., $\sup_{\tau \in T} \{v_F(\tau)\}$. The latter distribution is stochastically larger than the limiting distribution of CF_N (and hence that of $CF_{i,b}^U$) under the null hypothesis, i.e., $\sup_{\tau \in T_0} \{v_F(\tau)\}$, where $T_0 = \{\tau \in T : \beta(\tau) = 0\}$ is the contact set. Therefore, there may exist some alternatives against which $CF_{i,b}^U$ is more powerful than $CF_{i,b}$; see Sections 2.2.2 and 3.1.1 for this point. In practice, there is usually little information about the alternatives and it is recommended to consider both (recentered and non-centered) subsample critical values to enhance power performances.

2.2.5 Neyman's Smooth Tests

In nonparametric testing problems with a large number of alternatives, it is unlikely that there is a single test that is uniformly powerful against all alternatives (i.e., the negation of the null hypothesis). Therefore, in the absence of preliminary knowledge about a specific alternative, it is reasonable to construct a test that performs well across a broad range of alternatives. The main idea of Neyman (1937)'s smooth test is to embed the null model into finite (say d)-dimensional models and then to construct an asymptotically optimal test for the parametric testing problem. By letting the dimension d of the parametric model increase, one may ensure that the test is powerful against general alternatives. Several data-dependent procedures for choosing d are available in the literature. For a general introduction, see Lehmann and Romano (2005, section 14.4) and Ledwina (1994).

Ledwina and Wyłupek (2012a, LDWK) suggest a test of first-order stochastic dominance for independent samples based on the principle of Neyman's smooth test. Suppose that $\{X_{1,i} : i = 1, \ldots, N\}$ and $\{X_{2,i} : i = 1, \ldots, N\}$ are independent random samples from continuous distributions F_1 and F_2, respectively. (For simplicity, we consider the case of equal sample sizes. It is straightforward to allow for different sample sizes.) The hypotheses of interest are given by:

$$H_0 : F_1(x) \leq F_2(x) \text{ for all } x \in \mathbb{R},$$
$$H_1 : F_1(x) > F_2(x) \text{ for some } x \in \mathbb{R}.$$

Let

$$H(x) = \frac{1}{2} F_1(x) + \frac{1}{2} F_2(x)$$

denote the mixture distribution of F_1 and F_2. Then, the elements of the transformed (pooled) sample $\{H(X_{k,i}) : i = 1, \ldots, N; \; k = 1, 2\}$ take values in the unit interval $[0, 1]$. Define

$$B(z) = (F_1 - F_2) \circ H^{-1}(z) \text{ for } z \in [0, 1],$$

where $H^{-1}(x) = \inf\{x \in \mathbb{R} : H(x) \geq z\}$ with $B(0) = B(1) = 1$. Note that $B : [0, 1] \to \mathbb{R}$ is absolutely continuous with respect to Lebesgue measure λ on $[0, 1]$. The hypotheses of interest can be equivalently stated as

$$H_0' : B(z) \leq 0 \text{ for all } z \in [0, 1], \tag{2.2.76}$$
$$H_1' : B(z) > 0 \text{ for some } z \in [0, 1].$$

This representation allows one to reduce comparison of arbitrary continuous distributions on $\mathbb{R}$ to inference on two continuous distributions with the common support $[0, 1]$.

Let $\mathcal{U}_1$ be the class of all nondecreasing functions on $[0, 1]$. Then, from the property of the first-order stochastic dominance (Section 1.1.1), the null hypothesis H_0' holds if and only if

$$\int_0^1 u(z) dB(z) \geq 0 \text{ for all } u \in \mathcal{U}_1,$$

or equivalently

$$\int_0^1 u(z) \bar{s}(z) \lambda(dz) \geq 0 \text{ for all } u \in \mathcal{U}_1, \tag{2.2.77}$$

where $\bar{s} = dB/d\lambda$ is the density of B with respect to λ. LDWK call $\bar{s}$ the *control function*.

To check (2.2.77), LDWK suggest approximating $u \in \mathcal{U}_1$ by a system $\{u_j\}_{j=1}^\infty$ of non-decreasing functions on $[0, 1]$ given by

$$u_j(z) = -\sqrt{\frac{1 - a_j}{a_j}} 1\left(0 \leq z < a_j\right) + \sqrt{\frac{a_j}{1 - a_j}} 1\left(a_j \leq z \leq 1\right),$$

where $a_1, a_2, \ldots$ are successive points of the form $(2i - 1)/2^{l+1}$ for $l = 0, 1, \ldots, i$ and $i = 1, \ldots, 2^l$. We have $\int_0^1 u_j d\lambda = 0$ and $\int_0^1 u_j^2 d\lambda = 1$.

Now, let

$$\begin{aligned}
\gamma_j := \gamma_j(a_j) &= \int_0^1 u_j(z) \bar{s}(z) \lambda(dz) \\
&= -\sqrt{\frac{1 - a_j}{a_j}} \int_0^{a_j} dB(z) + \sqrt{\frac{a_j}{1 - a_j}} \int_{a_j}^1 dB(z) \\
&= \frac{1}{\sqrt{a_j(1 - a_j)}} \left\{(F_2 - F_1) \circ H^{-1}(a_j)\right\}
\end{aligned} \tag{2.2.78}$$

denote the jth Fourier coefficient of $\bar{s}$ in the system $\{u_j\}_{j=1}^{\infty}$. Since $\{a_j\}_{j \geq 1}$ lie densely in $(0, 1)$, the hypotheses of interest (2.2.76) can be equivalently stated as

$$H_0'' : \gamma_j \geq 0 \text{ for all } j \in \{1, 2, \ldots\}, \qquad (2.2.79)$$
$$H_1'' : \gamma_j < 0 \text{ for some } j \in \{1, 2, \ldots\}.$$

Let

$$\bar{B}(z) = \left(\bar{F}_1 - \bar{F}_2 \right) \circ \bar{H}^{-1}(z),$$

where $\bar{F}_1$, $\bar{F}_2$, and $\bar{H}$ denote the empirical CDFs based on the first, second, and the pooled sample $\{X_{1,1}, \ldots, X_{1,N}, X_{2,1}, \ldots, X_{2,N}\}$, respectively. LDWK suggest estimating γ_j by

$$\hat{\gamma}_j := \int_{1/(2N)}^{1} u_j \left(z - \frac{1}{4N} \right) d\bar{B}(z)$$
$$= A_N(j) + \frac{1}{\sqrt{a_j (1 - a_j)}} \left\{ \left(\bar{F}_2 - \bar{F}_1 \right) \circ \bar{H}^{-1}(\tilde{a}_j) \right\}, \qquad (2.2.80)$$

where $\tilde{a}_j = a_j + 1/(4N)$ and $A_N(j) = \left\{ \left(\bar{F}_2 - \bar{F}_1 \right) \circ \bar{H}^{-1}(1/(2N)) \right\} u_j$ $(1/(4N))$ and the equality follows from integration by parts. By a weak law of large numbers, it is easy to show that $\hat{\gamma}_j \to_p \gamma_j$ as $N \to \infty$. Also, since $A_N(j) = O(1/N)$, we can approximate

$$\hat{\gamma}_j \approx \frac{1}{\sqrt{a_j (1 - a_j)}} \left\{ \left(\bar{F}_2 - \bar{F}_1 \right) \circ \bar{H}^{-1}(a_j) \right\}, \qquad (2.2.81)$$

which shows that $\hat{\gamma}_j$ is close to the standard sample analogue estimator of γ_j defined by (2.2.78).

To test (2.2.79), LDWK consider

$$M_d = \min_{1 \leq j < d} \sqrt{\frac{N}{2}} \hat{\gamma}_j, \qquad (2.2.82)$$

where $d = 2^{l+1} - 1$. We may reject the null hypothesis if M_d is too small. LDWK show that the distribution of M_d under the least favorable case of the null hypothesis ($F_1 = F_2$) is pivotal in finite samples and hence can easily be simulated.

Let $c_1(\alpha)$ be the the largest value of c such that

$$P(M_d < c \mid F_1 = F_2) \leq \alpha$$

for $\alpha \in (0, 1)$. The following theorem shows that the test has a correct size in finite samples under the null hypothesis and is consistent against the alternative hypothesis (lemmas 1 and 2 of LDWK):

Theorem 2.2.14 *(a) For any $\alpha \in (0, 1)$ and any fixed N,*

$$P(M_d < c_1(\alpha)) \leq \alpha$$

under the null hypothesis H_0. (b) If $d = d(N)$ is a positive sequence such that $d(N)/N \to 0$ and $d(N) \to \infty$ as $N \to \infty$, then

$$\lim_{N \to \infty} P(M_d < c_1(\alpha)) = 1$$

under the alternative hypothesis H_1.

It is interesting to compare this test with some of the other tests mentioned earlier. In particular, the test statistic of Anderson (1996, section 2.2.1) in this context can be written as

$$AD_N = \min_{1 \leq j \leq J} \sqrt{\frac{N}{2}} \frac{\left(\bar{F}_2 - \bar{F}_1\right) \circ \bar{H}^{-1}(q_j)}{\sqrt{q_j\left(1 - q_j\right)}},$$

for some natural $J < \infty$, where $\{q_j\}_{j=1}^{J}$ are fixed grids chosen by the investigator. If J is fixed, then the test is not consistent against all alternatives. On the other hand, if $d = d(N)$ is not large compared to N, the test statistic M_d can be approximated by

$$M_d \approx \min_{1 \leq j \leq d} \sqrt{\frac{N}{2}} \frac{\left(\bar{F}_2 - \bar{F}_1\right) \circ \bar{H}^{-1}(a_j)}{\sqrt{a_j\left(1 - a_j\right)}}.$$

Therefore, one can see that the test statistic M_d is a variant of Anderson (1996)'s test statistic (section 2.2.1) by allowing the number of grids to increase as the sample size increases, which makes M_d consistent against all alternatives.

Another variant suggested by LDWK is

$$M_N^* = \inf_{Z_{(1)} \leq x \leq Z_{(2N)}} \sqrt{\frac{N}{2}} \frac{\left\{\bar{F}_2(x) - \bar{F}_1(x)\right\}}{\sqrt{\bar{H}(x)\left(1 - \bar{H}(x)\right)}},$$

where $Z_{(1)} \leq \cdots \leq Z_{(2N)}$ are ordered observations in the pooled sample. This is a weighted variant of the two-sample one-sided Kolmogorov–Smirnov statistic.

Ledwina and Wyłupek (2013) find in a simulation study that both M_d and M_N^* perform well in finite samples and, due to the weights built into them, they have equally high power in detecting differences in all parts of the underlying distributions.

One disadvantage of M_d is that it requires a choice of the number of grids d by an investigator, which can be arbitrary in practice. In view of this,

LDWK also suggest a Wald-type test statistic that uses a data-dependent rule to choose d.

Let $\mathcal{D} = \{2^{k+1} - 1 : k = 0, 1, \ldots, K\}$ be a finite set of grids, where K is a given number while $D = 2^{K+1} - 1$ is the maximal size of the grid. For $d \in \mathcal{D}$, define

$$Q_d = \frac{N}{2} \sum_{j=1}^{d} [-\hat{\gamma}_j]_+^2. \qquad (2.2.83)$$

So, under the alternative hypothesis H_1, we expect that Q_d takes large values. To choose d, LDWK suggest a data-dependent rule based on Schwarz (1978)'s Bayesian information criterion (BIC). Specifically, LDWK suggest choosing d that maximizes the penalized criterion function:

$$\max_{d \in \mathcal{D}} \{Q_d - \Pi_d\}, \qquad (2.2.84)$$

where

$$\Pi_d = \begin{cases} d \log(2N) & \text{if } M_d \geq -\sqrt{\eta \log(2N)} \\ 0 & \text{otherwise} \end{cases} \qquad (2.2.85)$$

and $\eta > 0$ is a tuning parameter. Let $\bar{d}$ denote the value d that maximizes (2.2.84). This rule assigns a higher penalty (and hence a smaller $\bar{d}$) if there exists empirical evidence for the null hypothesis, and a lower (zero) penalty (and hence a larger $\bar{d}$) if there is evidence for the alternative hypothesis. Since the value of Q_d is nondecreasing with respect to d, this implies that we have a smaller value of $M_{\bar{d}}$ under the null hypothesis and a larger value of $Q_{\bar{d}}$ under the alternative hypothesis. This strategy leads to a test with higher power, without affecting its size performance.

The distribution of $Q_{\bar{d}}$ under the least favorable case ($F_1 = F_2$) is distribution-free, since $Q_{\bar{d}}$ is a rank statistic. Therefore, the α-level critical values can be simulated by taking the smallest value of $c_2(\alpha)$ such that

$$P\left(Q_{\bar{d}} > c_2(\alpha)\right) \leq \alpha.$$

The following theorem shows that the test $Q_{\bar{d}}$ also has a correct size in finite samples under the null hypothesis and is consistent against the alternative hypothesis H_1 (lemmas 3 and 4 of LDWK):

Theorem 2.2.15 *(a) For any $\alpha \in (0, 1)$ and any fixed N,*

$$P(Q_{\bar{d}} > c_2(\alpha)) \leq \alpha$$

under the null hypothesis H_0. (b) If $D = d(N)$ is a positive sequence such that $d(N) \to \infty$ as $N \to \infty$, then

$$\lim_{N \to \infty} P(Q_{\bar{d}} > c_2(\alpha)) = 1$$

under the alternative hypothesis H_1.

Compared to M_d, the test $Q_{\bar{d}}$ has some advantages in that it allows a data-dependent choice of the number of grid points and may have better finite sample performances by adapting to the true relationship between distribution functions. However, $Q_{\bar{d}}$ still requires the tuning parameter η to be chosen in (2.2.85), on which the testing results might sensitively depend. It is a non-trivial question how to choose η optimally, but LDWK suggest a decision rule to choose η in a data-dependent way, which worked reasonably well in their simulations.

Ledwina and Wyłupek (2012b) extend the result of LDWK to test the null hypothesis of non-stochastic dominance against the alternative of stochastic dominance. The test is designed to reject the null hypothesis if all empirical Fourier coefficients $\{\hat{\gamma}_j\}_{j=1}^{d(N)}$ are simultaneously nonnegative and nonzero. As in LDWK, the test statistic is based on the data-dependent choice of the grid points. However, the test is not consistent against all alternatives and has asymptotic power strictly less than one under the alternative distributions with the population Fourier coefficient $\gamma_j = 0$ for some $j \in \{1, \ldots, D\}$, which essentially corresponds to the case of non-negligible contact set (see Theorem 1(ii) of Ledwina and Wyłupek, 2012b).

2.3 Null of Non-Dominance against Dominance

The most common approach to testing stochastic dominance in the literature is to consider the null hypothesis of dominance, following the usual convention of taking the theory of interest as the null and trying to find evidence against it. However, rejection of the null of dominance may sometimes be inconclusive in ranking distributions and non-rejection of dominance may be due to the low power of the test. Therefore, this approach has its limitations if one wishes to "establish" or try to find significant evidence of dominance.

An alternative way to test stochastic dominance is to posit the null of non-dominance. This approach has an advantage in the sense that if the null is rejected then one can infer stochastic dominance.[24] However, when the distributions are continuous, it is impossible to reject non-dominance in favor of dominance over the entire supports of the distributions, because two distribution functions always coincide at the tails; see Section 2.3.2 for a discussion.[25] Therefore, in order to test the null of non-dominance, it is necessary to put a restriction on the range over which the dominance relationship is investigated. Kaur, Rao, and Singh (1994), Davidson (2009), and Davidson and

---

[24] The two approaches are complementary in that positing a null of dominance cannot be used to infer dominance but can serve to infer non-dominance, while positing a null of nondominance cannot serve to infer non-dominance but can lead to inferring dominance (Davidson and Duclos, 2013, p. 87).

[25] For discrete distributions, it is possible to test the null of non-dominance over the full supports.

Duclos (2013) consider the hypothesis of so-called *restricted stochastic dominance* that restricts the domain of interest to some closed interval contained in the interior of the support of the distributions. In this section, we discuss their results.

2.3.1 Infimum t-Test

Kaur, Rao, and Singh (1994, KRS) consider testing second-order stochastic dominance between two different distributions over a finite interval $[a, b]$ which is assumed to be a strict subset of the union of the supports. Their hypotheses of interest are as follows:

$$H_0 : F_1^{(2)}(x) \leq F_2^{(2)}(x) \text{ for some } x \in [a, b],$$

$$H_1 : F_1^{(2)}(x) > F_2^{(2)}(x) \text{ for all } x \in [a, b],$$

where a, b are any two real numbers. The alternative hypothesis is that of strict stochastic dominance.

The hypotheses can be equivalently stated as

$$H_0 : \inf_{x \in [a,b]} D_{1,2}^{(2)}(x) \leq 0 \text{ vs. } H_1 : \inf_{x \in [a,b]} D_{1,2}^{(2)}(x) > 0, \tag{2.3.1}$$

where $D_{1,2}^{(2)}(x)$ is defined in (2.2.17) with $s = 2$.

The test statistic of KRS is based on the sample analogue of the expression in (2.3.1). For $k = 1, 2$, let $\{X_{k,i} : i = 1, .., N\}$ denote a random sample of size N from the distribution F_k and let $\bar{F}_k$ denote the empirical CDF. (KRS allow for different sample sizes.) For any fixed real value x, the sample analogue of $D_{1,2}^{(2)}(x)$ is given by

$$\bar{D}_{1,2}^{(2)}(x) := \bar{F}_1^{(2)}(x) - \bar{F}_2^{(2)}(x) = \frac{1}{N} \sum_{i=1}^{N} D_i(x),$$

where

$$D_i(x) = (x - X_{1,i}) \, 1\left[X_{1,i} \leq x\right] - (x - X_{2,i}) \, 1\left[X_{2,i} \leq x\right].$$

Define the standardized version of $\bar{D}_{1,2}^{(2)}(x)$:

$$Z_N(x) = \frac{\sqrt{N}\bar{D}_{1,2}^{(2)}(x)}{S_N(x)}, \tag{2.3.2}$$

where

$$S_N(x) = \sqrt{\frac{1}{N} \sum_{i=1}^{N} (D_i(x) - \bar{D}_{1,2}^{(2)}(x))^2}$$

is the sample variance. Thus, $Z_N(x)$ can be interpreted as a t-statistic for each x.

To test the null hypothesis H_0, KRS consider the minimum t-statistic:

$$KRS_N = \inf_{x \in [a,b]} Z_N(x).$$

Let $z_{1-\alpha}$ denote the $(1 - \alpha)$ quantile of the standard normal distribution for $\alpha \in (0, 1)$. KRS establish the following results:

Theorem 2.3.1 *Suppose that X_k has a nondegenerate distribution function F_k for $k = 1, 2$. (a) Under the null hypothesis H_0,*

$$\limsup_{N \to \infty} P\left[KRS_N > z_{1-\alpha}\right] \leq \alpha.$$

(b) If F_1 and F_2 are such that $D_{1,2}(x_0) = 0$ for some $x_0 \in [a, b]$ and $D_{1,2}^{(2)}(x) > 0$ for all $x \in [a, b] \backslash \{x_0\}$, then

$$\lim_{N \to \infty} P\left[KRS_N > z_{1-\alpha}\right] = \alpha.$$

(c) Under the alternative hypothesis H_1,

$$\lim_{N \to \infty} P\left[KRS_N > z_{1-\alpha}\right] = 1.$$

To explain the above results, write

$$Z_N(x) = \frac{\sqrt{N}\left[\bar{D}_{1,2}^{(2)}(x) - D_{1,2}^{(2)}(x)\right]}{S_N(x)} + \frac{\sqrt{N}D_{1,2}^{(2)}(x)}{S_N(x)} \qquad (2.3.3)$$
$$:= Z_{1,N}(x) + Z_{2,N}(x).$$

By a weak law of large numbers (WLLN), $S_N^2(x)$ converges in probability to $Var(D_i(x))$, which is assumed to be positive for all x. Therefore, by a CLT, the first term $Z_{1,N}(x)$ in (2.3.3) converges in distribution to the standard normal distribution for each x, while the second term $Z_{2,N}(x)$ diverges to ∞ when $D_{1,2}^{(2)}(x) > 0$, and diverges to $-\infty$ when $D_{1,2}^{(2)}(x) < 0$.

The test has an asymptotically correct size by the intersection-union principle. That is, under the null hypothesis H_0, there exists $x_0 \in [a, b]$ such that $D_{1,2}^{(2)}(x_0) \leq 0$. It follows that

$$P\left[\inf_{x \in [a,b]} Z_N(x) > z_{1-\alpha}\right]$$
$$\leq P\left[Z_N(x_0) > z_{1-\alpha}\right]$$
$$\leq P\left[\frac{\sqrt{N}\left[\bar{D}_{1,2}^{(2)}(x_0) - D_{1,2}^{(2)}(x_0)\right]}{S_N(x_0)} > z_{1-\alpha}\right]$$
$$\to P\left[N(0, 1) > z_{1-\alpha}\right] = \alpha,$$

where the second inequality holds because $D_{1,2}^{(2)}(x_0) \leq 0$ and the last convergence follows from a CLT. This establishes Theorem 2.3.1(a).

The test is generally conservative because the asymptotic rejection probability under the null hypothesis can be less than the nominal level α. However, in certain cases under the null hypothesis (Theorem 2.3.1(b)), the asymptotic rejection probability is equal to α (i.e., the test has an asymptotically exact size).

To illustrate the latter point, suppose that the distribution functions F_1 and F_2 satisfy $D_{1,2}^{(2)}(x_0) = 0$ for some $x_0 \in [a, b]$ and $D_{1,2}^{(2)}(x) > 0$ for all $x \in [a, b]\backslash\{x_0\}$. This case certainly satisfies the null hypothesis, because

$$\inf_{x \in [a,b]} D_{1,2}^{(2)}(x) = D_{1,2}^{(2)}(x_0) \leq 0.$$

In Equation 2.3.3, the second term is zero for $x = x_0$, but it diverges to ∞ for all $x \in [a, b]\backslash\{x_0\}$. Then, it is easy to see that the infimum of $Z_N(x)$ is achieved at $x = x_0$ asymptotically. Therefore, in this case, the asymptotic distribution of KRS_N is mainly determined by that of $Z_{1,N}(x)$ in (2.3.3) evaluated at $x = x_0$, which is the standard normal.

Theorem 2.3.1(c) shows that the test is consistent against the alternative hypothesis. It is because $Z_{2,N}(x)$ diverges to ∞ for all $x \in [a, b]$ under H_1 and hence $KRS_N \to \infty$ in probability.

The KRS test is practically attractive because it does not require a bootstrap or simulation procedure to compute critical values. Also, if it rejects the null hypothesis, we may have strong evidence of stochastic dominance between two distributions. However, the test can be applied only to a fixed closed subset of the domain of distributions, excluding the left tail, because $D_{1,2}^{(2)}(x) = 0$ for x in the left tail. Also, if the truncation point a is very close to the left tail, then the test would not be powerful in detecting alternatives in finite samples.

2.3.2 Empirical Likelihood Test

Let F_1 and F_2 be two continuous CDFs as in the previous section. The null hypothesis considered by Davidson and Duclos (2013, DD2) is that F_2 does not first-order stochastically dominate F_1. The alternative hypothesis is that F_2 first-order strictly stochastically dominates F_1. That is,

$$H_0 : F_1(x) \leq F_2(x) \text{ for some } x \in \mathcal{X}_0, \tag{2.3.4}$$

$$H_1 : F_1(x) > F_2(x) \text{ for all } x \in \mathcal{X}_0, \tag{2.3.5}$$

where $\mathcal{X}_0$ is a compact set that lies in the union $\mathcal{X}$ of the supports of two distributions.

It is critical that $\mathcal{X}_0$ is a *strict subset* of the joint support. To see this, consider the population quantity

$$d_* := \inf_{x \in \mathcal{X}} (F_1(x) - F_2(x)).$$

Then, the null hypothesis of non-dominance of distribution F_2 by F_1 over the whole support $\mathcal{X}$ can be expressed by the hypothesis $H_0' : d_* \le 0$. But if x^- denotes the lower limit of $\mathcal{X}$, then we have $F_1(x^-) - F_2(x^-) = 0$, whether or not H_0' is true. This implies that d_* may never be strictly greater than 0, though it can be less than 0. Therefore, a statistical test based on the sample analogue of d_* would never be significantly greater than 0, which would be required for a rejection of H_0'.[26] In fact, Berger (1988, theorem 4.1) shows that the uniformly most powerful test of the null hypothesis of H_0' against the alternative $H_1' : d_* > 0$ is the randomized "no data" test that rejects H_0' with probability α, regardless of the data; see also Álvarez-Esteban, del Barrio, Cuesta-Albertos, and Matrán (2016, ABCM) for this point. This motivates DD2 to restrict the domain of interest to $\mathcal{X}_0 \subset \mathcal{X}$ to test the null of non-dominance.

DD2 propose an empirical likelihood (EL) method to test the hypotheses (2.3.4) and (2.3.5). In particular, they consider both empirical likelihood ratio (ELR) statistic and the minimum t-statistic of KRS as test statistics and suggest using bootstrap critical values based on implied probabilities from the empirical likelihood procedure.

Let $\{X_{1,i} : i = 1, .., N\}$ and $\{X_{2,i} : i = 1, .., N\}$ be two random samples independently drawn from distributions F_1 and F_2, respectively. (For simplicity, we assume the equal size for the samples.) Let $\bar{F}_k$ be the empirical CDF for $k = 1, 2$.

The empirical likelihood method originally proposed by Owen (1988) assigns probability weights to each observation and tries to maximize empirical log likelihood function (ELF) subject to the constraint from the null hypothesis. If the null hypothesis is not true, then the empirical log likelihood ratio statistic, which is the difference between the maximum values of ELF with and without the constraints, will take a large value so that one can reject the null hypothesis.

To impose the null hypothesis, DD2 consider the constraint that there exists $x \in \mathcal{X}_0$ such that $F_1(x) = F_2(x)$. Then, consider the maximization problem:

$$\max_{\mathbf{p}_1, \mathbf{p}_2} \sum_{i=1}^{N} \log p_{1,i} p_{2,i}$$

---

[26] If the data are discrete or censored in the tails, then it is no longer impossible to reject the null H_0' if there is enough probability mass in the atoms at either end or over the censored areas of the distribution (see DD2, p. 96).

subject to

$$\sum_{i=1}^{N} p_{1,i} = \sum_{i=1}^{N} p_{2,i} = 1,$$

$$\sum_{i=1}^{N} p_{1,i} 1(X_{1,i} \leq x) = \sum_{i=1}^{N} p_{2,i} 1(X_{2,i} \leq x).$$

This problem has an explicit solution for the *implied probabilities*:

$$p_{k,i} := p_{k,i}(x) = \begin{cases} \frac{N_1(x)+N_2(x)}{2N \cdot N_1(x)} & \text{if } X_{k,i} \leq x \\ \frac{M_1(x)+M_2(x)}{2N \cdot M_1(x)} & \text{if } X_{k,i} > x \end{cases}, \qquad (2.3.6)$$

where $N_k(x) := \sum_{i=1}^{N} 1(X_{k,i} \leq x)$ and $M_k(x) := \sum_{i=1}^{N} 1(X_{k,i} > x)$ for $k = 1, 2$. The empirical log likelihood ratio (ELR) statistic $LR(x)$ is then given by

$$\frac{1}{2} LR(x) = \sum_{k=1}^{2} \left[N_k(x) \log N_k(x) + M_k(x) \log M_k(x) \right] \qquad (2.3.7)$$

$$- (N_1(x) + N_2(x)) \log (N_1(x) + N_2(x))$$
$$- (M_1(x) + M_2(x)) \log (M_1(x) + M_2(x)).$$

Finally, the minimum ELR statistic is given by

$$DD2_N = \inf_{x \in \mathcal{X}_0} LR(x). \qquad (2.3.8)$$

DD2 show that the least favorable case of the null hypothesis (or the frontier of non-dominance) corresponds to the case where there exists exactly one point x_0 in $\mathcal{X}_0$ such that $F_1(x_0) = F_2(x_0)$ and $F_1(x) > F_2(x)$ for all $x \in \mathcal{X}_0 \backslash \{x_0\}$, in the sense that probability of rejecting the null is no smaller on the frontier than any other case under the null hypothesis (theorem 2 of DD2). They also show that the minimum ELR statistic is asymptotically equivalent to the minimum t-statistic KRS_N (for the two independent samples) of Kaur, Rao, and Singh (1994), both under the least favorable case and under a sequence of local alternatives.

Although the asymptotic null distribution is pivotal (i.e., $N(0, 1)$), they recommend using bootstrap critical values based on the implied probabilities (2.3.6). That is, let $\hat{x}$ denote the value of x in $\mathcal{X}_0$ that minimizes the ELR statistic $LR(x)$ in (2.3.7) or the t-statistic $Z_N(x)$ in (2.3.2). Let the constrained empirical likelihood estimate of the CDF $F_k(x)$ be

$$\tilde{F}_k(x) = \sum_{i=1}^{N} p_{k,i}(\hat{x}) 1(X_{k,i} \leq x), \ k = 1, 2, \qquad (2.3.9)$$

where $p_{ki}(x)$ is defined in (2.3.6). This is a more efficient estimator of the CDF F_k than the standard empirical CDF because it embodies the null restrictions (Brown and Newey, 2002). Now, generate bootstrap samples from $\tilde{F}_k(x)$, $k = 1, 2$ and then, for each bootstrap sample, compute the minimum ELR or minimum t-statistic just as we do with the original data. The α-level bootstrap critical values are then computed as the $(1 - \alpha)$ quantile of the bootstrap distributions. Using simulations, DD2 show that the tests based on the bootstrap critical values are superior to those based on normal critical values in finite samples.

Davidson (2009) extends the results of DD2 to higher-order stochastic dominance with correlated samples. However, in this case, the implied probabilities do not have an explicit representation such as (2.3.6) and have to be computed numerically, which can be computationally intensive in some cases. He shows some simulation evidence that the bootstrap test tends to perform better than the asymptotic test in finite samples.

2.4 Null of Equality against Dominance

In statistics, there has been a large literature on testing the null of equal distributions against the alternative of (strict) dominance, that is

$$H_0 : F_1(x) = F_2(x) \text{ for all } x,$$
$$H_1 : F_1(x) < F_2(x) \text{ for all } x.$$

Various types of test statistics have been considered. Examples include Lee and Wolfe (1976) who consider a Mann–Whitney–Wilcoxon-type test statistic

$$\hat{\theta} = \int_{-\infty}^{\infty} \tilde{F}_2(x) d\tilde{F}_1(x),$$

where $(\tilde{F}_1, \tilde{F}_2)$ is the restricted maximum likelihood estimator of (F_1, F_2) obtained under the stochastic dominance restriction H_1. Their test is based on the property that

$$\theta := P(X_2 \leq X_1) = \int_{-\infty}^{\infty} F_2(x) dF_1(x) = 1/2$$

under H_0, while $\theta > 1/2$ under H_1. However, θ can be greater than $1/2$ even if H_1 does not hold. This implies that the test may reject the null of equality in favor of dominance even if there is no dominance.

Robertson and Wright (1981) propose likelihood ratio tests based on the restricted and unrestricted maximum likelihood estimators of the distributions which are assumed to be discrete (multinomial distributions) and show that the limit distributions are chi-bar square, a mixture of chi-square distributions (see Robertson, Wright, and Dykstra, 1988, for a general definition). Wang

(1996) extends this result to the case of comparing more than two distributions and suggests a bootstrap procedure to compute critical values. Dardanoni and Forcina (1998) extend the results of Wang (1996) to test uniform stochastic ordering and likelihood ratio ordering (see Section 5.5.2) as well as simple stochastic ordering (i.e., first-order stochastic dominance). Feng and Wang (2007) consider the same hypothesis and obtain the limit distribution of the likelihood ratio statistic using a different technique.

El Barmi and McKeague (2013) propose an empirical likelihood (EL)–based k-sample test for equal distributions against the alternatives that are stochastically ordered. The test statistic is given by integrating log empirical likelihood ratio statistic with respect to the empirical distribution of the pooled sample and its asymptotic null distribution is approximated by simulations.

Deshpande and Singh (1985) consider an integral-type test of second-order stochastic dominance for continuous distributions in a one sample setting. Their test is based on the population quantity

$$d_{DS} := \int_{-\infty}^{\infty} \int_{-\infty}^{x} (F_1(t) - F_0(t)) \, dt dF_0(x),$$

where F_0 is a known distribution. They observe that $d_{DS} = 0$ under $H_0 : F = F_0$, but $d_{DS} < 0$ under $H_1 : F$ dominates F_0. The test statistic is an empirical analogue of d_{DS} and is asymptotically normally distributed under the null. Eubank, Schechtman, and Yitzhaki (1993) extend this result to a two-sample setting, in which F_0 is replaced by an unknown distribution F_2. Bishop, Chakraborti, and Thistle (1989) consider a standardized sum statistic based on the difference between the estimates of finite number of coordinates of two generalized Lorenz curves, which is essentially testing the null of equal distributions against the alternative of second-order stochastic dominance. They show that the asymptotic null distribution is standard normal.

There exist many other important tests that are not mentioned above. However, as noted in Section 2.1, the tests in this category implicitly assume weak stochastic dominance as a maintained assumption, which is hard to justify in many applications. Also, since the alternative hypothesis is not the negation of the null hypothesis, it is possible that both H_0 and H_1 are false for some F_1 and F_2. For this reason, we shall not discuss them in more detail in this book.

2.5 Empirical Examples

2.5.1 Comparison of Income Distributions

The concepts of stochastic dominance relationships between income distributions are pivotal in social welfare or poverty rankings. In this section, based on the results of Barrett and Donald (2003, BD), we illustrate how to use a SD test

Table 2.1 *Canadian family income distributions: descriptive statistics*

	Before Tax		After Tax	
	1978	1986	1978	1986
Sample	8,526	9,470	8,526	9,470
Mean	35,535	36,975	29,840	30,378
Std. Dev.	22,098	24,767	16,873	18,346
Median	32,423	32,658	27,813	27,337

Table 2.2 *Stochastic dominance in Canadian before tax family income*

	1986 versus 1978			1978 versus 1986		
	FSD	SSD	TSD	FSD	SSD	TSD
KS2	0.010	0.350	0.503	0.000	0.000	0.000
KSB2	0.010	0.370	0.570	0.000	0.000	0.000
KSB3	0.010	0.280	0.480	0.000	0.000	0.000
MT(10)	0.018	0.216	0.388	0.000	0.001	0.001
MT(5)	0.156	0.194	0.353	0.000	0.000	0.000
W(10)	0.038	0.228	0.412	0.000	0.000	0.000
W(5)	0.157	0.189	0.369	0.000	0.000	0.001
MTA(10)	0.020	0.128	0.185	0.000	0.000	0.004
MTA(5)	0.154	0.159	0.157	0.000	0.000	0.005

in practice.[27] BD consider a data set from the Canadian Family Expenditure Survey for the years 1978 and 1986, which also have been extensively studied in the SD literature.

Table 2.1 shows the descriptive statistics of the data (before tax incomes).[28] A plot of the 1978 and 1986 empirical CDFs of income shows erratic differences, which implies that choice of specific finite grids can be important for the multiple comparison-based tests such as Anderson (1996) and Davidson and Duclos (2000).

Table 2.2 provides the p-values of various SD tests. KS2 correspond to the supremum test of BD based on the multiplier method: $KS2^*$ (defined in

---

[27] Tables 2.1 and 2.2 in this subsection are reprinted from tables IV and V, respectively, of Barrett, G. F. and Donald, S. G. (2003), "Consistent tests for stochastic dominance," *Econometrica* 71(1), 71–104, with permission of John Wiley and Sons.

[28] BD consider both "before tax" and "after tax" incomes in their empirical analysis. For simplicity, we discuss only the case of "before tax" incomes.

Equation 2.2.38). Also, KSB2 and KSB3 correspond to the same test based on the pooled sample bootstrap $KSB2^*$ (defined in Equation 2.2.39) and the recentered bootstrap $KSB3^*$ (defined in Equation 2.2.40), respectively. On the other hand, MT, W, and MTA correspond to the maximum t-test, the Wald test, and the Anderson test defined in (2.2.20), (2.2.19), and (2.2.9), respectively, where the numbers 5 and 10 in the parentheses refer to the number of grids (J).

First-, second-, and third-order dominance relations are examined. In Table 2.2, "1986 versus 1978" (the first panel) indicates that the income distribution of 1986 dominates that of 1978 and "1978 versus 1986" (the second panel) means the opposite. The results show that the 1986 income distribution second (and third) order dominates the 1978 income distribution for all types of tests. That is, in the first panel, all the p-values of SSD and TSD are larger than the conventional significance levels (0.1, 0.05, 0.01), while, in the second panel, they are almost zero except for the results of MTA (but the values are still smaller than 0.01).

With respect to FSD, one can reject the null of FSD in both cases, implying crossing of the CDFs, especially when the supremum-type tests are used. However, when only 5 $(= J)$ values are used to compute the MT, MTA, and W tests, the p-values for the hypothesis "1986 versus 1978" tend to be larger than the conventional significance levels. This may occur because the latter tests are based on the values that exclude the largest difference between the CDFs, emphasizing importance of considering the complete set of restrictions implied by stochastic dominance.[29]

2.5.2 Testing for Monday Effects in Stock Markets

The efficient market hypothesis (EMH) suggests that, at any given time, prices fully reflect all available information on a particular stock market.[30] Thus, according to the EMH, no investor has an advantage in predicting a return on a stock price since no one has access to information unavailable to everyone else. However, there are lots of findings against the EMH in the real world of investment. An example is the so-called *Monday effect* (or *weekend effect*),

---

[29] In a subsequent work using the same data, Donald and Hsu (2016) show that the power performance can be improved when the selective recentering (SR) method is used to compute critical values; see Section 3.1.2 for the SR method. In particular, they show that all the p-values of the tests based on the SR method are smaller than the standard BD tests (KS2, KSB2, KSB3). Especially, in the case of "1986 versus 1978," the p-values of the SR-based tests of DH for FSD are all less than 0.01, while those of the BD tests without recentering are greater than 0.01.

[30] Strictly speaking, there are three variants of the EMH: *weak, semi-strong*, and *strong* forms. The weak form of the EMH claims that prices reflect all publicly available past information (e.g., historical prices). The semi-strong form of the EMH claims that prices reflect not just all publicly available past information but also instantly reflect new public information (e.g., announcements of annual earnings, stock splits, etc.). The strong form of the EMH claims that prices instantly reflect even hidden "insider" information; see Fama (1970) for details.

which states that the Monday (close Friday to close Monday) stock returns, *on average*, are smaller than returns on any other day of the week. There are several explanations for differences in expected returns across days of week. They include data-snooping bias, market microstructure, different rates of flow of micro and macro information, and different trading patterns of various market participants.

Cho, Linton, and Whang (2007, CLW) empirically investigate the existence of the Monday effect in major stock markets using the SD criterion. The traditional approaches to analyzing the Monday effect are based on special cases of mean variance analysis, comparing either expected returns or Sharpe ratios. However, they have some limitations since there can be omitted risk factors that account for the differences in mean returns and the mean variance approach relies heavily on the assumption of normal returns or quadratic utility. In contrast, the SD approach is more satisfactory from the perspective of economic theory, since it is defined with reference to a much larger class of utility functions/return distributions.

Let X_1 denote the Monday returns and $X_2, \ldots, X_5$ denote the other weekday (i.e., Tuesday, $\ldots$, Friday, respectively) returns. The hypothesis usually tested in the literature is that $E(X_j) = E(X_k)$ for $j, k = 1, \ldots, 5$ against the alternative that $E(X_j) \neq E(X_k)$ for some $j, k \in \{1, \ldots, 5\}$. This is usually performed by a Wald or F-test from a regression of daily returns on daily dummies. Another hypothesis that is frequently used is $E(X_1) = 0$ against the one-sided alternative $E(X_1) < 0$, which can be done with a t-test on the Monday coefficient. However, neither approach really captures the essence of the Monday effect as either the alternative is too general or the null is too strong. The hypothesis of a Monday effect the literature has in mind is that

$$E(X_1) \leq E(X_j), \quad j = 2, \ldots, 5, \tag{2.5.1}$$

i.e., mean returns on Monday are lower than mean returns on the other days of the week, which can be tested using the result of Wolak (1987), who developed a test of multiple inequalities in a regression context.

CLW consider the following related hypothesis:

$$H_0^1 : \text{Monday is (stochastically) dominated by all the other weekdays,}$$
$$\tag{2.5.2}$$

with the alternative the negation of the null. This hypothesis is stronger than (2.5.1), i.e., (2.5.1) is necessary but not sufficient for (2.5.2). Therefore, if (2.5.2) is true, then so is (2.5.1).

To investigate the robustness of their results, CLW also consider the following additional null hypotheses:

$$H_0^2 : \text{Monday dominates at least one of the other weekdays;}$$

$$H_0^3 : \text{Monday dominates all the other weekdays;}$$

H_0^4 : Monday is dominated by at least one of the other weekdays;

H_0^5 : There exists at least one day that dominates all the others;

H_0^6 : There exists at least one day that is dominated by all the others;

H_0^7 : Either Monday or the rest of the weekdays dominates the other.

The alternative hypotheses are negations of the null hypotheses. The Monday effect is compatible with the null hypotheses H_0^1, H_0^4, H_0^6, and H_0^7. On the other hand, the reverse Monday effect is compatible with H_0^2, H_0^3, H_0^5, and H_0^7. For completeness, they also include the (rather strong) hypothesis of *equal* distributions, which is consistent with the EMH and therefore inconsistent with either the Monday or the reversed Monday effects, i.e.,

H_0^8 : All days have the same distribution of returns.

To express the above hypotheses using functionals of the CDFs of the returns, define

$$d_{1s} := \max_{k \neq 1} \sup_{x \in \mathcal{X}} \left[D_{k,1}^{(s)}(x) \right]; \quad d_{2s} := \min_{k \neq 1} \sup_{x \in \mathcal{X}} \left[D_{1,k}^{(s)}(x) \right];$$

$$d_{3s} := \max_{k \neq 1} \sup_{x \in \mathcal{X}} \left[D_{1,k}^{(s)}(x) \right]; \quad d_{4s} := \min_{k \neq 1} \sup_{x \in \mathcal{X}} \left[D_{k,1}^{(s)}(x) \right];$$

$$d_{5s} := \min_{k} \max_{l \neq k} \sup_{x \in \mathcal{X}} \left[D_{k,l}^{(s)}(x) \right]; \quad d_{6s} := \min_{k} \max_{l \neq k} \sup_{x \in \mathcal{X}} \left[D_{l,k}^{(s)}(x) \right];$$

$$d_{7s} := \min_{k} \left\{ \max_{k \neq 1} \sup_{x \in \mathcal{X}} \left[D_{k,1}^{(s)}(x) \right], \max_{k \neq 1} \sup_{x \in \mathcal{X}} \left[D_{1,k}^{(s)}(x) \right] \right\};$$

$$d_{8s} := \max_{k \neq 1} \sup_{x \in \mathcal{X}} \left| D_{1,k}^{(s)}(x) \right|,$$

where $s \geq 1$ is a given integer representing the order of stochastic dominance, $D_{k,1}^{(s)}$ denotes the difference between the integrated CDFs, and $\mathcal{X}$ denotes the support of X_k, $k = 1, \ldots, 5$. The null and alternative hypotheses can be stated now:

$$H_0^j : d_{js} \leq 0 \text{ vs. } H_1^j : d_{js} > 0 \text{ for } j = 1, \ldots, 8. \quad (2.5.3)$$

Let $\{X_{k,i} : i = 1, \ldots, N\}$ be the realizations of X_k, $k = 1, \ldots, 5$. The test statistics of CLW are based on the empirical analogues of d_{js}. For example, for the null hypothesis H_0^1, the test statistic is defined to be

$$D1_N^{(s)} = \max_{k \neq 1} \sup_{x \in \mathcal{X}} \sqrt{N} \left[\bar{D}_{k,1}^{(s)}(x) \right], \quad (2.5.4)$$

where $\bar{D}_{k,1}^{(s)}$ (for $k = 1, \ldots, 5$) is the difference between the integrated empirical CDFs. The other test statistics $D2_N^{(s)}, \ldots, D8_N^{(s)}$ are defined analogously. The critical values are computed using the subsampling and bootstrap procedures proposed by Linton, Maasoumi, and Whang (2005) (see Section 2.2.2).

A number of end-of-the-day indices are considered: Dow Jones Industrial Average (DJIA), S&P500, NASDAQ, Russell 2000, Nikkei 225, FTSE 100, and the CRSP indexes (EWX: equal weighted without dividends; VWX: value weighted without dividends; EWD: equal weighted with dividends; and VWD: value weighted with dividends) during the periods ranging from January 1, 1970 to December 31, 2004 (sample size $N = 1,573$). Daily returns are calculated as:

$$R_i = \ln(P_i/P_{i-1}),$$

where R_i is the daily return on day i, P_i and P_{i-1} are closing values of stock index on days i and $i - 1$, respectively.

To compare the methods with existing results, CLW first consider the traditional method that has been frequently used in the literature. That is, they estimate the linear regression

$$R_i = \alpha_1 D_{1i} + \alpha_2 D_{2i} + \alpha_3 D_{3i} + \alpha_4 D_{4i} + \alpha_5 D_{5i} + \varepsilon_i, \qquad (2.5.5)$$

where R_i is the stock return, D_{1i} is a dummy variable which takes the value 1 if day i is a Monday, and 0 otherwise, D_{2i} is a dummy variable which takes the value 1 if day i is a Tuesday, and 0 otherwise; and so forth.

Table 2.3 shows the OLS estimates for the equal weighted without dividends CRSP data (EWX); see CLW for the other daily indices.[31]

The standard errors are Newey and West (1987)'s HAC estimates with data dependent truncation. W1 is the Wald test statistic for the null hypothesis

$$H_0 : \alpha_1 = \alpha_2 = \alpha_3 = \alpha_4 = \alpha_5,$$

and W2 is that for

$$H_0 : \alpha_1 \leq \alpha_2, \ \alpha_1 \leq \alpha_3, \ \alpha_1 \leq \alpha_4, \ \alpha_1 \leq \alpha_5.$$

The alternatives are just their negations. The test of W2 is due to Wolak (1987). The results show that there exist strong evidence of Monday effects: (i) Monday returns are significantly negative on average; (ii) W1 indicates that they are significantly different from the other weekday returns; (iii) W2 indicates that we cannot reject that Monday returns are lower than the other weekday returns.

Daily stock return data is known to have quite heavy tails and so the linear regression results may be suspected. In view of this, CLW run quantile regressions (Koenker and Bassett, 1978) that are robust to heavy tailed errors and

---

[31] Tables 2.3, 2.4, and 2.5 in this subsection are reprinted from tables 1.1, 1.2, and 2, respectively, of Cho, Y.-H., Linton, O., and Whang, Y.-J. (2007), "Are there monday effects in stock returns?: A stochastic dominance approach," *Journal of Empirical Finance* 14(5), 736–755, with permission of Elsevier.

Table 2.3 *Monday effects: OLS estimates (EWX)*

	Mon.	Tue.	Wed.	Th.	Fri.	$W1$	$W2$
Mean(%)	−0.108	−0.010	0.111	0.114	0.205	180.08	0.000
t-value	−4.529	−0.519	5.840	5.996	11.610	[0.000]	[0.287]

Note: p-values are in the square brackets.

Table 2.4 *Monday effects: quantile regression estimates (EWX)*

τ	Mon.	Tue.	Wed.	Th.	Fri.
0.25	−0.428(0.025)	−0.318(0.021)	−0.200(0.022)	−0.171(0.021)	−0.084(0.020)
0.50	−0.039(0.018)	0.034(0.017)	0.151(0.016)	0.163(0.016)	0.256(0.015)
0.75	0.321(0.020)	0.357(0.017)	0.469(0.018)	0.470(0.016)	0.539(0.016)

Note: Standard errors are in parentheses.

outliers. Table 2.4 shows the results of linear quantile regressions for quantiles $q = 0.25, 0.5, 0.75$ for the EWX index. The results are similar to those of the mean regression. That is, Monday has the smallest coefficient.

CLW also consider indices other than EWX and different sample periods. To summarize, they find evidence for a Monday effect in some of the stock indices at least for some time periods. However, it is somewhat sensitive to period and the overall effect is more complex than can be captured in a simple mean regression specification. This motivates them to consider the distributional analysis based on the SD criteria.

CLW first compare the empirical CDFs and SDFs (integrated CDFs) of the five days for EWX. The Monday CDF lies above the CDFs for the other days until a very high level of returns is reached, where the Tuesday distribution crosses it. The other distributions are always well below the Monday distribution. None of the other SDFs cross the Monday SDF at all. This shows that bad news tends to work more severe on Mondays than on other days. Furthermore, the magnitude of the difference, measured by the horizontal distance between the distribution functions, is quite large.

To confirm the graphical findings, CLW perform a series of formal statistical tests based on $D1_N^{(s)}, \ldots, D8_N^{(s)}$ for $s = 1, 2, 3$. They consider both bootstrap and subsample critical values. For subsample tests, they compute the test statistics for 30 different subsample sizes b in the range $\left[N^{0.3}, N^{0.7} \right]$, and report the median of the corresponding p-values. Table 2.5 summarizes the median of p-values for the EWX data, in which I,...,VIII correspond to the hypothesis $H_0^1, \ldots, H_0^8$, respectively. It shows that there is strong evidence of Monday effect for EWX.

Table 2.5 *Monday effects: median of p-values of SD tests*

	I	II	III	IV	V	VI	VII	VIII
FSD	0.3192	0.0031	0.0000	0.5636	0.9993	0.1566	0.3116	0.0000
SSD	0.5931	0.0000	0.0000	0.4812	0.4631	0.5776	0.5931	0.0000

In conclusion, the testing results of CLW using the SD criteria confirm the earlier findings of a Monday effect for many series over the full sample. The analysis is based on a more generally acceptable approach to ranking investments than just looking at the means as was implicit in the earlier regression approach. The hypothesis tested is stronger than the usual one and the results suggest that regardless of investors' attitudes toward risk, degree of risk aversion, or seasonal variations in risk premia, Monday returns were too low to be equilibrium returns.

3 Tests of Stochastic Dominance: Further Results

This chapter discusses methods to improve power performances of SD tests. It also introduces several applications of stochastic dominance concepts to program evaluations. In particular, inference methods for distributional treatment effects and counterfactual policy effects are discussed. Some other issues of SD tests, such as the problem of unbounded supports, classification rules for SD relations, and large deviation approximation methods, are also discussed. The final section provides two empirical examples to illustrate the practical usefulness of the theoretical results.

3.1 Stochastic Dominance Tests with Improved Power

Many of early tests of stochastic dominance consider the least favorable case (LFC) of the null hypothesis to compute critical values. However, it is often the case that their asymptotic distributions depend on the "contact set" over which the two distributions are equal (see Equations 2.2.41 and 3.1.6). If the contact set is a strict subset of the full support, then the asymptotic distributions are stochastically dominated by those under the LFC. Therefore, it is conceivable that one can improve powers by directly estimating the asymptotic distributions themselves (rather than their upper bounds), since they will yield smaller critical values. This requires estimation of the contact set. There are mainly two approaches suggested in the literature: the *Contact Set Approach* and the *Selective Recentering Approach*.[1] We discuss their main ideas below.

3.1.1 The Contact Set Approach

Linton, Song, and Whang (2010, LSW) propose an integral- (or Cramér–von Mises-) type test of stochastic dominance that improves power performances

---

[1] Other approaches are also available in the literature. Subsampling gives power improvements without estimating the contact set explicitly; see Sections 2.2.2 and 3.1.3 for this point. Lok and Tabri (2015) combine the idea of the contact set approach with that of the empirical likelihood method to improve power performances of SD tests.

compared to the traditional LFC-based tests. The hypotheses of interest are given by

$$H_0 : F_1^{(s)}(x) \leq F_2^{(s)}(x) \ \forall x \in \mathcal{X},$$

$$H_1 : F_1^{(s)}(x) > F_2^{(s)}(x) \text{ for some } x \in \mathcal{X},$$

where $\mathcal{X}$ denotes a set contained in the union of the supports of X_1 and X_2.

The main features of the LSW test are as follows: (1) SD of arbitrary order; (2) serially independent observations with general cross-sectional dependence; (3) bootstrap test with estimated contact set; (4) uniform size validity; (5) unbounded support; and (6) prospects from non/semi-parametric models.

Consider a one-sided Cramér–von Mises-type functional

$$d_s := \int_{\mathcal{X}} \max \left\{ q(x) D_{1,2}^{(s)}(x), 0 \right\}^2 dx,$$

where $D_{1,2}^{(s)}(x)$ denotes the difference between the two (integrated) CDFs (Equation 2.2.17) and q is a bounded weight function. Observe that the null or alternative hypothesis can be checked by looking at whether $d_s = 0$ or $d_s > 0$, respectively.

The weight function is to allow for unbounded $\mathcal{X}$, because $F_k^{(s)}(x)$ may not be integrable over an unbounded set when $s \geq 2$; see Horváth, Kokoszka, and Zitikis (2006, Section 3.3.1). For the integral-type test, LSW suggest to consider

$$q(x) = \begin{cases} 1 \text{ if } x \in [z_1, z_2] \\ a/(a + |x - z_2|^{(s-1)\vee(1+\delta)}) \text{ if } x > z_2 \\ a/(a + |x - z_1|^{(s-1)\vee(1+\delta)}) \text{ if } x < z_1 \end{cases} \tag{3.1.1}$$

for $z_1 < z_2$ and $a, \delta > 0$. Of course, if $\mathcal{X}$ is bounded or $s = 1$, one may set $q(x) = 1$.

LSW allow for the case where X_k depends on (possibly infinite-dimensional) unknown parameters:

$$X_k(\theta, \tau) = \varphi_k(W; \theta, \tau), \ k = 1, 2, \tag{3.1.2}$$

where W is a random vector in $\mathbb{R}^{d_W}$ and $\varphi_k(\cdot; \theta, \tau)$ is a real-valued function known up to the parameter $(\theta, \tau) \in \Theta \times \mathcal{T}$ with Θ contained in a finite-dimensional Euclidean space and $\mathcal{T}$ being an infinite-dimensional space. The specification $X_k(\theta, \tau)$ allows for many non/semi-parametric models. For example, the variable $X_k := X_k(\theta_0, \tau_0)$ may be the residual obtained from the partially linear regression $X_k(\theta, \tau) = Y_k - Z_{k,1}^{\mathsf{T}} \theta - \tau(Z_{k,2})$ or the single index framework $X_k(\theta, \tau) = Y_k - \tau(Z_k^{\mathsf{T}} \theta)$ with $W = (Y, Z)$.

Let $X_{k,i}(\theta, \tau) = \varphi_k(W_i; \theta, \tau)$, where $\{W_i\}_{i=1}^N$ is a random sample. Define

$$\bar{D}_{1,2}^{(s)}(x, \theta, \tau) = \bar{F}_1^{(s)}(x, \theta, \tau) - \bar{F}_2^{(s)}(x, \theta, \tau),$$

where

$$\bar{F}_k^{(s)}(x, \theta, \tau) = \frac{1}{N(s-1)!} \sum_{i=1}^{N} [x - X_{k,i}(\theta, \tau)]_+^{s-1}.$$

The test statistic is defined to be the weighted empirical analogue of d_s, namely,

$$T_N = N \int_{\mathcal{X}} \max \left\{ q(x)\bar{D}_{1,2}^{(s)}(x, \hat{\theta}, \hat{\tau}), 0 \right\}^2 dx, \tag{3.1.3}$$

where $\hat{\theta}$ and $\hat{\tau}$ are consistent estimators of θ and τ, respectively. The estimators are assumed to have asymptotically linear representations (Assumption 3(ii) of LSW), which are satisfied by many parametric and non/semi-parametric estimators.

We now discuss the asymptotic behavior of T_N under the null hypothesis. For simplicity and clarity of the arguments, we focus on the case in which there are no estimated parameters and $\mathcal{X}$ is bounded with $q(x) = 1$. We shall also delete the superscript s for notational simplicity, unless it is necessary. In this setup, the test statistic simplifies to

$$T_N = N \int_{\mathcal{X}} \max \left\{ \bar{D}_{1,2}(x), 0 \right\}^2 dx, \tag{3.1.4}$$

where $\bar{D}_{1,2}(x) = \bar{F}_1(x) - \bar{F}_2(x)$ with $X_{k,i}(\theta, \tau) = X_{k,i}$.

Let

$$\mathcal{C}_0 = \{x \in \mathcal{X} : D_{1,2}(x) = 0\} \tag{3.1.5}$$

denote the *contact set* on which the null hypothesis holds with equality. Denote $\mathcal{P}_0$ to be the collection of probabilities that satisfy the null hypothesis H_0 and let $\mathcal{P}_{00} := \{P \in \mathcal{P}_0 : \lambda(\mathcal{C}_0) > 0\}$ be the subset of $\mathcal{P}_0$ for which the contact set has positive Lebesgue measure λ.

Without the estimated parameters, the pointwise asymptotic behavior of the T_N under the null hypothesis can be analyzed using an argument analogous to those for (2.2.41). That is, by the functional CLT, we have the weak convergence

$$\sqrt{N} \left[\bar{D}_{1,2}(\cdot) - D_{1,2}(\cdot) \right] \Rightarrow \nu(\cdot),$$

where $\nu(\cdot)$ is a mean-zero Gaussian process on $\mathcal{X}$.

If $\mathcal{P}_{00}$ is nonempty, then, for each $P \in \mathcal{P}_{00}$, we have

$$T_N = \int_{\mathcal{X}} \max \left\{ \sqrt{N} \left[\bar{D}_{1,2}(x) - D_{1,2}(x) \right] + \sqrt{N} D_{1,2}(x), 0 \right\}^2 dx$$

$$= \int_{\mathcal{C}_0} \max \left\{ \sqrt{N} \left[\bar{D}_{1,2}(x) - D_{1,2}(x) \right], 0 \right\}^2 dx$$

$$+ \int_{\mathcal{X} \backslash \mathcal{C}_0} \max \left\{ \sqrt{N} \left[\bar{D}_{1,2}(x) - D_{1,2}(x) \right] + \sqrt{N} D_{1,2}(x), 0 \right\}^2 dx$$

$$= \int_{C_0} \max\left\{\sqrt{N}\left[\bar{D}_{1,2}(x) - D_{1,2}(x)\right], 0\right\}^2 dx + o_p(1)$$

$$\Rightarrow \int_{C_0} \max\{v(x), 0\}^2 dx, \tag{3.1.6}$$

where the fourth line holds because $\sqrt{N}D_{1,2}(x) \to -\infty$ for all $x \in \mathcal{X}\backslash\mathcal{C}_0$ under the null hypothesis; see (2.2.43)–(2.2.45) for a related discussion. On the other hand, for each $P \in \mathcal{P}_0\backslash\mathcal{P}_{00}$, $\sqrt{N}D_{1,2}(x) \to -\infty$ for all $x \in \mathcal{X}$ so that the test statistic degenerates to zero. More formally, LSW establish the following result.

Theorem 3.1.1 *Suppose that Assumptions 1–3 of LSW hold. Then, under the null hypothesis,*

$$T_N \quad \Rightarrow \quad \begin{cases} \int_{C_0} \max\{v(x), 0\}^2 dx, & \text{if } P \in \mathcal{P}_{00} \\ 0, & \text{if } P \in \mathcal{P}_0\backslash\mathcal{P}_{00}. \end{cases}$$

Theorem 3.1.1 suggests that for each $P \in \mathcal{P}_{00}$, T_N has a nondegenerate limit distribution, but for each $P \in \mathcal{P}_0\backslash\mathcal{P}_{00}$ it degenerates to zero. LSW call $\mathcal{P}_{00}$ the set of *boundary points* of $\mathcal{P}_0$ and $\mathcal{P}_0\backslash\mathcal{P}_{00}$ the set of *interior points* of $\mathcal{P}_0$.

Theorem 3.1.1 illustrates that there is a discontinuity in the limit distribution of the test statistic. However, in finite samples, there is no discontinuity in the distribution of the test statistic. This implies that the *pointwise* asymptotic results in Theorem 3.1.1 may not provide a good approximation to the finite sample distribution even if N is very large.[2] For example, suppose that P is an interior point but is very close to the boundary $\mathcal{P}_{00}$, namely suppose $D_{1,2}(x) = d(x)/\sqrt{N}$, where $d(x) < 0$ for all $x \in \mathcal{X}$. Clearly, this model is in $\mathcal{P}_0\backslash\mathcal{P}_{00}$, but (under additional regularity conditions) T_N may still converge weakly to a nondegenerate distribution. Theorem 3.1.1 does not explain this phenomenon and, in order to examine the asymptotic behavior of T_N more completely, LSW suggest using *uniform asymptotics*.

Let E_P denote the expectation under probability P.

Definition 3.1.1

    (a)   A test φ_α with a nominal level α has an asymptotically (uniformly) valid size if

---

[2] This phenomenon of discontinuity arises often in the recent literature on moment inequality models (e.g., Moon and Schorfheide, 2012; Chernozhukov, Hong, and Tamer, 2007; and Andrews and Guggenberger, 2009).

$$\limsup_{N \to \infty} \sup_{P \in \mathcal{P}_0} E_P \varphi_\alpha \leq \alpha. \tag{3.1.7}$$

(b) *A test φ_α has an asymptotically exact size if it satisfies (3.1.7) and there exists a nonempty subset $\mathcal{P}_0' \subset \mathcal{P}_0$ such that*

$$\limsup_{N \to \infty} \sup_{P \in \mathcal{P}_0'} |E_P \varphi_\alpha - \alpha| = 0. \tag{3.1.8}$$

(c) *When a test φ_α satisfies (3.1.8), we say that the test is asymptotically similar on $\mathcal{P}_0'$.*

How can we construct asymptotically valid critical values with reasonably good finite sample performances? Since the Gaussian process v in Theorem 3.1.1 depends on the true data generating process, the asymptotic distribution cannot be tabulated once and for all. As we discussed in the previous chapter, many of the existing SD tests use the (bootstrap or simulation) critical values (i.e., $D_{1,2}(x) = 0$ for all $x \in \mathcal{X}$) of the null hypothesis. However, when the true data generating process lies away from the LFC and yet still lies in the boundary points, the LFC-based tests can be conservative (in the sense that the rejection probability is strictly less than the nominal significance level α). This implies that the tests may not be asymptotically similar on the boundary of the null hypothesis (that is, asymptotically they may not have a constant rejection probability on the boundary). This in turn implies that the tests may be asymptotically biased (and hence are not powerful) against a (possibly large) class of alternatives.

To illustrate heuristically why an asymptotically non-similar test under a composite null hypothesis can be asymptotically biased, let us consider the following simple example in a finite-dimensional case.[3]

Example 3.1 Suppose that $\{X_i = (X_{0,i}, X_{1,i})^\mathsf{T} : i = 1, \ldots, N\}$ is a random sample from the normal distribution with unknown mean $\mu = (\mu_0, \mu_1)^\mathsf{T}$ and known variance $\Sigma = diag(1, 1)$. Consider the hypotheses of interest:

$$H_0 : \mu_0 \leq 0 \text{ and } \mu_1 \leq 0 \text{ vs. } H_1 : \mu_0 > 0 \text{ or } \mu_1 > 0. \tag{3.1.9}$$

The "boundary" of the null hypothesis is given by $\mathcal{C}_{BD} = \{(\mu_0, \mu_1) : \mu_0 \leq 0$ and $\mu_1 \leq 0\} \cap \{(\mu_0, \mu_1) : \mu_0 = 0 \text{ or } \mu_1 = 0\}$, while the "least favorable case (LFC)" is given by $\mathcal{C}_{LF} = \{(\mu_0, \mu_1) : \mu_0 = 0 \text{ and } \mu_1 = 0\} \subset \mathcal{C}_{BD}$. To test (3.1.9), one may consider a maximum t-statistic:

$$T_N = \max\{N^{1/2}\overline{X}_0, N^{1/2}\overline{X}_1\},$$

---

[3] For a related result in the context of comparing predictabilities of forecasting models, see Hansen (2005).

where $\overline{X}_k = \sum_{i=1}^{N} X_{k,i}/N$ for $k = 0, 1$. The asymptotic null distribution of T_N is nondegenerate if the true μ lies on the boundary $\mathcal{C}_{BD}$, but the distribution depends on the location of μ. That is,

$$T_N \Rightarrow \begin{cases} \max\{\mathbb{Z}_0, \mathbb{Z}_1\} & \text{if} \quad \mu = (0, 0) \\ \mathbb{Z}_0 & \text{if} \quad \mu_0 = 0, \mu_1 < 0, \\ \mathbb{Z}_1 & \text{if} \quad \mu_0 < 0, \mu_1 = 0 \end{cases}$$

where $\mathbb{Z}_0$ and $\mathbb{Z}_1$ are mutually independent standard normal random variables. On the other hand, T_N diverges to $-\infty$ in the "interior" of the null hypothesis. Suppose that z_α^* satisfies $P(\max\{\mathbb{Z}_0, \mathbb{Z}_1\} > z_\alpha^*) = \alpha$ for $\alpha \in (0, 1)$. Then, the test based on the LFC is asymptotically non-similar on the boundary because, for example, $\lim_{N\to\infty} P(T_N > z_\alpha^* | \mu = (0, 0)) \neq \lim_{N\to\infty} P(T_N > z_\alpha^* | \mu = (0, -1))$. Now consider the following sequence of local alternatives: for $\delta > 0$,

$$H_{1,N} : \mu_0 = \frac{\delta}{\sqrt{N}} \text{ and } \mu_1 < 0.$$

Then, under $H_{1,N}$, it is easy to see that $T_N \Rightarrow N(\delta, 1)$. However, the test based on the LFC critical value may be biased against these local alternatives, because $\lim_{N\to\infty} P(T_N > z_\alpha^*) = P(N(\delta, 1) > z_\alpha^*) < \alpha$ for some values of δ. ∎

LSW propose a bootstrap procedure that is asymptotically similar on a subset of the class of probabilities satisfying the null hypothesis, which includes the LFC only as a special case. Therefore, compared to the LFC-based test, the bootstrap procedure (based on the contact set estimation) can make the LSW test biased against a smaller class of alternatives. Specifically, the steps are as follows:

1. Draw $\{W_{i,b}^*\}_{i=1}^{N}$ with replacement from the empirical distribution of $\{W_i\}_{i=1}^{N}$.
2. Construct estimators $\hat{\theta}_b^*$ and $\hat{\tau}_b^*$ using the bootstrap sample $\{W_{i,b}^*\}_{i=1}^{N}$.
3. Compute $\tilde{X}_{k,i,b}^* = \varphi_k(W_{i,b}^*; \hat{\theta}_b^*, \hat{\tau}_b^*)$ for each $b = 1, \ldots, B$.
4. Compute the bootstrap counterpart of $\bar{D}_{1,2}(x)$

$$\bar{D}_{1,2,b}^*(x) = \frac{1}{N} \sum_{i=1}^{N} \left\{ h_x(\tilde{X}_{1,i,b}^*) - h_x(\tilde{X}_{2,i,b}^*) \right.$$

$$\left. - \frac{1}{N} \sum_{i=1}^{N} \{h_x(\hat{X}_{1,i}) - h_x(\hat{X}_{2,i})\} \right\},$$

where $\hat{X}_{k,i} = X_{k,i}(\hat{\theta}, \hat{\tau})$ for $k = 1, 2$ and

$$h_x(z) := \frac{(x - z)^{s-1} 1\{z \le x\} q(x)}{(s - 1)!}.$$

5. Take a sequence $c_N \to 0$ and $c_N\sqrt{N} \to \infty$, and construct the estimated contact set

$$\hat{\mathcal{C}} = \left\{ x \in \mathcal{X} : q(x)|\bar{D}_{1,2}(x)| < c_N \right\}. \tag{3.1.10}$$

6. Compute

$$T_{N,b}^* = \begin{cases} \int_{\hat{\mathcal{C}}} \max\left\{ q(x)\sqrt{N}\bar{D}_{1,2,b}^*(x), 0 \right\}^2 w(x)dx, \\ \qquad\qquad\qquad \text{if } \lambda(\hat{\mathcal{C}}) > 0 \\ \int_{\mathcal{X}} \max\left\{ q(x)\sqrt{N}\bar{D}_{1,2,b}^*(x), 0 \right\}^2 w(x)dx, \\ \qquad\qquad\qquad \text{if } \lambda(\hat{\mathcal{C}}) = 0. \end{cases}$$

$$\tag{3.1.11}$$

7. Repeat steps 1–6 for $b = 1, \ldots, B$ and get the α-level bootstrap critical value

$$c_{\alpha,N,B}^* = \inf\{t : B^{-1}\Sigma_{b=1}^B 1\{T_{N,b}^* \leq t\} \geq 1 - \alpha\}.$$

If there are no estimated parameters, one may define $W_i = (X_{1,i}, X_{2,i})^\mathsf{T}$ in step 1, omit steps 2 and 3 and compute $\bar{D}_{1,2,b}^*(x)$ in Step 4 with $\hat{X}_{k,i} = X_{k,i}$.

LSW establish that the bootstrap-based test has the following asymptotic properties.

Theorem 3.1.2 *Suppose that the conditions of theorem 2 of LSW hold and fix any $\alpha \in (0, 1/2]$.*

(a) *Under the null hypothesis H_0, for some class of probabilities $\tilde{\mathcal{P}}_0 \subset \mathcal{P}_0$,*

$$\limsup_{N\to\infty} \sup_{P\in\tilde{\mathcal{P}}_0} P\left(T_N > c_{\alpha,N,\infty}^*\right) \leq \alpha.$$

(b) *Under the null hypothesis H_0, for some subset $\tilde{\mathcal{P}}_{00,N} \subset \tilde{\mathcal{P}}_0$,*

$$\limsup_{N\to\infty} \sup_{P\in\tilde{\mathcal{P}}_{00,N}} \left|P\left(T_N > c_{\alpha,N,\infty}^*\right) - \alpha\right| = 0.$$

(c) *Under the fixed alternative $P \in \mathcal{P}\backslash\mathcal{P}_0$ such that $\int_{\mathcal{X}} \max\{q(x)D_{1,2}(x), 0\}^2 dx > 0$,*

$$\lim_{N\to\infty} P\left(T_N > c_{\alpha,N,\infty}^*\right) = 1.$$

This theorem shows that the test T_N has an asymptotically correct size uniformly over a class of "regular" probabilities $\tilde{\mathcal{P}}_0$ satisfying the null hypothesis and it characterizes a subset $\tilde{\mathcal{P}}_{00,N}$ of $\tilde{\mathcal{P}}_0$ on which T_N is asymptotically similar. The subset $\tilde{\mathcal{P}}_{00,N}$ consists of the probabilities with asymptotically non-negligible contact set.[4] The results (a) and (b) of Theorem 3.1.2 together imply that T_N has an exact asymptotic size equal to α. On the other hand, the result (c) shows that T_N is consistent against a fixed alternative.

LSW further consider a sequence of local alternatives P_N converging (at a rate of $N^{-1/2}$) to a set of probabilities in $\mathcal{P}_0$. In particular, they consider the sequence of CDFs

$$F_{k,N}(x) = F_k^0(x) + \delta_k(x)/\sqrt{N}, \ k = 1, 2 \tag{3.1.12}$$

such that $F_1^0(x) \leq F_2^0(x)$ for all $x \in \mathcal{X}$, the contact set $C_{0,0} := \{x \in \mathcal{X} : F_1^0(x) = F_2^0(x)\}$ has nonzero Lebesgue measure, and $\int_{C_{0,0}} [\delta_1(x) - \delta_2(x)]_+^2 w(x)dx > 0$. They compare the local power of their test with that of a bootstrap test based on the LFC, that is,

$$T_{N,b}^{*LF} = \int_{\mathcal{X}} \max\left\{q(x)\sqrt{N}\bar{D}_{1,2,b}^*(x), 0\right\}^2 w(x)dx.$$

Theorem 3.1.3 *Suppose that the conditions of theorem 4 of LSW hold. Then, under the local alternatives $P_N \in \mathcal{P}\backslash\mathcal{P}_0$ satisfying (3.1.12),*

$$\lim_{N\to\infty} P_N\left(T_N > c_{\alpha,N,\infty}^*\right) \geq \lim_{N\to\infty} P_N\left(T_N > c_{\alpha,N,\infty}^{*LF}\right), \tag{3.1.13}$$

where $c_{\alpha,N,\infty}^{*LF}$ denote the $(1-\alpha)$ quantile of $T_{N,b}^{*LF}$. Furthermore, the inequality in (3.1.13) is strict, provided $\int_{\mathcal{X}} \max\{v(x), 0\}^2 dx > \int_{C_{0,0}} \max\{v(x), 0\}^2 dx$.

This theorem shows that the LSW test is asymptotically locally more powerful than the bootstrap test based on the LFC of the null hypothesis. When the union of the closures of the contact sets is a proper subset of the interior of $\mathcal{X}$, the test strictly dominates the LFC-based bootstrap test uniformly over the Pitman local alternatives (3.1.12). This result implies that the LFC-based bootstrap test is asymptotically inadmissible.

3.1.2 The Selective Recentering Approach

Donald and Hsu (2014, hereafter DH) suggest a *Selective Recentering (SR)* method that improves power performances of Barrett and Donald (2003, BD)'s LFC-based bootstrap test. The recentering method is an extension of the method of Hansen (2005) for finite (multiple) inequalities to a continuum of inequality constraints and is closely related to the *Generalized Moment Selection (GMS)* method of Andrews and Shi (2013); see Section 4.3.4.

---

[4] The set $\bar{\mathcal{P}}_{00,N}$ excludes Pitman sequences such that $D_{1,2}(x) = \delta(x)/\sqrt{N}$ for $\delta(x) \in (-\infty, 0)$.

Consider the setup of BD (given in Section 2.2.2). Under the null hypothesis, BD show that the test statistic converges weakly to the supremum of a Gaussian process v_s:

$$BD_N \Rightarrow \sup_{x \in \mathcal{C}_0} \{v_s(x)\}, \tag{3.1.14}$$

where $\mathcal{C}_0 = \{x \in \mathcal{X} : F_1^{(s)}(x) = F_2^{(s)}(x)\}$ denotes the contact set (Equation 2.2.41). Instead of estimating the limiting distribution (3.1.14) directly, BD suggest approximating its upper bound $\sup_{x \in \mathcal{X}} \{v_s(x)\}$ using multiplier and bootstrap methods. However, these procedures might be too conservative, as we discussed in the previous section.

DH instead suggest a bootstrap method that tries to mimic the limit distribution (3.1.14) closely. Define

$$\mu(x) = \min\{D_{1,2}^{(s)}(x), 0\}.$$

Obviously, we have $\mu(x) = D_{1,2}^{(s)}(x)$ under the null hypothesis. Therefore, the limit null distribution of BD_N is the same as that of

$$BD_N^0 = \sup_{x \in \mathcal{X}} \left[\sqrt{N} \left(\bar{D}_{1,2}^{(s)}(x) - D_{1,2}^{(s)}(x) \right) + \sqrt{N}\mu(x) \right]. \tag{3.1.15}$$

The idea of DH is to introduce the sample analogue of $\mu(x)$ in the resampling procedure to compute the critical values. Let $\{a_N : N \geq 1\}$ be a negative sequence such that $a_N \to -\infty$ and $a_N/\sqrt{N} \to 0$. Define the recentering function

$$\hat{\mu}_N(x) = \begin{cases} \bar{D}_{1,2}^{(s)}(x), & \text{if } \bar{D}_{1,2}^{(s)}(x) < \frac{a_N}{\sqrt{N}} \\ 0, & \text{otherwise} \end{cases}. \tag{3.1.16}$$

DH show that this function approximates the true function $\mu(x)$ uniformly over x (lemma 3.2 of DH), i.e.,

Theorem 3.1.4 *Under regularity conditions,*

$$\sup_{x \in \mathcal{X}} |\hat{\mu}_N(x) - \mu(x)| \overset{P}{\to} 0.$$

Let v_s^* be any of the bootstrap distributions in (2.2.38), (2.2.39), and (2.2.40) that are designed to approximate the distribution of v_s, i.e.,

$$v_s^*(x) = \mathcal{J}_s(x, \mathcal{B}_1^* \circ \bar{F}_1) - \mathcal{J}_s(\cdot, \mathcal{B}_2^* \circ \bar{F}_2) \text{ or} \tag{3.1.17}$$

$$v_s^*(x) = \mathcal{J}_s(x, \bar{F}_1^*) - \mathcal{J}_s(x, \bar{F}_2^*) \text{ or} \tag{3.1.18}$$

$$v_s^*(x) = \left[\mathcal{J}_s(x, \bar{F}_1^*) - \mathcal{J}_s(x, \bar{F}_1) \right] \tag{3.1.19}$$
$$- \left[\mathcal{J}_s(x, \bar{F}_2^*) - \mathcal{J}_s(x, \bar{F}_2) \right].$$

Recall that (3.1.17), (3.1.18), and (3.1.19) correspond to the multiplier method, the pooled sample bootstrap method, and the recentered bootstrap method, respectively.

Let

$$BD_N^* = \sup_{x \in \mathcal{X}} \left[v_s^*(x) + \sqrt{N} \hat{\mu}_N(x) \right]. \tag{3.1.20}$$

Conditional on the original sample, the distribution of BD_N^* mimics that of BD_N^0. The critical values from BD_N^* are smaller than those from the LFC-based distribution $\sup_{x \in \mathcal{X}} \left[v_s^*(x) \right]$ since $\hat{\mu}_N(x) \le 0$ for each $x \in \mathcal{X}$, which is the main source for the power improvement.

Let $\hat{c}_\alpha$ be the $(1 - \alpha)$ quantile of the distribution of BD_N^*. As an α-level critical value, DH recommend using

$$\hat{c}_{\alpha,\eta} = \max\{\hat{c}_\alpha, \eta\},$$

where η is an arbitrary small positive constant, e.g., 10^{-6}. Introduction of η is needed to deal with the situation where the null hypothesis holds with strict inequality for all x (the interior case), because in that case both BD_N and BD_N^* degenerate to zero. In practice, the choice of η may not be very important. Rather, the choice of a_N can often be important, because it directly affects the finite sample power performance of the test. Unfortunately, however, there is no clear way of choosing a_N, though DH recommend using $a_N = -0.1\sqrt{\log\log(N)}$ based on their simulation experiments.

The size and power properties of the DH test are summarized in the following theorem.

Theorem 3.1.5 *Suppose that the conditions of theorem 6.2 of DH hold and fix any* $\alpha \in (0, 1/2)$.

(a)   *Under the null hypothesis* H_0, *if* $D_{1,2}^{(s)}(x) < 0$ *for all* $x \in \mathcal{X}$,

$$\lim_{N \to \infty} P\left(BD_N > \hat{c}_{\alpha,\eta} \right) = 0.$$

(b)   *Under the null hypothesis* H_0, *if* $D_{1,2}^{(s)}(x) = 0$ *for some* $x \in \mathcal{X}$,

$$\lim_{N \to \infty} P\left(BD_N > \hat{c}_{\alpha,\eta} \right) = \alpha.$$

(c)   *Under the alternative hypothesis* H_1,

$$\lim_{N \to \infty} P\left(BD_N > \hat{c}_{\alpha,\eta} \right) = 1.$$

By adopting the approach of Andrews and Shi (2013), DH discuss how to modify the above testing procedure to achieve the uniform size validity (theorem 6.1 of DH).

3.1.3 Remarks

The SR approach is closely related to the contact set approach, but there are subtle differences. To see this, let

$$\hat{\mathcal{C}}_{SR} = \left\{ x \in \mathcal{X} : \bar{D}_{1,2}^{(s)}(x) \geq -c_N \right\}, \tag{3.1.21}$$

where $c_N = -a_N/\sqrt{N}$ is a positive sequence converging to 0. Then, we have

$$BD_N^* = \max \left\{ \sup_{x \in \hat{\mathcal{C}}_{SR}} \bar{T}_s^*(x), \quad \sup_{x \in \mathcal{X} \backslash \hat{\mathcal{C}}_{SR}} \left[\bar{T}_s^*(x) + \sqrt{N} \bar{D}_{1,2}^{(s)}(x) \right] \right\}$$

$$\simeq \begin{cases} \sup_{x \in \hat{\mathcal{C}}_{SR}} \bar{T}_s^*(x) & \text{if } \hat{\mathcal{C}}_{SR} \neq \emptyset \\ \sup_{x \in \mathcal{X}} \left[\bar{T}_s^*(x) + \sqrt{N} \bar{D}_{1,2}^{(s)}(x) \right] & \text{if } \hat{\mathcal{C}}_{SR} = \emptyset \end{cases}$$

for N sufficiently large since $\sqrt{N} \bar{D}_{1,2}^{(s)}(x) \to -\infty$ for $x \in \mathcal{X} \backslash \hat{\mathcal{C}}_{SR}$ when $\hat{\mathcal{C}}_{SR}$ is nonempty. Approximately, the critical value of the SR approach is equal to the $(1 - \alpha)$ quantile of $\sup_{x \in \hat{\mathcal{C}}_{SR}} v_s^*(x)$ when $\hat{\mathcal{C}}_{SR} \neq \emptyset$, while it is the maximum of the $(1 - \alpha)$ quantile of $\sup_{x \in \mathcal{X}} \left[v_s^*(x) + \sqrt{N} \bar{D}_{1,2}^{(s)}(x) \right]$ and $\eta > 0$ when $\hat{\mathcal{C}}_{SR} = \emptyset$.

On the other hand, the estimate of the contact set $\mathcal{X}^*$ (assuming $q(x) = 1$ for notational simplicity) is given by

$$\hat{\mathcal{C}} = \left\{ x \in \mathcal{X} : \left| \bar{D}_{1,2}^{(s)}(x) \right| \leq c_N \right\}.$$

The critical value based on the contact set approach corresponds to the $(1 - \alpha)$ quantiles of $\sup_{x \in \hat{\mathcal{C}}} v_s^*(x)$ when $\hat{\mathcal{C}} \neq \emptyset$, while it is that of $\sup_{x \in \mathcal{X}} \left[v_s^*(x) \right]$ when $\hat{\mathcal{C}} = \emptyset$.

Since $\hat{\mathcal{C}} \subseteq \hat{\mathcal{C}}_{SR}$, the critical values of the SR approach are generally larger than those of the contact set approach when $\hat{\mathcal{C}}$ is nonempty, but the SR critical values are smaller than the contact-set-based critical values when $\hat{\mathcal{C}}$ is empty. Therefore, both approaches are less conservative than the LFC-based test, but their relative power performances may depend on specific alternative distributions.

Related to the power properties, DH propose that their test is asymptotically more powerful than the subsampling approach of LMW against some local alternatives of the following form:

$$H_{1,N} : D_{1,2,N}^{(s)}(x) = D_{1,2}^{(s)}(x) + \delta_N(x),$$

where

$$\delta_N(x) = \begin{cases} \delta(x)/\sqrt{N} & \text{if } \delta(x) \geq 0 \\ \delta(x)/\sqrt{d_N} & \text{if } \delta(x) < 0 \end{cases}.$$

Such a result requires the assumption that $d_N \to \infty$, $d_N/N \to 0$, $b_N/d_N \to 0$, and $d_N a_N^2/N \to 0$ as $N \to \infty$, where b_N is the subsample size. To discuss the main idea, consider the following simple two-dimensional example.

Example 3.2 Let $\{X_i = (X_{0,i}, X_{1,i}) : i = 1, \ldots, N\}$ be i.i.d. normal random variables with unknown mean $\mu = (\mu_0, \mu_1)$ and known variance $\Sigma = diag(1, 1)$. Let the hypotheses of interest be given by:

$$H_0 : \mu_0 \leq 0 \text{ and } \mu_1 \leq 0.$$

Consider the local alternatives:

$$H_{1,N} : \mu_{0,N} = \delta_0/\sqrt{N} \text{ or } \mu_{1,N} = \delta_1/\sqrt{d_N},$$

where $\delta_0 > 0$ and $\delta_1 < 0$. Consider the maximum t-statistic

$$T_N = \max\left\{\sqrt{N}\bar{X}_0, \sqrt{N}\bar{X}_1\right\}.$$

It is easy to see that under the local alternative $H_{1,N}$, T_N converges in distribution to $N(\delta_0, 1)$ under the assumption $d_N/N \to 0$.

Consider the recentering sequence

$$\hat{\mu}_{k,N} = \begin{cases} \bar{X}_k, & \text{if } \bar{X}_k < \frac{a_N}{\sqrt{N}} \\ 0, & \text{otherwise.} \end{cases}, \quad k = 0, 1.$$

Clearly, $\sqrt{N}\hat{\mu}_{0,N} = 0$ with probability that goes to one. Also, under the assumption $d_N a_N^2/N \to 0$,

$$\sqrt{N}\bar{X}_1 = \sqrt{N}\left(\bar{X}_1 - \mu_{1,N}\right) + \sqrt{N}\delta_1/\sqrt{d_N}$$
$$= \sqrt{N}\delta_1/\sqrt{d_N} + O_p(1) < a_N$$

with probability that goes to 1, so that $\sqrt{N}\hat{\mu}_{1,N} \to -\infty$. Therefore, conditional on the original sample, the bootstrap statistic

$$T_N^* = \max_{k \in \{0,1\}}\left\{\sqrt{N}\left(\bar{X}_k^* - \bar{X}_k\right) + \sqrt{N}\hat{\mu}_{k,N}\right\}$$

converges in distribution to $\mathbb{Z} \sim N(0, 1)$ almost surely. Since the distribution $N(\delta_0, 1)$ is stochastically larger than $N(0, 1)$, the test based on the SR approach has asymptotically nontrivial local power.

On the other hand, consider the subsample test statistic

$$T_{N,b} = \max\left\{\sqrt{b_N}\bar{X}_{0,b}, \sqrt{b_N}\bar{X}_{1,b}\right\},$$

where the sample means $\bar{X}_{k,b}$, $k = 0, 1$ are based on the subsample of size $b = b_N$. Write

$$\sqrt{b_N}\bar{X}_{k,b} = \sqrt{b_N}\left(\bar{X}_{k,b} - \mu_{k,N}\right) + \sqrt{b_N}\mu_{k,N}, \quad k = 0, 1.$$

Clearly, $b_N/N \to 0$ implies that $\sqrt{b_N}\bar{X}_{0,b}$ converges in distribution to $\mathbb{Z}_1 \sim N(0, 1)$. Also, $b_N/d_N \to 0$ implies that $\sqrt{b_N}\bar{X}_{1,b}$ converges in distribution to $\mathbb{Z}_2 \sim N(0, 1)$. Therefore, if both $d_N/N \to 0$ and $b_N/d_N \to 0$, the subsample test statistic converges in distribution to $\max\{\mathbb{Z}_1, \mathbb{Z}_2\}$, which is stochastically larger than $\mathbb{Z}$.   ∎

The above example shows that the SR test can be asymptotically more powerful than the subsample test against the sequences of local alternatives satisfying the assumption that $d_N \to \infty$, $d_N/N \to 0$, $b_N/d_N \to 0$, and $d_N a_N^2/N \to 0$. However, there are other sequences of local alternatives such that the result may no longer hold. For example, if $d_N a_N^2/N$ converges to a positive constant or diverges to ∞, then, conditional on the original sample, T_N^* also converges in distribution to $\max\{\mathbb{Z}_1, \mathbb{Z}_2\}$. Also, if b_N and d_N take values such that $b_N/d_N \to \infty$, then the asymptotic distribution of $T_{N,b}$ follows the standard normal. In these cases, the relative advantage of the SR test over the subsampling test is not obvious.

3.1.4 A Numerical Example

In this subsection, we present a numerical example which illustrates the power improvements of a SD test (LSW test) with contact set estimation over a standard test (BD test) with conservative critical values.

First, consider the following design under which F_1 first-order stochastically dominates F_2:

$$F_1(x) = x \cdot 1(0 \le x < L) + L \cdot 1(L < x \le L + 0.1)$$
$$+ (x - 0.1) \cdot 1(L + 0.1 \le x < 1) + 1(1 \le x)$$
$$F_2(x) = x \cdot 1(0 \le x < 1) + 1(1 \le x),$$

where $L \in (0, 1)$. For $L = 1$, we define F_1 to be the same function as F_2. The contact set refers to the set of points satisfying $F_1(x) = F_2(x)$. In this design, the contact set is $[0, L]$ and L determines the "size" of the contact set.

Next, consider the second design under which F_1 does not first-order stochastically dominate F_2:

$$F_1(x) = (x + 0.1) \cdot 1(0 \le x < L) + L \cdot 1(L < x \le L + 0.1)$$
$$+ (x - 0.1) \cdot 1(L + 0.1 \le x < 1) + 1(1 \le x)$$
$$F_2(x) = x \cdot 1(0 \le x < 1) + 1(1 \le x).$$

Figure 3.1 presents the distribution functions under the above two designs.

For the simulation, we implement BD and LSW tests (discussed in Sections 2.2.2 and 3.1.1, respectively) and compute rejection frequencies based on 1,000 repetitions at the significance level 0.05. At each repetition, we draw a sample of size $N = 200$ from each distribution. The number of bootstrap

Table 3.1 *SD tests with power improvements:*
Rejection probabilities (Size)

L	0.2	0.4	0.6	0.8	1
BD	0.002	0.027	0.037	0.044	0.055
LSW	0.000	0.012	0.036	0.048	0.047

Table 3.2 *SD tests with power improvements:*
Rejection probabilities (Power)

L	0.2	0.4	0.6	0.8
BD	0.494	0.664	0.748	0.816
LSW	0.468	0.736	0.807	0.882

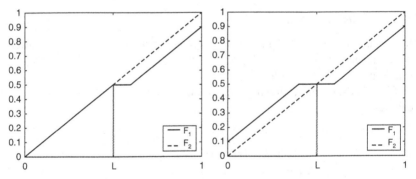

Figure 3.1 CDFs of the first (left) and second (right) designs

repetitions is $B = 500$. For the tuning parameter of the LSW test, we choose $c_N = c \log \log(N)/\sqrt{N}$, with coefficient $c = 0.8$.

Table 3.1 presents rejection probabilities of the two tests under the null hypothesis that F_1 first-order stochastically dominates F_2. The values are generally less than the nominal level 0.05. They are close to zero for small L values and increase to 0.05, as L approaches to 1. Overall, the rejection probabilities of the LSW test tend to be slightly less than those of BD.

Table 3.2 shows rejection probabilities under the second design, which correspond to the power of the tests. As L increases, so does the extent of violation of the null hypothesis. Thus the rejection probabilities increase as the value L increases. For values L exceeding 0.2, the rejection probabilities of the LSW test exceed those of the BD test, which implies that the contact-set-based test has overall superior power compared to the standard test based on conservative critical values.

3.2 Program Evaluation and Stochastic Dominance

3.2.1 Distributional Treatment Effects

Evaluation of causal effects of programs or policies has been of great interest in empirical research in economics and other social sciences; see Imbens and Wooldridge (2009) and Athey and Imbens (2017) for a recent review of the literature. Much of the literature has focused on the estimation of differences in *mean* outcomes, but there also has been active research on estimating the impact of a treatment on the entire *distribution* of outcomes; see, e.g., Bitler, Gelbach, and Hoynes (2006) for important empirical findings. The *distributional treatment effects* can provide a full picture of treatment effects. In general, distributional treatment effects can be assessed by comparing distributions of potential outcomes, which necessarily include unobserved counterfactual distributions. Therefore, standard tests of stochastic dominance are not directly applicable in this context. In this section, we discuss some methods available in the literature.

Potential Outcome Framework We first introduce the *potential outcome framework* commonly used in the treatment effect literature. Let $Y_i(0)$ be the potential outcome for individual i without treatment and $Y_i(1)$ be the potential outcome for the same individual with treatment, with distributions F_0 and F_1, respectively. Let D_i denote the indicator variable for the treatment, with $D_i = 1$ if the individual i is treated and $D_i = 0$ if the individual is not treated. The investigator does not observe both $Y_i(0)$ and $Y_i(1)$ for any individual i, since one of the potential outcomes should be counterfactual, but observes only the realized outcome $Y_i = Y_i(1) \cdot D_i + Y_i(0) \cdot (1 - D_i)$.

Definition 3.2.1 *The distributional treatment effect (for the whole population) is defined by the difference between the distributions of the potential outcomes*

$$\Delta_F(y) := P(Y_i(1) \leq y) - P(Y_i(0) \leq y) \tag{3.2.1}$$

for $y \in \mathbb{R}$.

If $\Delta_F(y) \leq 0$ for all y, then there exists a positive effect of the treatment on the distribution of potential outcomes, in the sense that the potential outcomes with treatment $Y(1)$ (first-order) stochastically dominate the potential outcomes without treatment $Y(0)$. In general, however, $\Delta_F(y)$ is not identified without further assumptions.

Inference under Unconfoundedness Suppose that we observe a covariate X_i for individual i. Then, the distributional treatment effect $\Delta_F(y)$ (defined in Equation 3.2.1) is identified under the *Unconfoundedness* (also referred to as *Exogeneity, Ignorability,* or *Selection on Observable*) assumption:

Assumption 3.2.1 *(Unconfoundedness): $(Y(0), Y(1))$ is independent of D conditional on X.*

Theorem 3.2.1 *Under the unconfoundedness assumption, the distributional treatment effect is given by*

$$\Delta_F(y) = E\left[\frac{D1(Y \leq y)}{p(X)}\right] - E\left[\frac{(1-D)1(Y \leq y)}{1 - p(X)}\right]. \qquad (3.2.2)$$

Notice that the expression (3.2.2) depends only on the joint distribution of the observed random variables $\{Y, D, X\}$. This theorem holds because the distribution of the potential outcome $Y(1)$ is given by

$$
\begin{aligned}
F_1(y) &:= P\left(Y_i(1) \leq y\right) \\
&= E\left\{E\left[1\left(Y(1) \leq y\right) |X\right]\right\} \\
&= E\left\{\frac{E\left[1\left(Y(1) \leq y\right) |X\right] \cdot p(X)}{p(X)}\right\} \\
&= E\left\{\frac{E\left[1\left(Y(1) \leq y\right) |X, D = 1\right] \cdot p(X)}{p(X)}\right\} \\
&= E\left\{\frac{E\left[D1\left(Y \leq y\right) |X\right]}{p(X)}\right\} \\
&= E\left[\frac{D1\left(Y \leq y\right)}{p(X)}\right],
\end{aligned}
\qquad (3.2.3)
$$

where $p(x) = P(D = 1|X = x)$ denotes the *propensity score function*, the second and the last lines follow by the law of iterated expectations, the fourth line holds by unconfoundedness, and the fifth line holds because $Y(1) = Y$ when $D = 1$. Likewise, the distribution of the potential outcome $Y(0)$ is

$$
\begin{aligned}
F_0(y) &:= P\left(Y_i(0) \leq y\right) \\
&= E\left[\frac{(1-D)1(Y \leq y)}{1 - p(X)}\right].
\end{aligned}
\qquad (3.2.4)
$$

Therefore, by combining (3.2.3) and (3.2.4), the distributional treatment effect is identified as (3.2.2).

The hypotheses of interest are

$$H_0 : \Delta_F(y) \leq 0 \ \forall y \in \mathcal{Y}, \qquad (3.2.5)$$
$$H_1 : \Delta_F(y) > 0 \text{ for some } y \in \mathcal{Y},$$

where $\mathcal{Y}$ denotes the union of the supports of $Y(1)$ and $Y(0)$. To test the hypothesis, we first have to estimate the distribution functions F_1 and F_0. One of the popular estimators is the *inverse probability weighting (IPW) estimator* suggested by Hirano, Imbens, and Ridder (2003):

$$\hat{F}_1(y) = \left(\sum_{i=1}^{N} \frac{D_i \mathbb{1}\,(Y_i \leq y)}{\hat{p}(X_i)} \right) \bigg/ \left(\sum_{i=1}^{N} \frac{D_i}{\hat{p}(X_i)} \right), \qquad (3.2.6)$$

$$\hat{F}_0(y) = \left(\sum_{i=1}^{N} \frac{(1 - D_i)\,\mathbb{1}\,(Y_i \leq y)}{1 - \hat{p}(X_i)} \right) \bigg/ \left(\sum_{i=1}^{N} \frac{(1 - D_i)}{1 - \hat{p}(X_i)} \right),$$

where $\hat{p}(x)$ is the nonparametric series logit estimator of $p(x)$.

Consider the supremum type statistic to test the hypothesis (3.2.5):

$$T_N = \sqrt{N} \sup_{y \in \mathcal{Y}} \left(\hat{F}_1(y) - \hat{F}_0(y) \right). \qquad (3.2.7)$$

The asymptotic null distribution under the least favorable case ($F_0 = F_1$) can be shown to be a functional of a Gaussian process.

Maier (2011) suggests approximating the critical values by a bootstrap procedure based on the pooled sample.[5] On the other hand, Donald and Hsu (2014) suggest a multiplier method. The latter method is based on the expression for the "influence functions"[6] of $\sqrt{N}(\hat{F}_1(y) - F_1(y))$ and $\sqrt{N}(\hat{F}_0(y) - F_0(y))$, so that it requires simulating the processes

$$\Psi_1^U(y) = \frac{1}{\sqrt{N}} \sum_{i=1}^{N} \varepsilon_i \left[\frac{D_i \mathbb{1}\,(Y_i \leq y)}{\hat{p}(X_i)} - \hat{F}_1(z) \right.$$

$$\left. - (D_i - \hat{p}(X_i)) \frac{\hat{F}_1(y|X_i)}{\hat{p}(X_i)} \right],$$

$$\Psi_0^U(y) = \frac{1}{\sqrt{N}} \sum_{i=1}^{N} \varepsilon_i \left[\frac{(1 - D_i)\,\mathbb{1}\,(Y_i \leq y)}{1 - \hat{p}(X_i)} - \hat{F}_0(z) \right.$$

$$\left. + (D_i - \hat{p}(X_i)) \frac{\hat{F}_0(y|X_i)}{1 - \hat{p}(X_i)} \right],$$

where $\{\varepsilon_i\}_{i=1}^{N}$ are i.i.d. random variables with mean 0 and variance 1 which are independent of the original sample $\{Y_i, D_i, X_i\}_{i=1}^{N}$, and $\hat{F}_1(y|x)$ and $\hat{F}_0(y|x)$

---

[5] The test statistic of Maier (2011) uses $\sqrt{N/2}$ instead of $\sqrt{N}$ to guarantee that the asymptotic null distribution is a standard Brownian bridge under the least favorable case. However, since the critical values are calculated by bootstrap procedures, this difference is inconsequential in practice.

[6] The influence function is a measure of the dependence of an estimator on a single observation, and was originally suggested in the robust estimation literature; see Hampel (1974).

denote the nonparametric series estimators of the conditional distributions of $Y(1)$ and $Y(0)$ given $X = x$, respectively.[7]

Under regularity conditions, it is shown that both tests are asymptotically valid under the null hypothesis and are consistent against the alternative H_1. The bootstrap procedure of Maier (2011) is relatively simple because it does not require the knowledge of the influence functions, but it can be computationally more expensive because the nonparametric estimator $\hat{p}$ should be computed at each bootstrap step. However, both tests are conservative because the critical values are based on the least favorable case of the null hypothesis.

Inference with Instrumental Variables Abadie (2002) proposes tests for distributional treatment effects in observational studies, where treatment intake is possibly nonrandomized (endogenous) but a binary instrument is available for the researcher. For example, in studying the effects of Vietnam veteran status on the distribution of civil earnings, the eligibility of the Vietnam era draft lottery can be a useful instrument; see Section 3.4.1.

To explain his test, consider the potential outcome framework introduced earlier in this section. Suppose that there exists a binary variable (*instrument*) Z_i that is independent of the responses $Y_i(0)$ and $Y_i(1)$, but is correlated with D_i in the population. Denote $D_i(z)$ the value that D_i would have taken if $Z_i = z$ for $z = 0, 1$. In practice, the investigator does not observe both $D_i(0)$ and $D_i(1)$ simultaneously, and observes only the realized treatment $D_i = D_i(1) \cdot Z_i + D_i(0) \cdot (1 - Z_i)$. Also, the investigator observes only the realized outcome $Y_i = Y_i(1) \cdot D_i + Y_i(0) \cdot (1 - D_i)$. In this setup, Abadie (2002) shows that the distributional treatment effect for the subpopulation of "compliers" can be identified under the following assumptions:[8]

Assumption 3.2.2 *(i) Z is independent of $(Y(0), Y(1), D(0), D(1))$; (ii) $0 < P(Z = 1) < 1$ and $P(D(1) = 1) > P(D(0) = 1)$; (iii) $P(D(1) \geq D(0)) = 1$.*

Theorem 3.2.2 *Under Assumption 3.2.2, the distributional treatment effect for the compliers is given by*

$$\begin{aligned}
\Delta_F^C(y) &:= P\left(Y_i(1) \leq y \mid D_i(0) = 0, \ D_i(1) = 1\right) \\
&\quad - P\left(Y_i(0) \leq y \mid D_i(0) = 0, \ D_i(1) = 1\right) \\
&:= F_{(1)}^C(y) - F_{(0)}^C(y) \\
&= \frac{P(Y_i \leq y \mid Z_i = 1) - P(Y_i \leq y \mid Z_i = 0)}{E[D_i \mid Z_i = 1] - E[D_i \mid Z_i = 0]}.
\end{aligned} \tag{3.2.8}$$

---

[7] See Donald and Hsu (2014, p. 386) for the definition of the series estimators.

[8] Compliers are the individuals who (always) comply with their assignment, i.e., take the treatment if assigned to it and do not take it if assigned to the control group. Therefore, by definition, individual i is a complier if $D_i(0) = 0$ and $D_i(1) = 1$.

This theorem holds because, under Assumption 3.2.2, the CDFs of the potential outcomes for the compliers can be expressed as (Abadie, 2002, lemma 2.1)

$$F_{(1)}^C(y) = \frac{E\left[1\,(Y_i \le y)\,D_i \mid Z_i = 1\right] - E\left[1\,(Y_i \le y)\,D_i \mid Z_i = 0\right]}{E\left[D_i \mid Z_i = 1\right] - E\left[D_i \mid Z_i = 0\right]}$$

(3.2.9)

and

$$F_{(0)}^C(y) = \frac{E\left[1\,(Y_i \le y)\,(1 - D_i)\,|Z_i = 1\right] - E\left[1\,(Y_i \le y)\,(1 - D_i)\,|Z_i = 0\right]}{E\left[(1 - D_i)\,|Z_i = 1\right] - E\left[(1 - D_i)\,|Z_i = 0\right]}.$$

(3.2.10)

Since the denominator of (3.2.8) is positive by Assumption 3.2.2 (ii), the hypothesis

$$H_0 : \Delta_F^C(y) \le 0 \text{ for all } y \in \mathbb{R}$$

holds if and only if

$$H_0 : F_{Y|Z=1}(y) - F_{Y|Z=0}(y) \le 0 \text{ for all } y \in \mathbb{R},$$

(3.2.11)

where $F_{Y|Z=z}(y) = P(Y_i \le y \mid Z_i = z)$ for $z \in \{0, 1\}$ (Abadie, 2002, proposition 2.1). Higher-order distributional treatments for the compliers are defined analogously.

Divide the random sample $\{Y_1, \ldots, Y_N\}$ into two subsamples $\{Y_{1,1}, \ldots, Y_{1,N_1}\}$ and $\{Y_{0,1}, \ldots, Y_{0,N_0}\}$, corresponding to the observations with $Z_i = 1$ and $Z_i = 0$, respectively. Here, $N_1 = \sum_{i=1}^{N} Z_i$ and $N_0 = \sum_{i=1}^{N} (1 - Z_i)$. Then $F_{Y|Z=1}$ and $F_{Y|Z=0}$ can be estimated by the empirical CDFs of the subsamples:

$$\bar{F}_{Y|Z=1}(y) = \frac{1}{N_1} \sum_{i=1}^{N_1} 1\left(Y_{1,i} \le y\right),$$

$$\bar{F}_{Y|Z=0}(y) = \frac{1}{N_0} \sum_{i=1}^{N_0} 1\left(Y_{0,i} \le y\right).$$

Based on the CDF estimators, Abadie suggests the following supremum-type test statistic to test the null hypothesis (3.2.11):

$$ABD_N = \left(\frac{N_1 N_0}{N}\right)^{1/2} \sup_{y \in \mathbb{R}} \left(\bar{F}_{Y|Z=1}(y) - \bar{F}_{Y|Z=0}(y)\right).$$

(3.2.12)

Test statistics for higher-order distributional treatment effects can be defined similarly by replacing the empirical CDFs with the integrated CDFs. The critical values can be estimated by a bootstrap procedure (e.g., a pooled sample bootstrap or a recentered bootstrap), as we discussed in Section 2.2.2.

Inference under Rank Preservation Chernozhukov and Hansen (2006, CH) suggest an alternative inference method for distributional treatment effects when treatment intake is endogenous. Their results are based on the identification strategy of Chernozhukov and Hansen (2005), who show that quantile treatment effects can be identified if the relative rankings of individual heterogeneity are invariant in some sense across potential outcome distributions. Therefore, in contrast to Abadie (2002), who tries to identify the *local* distributional treatment effects for compliers, CH try to recover the distributional treatment effects for the *entire* population satisfying the rank preservation assumption (defined below). CH provide a general inference method on *quantile* treatment effect models (with endogeneity) and apply it to test many interesting hypotheses, including the stochastic dominance hypothesis.

Consider the potential outcome framework, where potential outcomes $Y(d)$ are indexed by potential values $d \in \{0, 1\}$ of the endogenous treatment variable D. The potential outcomes $\{Y(d) : d \in \{0, 1\}\}$ are latent because we only observe $Y = D \cdot Y(1) + (1 - D) \cdot Y(0)$ for each individual. Define the *quantile treatment response function*

$$Q(x, d, \tau) := Q_{Y(d)|X=x}(\tau)$$

to be the τ quantile of potential outcome Y_d conditional on observed characteristic $X = x$. Then, the *quantile treatment effect (QTE)* at (x, τ) is defined as

$$Q(x, 1, \tau) - Q(x, 0, \tau). \tag{3.2.13}$$

Conditional on $X = x$, the potential outcome $Y(d)$ can be represented by its conditional quantile function:[9]

$$Y(d) = Q(x, d, U_d), \text{ where } U_d \sim U(0, 1). \tag{3.2.14}$$

The variable U_d is referred to as the "rank variable," which characterizes heterogeneity of individuals with the same observed characteristic x and treatment d and represents some unobserved characteristics such as abilities. CH assume the following conditions:

Assumption 3.2.3 *(i) Conditional on* $X = x$*, for each* d*,* $Y(d) = Q(x, d, U_d)$*, where* $Q(x, d, \tau)$ *is strictly increasing in* τ *and* $U_d \sim U(0, 1)$*; (ii) Conditional on* $X = x$*,* $\{U_d : d \in \{0, 1\}\}$ *is independent of* Z*; (iii)* $D = \delta(X, Z, V)$ *for some unknown function* δ *and random vector* V*; (iv) Conditional on* $X = x$*,* $Z = z$*, either (a)* $U_0 = U_1$ *(Rank Invariance) or*

---

[9] This follows from the Skorohod representation theorem. That is, for a random variable X with cdf F_X, $Q_X(U) = F_X^{-1}(U)$ for $U \sim U(0, 1)$ has the same distribution as X because $P(Q_X(U) \le x) = P(U \le F_X(x)) = F_X(x)$, see Appendix A for details.

(b) U_0 and U_1 are identically distributed, conditional on V (Rank Similarity);
(v) Observed variables consist of $Y = Q(X, D, U_D)$, D, X, and Z.

Theorem 3.2.3 *(theorem 1, CH): Under Assumption 3.2.3,*

$$P\,[Y \leq Q(X, D, \tau)|X, Z] = \tau \ a.s. \ for \ all \ \tau \in (0, 1). \qquad (3.2.15)$$

This theorem gives the basis for inference on the quantile response function. To verify (3.2.15), the rank preservation assumption (Assumption 3.2.3(iv)) is crucial. To see this, notice that, under the rank invariance $U_0 = U_1 := U$, (3.2.15) holds because the event $\{Y \leq Q(X, D, \tau)\}$ is equivalent to $\{U \leq \tau\}$. On the other hand, under the rank similarity, (3.2.15) holds because

$$
\begin{aligned}
E\,[1(Y &\leq Q(X, D, \tau)|X, Z] \\
&= E\,[1(Q(X, D, U_D) \leq Q(X, D, \tau)|X, Z] \\
&= E\,[1(U_D \leq \tau)|X, Z] \\
&= E\,\{E\,[1(U_D \leq \tau)|X, Z, V]\mid X, Z\} \\
&= E\,\{E\,[1(U_0 \leq \tau)|X, Z, V]\mid X, Z\} \\
&= E\,[1(U_0 \leq \tau)|X, Z] \\
&= E\,[1(U_0 \leq \tau)|X] = \tau,
\end{aligned}
$$

where the second equality holds by the monotonicity of Q in τ, the third and fifth equalities follow from the law of iterated expectations, the fourth equality uses the rank similarity assumption, and the sixth equality holds by conditional independence assumption in Assumption 3.2.3(ii).

For the purpose of estimation, CH consider the linear quantile regression model

$$Q(x, d, \tau) = x^{\mathsf{T}}\alpha(\tau) + d \cdot \beta(\tau), \qquad (3.2.16)$$

where d is a scalar treatment variable (CH allow a vector of treatment variables, but for simplicity we shall discuss only the scalar case) and x is a $k \times 1$ vector of covariates. In model (3.2.16), the quantile treatment effect (QTE) at $\tau \in (0, 1)$ is given by the parameter $\beta(\tau)$ and hence the hypothesis of stochastic dominance is equivalent to

$$H_0 : \beta(\tau) \geq 0 \text{ for all } \tau \in \mathcal{T} \qquad (3.2.17)$$

where $\mathcal{T}$ is a closed subinterval of $(0, 1)$.

Notice that (3.2.15) implies that, conditional on (X, Z), the τ quantile of $Y - Q(X, D, \tau)$ is 0. This in turn implies that the solution to the (population) quantile regression of $Y - Q(X, D, \tau)$ on (X, Z) is 0. CH refer to the latter regression as the *instrumental variable quantile regression (IVQR)*. Based on this result, CH suggest considering the following sample quantile regression objective function:

$$S_N(\alpha, \beta, \gamma, \tau) = \frac{1}{N} \sum_{i=1}^{N} \rho_\tau \left(Y_i - X_i^\mathsf{T}\alpha - D_i\beta - \hat{\Phi}_i(\tau)\gamma \right) \quad (3.2.18)$$

where $\rho_\tau(u) = u\,(\tau - 1\,(u < 0))$ is the check function, $\hat{\Phi}_i(\tau) = \hat{\Phi}(X_i, Z_i, \tau)$ is an instrument (e.g., the least squares projection of D_i on Z_i and X_i). To choose $\theta = (\alpha^\mathsf{T}, \beta)^\mathsf{T}$ such that the solution to γ that minimizes the objective function, S_N, is close to 0, CH suggest a two-step procedure:

1. For each $(\beta, \tau) \in \mathcal{B} \times \mathcal{T}$, minimize $S_N(\alpha, \beta, \gamma, \tau)$ with respect to $(\alpha, \gamma) \in \mathcal{A} \times \Gamma$ to get $(\hat{\alpha}(\beta, \tau), \hat{\gamma}(\beta, \tau))$.
2. For each $\tau \in \mathcal{T}$, choose $\beta \in \mathcal{B}$ that minimizes $\left| \hat{\gamma}(\beta, \tau) \right|$ to get $\hat{\beta}(\tau)$.

The parameter estimates are now given by

$$\hat{\theta}(\tau) = \left(\hat{\alpha}(\tau)^\mathsf{T}, \hat{\beta}(\tau) \right)^\mathsf{T} := \left(\hat{\alpha}(\hat{\beta}(\tau), \tau)^\mathsf{T}, \hat{\beta}(\tau) \right)^\mathsf{T}. \quad (3.2.19)$$

In practice, the minimization can be carried out over discretized parameter spaces, e.g., $\mathcal{B} = \{b_j : j = 1, \ldots, J\}$, $\mathcal{T} = \{0.1, \ldots, 0.9\}$, and the standard quantile regression algorithms can be used for the first step.

Suppose that the observations $\{(Y_i, X_i, D_i, Z_i) : i = 1, \ldots, N\}$ are i.i.d. Under some regularity conditions (including the nonsingularity of the Jacobian matrix $H(\tau)$ defined below, which is necessary for the identification of Q), it can be shown that the IVQR parameters have the uniform Bahadur representation (theorem 3 of CH):

$$\sqrt{N} \left(\hat{\theta}(\tau) - \theta(\tau) \right) = -H(\tau)^{-1} \frac{1}{\sqrt{N}} \sum_{i=1}^{N} l_i\,(\tau, \theta(\tau))\,\Psi_i\,(\tau) + o_p(1)$$

$$(3.2.20)$$

uniformly over $\tau \in \mathcal{T}$, where $W = (X^\mathsf{T}, D)^\mathsf{T}$, $\Psi(\tau) = (X^\mathsf{T}, \Phi(\tau))^\mathsf{T}$, $l_i\,(\tau, \theta) = \left[\tau - 1\left(Y_i \leq W_i^\mathsf{T}\theta \right) \right]$ and $H(\tau) = E\left[f_{Y|X,D,Z}\,(W^\mathsf{T}\theta(\tau))\,\Psi\,(\tau)\,W^\mathsf{T} \right]$.

By the Donsker theorem,

$$\sqrt{N} \left(\hat{\theta}(\cdot) - \theta(\cdot) \right) \Rightarrow b(\cdot),$$

where $b(\cdot)$ is a $(k + 1)$-dimensional Gaussian process with mean zero and covariance kernel,

$$Eb(\tau_1)b(\tau_2)^\mathsf{T}$$

$$= (\min\{\tau_1, \tau_2\} - \tau_1\tau_2) \cdot H(\tau_1)^{-1} J(\tau_1, \tau_2) \left[H(\tau_2)^{-1} \right]^\mathsf{T},$$

where $J(\tau_1, \tau_2) = E\left[\Psi(\tau_1)\Psi(\tau_2)^\mathsf{T} \right]$. Therefore, we have

$$\sqrt{N}\left[R\Omega(\cdot)R^{\mathsf{T}}\right]^{-1/2}\left[\hat{\beta}(\cdot)-\beta(\cdot)\right]\Rightarrow \nu_1(\cdot), \tag{3.2.21}$$

where $R=\left[0_k^{\mathsf{T}},1\right]^{\mathsf{T}}$, $\Omega(\tau)=H(\tau)^{-1}J(\tau,\tau)\left[H(\tau)^{-1}\right]^{\mathsf{T}}$ and ν_1 is a one-dimensional standard Brownian bridge. With a consistent estimator of $\Omega(\tau)$, (3.2.21) thus implies that a distribution free inference of H_0 is possible as in Koenker and Xiao (2002) (Section 2.2.4).

To test the hypothesis (3.2.17), CH consider both (one-sided) supremum and integral-type tests:

$$CH_N = \sqrt{N}\sup_{\tau\in\mathcal{T}}\left[-\hat{\beta}(\tau)\right]_+ \text{ or } N\int_{\mathcal{T}}\left[-\hat{\beta}(\tau)\right]_+^2 d\tau. \tag{3.2.22}$$

To compute critical values, CH recommend using a *score subsampling* procedure, which is a subsampling version of the multiplier method. Specifically, let $\mathcal{S}=\left\{\left(Y_i,X_i^{\mathsf{T}},D_i,Z_i^{\mathsf{T}}\right)^{\mathsf{T}}:i=1,\ldots,N\right\}$ denote the full sample. CH show that the following testing procedure has an asymptotically correct size under the null hypothesis and is consistent against the fixed alternative.

1. Generate B_N randomly chosen subsets of $\{1,\ldots,N\}$ of size b, which satisfies $b\to\infty$ and $b/N\to 0$. Denote such subsets as $\{\mathcal{I}_j:j=1,\ldots,B_N\}$.

2. Define

$$v_{j,b,N}(\tau)=\frac{1}{b}\sum_{i\in\mathcal{I}_j}\hat{z}_i(\tau),$$

where

$$\hat{z}_i(\tau)=R\left[\hat{H}(\tau)^{-1}l_i\left(\tau,\hat{\theta}(\tau)\right)\hat{\Psi}_i(\tau)\right],$$

$$\hat{H}(\tau)=\frac{1}{2Nh_N}\sum_{i=1}^{N}\left[1\left\{\left|Y_i-W_i^{\mathsf{T}}\hat{\theta}(\tau)\right|\le h_N\right\}\hat{\Psi}_i(\tau)W_i^{\mathsf{T}}\right],$$

and $h_N\to 0$ as $N\to\infty$. Since $\hat{z}_i(\tau)$ is the (estimated) score function of the quantile process $\hat{\beta}(\tau)$ (3.2.20), it can be directly used to approximate the distribution of $\hat{\beta}(\tau)$.

3. Define the subsample test statistic

$$CH_{j,b,N}=\sqrt{b}\sup_{\tau\in\mathcal{T}}\left[v_{j,b,N}(\tau)\right]_+ \text{ or}$$

$$=b\int_{\mathcal{T}}\left[v_{j,b,N}(\tau)\right]_+^2 d\tau.$$

4. The subsample critical value $g_{N,b}(1-\alpha)$ is defined to be the $(1-\alpha)$ quantile of the subsampling distribution of $\{CH_{j,b,N}:j=1,\ldots,B_N\}$.

5. Reject the hypothesis H_0 if $CH_N > g_{N,b}(1-\alpha)$.

The score subsampling procedure is similar to the multiplier method that is based on the score function multiplied by a Gaussian normal random variable. Therefore, it also has a computational advantage in that the parameters need not be estimated repeatedly. On the other hand, in contrast to the standard subsampling, the score subsampling procedure requires estimation of the score function and hence the performance may be sensitive to the choice of the tuning parameter h_N.

Inference with Repeated Measurements When treatment decisions depend on unobserved characteristics, the potential outcome distributions and hence distributional treatment effects, can be identified if repeated measurements (e.g., panel data) are available; see Wooldridge (2005), Abrevaya (2006), and Arellano and Bonhomme (2012).

Jun, Lee, and Shin (2016, JLS) show that, under the assumption of "time homogeneity," the potential outcome distributions are identified in a nonparametric setup and suggest an inference method for the stochastic dominance hypothesis between potential outcome distributions that may only be *partially identified*.

Consider the panel data $\{(Y_{it}, D_{it}, X_{it}) : i = 1, \ldots, N, t = 1, \ldots, T\}$, where Y_{it} is an outcome, D_{it} is a binary treatment, and X_{it} is a vector of strictly exogenous covariates. Assume that the observations are identically distributed across i, and T is small and fixed. The observed outcome Y_{it} is related to the potential outcomes $Y_{it}(1)$ and $Y_{it}(0)$ corresponding to $D_{it} = 1$ and 0, respectively, via

$$Y_{it} = D_{it} Y_{it}(1) + (1 - D_{it}) Y_{it}(0).$$

For $d \in \{0, 1\}$, let

$$F_t^d(y) := P(Y_{it}(d) \le y), \quad y \in \mathbb{R} \tag{3.2.23}$$

denote the marginal distribution of the potential outcome. For identification of F_t^d, JLS assume:

Assumption 3.2.4 *(i) There exists a vector α_i of time invariant unobserved confounding factors such that for $d = 0, 1$ and for $t = 1, \ldots, T$, $Y_{it}(d)$ is independent of $\boldsymbol{D}_{it} := (D_{i1}, \ldots, D_{it})$ conditional on α_i; (ii) For $d = 0, 1$ and for $t = 1, \ldots, T$, $Y_{it}(d)$ and $Y_{i1}(d)$ have the same distribution conditional on α_i.*

Assumption 3.2.4(i) is the standard assumption of selection on unobservables. Assumption 3.2.4(ii) is the time homogeneity assumption, which allows one to write $F_t^d(y)$ as $F^d(y)$ and is crucial in the identification strategy of JSL.[10]

Theorem 3.2.4 *(theorem 1, JLS): Under Assumption 3.2.4, the potential distribution is partially identified as*

$$0 \leq L^d(y) \leq F^d(y) \leq U^d(y) \leq 1, \quad y \in \mathbb{R} \tag{3.2.24}$$

for $d \in \{0, 1\}$, where L^d and U^d are the lower and upper bounds, respectively.

For example, when $T = 2$, the bounds are given by

$$L^d(y) = P\,(Y_{i1} \leq y,\ D_{i1} = d) \tag{3.2.25}$$
$$+ P\,(Y_{i2} \leq y,\ D_{i1} = 1 - d,\ D_{i2} = d)$$
$$U^d(y) = L^d(y) + P\,(D_{i1} = D_{i2} = 1 - d) \tag{3.2.26}$$

for $d \in \{0, 1\}$.

Define the distributional treatment effect parameter

$$\Delta_F(y) = F^1(y) - F^0(y). \tag{3.2.27}$$

The standard inference method is not directly applicable because the parameter $\Delta_F(y)$ is only partially identified. That is, rewriting (3.2.24), it satisfies the following moment inequalities:

$$A \cdot \theta(y) \leq b(y), \text{ for all } y \in \mathbb{R}, \tag{3.2.28}$$

where

$$A = \begin{pmatrix} -1 & 1 \\ 1 & -1 \\ -1 & 0 \\ 1 & 0 \end{pmatrix}, \quad \theta(y) = \begin{pmatrix} F^1(y) \\ \Delta_F(y) \end{pmatrix}, \quad b(y) = \begin{pmatrix} -L^0(y) \\ U^0(y) \\ -L^1(y) \\ U^1(y) \end{pmatrix}.$$

For a given $y \in \mathbb{R}$, let $\Theta(y)$ denote the set of $\theta(y)$ that satisfies (3.2.28). It is the identified set. Consider the stochastic dominance hypothesis $\Delta_F(y) \leq 0$ for all $y \in \mathbb{R}$. Since Δ_F is only partially identified, we cannot test the hypothesis directly. Instead, we may consider the two possibilities:

$$H_0^A : \forall \theta(y) \in \Theta(y),\ \Delta_F(y) \leq 0 \text{ for all } y \in \mathbb{R} \tag{3.2.29}$$

and

$$H_0^B : \exists\ \theta(y) \in \Theta(y),\ \Delta_F(y) \leq 0 \text{ for all } y \in \mathbb{R}. \tag{3.2.30}$$

---

[10] This assumption can be restrictive in some applications, but JSL (theorem 2) show that it can be relaxed in a limited sense.

JLS show that the hypotheses (3.2.29) and (3.2.30) are equivalent to

$$H_0^A : U^1(y) \le L^0(y) \text{ for all } y \in \mathbb{R} \tag{3.2.31}$$

and

$$H_0^B : L^1(y) \le U^0(y) \text{ for all } y \in \mathbb{R}, \tag{3.2.32}$$

respectively. The alternative hypotheses are their negations.

Let $\hat{L}^d(y)$ and $\hat{U}^d(y)$ denote the nonparametric estimators of $L^d(y)$ and $U^d(y)$, respectively. In practice, they can be estimated by the empirical CDFs of the relevant subpopulations. To test the hypotheses, JLS suggest using the Cramér–von Mises-type test of Linton, Song, and Whang (2010) (Section 3.1.1). In the case of (3.2.31), the test statistic is defined by

$$JLS_N = N \int \left[\hat{U}^1(y) - \hat{L}^0(y) \right]_+^2 w(y) dy,$$

where $w(y)$ is a weight function. They suggest computing the critical values using the contact set-based bootstrap procedure; see Section 3.1.1.

3.2.2 Counterfactual Policy Analysis

Tests of stochastic dominance can be used to evaluate counterfactual policy effects. Let $X \in \mathbb{R}^k$ denote a vector of covariates that determine an outcome variable of interest Y. In a policy analysis, we are often interested in the effects of a counterfactual change of the distribution of X (or a counterfactual change of the conditional distribution of Y given X) on the distribution of Y. Since the latter distribution is not directly observable, we call such analysis *counterfactual analysis*.

For example, we are interested in the effect of cleaning up a local hazardous waste site (X) on the distribution of the housing prices (Y); the effect of a public policy to reduce smoking (X) on the distribution of infant birth weights (Y); or the effect of the change in the minimum wage, which changes the conditional distribution $F_{Y|X}$, on the distribution of wages (Y).

To explain counterfactual policy effects, we use the framework of Chernozhukov, Fernández-Val, and Melly (2013, CFM), who present a general inference method for counterfactual distributions.

Let F_{Y_j}, F_{X_j}, and $F_{Y_j|X_j}$ denote the marginal distributions of Y_j, X_j, and the conditional distribution of Y_j given X_j, respectively, for $j = 1, 2$. Let the *counterfactual distribution* be defined by

$$F_{Y\langle j|k\rangle}(y) := \int_{\mathcal{X}_k} F_{Y_j|X_j}(y|x) dF_{X_k}(x) \text{ for } j, k \in \{1, 2\}, \ j \ne k, \tag{3.2.33}$$

where $\mathcal{X}_k$ denotes the support of X_k. For example, let the index 1 and 2 denote the population of men and women, respectively, and suppose that Y_j and

X_j denote wages and job market characteristics that affect wages, respectively, for the population $j \in \{1, 2\}$. Then, $F_{Y(1|1)} = F_{Y_1}$ and $F_{Y(2|2)} = F_{Y_2}$ are the (observed) distributions of wages for men and women, respectively. On the other hand, $F_{Y(1|2)}$ refers to the counterfactual distribution of wages that would have prevailed for women, had they faced the men's wage schedule $F_{Y_1|X_1}$. In another thought experiment, $F_{Y(1|2)}$ may be interpreted as the counterfactual distribution of wages that would have prevailed for men, had they had the women's job market characteristics F_{X_2}. Therefore, depending on the contexts, the counterfactual distributions may have different meanings.

To evaluate the counterfactual policy effects, we are interested in the stochastic dominance hypothesis on the counterfactual distributions:

$$F_{Y(j|k)}(y) \leq F_{Y(l|m)}(y) \text{ for all } y \in \mathbb{R} \tag{3.2.34}$$

for $j, k, l, m \in \{1, 2\}$. For notational simplicity, we shall focus on the case $(j, k, l, m) = (1, 1, 1, 2)$ (the other cases are similar), i.e.,

$$H_0 : F_{Y_1}(y) \leq F_{Y(1|2)}(y) \text{ for all } y \in \mathbb{R}. \tag{3.2.35}$$

Before we discuss the inference problem, we briefly mention about the identification issues of counterfactual distributions. The counterfactual policy effects may have a causal interpretation under additional assumptions.

CFM (lemma 2.1) show that if the policy (of changing the conditional distribution $F_{Y|X}$ or the marginal distribution F_X) is independent of the potential outcomes given the covariate, the counterfactual policy has a causal interpretation.

Rothe (2010) also presents identification conditions for the causal effect of a policy which changes marginal distributions. Specifically, Rothe (2010) considers the following nonseparable model:

$$Y_1 = m(X_1, \varepsilon), \tag{3.2.36}$$

where Y_1 is the outcome variable of interest, X_1 is a vector of policy variables, and ε denotes an unobserved error term that represents individual heterogeneity. He was interested in how the distribution of Y would change if a policy maker could exogenously shift the values of X_1 to some X_2. (Using our previous notation, this policy corresponds to changing F_{X_1} to F_{X_2} for the population 1.) The policy would generate the counterfactual random variable

$$Y_2 = m(X_2, \varepsilon). \tag{3.2.37}$$

The main research question is to compare the distribution of Y_1 with that of Y_2. For the causal interpretation, it is important that the policy does not affect the model structure (that is, the functional form of $m(\cdot, \cdot)$ or the distribution of ε). Rothe (2010, proposition 1) establishes the following identification result:

Theorem 3.2.5 *Assume that ε is independent of both X_1 and X_2 and the support of X_2 is a subset of X_1. Then,*

$$F_{Y_2}(y) = \int_{\mathcal{X}_2} F_{Y_1|X_1}(y|x)\,dF_{X_2}(x)\ \text{for all } y \in \mathbb{R} \qquad (3.2.38)$$

and is thus identified.

The proof of Theorem 3.2.5 is straightforward because

$$
\begin{aligned}
F_{Y_2}(y) &= P\left(m(X_2, \varepsilon) \le y\right) \\
&= \int P\left(m(X_2, \varepsilon) \le y | X_2 = x\right) dF_{X_2}(x) \\
&= \int P\left(m(x, \varepsilon) \le y\right) dF_{X_2}(x) \\
&= \int P\left(m(X_1, \varepsilon) \le y | X_1 = x\right) dF_{X_2}(x) \\
&= \int F_{Y_1|X_1}(y|x)\,dF_{X_2}(x), \qquad (3.2.39)
\end{aligned}
$$

where the third equality follows from the exogeneity assumption of ε in the theorem.[11]

Rothe (2012) extends this result to evaluate *partial* distributional policy effects under a more general identification strategy. Consider the model (3.2.36) with $X_1 = (W_1, Z^\mathsf{T})^\mathsf{T} \in \mathbb{R}^k$, where W_1 is a one-dimensional policy variable whose unconditional distribution is going to be changed and $Z = (Z_1, \ldots, Z_{k-1})^\mathsf{T}$ is a $(k-1)$-dimensional vector of the remaining covariates. Assume that W_1 is a continuous random variable.[12] Let Q_S denote the quantile function of a random variable S. By the Skorohod representation theorem, one can express the elements of X using their quantile functions, i.e.,

$$X_1 = \left(Q_{W_1}(U_1), Q_{Z_1}(U_2), \ldots, Q_{Z_{k-1}}(U_k)\right)$$

for some $U_i \sim U(0, 1)$, $i = 1, \ldots, k$; see Section 3.2.1. The quantile functions determine the shape of the marginal distributions of the elements of X, while the vector of "rank variables" U determines its dependence structure.[13]

Consider a policy experiment in which the distribution F_{W_1} is changed to the distribution F_{W_2} of another random variable W_2, with everything else held constant. Then, the counterfactual outcome becomes

---

[11] The strict exogeneity assumption can be restrictive in some applications and can be relaxed to conditional exogeneity given some other random variable.

[12] If W_1 is discrete, then the counterfactual effect discussed below is only partially identified (Rothe, 2012).

[13] The joint CDF of U is the copula function C of F_X, i.e., $P(U \le u) = P(Q_W(U_1) \le u_1, \ldots, Q_{Z_{1,k-1}}(U_k) \le u_k) = P\left(U_1 \le F_W(u_1), \ldots, U_k \le F_{Z_{1,k-1}}(u_k)\right) = C\left(F_W(u_1), \ldots, F_{Z_{1,k-1}}(u_k)\right)$.

$$Y_2 = m(X_2, \varepsilon),$$

where

$$X_2 = \left(Q_{W_2}(U_1), Q_{Z_1}(U_2), \ldots, Q_{Z_{k-1}}(U_k) \right).$$

In this experiment, the rank variable U_1 is assumed to be invariant. This condition requires that the unconditional distribution of W_1 is changed in such a way that the joint distribution of ranks of X remains unaffected. This condition is crucial for the identification of the partial counterfactual policy effect. If ε is independent of U_1 conditional on Z and some support conditions hold, then an argument similar to (3.2.39) yields that the unconditional distribution of the counterfactual random variable Y_2 is identified (theorem 1 of Rothe, 2012) as

$$F_{Y_2}(y) = \int_{\mathcal{X}_1} F_{Y_1|X_1}\left[y \mid Q_{W_2}\left(F_{W_1}(w) \right), z \right] d F_{X_1}(w, z) \text{ for all } y \in \mathbb{R}.$$

$$(3.2.40)$$

We now discuss the testing problem. Consider the null hypothesis (3.2.35), where the counterfactual distribution $F_{Y(1|2)}(y)$ is given by F_{Y_2} in (3.2.39). (The case for (3.2.40) will be discussed later.) Suppose that there are two samples $\mathcal{S}_j = \{(Y_{j,i}, X_{j,i}) : i = 1, \ldots, N_j\}$ which are i.i.d. copies of (Y_j, X_j) for the population $j = 1, 2$.

Two types of populations are considered:

1. *Type I*: The populations may correspond to different demographic groups (e.g., men and women) or time periods. In this case, the samples $\mathcal{S}_1$ and $\mathcal{S}_2$ are both observed and are assumed to be mutually independent. This case is useful in the decomposition analysis (e.g., DiNardo, Fortin, and Lemieux, 1996; Fortin, Lemieux, and Firpo, 2011).

2. *Type II*: We may create population 2 artificially by transforming population 1, e.g., by changing X_1 to $X_2 = X_1 + 1$. In this case, only $\{Y_{1,i}, X_{1,i}, X_{2,i}\}$ are observed, $\{Y_{2,j}\}$ is not observed, and the samples $\mathcal{S}_1$ and $\mathcal{S}_2$ are dependent. This case is useful when we wish to evaluate the counterfactual policy effect of changing the distribution of the covariates on the outcome variable (e.g., Stock, 1991).

Although the two cases are conceptually different, their econometric analyses are very similar. Below, we shall focus on the Type II population with $N_1 = N_2 = N$, because the Type I population has been fully discussed in CFM and Rothe (2010, 2012).

Let

$$\hat{F}_{Y_2}(y) = \int_{\mathcal{X}_2} \hat{F}_{Y_1|X_1}(y|x) d\bar{F}_{X_2}(x), \tag{3.2.41}$$

be an estimator of the counterfactual distribution F_{Y_2} defined in (3.2.35), where

$$\bar{F}_{X_2}(x) = \frac{1}{N} \sum_{i=1}^{N} 1(X_{2,i} \le x) \tag{3.2.42}$$

is the empirical CDF of $\{X_{2,i}\}$ and $\hat{F}_{Y_1|X_1}$ is an estimator of $F_{Y_1|X_1}$.

To estimate $F_{Y_1|X_1}$, CFM suggest two semiparametric estimators. The first estimator is based on the *distribution regression*

$$\hat{F}_{Y_1|X_1}^A(y|x) = \Lambda\left(P(x)^{\mathsf{T}}\hat{\beta}(y)\right), \tag{3.2.43}$$

where Λ is a known link function (e.g., $\Lambda(v) = 1 - \exp(-\exp(v))$), $P(x)$ is a vector of transformation of x (e.g., polynomials or B-splines), and $\hat{\beta}(\cdot)$ is the estimator of the unknown function-valued parameter $\beta(\cdot)$, which satisfies

$$\hat{\beta}(y) = \arg\max_b \sum_{i=1}^{N} \left\{ 1(Y_{1,i} \le y) \ln\left[P(X_{1,i})^{\mathsf{T}}b\right] \right.$$
$$\left. + 1(Y_{1,i} > y) \ln\left[1 - P(X_{1,i})^{\mathsf{T}}b\right] \right\}.$$

The second estimator is based on the quantile regression and takes the form

$$\hat{F}_{Y_1|X_1}^B(y|x) = \varepsilon + \int_{\varepsilon}^{1-\varepsilon} 1\left(P(x)^{\mathsf{T}}\tilde{\beta}(\tau) \le y\right) d\tau, \tag{3.2.44}$$

where

$$\tilde{\beta}(\tau) = \arg\min_b \sum_{i=1}^{N} \rho_\tau\left(Y_{1,i} - P(X_{1,i})^{\mathsf{T}}b\right),$$

$\rho_\tau(u) = u(\tau - 1(u \le 0))$ is the check function and $\varepsilon > 0$ is a small constant.

On the other hand, Rothe (2010) suggests a nonparametric kernel estimator of $F_{Y_1|X_1}$:

$$\hat{F}_{Y_1|X_1}^C(y|x) = \frac{\sum_{i=1}^{N} 1\left(Y_{1,i} \le x\right) K_h\left(x - X_{1,i}\right)}{\sum_{i=1}^{N} K_h\left(x - X_{1,i}\right)}, \tag{3.2.45}$$

where $K_h(v) = h^{-k} K(v/h)$, $h = h_N$ is a bandwidth such that $h_N \to 0$ as $N \to \infty$, and K is a (higher-order) kernel function.[14]

---

[14] The higher-order kernel is used to make the bias of the nonparametric estimator converge to zero at a faster rate. However, it may make the estimator $\hat{F}_Y(y)$ not monotonically increasing in finite samples. See Rothe (2010) for a modified estimator that has the monotonicity property.

Rewrite the estimator (3.2.41) as

$$\hat{F}_{Y_2}(y) = \frac{1}{N} \sum_{i=1}^{N} \hat{F}_{Y_1|X_1}(y|X_{2,i}), \tag{3.2.46}$$

where $\hat{F}_{Y_1|X_1}(y|x)$ denotes $\hat{F}_{Y_1|X_1}^A(y|x)$, $\hat{F}_{Y_1|X_1}^B(y|x)$, or $\hat{F}_{Y_1|X_1}^C(y|x)$. It is interesting that, under some regularity conditions, this estimator has the Donsker property, i.e.,

$$\sqrt{N}\left(\hat{F}_{Y_2}(\cdot) - F_{Y_2}(\cdot)\right) \Rightarrow \nu_2(\cdot), \tag{3.2.47}$$

where ν_2 is a mean-zero tight Gaussian process. This result follows mainly because the estimator $\hat{F}_{Y_1|X_1}^A(y|x)$ (or $\hat{F}_{Y_1|X_1}^B(y|x)$) is based on a semiparametric model and hence is $\sqrt{N}$-consistent. On the other hand, although $\hat{F}_{Y_1|X_1}^C(y|X_{2,i})$ is not $\sqrt{N}$-consistent for each i, its sample average $\hat{F}_{Y_2}(y)$ is $\sqrt{N}$-consistent and asymptotically normal because the sample average takes the form of the U-statistic (theorem 1 of Rothe, 2010).

To test (3.2.35), consider a one-sided Kolmogorov–Smirnov-type test statistic:

$$CR_N = \sup_{y \in \mathbb{R}} \left(\hat{F}_{Y_1}(y) - \hat{F}_{Y_2}(y)\right), \tag{3.2.48}$$

where $\hat{F}_{Y_1}(y) = (1/N) \sum_{i=1}^{N} 1(Y_{1,i} \leq y)$ and $\hat{F}_{Y_2}(y)$ is as defined in (3.2.46). Combining the above results and using the continuous mapping theorem, it can be established that, under the least favorable case of the null hypothesis,

$$CR_N \Rightarrow \sup_{y \in \mathbb{R}} \nu_{12}(y),$$

where ν_{12} denotes a mean-zero tight Gaussian process.

Since the limiting distribution is not pivotal, the critical values need to be computed using a simulation or bootstrap procedure. CFM suggest an *exchangeable bootstrap* which covers the standard nonparametric, weighted, and M out of N bootstrap and subsampling.

For example, consider the standard nonparametric bootstrap.

1. In the case of type II population, draw a bootstrap sample $\mathcal{S}^* = \{(Y_{1,i}^*, X_{1,i}^*, X_{2,i}^*) : i = 1, \ldots, N\}$ from $\{(Y_{1,i}, X_{1,i}, X_{2,i}) : i = 1, \ldots, N\}$ without replacement. (In the case of type I population, draw bootstrap samples $\mathcal{S}_1^* = \{(Y_{1,i}^*, X_{1,i}^*) : i = 1, \ldots, N_1\}$ and $\mathcal{S}_2^* = \{(Y_{2,i}^*, X_{2,i}^*) : i = 1, \ldots, N_2\}$ independently from $\mathcal{S}_1$ and $\mathcal{S}_2$ without replacement, respectively.)

2. Compute the estimators $\hat{F}_{Y_1}^*$ and $\hat{F}_{Y_2}^*$ using the bootstrap sample and then construct the recentered bootstrap test statistic:

$$CR_N^* = \sup_{y \in \mathbb{R}} \left\{ (\hat{F}_{Y_1}^*(y) - \hat{F}_{Y_2}^*(y)) - (\hat{F}_{Y_1}(y) - \hat{F}_{Y_2}(y)) \right\}.$$

$$(3.2.49)$$

3. Reject the null hypothesis at the significance level α, if CR_N is greater than the $(1 - \alpha)$ quantile of the bootstrap distribution of CR_N^*.

An analogous result can be established in the *partial* counterfactual policy experiment. In this case, the counterfactual distribution (3.2.40) can be estimated by

$$\hat{F}_{Y_2}(y) = \frac{1}{N} \sum_{i=1}^{N} \hat{F}_{Y_1|X_1} \left[y \mid \hat{Q}_{W_2} \left(\bar{F}_{W_1}(W_i) \right), Z_i \right], \qquad (3.2.50)$$

where $\bar{F}_{W_1}$ and $\hat{Q}_{W_2}$ denote the empirical CDF and the empirical quantile function of $\{W_{2,i}\}$, respectively, and $\hat{F}_{Y_1|X_1}(\cdot|\cdot)$ denotes $\hat{F}_{Y_1|X_1}^A(y|x)$, $\hat{F}_{Y_1|X_1}^B(y|x)$ or $\hat{F}_{Y_1|X_1}^C(y|x)$. Under some regularity conditions, this estimator also has the Donsker property (theorem 6 of Rothe, 2012). A nonparametric bootstrap can be used to compute critical values.

The above results can be extended to inferences using functionals of the counterfactual distributions. For example, counterfactual policy effects based on quantiles, Lorenz curve, or Gini coefficient can be developed without much additional work.[15]

3.3 Some Issues of Stochastic Dominance Tests

3.3.1 Stochastic Dominance Tests with Unbounded Supports

Horváth, Kokoszka, and Zitikis (2006, HKZ) show that, if the supports are unbounded, using a *weighted* version of the (Kolmogorov–Smirnov-type) test statistic may be necessary for obtaining a nondegenerate asymptotic distribution. Below we discuss their main idea.

Let X_1 and X_2 be two continuous random variables with CDFs F_1 and F_2, respectively. For $s \geq 2$, consider the null hypothesis of the sth-order stochastic dominance over the *whole* real line:

$$H_0 : F_1^{(s)}(x) \leq F_2^{(s)}(x) \text{ for all } x \in \mathbb{R}. \qquad (3.3.1)$$

Using integration by parts, it is easy to see that the hypothesis H_0 can be equivalently stated as

$$H_0 : \Lambda_1(s, x) \leq \Lambda_2(s, x) \text{ for all } x \in \mathbb{R},$$

---

[15] It is because they are Hadarmard differentiable functions of the counterfactual distributions and so the functional delta method can be used to analyze their asymptotic properties.

where

$$\Lambda_k(s, x) := \int_{-\infty}^{x} (x - t)^{s-2} F_k(t) dt, \ k = 1, 2. \tag{3.3.2}$$

Let $\{X_{1,i}\}_{i=1}^{N_1}$ and $\{X_{2,i}\}_{i=1}^{N_2}$ be two independent random samples from the distributions F_1 and F_2, respectively. Consider the weighted Kolmogorv–Smirnov-type test statistic:

$$T_N(s, q) = \sqrt{\frac{N_1 N_2}{N}} \sup_{x \in \mathbb{R}} q(x) \left[\hat{\Lambda}_{1,N}(s, x) - \hat{\Lambda}_{2,N}(s, x) \right], \tag{3.3.3}$$

where $N = N_1 + N_2$, $q : \mathbb{R} \to [0, \infty)$ is a weight function, and

$$\hat{\Lambda}_{k,N}(s, x) = \int_{-\infty}^{x} (x - t)^{s-2} \bar{F}_k(t) dt, \ k = 1, 2 \tag{3.3.4}$$

is the empirical analog of $\Lambda_k(s, x)$ in (3.3.2). When $q(x) = 1$ ($0 \le x \le \bar{x}$) for $\bar{x} < \infty$, then the test statistic $T_N(s, q)$ corresponds to that of Barrett and Donald (2003).

However, if $q(x) = 1$, then the statistic $T_N(s, q)$ may be infinite and hence may not be well defined. To see this, consider the simple case $N_1 = N_2 = 1$. Then, we have

$$\hat{\Lambda}_{1,1}(s, x) - \hat{\Lambda}_{2,1}(s, x) = \int_{-\infty}^{x} (x - t)^{s-2} \left[1 (X_1 \le t) - 1(X_2 \le t) \right] dt$$

$$= \frac{1}{s - 1} \left\{ [x - X_1]_+^{s-1} - [x - X_2]_+^{s-1} \right\}. \tag{3.3.5}$$

Notice that the supremum over $x \in \mathbb{R}$ of the right-hand side of (3.3.5) is infinite for any $s > 2$. This implies that, to make the $T_N(s, q)$ statistic well defined, we need to use a weight function q such that $q(x) \to 0$ as $x \to \infty$.

Specifically, HKZ assume that the weight function satisfies the condition:

$$\sup_{x \in \mathbb{R}} q(x) \left(1 + [x]_+ \right)^{s-2} < \infty. \tag{3.3.6}$$

For example, for some fixed constants z and a, one may choose $q(x) = 1$ for all $x \le z$ and $q(x) = a/(a + x - z)$ for all $x > z$.

HKZ (theorem 1) show that, under an additional condition for CDFs, the weighted KS test statistic $T_N(s, q)$ converges weakly to the supremum of a mean zero Gaussian process under the LFC of the null hypothesis:

Theorem 3.3.1 *Let $s \ge 2$. Suppose that the weight function q satisfies the condition (3.3.6) and the CDFs F_1 and F_2 satisfy*

$$\int_{-\infty}^{\infty} \left(1 + [t]_-^{s-2} \right) \sqrt{F_k(t) \left(1 - F_k(t) \right)} dt < \infty, \ k = 1, 2.$$

Furthermore, assume that $N_1/N \to \lambda \in (0, 1)$ as $N_1, N_2 \to \infty$. Then, under the LFC of the null hypothesis ($F_1 = F_2$),

$$T_N(s, q) \Rightarrow \sup_{x \in \mathbb{R}} q(x)\Gamma_{s,\lambda}(x),$$

where

$$\Gamma_{s,\lambda}(x) := \int_{-\infty}^{x} (x - t)^{s-2} \left[\sqrt{1 - \lambda}\mathcal{B}_1\left(F_1(t)\right) - \sqrt{\lambda}\mathcal{B}_2\left(F_2(t)\right) \right] dt$$

and $\mathcal{B}_1$ and $\mathcal{B}_2$ are two independent standard Brownian bridges.

HKZ (section 5) suggest (conservative) bootstrap critical values based on the pooled sample, analogous to (2.2.39).

The idea of introducing a weight function to test higher-order SD hypotheses by HKZ is useful, because many well-known distributions including normals do not have compact supports.[16] The idea of weighting can also be applied to other types of test statistics. For example, Linton, Song, and Whang (2010) also introduce a weight function to an integral-type test to allow unbounded supports (Equation 3.1.1 in Section 3.1.1).

3.3.2 Classification of Stochastic Dominance Relations

Partial orders such as stochastic dominance have frequently been used to characterize rankings of poverty, inequality, and welfare. It is known that most welfare indices agree on the rankings of inequality or poverty if there is strict dominance between two income distributions (Atkinson, 1970 and Foster and Shorrocks, 1988). However, if there are crossings of the distributions, the conclusions based on the summary indices may be misleading. Therefore, it is of interest to determine the relationship between two population distributions, say F_1 and F_2, given observed samples.

The relationship can be classified into 4 cases:[17] (1) F_1 equals F_2 (or $F_1 = F_2$); (2) F_1 lies above F_2 (or $F_2 < F_1$); (3) F_2 lies above F_1 (or $F_1 < F_2$); (4) F_1 crosses F_2 (or $F_1 \bowtie F_2$).

The usual practice in the literature is as follows:[18] first perform two tests with the null hypotheses of $H_A : F_1$ dominates F_2 and $H_B : F_2$ dominates F_1 against their negations and then decide that F_1 equals F_2 if neither H_A nor H_B are rejected; F_1 lies above F_2 if H_A is rejected and H_B is not rejected; F_2 lies above F_1 if H_A is not rejected and H_B is rejected; and F_1 crosses F_2 if

---

[16] Some researchers argue that the compactness assumption is innocuous in practice because most of the observed data lie in (sufficiently large) bounded intervals.

[17] Here, "F_1 lies above F_2" means that "$F_2(x) \le F_1(x)$ for all x, with strict inequality for some x."

[18] Below, for the purpose of explanation, we focus on first-order stochastic dominance relationship in the classification problem. However, the basic idea is the same for the other partial orderings such as higher-order dominance or Lorenz dominance, etc.

both H_A and H_B are rejected. This procedure is simple and easy to use, but computation of the classification errors of the decisions is complicated due to dependence between the tests.

As for the critical values, the original procedure proposed by Bishop, Formby, and Thistle (1989, BFT) suggests to use the upper α quantile of the distribution of the test statistic to test the null hypothesis of equal distributions $F_1 = F_2$.[19] However, it is criticized that the BFT procedure may hastily decide dominance – (2) or (3) – when in fact the two distributions cross – (4); see Dardanoni and Forcina (1999) and Gastwirth and Nayak (1989).

Bennett (2013) argues that this happens because the above procedure does not control over how the total type I error under the null of equality is allocated to the various classifications of dominance and crossings, and suggests a two-step procedure, described below.

For $k = 1, 2$, let $\{X_{k,i} : i = 1, \ldots, N\}$ be a random sample of size N from the distribution F_k. Consider the Kolmogorov–Smirnov-type test statistics A_N and B_N for the null hypotheses H_A and H_B, respectively:

$$A_N = \sup_{x \in \mathcal{X}} \sqrt{N} \left(\bar{F}_1(x) - \bar{F}_2(x) \right)$$

$$B_N = \sup_{x \in \mathcal{X}} \sqrt{N} \left(\bar{F}_2(x) - \bar{F}_1(x) \right).$$

We expect that both A_N and B_N are close to zero when $F_1 = F_2$, A_N is small and B_N is large when $F_1 < F_2$, A_N is large and B_N is small when $F_2 < F_1$, and both A_N and B_N are large when $F_1 \bowtie F_2$.

Bennett (2013) suggests the following procedure:

(1) If $A_N \leq a(\alpha)$ and $B_N \leq a(\alpha)$, then decide $F_1 = F_2$

(2) If $A_N \leq b(\alpha, \beta)$ and $B_N > a(\alpha)$, then decide $F_1 < F_2$

(3) If $A_N > a(\alpha)$ and $B_N \leq b(\alpha, \beta)$, then decide $F_2 < F_1$

(4) If $A_N > b(\alpha, \beta)$ and $B_N > b(\alpha, \beta)$, then decide $F_2 \bowtie F_1$,

where $a(\alpha)$ and $b(\alpha, \beta)$ satisfy

$$P\left[\max\{v_A, v_B\} > a(\alpha)\right] = \alpha, \qquad (3.3.7)$$

$$P\left[\max\{v_A, v_B\} > a(\alpha), \min\{v_A, v_B\} > b(\alpha, \beta)\right] = \alpha \times \beta \qquad (3.3.8)$$

for $\alpha, \beta \in (1, 0)$, $v_A = \sup_{t \in [0,1]} \mathcal{B}(t)$, $v_B = -\inf_{t \in [0,1]} \mathcal{B}(t)$, and $\mathcal{B}$ is a standard Brownian bridge.

What would be the probabilities of misclassification from this procedure? Suppose that $F_1 = F_2$ is true. Then, by the functional CLT and continuous mapping theorem, the probability of incorrect decision is given by

---

[19] BFT consider tests based on finite grid points and the critical values are from the studentized maximum modulus (SMM) distribution.

$$\lim_{N \to \infty} P\left[A_N > a(\alpha) \text{ or } B_N > a(\alpha) | F_1 = F_2\right]$$

$$= P\left[\max\{\nu_A, \nu_B\} > a(\alpha)\right] = \alpha.$$

Now, by (3.3.8), this total error probability α under $F_1 = F_2$ is apportioned to dominance ($F_1 < F_2$ or $F_2 < F_1$) and crossing ($F_1 \bowtie F_2$) with probability $\alpha(1 - \beta)$ and $\alpha\beta$, respectively (theorem 2 of Bennett, 2013).

Next, suppose that $F_1 < F_2$ is true. Then, the probability of making correct decision (i.e., $F_1 < F_2$) is asymptotically bounded below by $F_{\min}(b(\alpha, \beta))$, where

$$F_{\min}(b) = 2(1 - e^{-2b^2}) - \left(1 - 2\sum_{k=1}^{\infty}(-1)^{k+1}e^{-2k^2b^2}\right).$$

In this case, the error of classifying as $F_1 = F_2$ or $F_2 < F_2$ is zero and that of classifying as $F_1 \bowtie F_2$ is bounded above by $1 - F_{\min}(b(\alpha, \beta))$.

Finally, when there is crossing ($F_1 \bowtie F_2$), the probability of making incorrect classification is asymptotically zero in all the other cases. This implies that the test is consistent in the sense that a crossing can be detected with probability tending to one as $N \to \infty$.

To sum up, the procedure of Bennett (2013) can be useful in practice when one is interested in classifying distributions into four different cases. A caveat is that the choice of β can be arbitrary and probabilities of misclassification may heavily depend on β. If there is an economic theory or a priori reasoning available that restricts the relationship between the distributions, then one may consider a more directed test and reduce the misclassification errors (or, equivalently, improve the power of the tests). Also, as mentioned in Bennett (2013, p. 1316), the probability of making a correct decision when there is dominance largely depends on the contact set $C_0 = \{x \in \mathcal{X} : F_1(x) = F_2(x)\}$. It appears that in this case the misclassification error can be reduced if the inference procedure employs an estimated contact set.

3.3.3 Large Deviation Approximation

Parker (2015) proposes a large deviation approximation to the asymptotic distribution of the supremum-type test of sth-order stochastic dominance for $s \geq 2$.

Consider the Barrett–Donald test statistic BD_N. Under the null hypothesis of stochastic dominance over a compact set $\mathcal{X} = [x_L, x_U]$, it is known that

$$BD_N \Rightarrow \sup_{x \in C_0} \{\nu_s(x)\},$$

where ν_s is a mean zero Gaussian process and $C_0 = \{x \in \mathcal{X} : F_1^{(s)}(x) = F_2^{(s)}(x)\}$ is the contact set (see Equation 2.2.41). Let x_U^* be the right endpoint of C_0.

Parker (2015) establishes that, under the conditions of Linton, Song, and Whang (2010),

$$\lim_{u \to \infty} \lim_{N \to \infty} \frac{P\left[\sup_{x \in [x_L, x_U^*]} \bar{T}_s(x) > u\right]}{1 - \Phi(u/\sigma(x_U^*))} = 1,$$

where $\sigma^2(x) = Var(v_s(x))$ and Φ denotes the CDF of the standard normal distribution. This implies that the *tail* probabilities of the asymptotic null distribution of BD_N can be approximated by those of the standard normal distribution.

Parker (2015) suggests estimators of $\sigma^2(\cdot)$ and x_U^* and shows that their finite sample performances are comparable to those of resampling based tests (e.g., Barrett and Donald, 2003, and Linton, Maasoumi, and Whang, 2005).

This approach is promising because it has an obvious computational advantage over resampling based methods. However, its finite sample and theoretical properties may depend sensitively on estimates of the right endpoint of the contact set.

3.4 Empirical Examples

3.4.1 Distributional Treatment Effects of Veteran Status

In this section, we illustrate the empirical application of Abadie (2002), who studies the impact of Vietnam veteran status on the distribution of civilian earnings. The data consists of a sample of 11,637 white men, born in 1950–1953, from the March Current Population Surveys of 1979 and 1981–5.

Figure 3.2 shows the empirical distributions of the realized annual earnings for veterans and nonveterans. Using the notation of Section 3.2.1, they are estimators of CDFs $F_{Y|D=1}$ and $F_{Y|D=0}$, respectively. In the figure, it is easy to observe that the distribution of the realized earnings of veterans has higher low quantiles and lower high quantiles than that for nonveterans, although the difference between the distributions appears to be minor. On average, the annual earnings of veterans were less than those of nonveterans.

However, it is hard to draw causal inference on distributional treatment effects simply by comparing the distributions of the realized earnings between the two population groups, because the veteran status was not randomly assigned in the population and there was a strong self-selection in the enrollment for military service during the Vietnam era. In view of this, Abadie (2002) proposes using *draft eligibility* as an instrument, because it is randomly assigned in the population (hence is independent of potential outcomes) and is also closely related to treatment intake (military enrollment).

Figure 3.3 plots the sample analogs of the potential outcome distributions $F_{(1)}^C$ and $F_{(0)}^C$ defined in (3.2.9) and (3.2.10), respectively. There is a notable

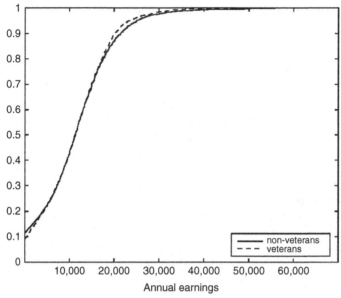

Annual earnings

Figure 3.2 Empirical CDFs of earnings of veterans and nonveterans
Note: Reprinted from Figure 1 of Abadie, A. (2002), "Bootstrap tests for distributional treatment effects in instrumental variable models," *Journal of the American Statistical Association* 97(457), 284–292, with permission of the American Statistical Association, www.amstat.org

difference between Figures 3.2 and 3.3. The distribution of potential earnings of the veterans for compliers has now lower low quantiles than the distribution for the nonveterans, while high quantiles are not affected very much.[20]

Based on this finding, Abadie (2002) tests the null hypothesis of stochastic dominance of potential outcomes of nonveterans over those of veterans, using the test statistic (3.2.12) (with $Z = 1$ and $Z = 0$ now interchanged). He finds that the bootstrap p-values for the first- and second-order stochastic dominance hypotheses are 0.8260 and 0.7415, respectively. This suggests that he cannot reject the hypothesis that there have been negative effects of military service for compliers during the Vietnam era in the sense of stochastic dominance.

3.4.2 Returns to Schooling: Quantile Treatment Effects

The impacts of education on earnings have been extensively studied in labor economics. The standard regression methods may not be directly applicable due to the possible endogenous relationship between education and earnings.

---

[20] This motivates the concept of *initial dominance*; see Section 5.2.3 for details.

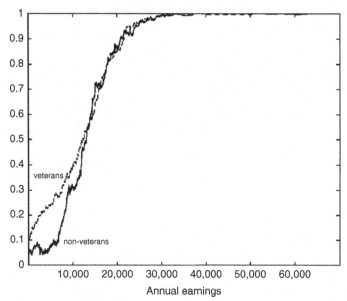

Figure 3.3 Estimated distributions of potential earnings for compliers
Note: Reprinted from Figure 2 of Abadie, A. (2002), "Bootstrap tests for distributional treatment effects in instrumental variable models," *Journal of the American Statistical Association* 97(457), 284–292, with permission of the American Statistical Association, www.amstat.org

Furthermore, it is believed that there is substantial heterogeneity in returns to schooling across different individuals.

Chernozhukov and Hansen (2006) use the data of Angrist and Keueger (1991) to estimate the quantile treatment effects (QTE) of schooling on earnings. The data set consists of 329,509 males from the 1980 US Census who were born between 1930 and 1939. They consider the linear quantile regression model

$$Q(X, D, \tau) = X^{\mathsf{T}}\alpha(\tau) + D \cdot \beta(\tau), \tag{3.4.1}$$

where $Y = Q(X, D, U_D)$ is the log of weekly wage, D is the reported years of schooling and X is a vector of covariates consisting of state and year of birth fixed effects. Quarter of birth was used as an instrument for education.

Figure 3.4 shows the IV-QR and QR estimates of the schooling coefficients $\beta(\tau)$ for $\tau \in [0.05, 0.95]$. The shaded region in each panel is the 95% confidence interval. It shows that returns to schooling vary over the earnings distribution. In other words, there is considerable heterogeneity in the quantile treatment effects. In particular, the IV-QR estimates, which are robust to the possibility of endogeneity, show that the returns to schooling decrease as the

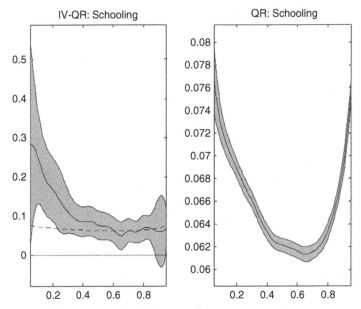

Figure 3.4 Estimates of schooling coefficients
Note: Reprinted from Figure 1 of Chernozhukov, V. and Hansen, C. (2006), "Instrumental quantile regression inference for structural and treatment effect models," *Journal of Econometrics* 132(2), 491–525, with permission of Elsevier

quantile index increases toward the middle of the distribution and then tend to be constant. This result is consistent with the common belief that people with high unobserved "ability"(as measured by the quantile index τ) will get high earnings regardless of their education level, while people with lower "ability" gain more from education.

Chernozhukov and Hansen (2006) also test the null hypothesis of stochastic dominance

$$H_0 : \beta(\tau) \geq 0 \text{ for all } \tau \in \mathcal{T}$$

using the supremum-type test statistic (3.2.22). The value of the test statistic was 0.000, while 90% and 95% subsampling critical values were 2.185 and 2.549, respectively, when the subsample size was $b = 5N^{2/5}$. This result suggests that they cannot reject the hypothesis of stochastic dominance, confirming the intuition that schooling increases earnings across the ability distribution.

4   Stochastic Dominance with Covariates

4.1 Introduction

In many economic examples, it is often of interest to compare distributions of two population subgroups defined by some observed covariates. For example, we wish to compare the distribution of the length of unemployment spell for the workers who received a job training program (Y_1) with that of the workers who did not receive the job training program (Y_2), after controlling for worker characteristics (X) such as age, education, and wealth at a specific level.

If all elements of the covariates X are discrete, then the inference procedure for comparing conditional distributions is essentially equivalent to that for comparing unconditional distributions, by treating each sample as the set of realizations from the population subgroup with a specific value of the covariates. This amounts to, for example, grouping the whole sample into subsets, say of families with different sizes, by educational attainment, or subgroups of funds by investment goals, and then making comparisons across homogenous subsamples.[1] If some elements of X are continuous, however, then we need an inference procedure fundamentally different from those developed for unconditional distributions (i.e., those discussed in Chapters 2 and 3). Therefore, in this chapter, we shall focus on the cases where some elements of X are continuous.

Let $F_1(y|x)$ and $F_2(y|x)$ denote the conditional CDFs of random variables Y_1 and Y_2, respectively, given $X = x$. We consider two forms of *conditional stochastic dominance*:

---

[1] For example, Lefranc, Pistolesi, and Trannoy (2008, 2009) consider the hypothesis of conditional stochastic dominance when the covariates are discrete. Specifically, they were interested in testing the equality of opportunity by comparing the conditional distributions of individual incomes (Y) given parental education or occupation (X) in different countries. By partitioning the whole sample into three categories based on parental education (or occupation) levels, they apply the standard test of Davidson and Duclos (2000, section 2.2.1) for unconditional distributions.

1. The first hypothesis is that the distribution of Y_1 stochastically dominates the distribution of Y_2, conditional on a *fixed* value of $X = x_0$.

$$H_0^A : F_1(y|x_0) \leq F_2(y|x_0) \text{ for all } y. \tag{4.1.1}$$

2. The second hypothesis is that the distribution of Y_1 stochastically dominates the distribution of Y_2, conditional on *all* values of X.

$$H_0^B : F_1(y|x) \leq F_2(y|x) \text{ for all } (y, x). \tag{4.1.2}$$

The hypotheses H_0^A and H_0^B can be tested based on estimators of the conditional CDFs.[2] For the hypothesis H_0^A, the asymptotic properties of the test statistics (introduced below) based on conditional CDF estimators at a fixed value of X can be analyzed using the standard empirical process method (such as the Donsker theorem, etc.). However, to test the hypothesis H_0^B, we need a technical tool different from the standard method, mainly because nonparametric (or smoothed) conditional CDF estimators, as stochastic processes with respect to x, typically do not satisfy a weak convergence property; see Section A.3 for details. In this chapter, we introduce four different approaches suggested in the literature to deal with this problem.

4.2 Conditional Stochastic Dominance at Fixed Values of Covariates

4.2.1 Quantile-Based Tests

For $k = 1, 2$, let $(Y_k, X_k^\mathsf{T})^\mathsf{T} \in \mathbb{R} \times \mathbb{R}^d$ denote a $(d + 1)$-dimensional random vector with the conditional CDF $F_k(y|x)$ and the conditional quantile function of Y_k given $X_k = x$ for $\tau \in (0, 1)$

$$Q_k(\tau|x) := F_k^{-1}(\tau|x) = \inf\{y : F_k(y|x) \geq \tau\}.$$

The null hypothesis of interest is

$$H_0^A : Q_1(\tau|x_0) \geq Q_2(\tau|x_0) \text{ for each } \tau \in \mathcal{T}, \tag{4.2.1}$$

where $\mathcal{T}$ is a closed subinterval of $(0, 1)$. The alternative hypothesis is the negation of H_0^A. Below, we discuss the result of Qu and Yoon (2015, QY), who suggest a fully nonparametric test of the hypothesis (4.2.1).

---

[2] The concept of conditional stochastic dominance in this chapter is different from that of Linton, Maasoumi, and Whang (2005, LMW) or Chernozhukov and Fernández-Val (2005, CF). To illustrate this in a simple setting, suppose $Y_j = \alpha_j + X_j\beta + \varepsilon_j$ for $j = 1, 2$, where ε_j is independent of X_j and has mean 0. Then, both LMW and CF compare the unconditional distributions $P(Y_j - X_j\beta \leq y) = F_{\varepsilon_j}(y - \alpha_j)$ at each y for $j = 1, 2$. On the other hand, the conditional dominance hypothesis in this chapter compares the distributions $P(Y_j \leq y|X_j = x) = F_{\varepsilon_j}(y - \alpha_j - x\beta)$ at each y or (y, x).

QY consider a two-sample setting. Let $\mathcal{S}_1 = \{(Y_{1,i}, X_{1,i}) : i = 1, \ldots, N_1\}$ and $\mathcal{S}_2 = \{(Y_{2,i}, X_{2,i}) : i = 1, \ldots, N_2\}$ denote independent i.i.d. copies of (Y_1, X_1) and (Y_2, X_2), respectively.

The testing procedure of QY is based on the local linear estimator of $Q_k(\tau|x_0)$, denoted by $\hat{\alpha}_k(\tau)$, which is determined via

$$\left(\hat{\alpha}_k(\tau), \hat{\beta}_k(\tau)\right)$$

$$= \arg\min_{\alpha, \beta} \sum_{i=1}^{N_k} \left[Y_{k,i} - \alpha - \left(X_{k,i} - x_0\right)^\mathsf{T} \beta\right] \cdot K\left(\frac{X_{k,i} - x_0}{h_N}\right),$$

(4.2.2)

for $k = 1, 2$, where $\rho_\tau(u) = u\left(\tau - 1\left(u \leq 0\right)\right)$ is the check function, K is a kernel function, and h_N is the bandwidth; see, e.g., Fan and Gijbels (1996) for the general properties of local polynomial estimators.[3]

In finite samples, however, the unrestricted estimate $\hat{\alpha}_k(\tau)$ for $\tau \in \mathcal{T}$ from (4.2.2) may not have the desired monotonicity property (of the quantile function) with respect to $\tau \in \mathcal{T}$. To get a monotone estimator, QY suggest two estimators:

1. Partition $\mathcal{T}$ into a grid of equally spaced quantiles $\mathcal{T}_M = \{\tau_1, \ldots, \tau_M\}$ and minimize the sum of the objective functions (4.2.2) with different τ_m's for $m = 1, \ldots, M$ under the restriction $\alpha_k(\tau_1) \leq \cdots < \alpha_k(\tau_M)$. Then, linearly interpolate the estimates of $\{\alpha_k(\tau_m) : m = 1, \ldots, M\}$ to obtain an estimator of the quantile process $\{\alpha_k(\tau) : \tau \in \mathcal{T}\}$.

2. Partition $\mathcal{T}$ into a grid of equally spaced quantiles $\mathcal{T}_M = \{\tau_1, \ldots, \tau_M\}$, minimize the objective function (4.2.2) at each τ_m for $k = 1, \ldots, M$, and linearly interpolate the estimates of $\{\alpha_k(\tau_m) : m = 1, \ldots, M\}$. Then, apply rearrangement to the latter estimates as in Chernozhukov, Fernández-Val, and Galichon (2010).

Below, we denote the monotonized quantile process estimate from either 1 or 2 above as $\{\tilde{\alpha}_k^*(\tau) : \tau \in \mathcal{T}\}$. Also, unless it is necessary, we shall suppress the subscript k for notational simplicity. The asymptotic properties of $\hat{\alpha}(\tau)$ depend on whether x_0 is close to the boundary of the support or not. QY discuss both cases, but, for simplicity, we shall discuss only the case where x_0 is an interior point.

Let f_X and $f_{Y|X}$ be marginal density of X and conditional density of Y given X, respectively. QY (theorem 1) first establish the following uniform (in τ) Bahadur representation for the unrestricted estimator $\hat{\alpha}(\tau)$:

---

[3] QY allow h_N to depend on τ, but we shall suppress the dependence for notational simplicity.

Theorem 4.2.1 *Let x_0 be an interior point. Under regularity conditions, the following result holds uniformly over $\tau \in \mathcal{T}$:*

$$\sqrt{Nh_N^d}\left(\hat{\alpha}(\tau) - Q(\tau|x_0) - d_\tau h_N^2\right)$$

$$= H(\tau)^{-1}\frac{1}{\sqrt{Nh_N^d}}\sum_{i=1}^{N} l_i\,(\tau)\,K\left(\frac{X_i - x_0}{h_N}\right) + o_p(1),$$

where $l_i\,(\tau) = [\tau - 1\,(Y_i \le Q(\tau|X_i))]$, $H(\tau) = f_X(x_0)\cdot f_{Y|X}\,[Q(\tau|x_0)|x_0]$, and $d_\tau = \frac{1}{2}tr\left(\frac{\partial^2 Q(\tau|x_0)}{\partial x \partial x^\mathsf{T}}\int uu^\mathsf{T} K(u)du\right)$ is the asymptotic bias term.

Using this representation and the result that the linear interpolations in 1 or 2 above do not affect the first-order asymptotic distribution of $\tilde{\alpha}^*(\tau)$ if $M/\left(Nh^d\right)^{1/4} \to \infty$ as $N \to \infty$, it is possible to establish the weak convergence result:

$$\sqrt{Nh_N^d}\,f_X(x_0)f_{Y|X}\,[Q(\tau|x_0)|x_0]\left(\tilde{\alpha}^*(\tau) - Q(\tau|x_0) - d_\tau h_N^2\right)$$

$$\Rightarrow \kappa_2^{1/2} \cdot \mathcal{B}(\tau), \tag{4.2.3}$$

where $\kappa_2 = \int K^2(u)du$ and $\mathcal{B}(\cdot)$ is a standard Brownian bridge (QY, theorem 3).

The result (4.2.3) implies that a distribution free inference on $Q(\tau|x_0)$ is possible, after estimating the unknown functions f_X, $f_{Y|X}$, $Q(\tau|x)$, and the bias term d_τ using, e.g., the local polynomial estimators. Alternatively, a simulation method can be used to approximate the limiting distribution.

We now turn to the testing problem for the hypothesis (4.2.1). QY do not provide the details of the test, but we briefly sketch the main steps, following their idea.

Let $\hat{Q}_k(\tau|x_0)$ denote $\tilde{\alpha}_k^*(\tau)$ for $k = 1, 2$. Consider a supremum-type test statistic

$$QY_N = \sqrt{\frac{N_1 N_2}{N}h_N^d}\,\sup_{\tau\in\mathcal{T}}\left\{\hat{Q}_2(\tau|x_0) - \hat{Q}_1(\tau|x_0) - \hat{b}_N\right\}, \tag{4.2.4}$$

where $N = N_1 + N_2$, $b_N = \left(\hat{d}_{1,\tau} + \hat{d}_{2,\tau}\right)h_N^2$, and

$$\hat{d}_{k,\tau} = \frac{1}{2}tr\left(\frac{\partial^2 \hat{Q}_k(\tau|x_0)}{\partial x \partial x^\mathsf{T}}\int uu^\mathsf{T} K(u)du\right), \quad k = 1, 2.$$

In practice, $\frac{\partial^2 \hat{Q}_k(\tau|x_0)}{\partial x \partial x^\mathsf{T}}$ can be estimated by a local cubic estimator (i.e., the estimator of the coefficient of the additional quadratic term in Equation 4.2.2).

From (4.2.3), we can characterize the asymptotic null distribution of QY_N:

Theorem 4.2.2 *Suppose that $N_1/N \to \lambda \in (0, 1)$ as $N_1, N_2 \to \infty$ and additional regularity conditions hold. Then, under the least favorable case ($Q_1(\tau|x_0) = Q_2(\tau|x_0)$ for all $\tau \in \mathcal{T}$) of the null hypothesis H_0^A, we have*

$$QY_N \Rightarrow \sup_{\tau \in \mathcal{T}} \left(\sqrt{\lambda} v_2(\tau) - \sqrt{1-\lambda} v_1(\tau) \right), \tag{4.2.5}$$

where

$$v_k(\tau) = \frac{G_k(\tau)}{\sqrt{f_{X_k}(x_0)} f_{Y_k|X_k}[Q_k(\tau|x_0)|x_0]}, \quad k = 1, 2,$$

and $G_1(\tau)$ and $G_2(\tau)$ are independent copies of $G(\tau) = \kappa_2^{1/2} \cdot \mathcal{B}(\tau)$.

We can simulate the process $v_k(\tau)$ via

$$v_k^*(\tau) = \hat{H}_k(\tau)^{-1} \frac{1}{\sqrt{N h_N^k}} \sum_{i=1}^{N_k} \left[\tau - 1 \left(U_{k,i}^0 \le 0 \right) \right] K \left(\frac{X_{k,i} - x_0}{h_N} \right), \tag{4.2.6}$$

where $\{U_{k,i}^0 : i = 1, \ldots, N_k, \ k = 1, 2\}$ are i.i.d. $U(0, 1)$ random variables and

$$\hat{H}_k(\tau) = \hat{f}_{X_k}(x_0) \cdot \hat{f}_{Y_k|X_k} \left[\hat{Q}_k(\tau|x_0)|x_0 \right],$$

$$\hat{f}_{X_k}(x) = \frac{1}{N_k} \sum_{i=1}^{N_k} K \left(\frac{X_{k,i} - x_0}{h_N} \right),$$

$$\hat{f}_{Y_k|X_k}(y|x) = \frac{1}{h_N} \int K \left(\frac{y - z}{h_N} \right) d\hat{F}_k(z|x),$$

$$\hat{F}_k(z|x) = \sup \left\{ \tau \in (0, 1) : \hat{Q}_k(\tau|x) \le z \right\}.$$

Therefore, we can simulate the limit distribution in (4.2.5) by

$$QY_N^* = \sup_{\tau \in \mathcal{T}} \left(\sqrt{\frac{N_1}{N}} v_2^*(\tau) - \sqrt{\frac{N_2}{N}} v_1^*(\tau) \right). \tag{4.2.7}$$

The simulated critical value $g_N(1-\alpha)$ is defined as the $(1-\alpha)$ sample quantile of the distribution of QY_N^* conditional on the original samples $\{\mathcal{S}_1, \mathcal{S}_2\}$ and we may reject the hypothesis H_0 if $QY_N > g_N(1-\alpha)$. Under suitable regularity conditions, it is possible to show that the test has an asymptotically correct size under the null hypothesis and is consistent against all alternatives.

4.2.2 Cumulative Distribution Function-Based Tests

Consider the two sample settings in the previous section. The conditional stochastic dominance hypothesis H_0^A can be equivalently stated using conditional CDFs:

$$H_0^A : F_1(y|x_0) \le F_2(y|x_0) \text{ for each } y \in \mathcal{Y}, \tag{4.2.8}$$

where $\mathcal{Y}$ denotes the union of the supports of Y_1 and Y_2. For $k = 1, 2$, define the kernel estimator of the conditional CDF $F_k(y|x_0)$ based on the sample $\mathcal{S}_k$ to be

$$\hat{F}_k(y|x_0) = \frac{\sum_{i=1}^{N_k} K\left(\frac{X_{k,i}-x_0}{h_N}\right) 1\left(Y_{k,i} \le y\right)}{\sum_{i=1}^{N_k} K\left(\frac{X_{k,i}-x_0}{h_N}\right)}.$$

By the Donsker theorem, it is straightforward to show that the CDF process (in y) converges weakly to a Gaussian process (Shen, 2017, theorem 1):

Theorem 4.2.3 *Under regularity conditions, for each* $x_0 \in \mathcal{X}$,

$$\sqrt{N h_N^d f_{X_k}(x_0)}\left(\hat{F}_k(\cdot|x_0) - F_k(\cdot|x_0)\right) \Rightarrow \kappa_2^{1/2} \cdot \mathcal{B}_k(F_k(\cdot|x_0)), \tag{4.2.9}$$

where $\kappa_2 = \int K^2(u)du$, *and* $\mathcal{B}_1$ *and* $\mathcal{B}_2$ *are independent standard Brownian bridges.*

To test the null hypothesis H_0^A in (4.1.1), consider a supremum-type test statistic:

$$SH_N = \kappa_2^{-1/2}\left(\frac{N h_N^d \hat{f}_{X_1}(x_0)\hat{f}_{X_2}(x_0)}{\hat{f}_{X_1}(x_0) + \hat{f}_{X_2}(x_0)}\right)^{1/2}$$
$$\times \sup_{y \in \mathcal{Y}}\left\{\hat{F}_1(y|x_0) - \hat{F}_2(y|x_0)\right\},$$

where

$$\hat{f}_{X_k}(x_0) = \frac{1}{N_k h_N^d}\sum_{i=1}^{N_k} K\left(\frac{X_{k,i} - x_0}{h_N}\right).$$

From (4.2.9), we can see that the distribution of SH_N is asymptotically pivotal under the LFC of the null hypothesis:

Theorem 4.2.4 *Under the least favorable case* $(F_1(y|x_0) = F_2(y|x_0)$ *for all* $y \in \mathcal{Y})$ *of* H_0^A,

$$SH_N \Rightarrow \sup_{t \in [0,1]} \mathcal{B}(t), \tag{4.2.10}$$

where $\mathcal{B}$ *is a standard Brownian bridge.*

Recall that the limiting distribution $\sup_{t \in [0,1]} \mathcal{B}(t)$ is tabulated and its critical values for $10\%, 5\%$, and 1% significance levels are given by $1.073, 1.2239$, and 1.5174, respectively (Equation 2.2.26 in Section 2.2.2).

For higher-order stochastic dominance, Shen (2017, section 2.4) suggests a simulation method (similar to the simulation method in the previous subsection) to compute critical values. She also discusses extensions to semiparametric single index models and stratified sampling.

4.3 Conditional Stochastic Dominance at All Values of Covariates

Consider the hypothesis of conditional stochastic dominance for *all* values of the covariates:

$$H_0^B : F_{Y_1|X}(y|x) \leq F_{Y_2|X}(y|x) \text{ for all } (y, x) \in \mathcal{Y} \times \mathcal{X},$$

A natural way of testing the hypothesis H_0^B would be to consider a supremum or integral-type test statistic based on a nonparametric estimator, say $\hat{F}_{Y_k|X}$, of $F_{Y_k|X}$ for $k = 1, 2$. However, unlike the empirical CDF (i.e., the nonparametric estimator of *unconditional* CDF), it is known that the random process $(x, y) \longmapsto r_N \left(\hat{F}_{Y_1|X}(y|x) - E\hat{F}_{Y_1|X}(y|x) \right)$ in a function space does not converge weakly to a nondegenerate limit, where $r_N \to \infty$ is a nonrandom sequence.[4] This makes the asymptotic analysis of the test statistic complicated and nonstandard. In this section, we introduce several different approaches to overcoming the difficulty.

4.3.1 The Poissonization Approach

In this section, we discuss the Poissonization approach to test the hypothesis of conditional stochastic dominance; see Section A.3 in Appendix A for the main idea of the Poissonization method. Lee and Whang (2009, LW) and Chang, Lee, and Whang (2015) use a Poissonization method to test the hypothesis of *Conditional Distributional Treatment Effect (CDTE)*. Since CDTE is one of the main applications of conditional stochastic dominance, we briefly discuss their results below.

Consider the potential outcome framework (Section 3.2.1), where $Y(0)$ and $Y(1)$ denote the potential outcomes without and with treatment, respectively, and D denotes the treatment indicator variable. The realized outcome is given by $Y = Y(1) \cdot D + Y(0) \cdot (1 - D)$. Assume that independent and identically distributed (i.i.d.) observations $\{(Y_i, D_i, X_i) : i = 1, \ldots, N\}$ of (Y, D, X) are available, where X denotes a vector of covariates.

The conditional distributional treatment effect for the population subgroup with $X = x$ is defined by the difference between the conditional distributions of the potential outcomes

$$\tau_0(y, x) := P\left(Y(1) \leq y | X = x\right) - P\left(Y(0) \leq y | X = x\right) \quad (4.3.1)$$
$$= P\left(Y(1) \leq y | X = x, D = 1\right)$$
$$- P\left(Y(0) \leq y | X = x, D = 0\right)$$

for $(y, x) \in \mathbb{R} \times \mathbb{R}^k$, where the last equality holds under randomized experiments or the unconfoundedness assumption (see Section 3.2.1).

---

[4] See Section A.3 for a related discussion.

The hypotheses of interest are

$$H_0 : \tau_0(y, x) \leq 0 \text{ for all } (y, x) \in \mathcal{Z}, \tag{4.3.2}$$
$$H_1 : \tau_0(y, x) > 0 \text{ for some } (y, x) \in \mathcal{Z},$$

where $\mathcal{Z} \subset \mathbb{R} \times \mathbb{R}^k$ denotes a subset on which one wishes to evaluate the treatment effects.

To test H_0, LW consider a class of tests based on the one-sided L_1 norm:

$$T_N = \int_{\mathcal{Z}} \sqrt{N} \left[\hat{\tau}(y, x) \right]_+ \hat{w}(y, x) d(y, x), \tag{4.3.3}$$

where $\hat{\tau}(y, x)$ is a uniformly consistent estimator of $\tau_0(y, x)$ and $\hat{w}(y, x)$ is a possibly data-dependent weight function that is strictly positive on $\mathcal{Z}$. (For simplicity, we shall assume $\hat{w}(y, x) = 1$.)

To construct the test statistic T_N, it is necessary to estimate $\tau_0(y, x)$. LW consider a kernel estimator of $\tau_0(y, x)$. Define

$$p_d(x) = P(D = d | X = x) f(x), \ d = 0, 1,$$
$$\phi(x, D) = \frac{1(D = 1)}{p_1(x)} - \frac{1(D = 0)}{p_0(x)},$$

where $f(x)$ denotes the density of X. Then, the kernel estimator of $\tau_0(y, x)$ is given by

$$\hat{\tau}(y, x) = \frac{1}{N} \sum_{i=1}^{N} 1(Y_i \leq y) \hat{\phi}(x, D_i) K_h(x - X_i),$$

where $\hat{\phi}(x, D)$ is $\phi(x, D)$ with p_d replaced by $\hat{p}_d$, $K_h(\cdot) := K(\cdot / h) / h^k$, and

$$\hat{p}_d(x) = \frac{1}{N} \sum_{i=1}^{N} 1(D_i = d) K_h(x - X_i), d = 0, 1. \tag{4.3.4}$$

Here, K is a k-dimensional kernel function and h is a bandwidth.

What would be the asymptotic distribution of T_N under the null hypothesis? The answer is not straightforward because T_N in (4.3.3) depends on the non-parametric kernel estimator $\hat{\tau}(\cdot, \cdot)$ in a nonlinear and non-differentiable fashion and the process $(x, y) \mapsto \hat{\tau}(x, y)$ does not have a weak convergence to a nondegenerate limit distribution. In view of this, LW suggest using the Poissonization technique (Section A.3) to characterize the asymptotic distribution of T_N.

Let

$$K_*(\lambda) = \int K(\xi) K(\xi + \lambda) d\xi \text{ and } \rho_0(\lambda) = \frac{K_*(\lambda)}{K_*(0)}.$$

For y, y', x, define

$$\mu_1(y_1, y_2, x)$$
$$= \sum_{d \in \{0,1\}} \frac{E[1(Y \le y_1)1(Y \le y_2)|X = x, D = d]}{p_d(x)},$$
$$\mu_2(y_1, y_2, x)$$
$$= \sum_{d \in \{0,1\}} \frac{E[1(Y \le y_1)|X = x, D = d]E[1(Y \le y_2)|X = x, D = d]}{p_d(x)}.$$

Also, define

$$\rho_1(y, y', x, \lambda) = \{\mu_1(y, y', x) - \mu_2(y, y', x)\} K_*(\lambda),$$
$$\rho_2(y, x) = \{\mu_1(y, y, x) - \mu_2(y, y, x)\} K_*(0),$$
$$\rho(y, y', x, \lambda) = \frac{\rho_1(y, y', x, \lambda)}{\sqrt{\rho_2(y, x)\rho_2(y', x)}}.$$

LW show that under the least favorable case of the null hypothesis, a standardized version of T_N is asymptotically normally distributed.

Theorem 4.3.1 *If* $\tau_0(y, x) = 0 \; \forall \; (y, x) \in \mathcal{Z}$, *then*

$$\frac{T_N - a_N}{\sigma_0} \Rightarrow N(0, 1),$$

where

$$a_N = \frac{1}{h^{k/2}\sqrt{2\pi}} \int_{\mathbb{R}^k} \int_{\mathbb{R}} \sqrt{\rho_2(y, x)} d(y, x),$$
$$\sigma_0^2 = \int_{\Delta_0} \int_{\mathbb{R}^k} \int_{\mathbb{R}} \int_{\mathbb{R}} F\left[\rho(y, y', x, \lambda)\right] \sqrt{\rho_2(y, x)\rho_2(y', x)} d(y, y', x, \lambda)$$
$$F(\rho) = Cov\left(\left[\sqrt{1-\rho}\mathbb{Z}_1 + \rho\mathbb{Z}_2\right]_+, [\mathbb{Z}_2]_+\right),$$
$$\Delta_0 = \{\lambda \in \mathbb{R}^k : \|\lambda\| \le 1\}.$$

In practice, a_N and σ_0 should be estimated and both ρ and ρ_2 can be estimated by nonparametric kernel estimators. On the other hand, $F(\rho)$ that appears in the definition of σ_0^2 can be approximated for each value of ρ with arbitrary accuracy by simulating a large number of independent standard normal random variables ($\mathbb{Z}_1, \mathbb{Z}_2$).

A feasible version of the test statistic is then given by

$$S_N = \frac{T_N - \hat{a}_N}{\hat{\sigma}},$$

where $\hat{a}_N$ and $\hat{\sigma}$ denote the estimators of a_N and σ, respectively.

LW suggest rejecting H_0 if $S_N > z_{1-\alpha}$, at the nominal significance level α, where $z_{1-\alpha}$ is the $(1 - \alpha)$ quantile of the standard normal distribution for $0 < \alpha < 1$. They also show that the test is consistent against all alternatives and is powerful against some, though not all, $N^{-1/2}$-local alternatives.

The advantage of the LW test is its computational simplicity, because it does not require a resampling procedure to compute critical values. However, the test based on the least favorable case of the null hypothesis can be too conservative. To improve the power performance, LW also suggest a test based on the estimated contact set

$$\hat{C} = \{(y, x) \in \mathcal{Z} : |\hat{\tau}(y, x)| \le \eta_N\},$$

where η_N is a sequence of positive constants that converge to zero. To implement the test, several tuning parameters such as the bandwidth h and η_N need to be chosen. In practice, LW suggest choosing $h = C_h \hat{s}_X N^{-2/(7k)}$ and $\eta_N = h \times N^{2/(7k)} \times N^{-11/56}$, where $\hat{s}_X$ is the sample standard deviation of X, which works well in their simulations and empirical applications; see Section 4.5.1 below.

4.3.2 The Least Concave Majorant Approach

Delgado and Escanciano (2013, DE) suggest a test of (first-order) conditional stochastic dominance using the *least concave majorant (LCM)* approach.

To illustrate the main idea of the LCM approach, consider the hypothesis of non-positivity of a real-valued function g,

$$g(x) \le 0 \text{ for all } x \in \mathbb{R}. \tag{4.3.5}$$

The hypothesis is equivalent to monotonicity of

$$D(x) = \int_{-\infty}^{x} g(s)ds$$

in x, which in turn is equivalent to concavity of

$$C(x) = \int_{-\infty}^{x} D(t)dt$$

in x, because $\partial^2 C(x)/\partial x^2 = \partial D(x)/\partial x = g(x) \le 0$. Let $\mathcal{T}C$ be the *least concave majorant* of C, that is the smallest concave function lying above the function C. For any concave function g, $\mathcal{T}g = g$. Therefore, the hypothesis (4.3.5) is equivalent to

$$\mathcal{T}C - C = 0.$$

Let $F_{Y_k|X}(y|x)$ denote the conditional CDF of Y_k given $X = x$, respectively, for $k = 1, 2$. Then, from the above discussion, it is easy to see that the null hypothesis of conditional stochastic dominance

$$H_0 : F_{Y_1|X}(y|x) \le F_{Y_2|X}(y|x) \text{ for all } y, x \tag{4.3.6}$$

is true if and only if

$$D(y, x) = \int_{-\infty}^{x} (F_{Y_1|X}(y|s) - F_{Y_2|X}(y|s)) F_X(ds)$$

is nonincreasing in x for all y, which in turn is equivalent to concavity of

$$C(y, u) = \int_0^u D(y, F_X^{-1}(t)) dt$$

in u for all y, using the fact that the quantile function F_X^{-1} is nondecreasing. Therefore, the null hypothesis (4.3.6) can be represented as

$$H_0 : \mathcal{T}C - C = 0.$$

To define the test statistic, let $\mathcal{S}_N = \{(Y_{1,i}, Y_{2,i}, X_i)^\mathsf{T}\}_{i=1}^N$ be i.i.d. observations of $Z = (Y_1, Y_2, X)^\mathsf{T}$. Let C_N be the empirical analog of C, that is

$$C_N(y, u)$$
$$= \frac{1}{N} \sum_{i=1}^N [1(Y_{1,i} \le y) - 1(Y_{2,i} \le y)](u - \bar{F}_X(X_i)) 1(\bar{F}_X(X_i) \le u),$$

where $\bar{F}_X$ denotes the empirical CDF of $\{X_i\}_{i=1}^N$. DE consider the supremum-type test statistic

$$DE_N = \sqrt{N} \sup_{y,u} \{\mathcal{T}C_N(y, u) - C_N(y, u)\}.$$

To compute the critical values, DE suggest a multiplier method. That is, generate the statistic

$$DE_N^* = \sqrt{N} \sup_{y,u} \{\mathcal{T}C_N^*(y, u) - C_N^*(y, u)\},$$

where

$$C_N^*(y, u)$$
$$:= \frac{1}{N} \sum_{i=1}^N [1(Y_{1i} \le y) - 1(Y_{2i} \le y)](u - \hat{F}_X(X_i)) 1(\hat{F}_X(X_i) \le u) V_i,$$

$\{V_i\}_{i=1}^N$ are i.i.d. random variables with mean zero and variance one, independently generated from the sample $\mathcal{S}_N$, with bounded support. The α-level simulation critical value $c_{N,\alpha}^*$ is then defined to be the $(1 - \alpha)$ quantile of the simulation distribution of DE_N^*.

The asymptotic properties of the DE test are summarized as follows:

Theorem 4.3.2 *Assume that F_X is continuous. (a) Under H_0,*

$$\limsup_{N \to \infty} P\left(DE_N > c^*_{N,\alpha}\right) \leq \alpha,$$

with equality when H_0 holds with equality. (b) Under H_1,

$$\lim_{N \to \infty} P\left(DE_N > c^*_{N,\alpha}\right) = 1.$$

The asymptotic validity of the DE test under the null hypothesis is based on the following arguments: by the functional CLT,

$$\sqrt{N}G_N := \sqrt{N}\left(C_N - C\right) \Rightarrow \nu_\infty,$$

where ν_∞ is a tight mean-zero Gaussian process. By the continuous mapping theorem,

$$\sqrt{N}\left(\mathcal{T}G_N - G_N\right) \Rightarrow \mathcal{T}\nu_\infty - \nu_\infty. \tag{4.3.7}$$

Since $\mathcal{T}G_N + C \geq C_N$ (from the property of the LCM operator $\mathcal{T}$) and $\mathcal{T}G_N + C$ is concave under H_0, we have $\mathcal{T}G_N + C \geq \mathcal{T}C_N$. Therefore,

$$\sqrt{N}(\mathcal{T}C_N - C_N) \leq \sqrt{N}\left(\mathcal{T}G_N - G_N\right). \tag{4.3.8}$$

Under the LFC, $C = 0$, and hence $G_N = C_N$, so the inequality (4.3.8) holds with equality. The continuous mapping theorem, bootstrap consistency, and Equations 4.3.7–4.3.8 now establish part (a) of Theorem 4.3.2.

DE also discuss extensions of the above results to tests of conditional moment inequalities

$$H_0 : E\left[m(Z, \theta_0)|X = x\right] \leq 0 \text{ for all } x \text{ and some } \theta_0.$$

The hypothesis can be tested using the test statistic DE_N with

$$C_N(y, u) = \frac{1}{N} \sum_{i=1}^{N} m(Z_i, \hat{\theta})(u - \bar{F}_X(X_i))1(\bar{F}_X(X_i) \leq u),$$

where $\hat{\theta}$ is an $N^{-1/2}$-consistent estimator of θ_0 satisfying a linear expansion. The bootstrap critical values can be defined similarly.

The DE test based on the LCM approach is computationally more demanding than the LW test based on the Poissonization approach, because it requires a resampling procedure. However, it is attractive in that it does not require a choice of smoothing parameters.

4.3.3 The Strong Approximation Approach

Gonzalo and Olmo (2014, GO) suggest a test of (possibly higher-order) conditional stochastic dominance in a *dynamic* setting. The test result can be used to evaluate optimality of an investor's decision as the information set varies over time. The test allows for general forms of unknown serial and mutual dependence between random variables. A multiplier-type bootstrap procedure is suggested to estimate critical values under the LFC of the null hypothesis.

Let $(Y_{1,i}, Y_{2,i}, Q_i)_{i \geq 1} \in \mathbb{R}^{k+2}$ denote a strictly stationary and β-mixing multivariate time series process.[5] Let

$$X_i = \{(Y_{1,l-1}, Y_{2,l-1}, Q_l) : i - m + 1 \leq l \leq i\}$$

be the information set at time i, defined on a compact set $\mathcal{X} \subset \mathbb{R}^q$ with $q = (k+2)m$.

The null hypothesis is that $Y_{1,i}$ stochastically dominates $Y_{2,i}$ at order s conditional on X_i for all $i \geq 1$. Under the stationarity assumption, the hypotheses of interest can be stated as follows:

$$H_0 : g^{(s)}(z) \leq 0 \text{ for all } z := (x, y) \in \mathcal{X} \times \mathcal{Y} := \mathcal{Z}, \qquad (4.3.9)$$

$$H_1 : g^{(s)}(z) > 0 \text{ for some } z \in \mathcal{Z},$$

where

$$g^{(s)}(z) = E\left[D_i^{(s)}(y) | X_i = x\right], \qquad (4.3.10)$$

$$D_i^{(s)}(y) = G_s(Y_{1,i}, y) - G_s(Y_{2,i}, y), \qquad (4.3.11)$$

$$G_s(Y, y) = (y - Y)^{s-1} 1 (Y \leq y). \qquad (4.3.12)$$

The conditional expectation $g^{(s)}(z)$ can be estimated by the Nadaraya–Watson kernel estimator:

$$\hat{g}^{(s)}(z) = \frac{\sum_{i=1}^N K_h(x - X_i) D_i^{(s)}(y)}{\sum_{i=1}^N K_h(x - X_i)},$$

where $K_h(\cdot) = K(\cdot/h)/h^q$. The test statistic of GO is given by

$$GO_N = \sup_{z \in \mathcal{Z}} \left(Nh^q\right)^{1/2} \left\{\hat{g}^{(s)}(z)\right\}.$$

The asymptotic behavior of GO_N depends on the stochastic process

$$v_N(z) = \left(Nh^q\right)^{1/2} \left[\hat{g}^{(s)}(z) - g^{(s)}(z)\right].$$

GO suggest approximating $v_N(\cdot)$ by a Gaussian process by extending the strong approximation result for i.i.d. data to a time series context.[6] In particular, they combine the results of Neumann (1998) and Chernozhukov, Lee, and Rosen (2013) to get the desired strong approximation. Their method requires $D_i^{(s)}(y)$ to satisfy the following model:

$$D_i^{(s)}(y) = g^{(s)}(X_i, y) + u_i(y), \qquad (4.3.13)$$

---

[5] See Definitions A.2.7 and A.2.12.

[6] In an i.i.d. setting, a strong approximation (or a Skorohod-type embedding) is originally used by Bickel and Rosenblatt (1973) to obtain limit theorems for L_∞ and L_2-distances between a nonparametric kernel density estimate and the true function.

where the errors $u_i(y)$, $i \geq 1$ are i.i.d. for each $y \in \mathcal{Y}$.[7]

Under (4.3.13) and some additional assumptions, the following result can be established:

Theorem 4.3.3 *Under Assumptions 1–7 of GO,*

$$\sup_{z \in \mathcal{Z}} |v_N(z) - \tilde{v}_N(z)| = o_p(\delta_N),$$

where $\{\tilde{v}_N(\cdot) : N \geq 1\}$ is a sequence of mean zero Gaussian processes with continuous sample paths over $z \in \mathcal{Z}$ and δ_N is such that $N^{-1/(2q+2)}$ $(h^{-1} \log N)^{1/2} + (Nh^q)^{-1/2} \log^{3/2} N = o(\delta_N)$.

Theorem 4.3.3 shows that critical values of GO_N can be approximated by the quantiles of $\sup_{z \in \mathcal{Z}} \{\tilde{v}_N(z)\}$ for sufficiently large N. Their main results are as follows:

Theorem 4.3.4 *Let $c_{N,\alpha}$ denote the $(1-\alpha)$ quantile of $\sup_{z \in \mathcal{Z}} \{\tilde{v}_N(z)\}$. Under the assumptions of Theorem 4.3.3, (a) if H_0 is true,*

$$\limsup_{N \to \infty} P\left(GO_N > c_{N,\alpha}\right) \leq \alpha$$

with equality under the LFC $\left(i.e., g^{(s)}(z) = 0 \text{ for all } z\right)$; (b) if H_1 is true,

$$\lim_{N \to \infty} P\left(GO_N > c_{N,\alpha}\right) = 1.$$

In practice, $c_{N,\alpha}$ can be estimated using a multiplier method

$$GO_N^* = \sup_{z \in \mathcal{Z}} (Nh^q)^{1/2} \left\{\hat{g}^{(s)*}(z)\right\},$$

where

$$\hat{g}^{(s)*}(z) = \frac{\sum_{i=1}^N K_h(x - X_i) D_i^{(s)}(y) V_i}{\sum_{i=1}^N K_h(x - X_i)}$$

and $\{V_i\}_{i=1}^N$ are i.i.d. random variables with mean zero and variance one, independently generated from the original sample $\{(Y_{1,i}, Y_{2,i}, Q_i)\}_{i=1}^N$.

Theorem 4.3.5 *Under the assumptions of Theorem 4.3.3,*

$$P^*\left[\sup_{z \in \mathcal{Z}} \left|(Nh^q)^{1/2} \hat{g}^{(s)*}(z) - \tilde{v}_N^*(z)\right| > o(\zeta_N)\right] = o(1),$$

---

[7] The i.i.d. property is assumed to apply the strong approximation result of Neumann (1998), but can be restrictive in dynamic settings.

where $\tilde{v}_N^*$ denotes an independent copy of the Gaussian process $\tilde{v}_N$, $\zeta_N = o(1)$, and P^* denotes the simulated probability conditional on the original sample.

Theorem 4.3.5 implies that the asymptotic α-level critical value can be approximated by the $(1 - \alpha)$ quantile of the bootstrap distribution of GO_N^*.

GO apply their test to US sectoral portfolios conditional on the dynamics of market portfolio. The test result can be used to evaluate optimality of an investor's decision as the information set varies over time. The data set consists of monthly excess returns on the ten equally weighted industry portfolios and market portfolios (value-weighted returns on all NYSE, AMEX, and NAS-DAQ stocks minus one-month Treasury bill rate) during the period of January 1960–December 2009. They find that the telecommunications sector (second- and third-order) stochastically dominates the high-tech and shop sectors, while the unconditional SD tests of Barrett and Donald (2003) suggest a completely different ordering of the investment strategies.

4.3.4 The Unconditional Moment Representation Approach

Andrews and Shi (2017, AS) consider inference on models defined by many moment inequalities and/or equalities. The result is an extension of Andrews and Shi (2013) who consider finite conditional moment restrictions to cover models with many (countable and uncountable) conditional moment restrictions.

The idea is to transform each conditional moment restriction into infinitely many unconditional moment functions using "instrument" functions. The method requires the "manageability" assumption on the class of conditional moment functions. With this assumption, AS show that the class of transformed unconditional moment inequalities/equalities are also manageable, so that the previous results of Andrews and Shi (2013) can be applied. The inference method is very general and can be applied to many different contexts.

One of the main examples discussed intensively by AS is *conditional stochastic dominance*.[8] The method also can be easily extended to time series contexts.[9] Let $W = (Y_1, Y_2, X^\mathsf{T})^\mathsf{T} \in \mathbb{R} \times \mathbb{R} \times \mathbb{R}^k$. For simplicity, assume that $k = 1$. The null hypothesis is that Y_1 stochastically dominates Y_2 at order s conditional on X. The hypothesis can be written as conditional moment inequalities:

---

[8] Other examples include inference on random-coefficient binary choice models with instrumental variables, convex moment prediction models, ordered choice models with endogeneity and instruments, and discrete games identified by revealed preference.

[9] However, the unconditional moment representation method is not easily applicable to test a continuum of inequalities that are not moment inequalities, e.g., Lorenz dominance, likelihood ratio ordering, or quantile treatment effects with covariates; see Section 6.2 for a test of more general functional inequalities.

$$H_0 : E\left[G_s(Y_1, y) - G_s(Y_2, y)|X\right] \leq 0 \text{ a.s. } \forall y \in \mathcal{Y},$$

where $G_s(Y, y)$ is as defined in (4.3.12) and $\mathcal{Y}$ denotes a compact set containing the supports of Y_1 and Y_2.

The *conditional* moment inequalities can be transformed into equivalent *unconditional* moment inequalities using instrumental functions:

$$H_0 : E\left[\{G_s(Y_1, y) - G_s(Y_2, y)\} g(X)\right] \leq 0 \; \forall y \in \mathcal{Y} \text{ and } \forall g \in \mathcal{G},$$
(4.3.14)

where g is an instrument that depends on X, and $\mathcal{G}$ is a collection of instruments.

Without loss of generality, we can transform each element of X to lie in $[0, 1]$. Examples of $\mathcal{G}$ include the class of indicator functions of cubes that partition $[0, 1]$:

$$\mathcal{G} = \left\{g_{a,r} : g_{a,r}(x) := 1\left(x \in C_{a,r}\right) \text{ for } C_{a,r} \in \mathcal{C}\right\}, \text{ where}$$
$$\mathcal{C} = \left\{C_{a,r} := \left[(a-1)/(2r), a/(2r)\right] : a \in \{1, 2, \ldots, 2r\} \text{ and}\right.$$
$$\left. r = r_0, r_0 + 1, \ldots\right\}$$

for some positive integer r_0.

Define

$$\bar{m}_N(y, g) = \frac{1}{N}\sum_{i=1}^{N} m(W_i, y, g), \text{ where}$$
$$m(W_i, y, g) = \left\{G_s(Y_{1,i}, y) - G_s(Y_{2,i}, y)\right\} g(X_i).$$

and

$$\bar{\sigma}_N^2(y, g) = \hat{\sigma}_N^2(y, g) + \varepsilon \cdot s_N^2, \text{ where } \varepsilon = 1/20,$$
$$\hat{\sigma}_N^2(y, g) = \frac{1}{N}\sum_{i=1}^{N} \{m(W_i, y, g) - \bar{m}_N(y, g)\}^2,$$
$$s_N^2 = \frac{1}{N}\sum_{i=1}^{N} \left\{\left(Y_{1,i} - \bar{Y}_1\right)^2 + \left(Y_{2,i} - \bar{Y}_2\right)^2\right\},$$
$$\bar{Y}_j = \frac{1}{N}\sum_{i=1}^{N} Y_{j,i} \text{ for } j = 1, 2.$$

AS suggest two types of test statistics:

1. A Cramér–von Mises (CvM)-type statistic

$$AS_N^{CM}$$
$$= \sup_{y \in \mathcal{Y}} \sum_{r=1}^{r_{1,N}} \sum_{a=1}^{2r} w(r)(2r)^{-1}\left[\sqrt{N}\bar{m}_N(y, g_{a,r})/\bar{\sigma}_N(y, g_{a,r})\right]_+^2,$$

where $w(r) = (r^2 + 100)^{-1}$ is a weight function and $r_{1,N} \to \infty$ as $N \to \infty$;

2. A Kolmogorov–Smirnov (KS)-type statistic

$$AS_N^{KS} = \sup_{y \in \mathcal{Y}} \sup_{g_{a,r} \in \mathcal{G}_{r_{1,N}}} \left[\sqrt{N} \bar{m}_N(y, g_{a,r}) / \bar{\sigma}_N(y, g_{a,r}) \right]_+^2,$$

where $\mathcal{G}_{r_{1,N}} = \{g_{a,r} \in \mathcal{G} : r \le r_{1,N}\}$.

In practice, the supremum over $\mathcal{Y}$ can be computed by discretization. Specifically, AS suggest approximating $\mathcal{Y}$ by $1/(M+1), \ldots, M/(M+1)$ percentile points of the pooled observations of $\{Y_{1,i}\}_{i=1}^N$ and $\{Y_{2,i}\}_{i=1}^N$ for some $M < \infty$.

To compute critical values, AS suggest the following steps:

1. Compute

$$\bar{\varphi}_N(y, g) = B_N 1 \left(\xi_N(y, g) < \kappa_N \right), \text{ where}$$

$$\xi_N(y, g) = \sqrt{N} \bar{m}_N(y, g) / \bar{\sigma}_N(y, g),$$

$$\kappa_N = -(0.3 \ln N)^{1/2} \text{ and}$$

$$B_N = -(0.4 \ln N / \ln (\ln N))^{1/2}.$$

2. Generate a bootstrap sample $\{W_i^*\}_{i=1}^N$ by drawing randomly with replacement from $\{W_i\}_{i=1}^N$ and compute $\bar{m}_N^*(y, g_{a,r})$ and $\bar{\sigma}_N^*(y, g_{a,r})$ using the bootstrap sample.

3. Compute the bootstrap test statistic with $\sqrt{N} \bar{m}_N(y, g_{a,r}) / \bar{\sigma}_N(y, g_{a,r})$ replaced by

$$\sqrt{N} \left\{ \bar{m}_N^*(y, g_{a,r}) - \bar{m}_N(y, g_{a,r}) \right\} / \bar{\sigma}_N^*(y, g_{a,r}) + \bar{\varphi}_N(y, g_{a,r}).$$

4. Repeat steps 2–3 B times and take the bootstrap GMS (generalized moment selection) critical values $c_{N,\alpha}^*$ to be the $(1 - \alpha + \eta)$ sample quantile of the bootstrap distribution plus η, where $\eta = 10^{-6}$.

Intuitively, in the above procedure, the recentering function $\bar{\varphi}_N(y, g)$ plays the role of selecting (approximately) the "boundary points" (y, g) at which the moment inequalities in Equation 4.3.14 are binding (i.e., hold with equality). By eliminating the "interior points" at which the inequalities are strict in computing the bootstrap test statistic in step 3, one may have smaller critical values and hence a test with higher power.[10,11]

AS show that, under suitable conditions, the test has a correct uniform asymptotic size under the null hypothesis and is consistent against all fixed alternatives. Also, the test is asymptotically more powerful than the test based

[10] The selective recentering (SR) approach in Section 3.1.2 essentially follows this idea.
[11] Introduction of the tuning parameter η is to ensure the uniform validity of test under the null hypothesis.

on the LFC of the null hypothesis, which takes $\bar{\varphi}_N(y, g) = 0$ because $\bar{\varphi}_N(y, g) \leq 0$ for all y, g and $[\cdot]_+$ is nondecreasing in its argument. For an application of this approach, see Section 4.5.2.

4.4 Stochastic Monotonicity

Let Y and X denote two random variables whose joint distribution is absolutely continuous with respect to Lebesgue measure on $\mathbb{R}^2$. Let $F_{Y|X}(\cdot|x)$ denote the distribution of Y conditional on $X = x$. The hypothesis of *stochastic monotonicity* (SM) is defined to be

$$H_0 : \text{For each } y \in \mathcal{Y}, \ F_{Y|X}(y|x) \leq F_{Y|X}(y|x'),$$

whenever $x \geq x'$ for $x, x' \in \mathcal{X}$, where $\mathcal{Y}$ and $\mathcal{X}$ are the supports of Y and X, respectively. The hypothesis is a continuum version of the stochastic dominance hypothesis for conditional distributions.

The SM hypothesis can be of interest in many applications in economics. For example, if X is some policy or other input variable, it amounts to testing whether its effect on the distribution of Y is increasing. This concept has also been used frequently in economic theories. Examples include Blundell, Gosling, Ichimura, and Meghir (2007), who used SM to get tighter bounds on unobservable wage distributions; Lucas and Stokey (1989) and Hopenhayn and Prescott (1992) who exploited SM to ensure the existence of a stationary equilibrium under weak conditions in dynamic macro models; Pakes (1986) who assumed SM in a study of optimal renewal policy of patents, etc.

Despite its important role in economics, however, few results have been made available for testing the SM hypothesis until the work of Lee, Linton, and Whang (2009, LLW). In this subsection, we briefly discuss the latter result and the subsequent work.

LLW consider a test statistic based on the supremum of a rescaled *second-order U-process* indexed by two parameters x and y. The test is a generalization of the test of Ghosal, Sen, and van der Vaart (2000) for the hypothesis of monotonicity of a mean regression function. Their test is applicable to i.i.d. data or a Markov time series. They prove that the asymptotic distribution of the test statistic is a Gumbel with certain nonstandard norming constants, and provide a higher-order analytic approximation to the limiting distribution to improve finite sample performances, which works quite well in simulations. They show that the test is consistent against all alternatives.

To explain the testing procedure of LLW, let $\{(Y_i, X_i) : i = 1, \ldots, N\}$ denote a random sample of (Y, X). X is allowed to be indexed by an unknown parameter to control for the influence of other factors. Specifically, assume that $X_i = \psi(W_i, \theta_0)$ is a known function of observable W_i for some unknown θ_0. Let $\widehat{X}_i = \psi(X_i, \hat{\theta})$, where $\hat{\theta}$ is a $\sqrt{N}$-consistent estimator of θ_0. Consider the U-process:

$$\widehat{U}_N(y, x) = \frac{2}{N(N-1)} \sum_{1 \leq i < j \leq N} [1(Y_i \leq y) - 1(Y_j \leq y)] \mathrm{sgn}(\widehat{X}_i - \widehat{X}_j)$$
$$\times K_{h_N}(\widehat{X}_i - x) K_{h_N}(\widehat{X}_j - x),$$

where $K_h(\cdot) = K(\cdot/h)/h$ and $\mathrm{sgn}(x)$ denotes sign of x. $\widehat{U}_N(y, x)$ is a locally weighted version of *Kendall's τ statistic*, applied to $1(Y \leq y)$.

Define $U_N(y, x)$ to be $\widehat{U}_N(y, x)$ with $\widehat{X}$ replaced by X. Since the rate of convergence of $\hat{\theta}$ to θ_0 is assumed to be sufficiently fast, it can be seen that the asymptotic distribution of $U_N(y, x)$ is the same as that of $\widehat{U}_N(y, x)$.

Under some regularity conditions, as $N \to \infty$,

$$h_N^{-1} E U_N(y, x) \to F_x(y|x) \left(\int \int |u_1 - u_2| K(u_1) K(u_2) du_1 du_2 \right)$$
$$\times [f_X(x)]^2,$$

where $F_x(y|x)$ is a partial derivative of $F_{Y|X}(y|x)$ with respect to x. Therefore, under the null hypothesis such that $F_x(y|x) \leq 0$ for all $(y, x) \in \mathcal{Y} \times \mathcal{X}$, $\widehat{U}_N(y, x)$ is less than or equal to zero on average for large N. On the other hand, under the alternative hypothesis such that $F_x(y|x) > 0$ for some $(y, x) \in \mathcal{Y} \times \mathcal{X}$, a suitably normalized version of $\widehat{U}_N(y, x)$ can be very large.

In view of this, LLW consider a supremum test statistic

$$S_N = \sup_{(y,x) \in \mathcal{Y} \times \mathcal{X}} \frac{\widehat{U}_N(y, x)}{c_N(x)} \tag{4.4.1}$$

where

$$c_N(x) = \hat{\sigma}_N(x)/\sqrt{N},$$
$$\hat{\sigma}_N^2(x) = \frac{4}{N(N-1)(N-2)} \sum_{i \leq i \neq j \neq k \leq N} \mathrm{sgn}(\widehat{X}_i - \widehat{X}_j) \mathrm{sgn}(\widehat{X}_i - \widehat{X}_k)$$
$$\times K_{h_N}(\widehat{X}_j - x) K_{h_N}(\widehat{X}_k - x) [K_{h_N}(\widehat{X}_i - x)]^2.$$

Alternatively, one may use a scaling factor

$$c_N(x) = \tilde{\sigma}_N(x)/\sqrt{N},$$

where

$$\tilde{\sigma}_N(x) = 4 h_N^{-1} \left[\int q^2(u) K^2(u) du \right] \times \hat{f}_X^3(x).$$

$\tilde{\sigma}_N(x)$ is asymptotically equivalent to $\hat{\sigma}_N(x)$ and easier to compute. But it may be less accurate in finite samples.

Although the test S_N is easy to implement, the asymptotic theory for the test involves several lengthy steps:

1. Asymptotic approximation of $\widehat{U}_N(y, x)/c_N(x)$ by a Gaussian process.
2. Asymptotic approximation of the excursion probability of the supremum of the Gaussian process on a fixed set.
3. Asymptotic approximation of the excursion probability of the supremum of the Gaussian process on an increasing set.

None of these steps is trivial and, in particular, step 2 requires the development of a new result for the excursion probability of the supremum of the Gaussian process that has a nonstandard covariance function because the approximating Gaussian process contains both stationary and nonstationary parts.

Let $q(u) = \int \text{sgn}(u - w)K(w)dw$ and β_N be the largest solution to the equation:

$$h_N^{-1}\left(\frac{8\lambda}{\pi}\right)^{1/2}\beta_N \exp(-2\beta_N^2) = 1, \quad \text{where} \tag{4.4.2}$$

$$\lambda = -\frac{6\int q(x)K^2(x)K'(x)dx + \int q^2(x)K(x)K''(x)dx}{\int q^2(x)K^2(x)dx}.$$

One may solve (4.4.2) numerically or use the following approximation to β_N: letting $c^* = (8\lambda/\pi)^{1/2}$,

$$\beta_N \simeq \left(\frac{1}{2}\log\left[\frac{c^*}{h_N}\right]\right)^{1/2} + \frac{\log\left[\frac{1}{2}\log\left[\frac{c^*}{h_N}\right]\right]}{8\left(\frac{1}{2}\log\left[\frac{c^*}{h_N}\right]\right)^{1/2}}. \tag{4.4.3}$$

LLW (theorem 3.1) establish the asymptotic distribution of S_N under the least favorable case (i.e., $F_{Y|X}(y|x) = F_Y(y)$ for any (y, x) or equivalently Y is independent of X).

Theorem 4.4.1 *Let Assumption 3.1 of LLW hold. Let h_N satisfy $h_N \log N \to 0$, $Nh_N^3/(\log N) \to \infty$, and $Nh_N^2/(\log N)^4 \to \infty$. Then, for any $x \in \mathbb{R}$,*

$$P\left(4\beta_N(S_N - \beta_N) < x\right)$$

$$= \exp\left\{-\exp\left(-x - \frac{x^2}{8\beta_N^2}\right)\left[1 + \frac{x}{4\beta_N^2}\right]\right\} + o(1). \tag{4.4.4}$$

In particular,

$$\lim_{N\to\infty} P\left(4\beta_N(S_N - \beta_N) < x\right) = \exp\left(-e^{-x}\right). \tag{4.4.5}$$

The approximation in (4.4.4) gives a higher-order refinement to the asymptotic distribution of S_N and performs significantly better in finite samples than the first-order Gumbel approximation (4.4.5). Alternatively, one may use bootstrap critical values which may also give asymptotic refinements but it is usually computationally more demanding than the analytic critical values based on (4.4.4).

LLW apply the results to empirically investigate the issue of intergenerational income mobility. In particular they test the stochastic monotonicity between sons' incomes (Y) and parental incomes (X) using data from the Panel Study of Income Dynamics (PSID), as in Solon (1992) and Minicozzi (2003). The problem is of interest because if one fails to reject the hypothesis, then that would imply that the incomes of sons with high parental incomes are higher not only on average but also in the stochastic dominance sense than those with low parental incomes. They find no evidence to reject the null hypothesis of stochastic monotonicity at any conventional significance level, which strengthens the existing findings based on mean regressions. See also Dardanoni, Fiorini, and Forcina (2012) for a related result.

We now discuss the pros and cons of the LLW test. The main advantage lies in its computational simplicity because the critical values can be computed analytically and yet perform pretty well in finite samples. However, the procedure requires a choice of smoothing parameter h_N for which not much guidance is available yet. Also, the critical values are based on the least favorable case of the null hypothesis and hence the test can be conservative against some alternatives.

Subsequently, Delgado and Escanciano (2012) developed a test of stochastic monotonicity that does not require smoothing parameters. Their main idea is that, under the null hypothesis of stochastic monotonicity, the copula function

$$C(u, v) := F_{Y,X}\left(F_Y^{-1}(u), F_X^{-1}(v)\right)$$

$$= \int_0^v F_{Y|X}\left(F_Y^{-1}(u) \mid F_X^{-1}(w)\right) dw$$

for $(u, v) \in [0, 1]^2$ is concave in v and hence should be equal to its least concave majorant $\mathcal{T}C$ (the smallest concave function lying above C) for each $u \in [0, 1]$.[12] The test statistic of Delgado and Escanciano (2012) is based on the sup-norm of the difference between the empirical copula function and its least concave majorant with respect to the explanatory variable. Under the least favorable case of the null hypothesis (independence of Y and X), the limit distribution of the test statistic is a functional of a Brownian sheet which can be tabulated.

Extensions of the above results are also available. For example, Seo (2016) extends the results of Delgado and Escanciano (2012) and suggests a testing procedure with improved power properties by incorporating the contact set

---

[12] See Section 4.3.2 for the least concave majorant approach in a different context.

approach of Linton, Song, and Whang (2010). To show its asymptotic validity, she draws on the Hadamard directional differentiability of the LCM operator (Beare and Moon, 2015) and the functional delta method with directionally differentiable operators (Fang and Santos, 2016); see Sections 3.1.1 and 5.5.1 for the concepts and related discussions.

On the other hand, Shen (2017) considers a test of stochastic monotonicity with respect to a subset of conditioning variables. Let $F_{Y|X}(y|x)$ denote the conditional CDF of the outcome variable $Y \in \mathbb{R}$ conditional on $X := (X_1, X_2) = (x_1, x_2) := x$, where $X_1 \in \mathbb{R}$ and $X_2 \in \mathbb{R}^d$ are continuous random variables. She considers the *partial* stochastic monotonicity of the conditional distribution of Y with respect to X_1 given X_2 at a fixed value of $X = x$, i.e.,

$$H_0 : \text{For each } y \in \mathcal{Y}, \ \frac{\partial}{\partial x_1} F_{Y|X}(y|x) \le 0.$$

She considers a supremum-type test statistic, which is based on the supremum (over y) of the nonparametric kernel estimator of the partial derivative $\frac{\partial}{\partial x_1} F_{Y|X}(y|x)$. Given that the conditioning variable x is fixed, the estimated process $\frac{\partial}{\partial x_1} \hat{F}_{Y|X}(\cdot|x)$ has the Donsker property and a standard argument can be used to show that a suitably normalized version of the test statistic converges weakly to a functional of a Gaussian process, whose paths can be simulated with a simulation method.

4.5 Empirical Examples

4.5.1 Testing for Conditional Treatment Effects

Chang, Lee, and Whang (2015, CLW2) investigate the effects of single-sex schooling on the distribution of academic achievements. Their result is an application of the conditional stochastic dominance test of Lee and Whang (2009) discussed in Section 4.3.1.

The merits of single-sex schools have been fiercely debated in Korea, where single-sex schools are much more prevalent than in other countries. The case of Korea is perfectly suited for analyzing the influence of single-sex and co-educational schools because students are quite randomly assigned to high schools. This feature is suitable for studying the effects of single-sex schooling in contrast to other countries, where most single-sex schools are private or parochial, thereby resulting in selection issues and many confounding factors.

Using Korean data on secondary education, CLW2 attempt to analyze how students' academic achievements, represented by the Korean college scholastic ability test (CSAT), differ between coeducational and single-sex schools. To account for individual heterogeneity in the data, CLW2 use monthly household income as a covariate.

CLW2 use the Korean Education and Employment Panel (KEEP) data constructed by the Korea Research Institute for Vocational Education and Training

(KRIVET). In particular, they use the data of the middle school senior cohort who lived in the regions affected by the *Equalization Policy* and entered high school in 2005. These students received their CSAT scores in 2008. In 2008, the CSAT score was reported not in raw value but only in rank scale due to a temporary education policy. Therefore, they use a weighted average of test scores as the CSAT score variable giving the same weight to three primary subjects (Korean, Mathematics, and English) and average all selective tests a student took.

Figure 4.1 shows nonparametric kernel estimates of the conditional mean of Korean SAT scores as a function of monthly household income. Each conditional mean function is estimated separately across gender and school type, and each observation is superimposed as a plus symbol. The dotted line is for single-sex schools and the solid line is for coeducational schools. The kernel function used in estimation is

$$K(u) = \frac{3}{2}(1 - (2u)^2)1\left\{|u| \le \frac{1}{2}\right\}.$$

The bandwidth is chosen by the least square cross-validation.

The plot of the estimated conditional mean functions suggests that there is a negative conditional *average* treatment effect for male students, when assignment to coeducational schools is regarded as treatment, except for families with high incomes. However, the estimated functions cross each other and the gap between them is not substantial among females.

Let Y denote the weighted average score of a student and let X be his (or her) monthly household income. The treatment variable D can be either single-sex schooling or coeducational schooling. When we consider assignment to a single-sex school as treatment, for example, the null hypothesis of first-order conditional stochastic dominance can be stated as

$$H_0 : P[Y_{\text{coed}} \le y \mid X = x] \le P[Y_{\text{single-sex}} \le y \mid X = x]$$
$$\text{for all } (x, y) \in \mathcal{X} \times \mathcal{Y}.$$

The set $\mathcal{X}$ was constrained to be the interval between the 0.1 and 0.9 quantiles of each covariate. Likewise, $\mathcal{Y}$ was set to be the interval between the 0.1 and 0.9 quantiles of Y. For all tests, an inverse-standard-error weight function is used.

The testing results show that there is significant evidence against the null hypothesis that the test score for the boys' school group is stochastically dominated by that of the coeducational school group across all income levels. The null is rejected at the 5% nominal level among males whereas the null is not rejected among females.[13]

---

[13] The p-values for the males are in the range of [0.014, 0.020] when the bandwidth constant takes $C_h \in \{4.0, 4.5, .., 6.0\}$, while the p-values for the females are in [0.374, 0.475].

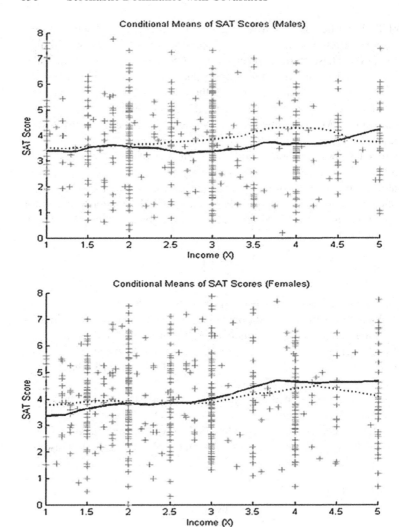

Figure 4.1 Conditional mean of CSAT scores (control: Income)
Note: Reprinted from Figure 1 of Chang, M., Lee, S., and Whang, Y.-J. (2015), "Nonparametric tests of conditional treatment effects with an application to single-sex schooling on academic achievements," *The Econometrics Journal* 18(3), 307–346, with permission of John Wiley and Sons

4.5.2 Testing for a Strong Leverage Hypothesis

The so-called *leverage hypothesis* (Black, 1976, and Christie, 1982) essentially indicates that negative shocks to stock prices affect their volatility more than positive shocks with the equal magnitude do. Whether this is attributable to changing financial leverage is still subject to dispute, but the terminology is in widespread use. Most of the existing tests of the leverage hypothesis typically involve fitting of a general parametric or semiparametric model to conditional volatility.

Linton, Whang, and Yen (2016, LWY) propose a way of testing the leverage hypothesis nonparametrically, without requiring a specific parametric or semiparametric model. The null hypothesis of LWY is that "the conditional distribution of volatility given negative returns and past volatility stochastically dominates in the first-order sense the distribution of volatility given positive returns and past volatility." This hypothesis is stronger in some sense than those considered previously since it refers to the distributions rather than just the means of the outcome. If the null hypothesis is satisfied then any investor who values volatility negatively would prefer the distribution of volatility that arises after positive shocks to returns to the distribution that arises after negative shocks. Another advantage of formulating the hypothesis in terms of distributions is that the tests are less sensitive to the existence of moments.

The main features of LWY test are as follows: they (i) extend the unconditional dominance test of Linton, Maasoumi, and Whang (2005) to conditional stochastic dominance in order to test the leverage hypothesis; (ii) propose an inference method based on subsampling and show that the test is consistent against a general class of alternatives; (iii) use *realized volatility* as a direct nonparametric measure of volatility, which allows for avoiding a specification of model for volatility and makes the test model-free; (iv) propose a double asymptotic framework ($n \to \infty$ and $T \to \infty$), where n and T denote the high-frequency and low-frequency time periods, and suggest a bias correction method under weaker conditions on n and T; and (v) find empirical evidence in favor of the strong leverage hypothesis. In this section, we briefly introduce the main idea of LWY.

Suppose that we observe a process $\{y_t, x_t, r_t\}_{t=1}^{T}$ for $y_t \in \mathbb{R}, x_t \in \mathbb{R}^{d_x}$, and $r_t \in \mathbb{R}$. Let

$$F^+(y|x) = P\left(y_t \leq y \mid r_{t-1} \geq 0, x_t = x\right),$$
$$F^-(y|x) = P\left(y_t \leq y \mid r_{t-1} < 0, x_t = x\right)$$

denote the conditional CDFs. Consider the hypothesis

$$H_0 : F^-(y|x) \leq F^+(y|x) \text{ a.s. for all } (y, x) \in \mathcal{X}_y \times \mathcal{X}_x,$$
$$H_1 : F^-(y|x) > F^+(y|x) \text{ for some } (y, x) \in \mathcal{X}_y \times \mathcal{X}_x,$$

where $\mathcal{X}_y \subset \mathbb{R}$ denotes the support of y_t and $\mathcal{X}_x \subset \mathbb{R}^{d_x}$ denotes the support of x_t. A leading example would be to take $y_t = \sigma_t^2$ and $x_t = \sigma_{t-1}^2$ with $d_x = 1$. One may also take $x_t = h(\sigma_{t-1}^2, \ldots, \sigma_{t-p}^2)$, where $h : \mathbb{R}^p \to \mathbb{R}^{d_x}$ for $1 \leq d_x < p$ is a known measurable function.

Let

$$\pi_0^+(x) = P(r_{t-1} \geq 0|x_t = x),$$

$$\pi_0^-(x) = P(r_{t-1} < 0 | x_t = x).$$

We can write the null hypothesis in the form of a conditional moment inequality:

$$H_0 : E\left[1(y_t \leq y)\left(\frac{1(r_{t-1} < 0)}{\pi_0^-(x_t)} - \frac{1(r_{t-1} \geq 0)}{\pi_0^+(x_t)} \right)\bigg| x_t = x \right] \leq 0$$

for all $(y, x) \in \mathcal{X}_y \times \mathcal{X}_x$. Equivalently, it can be written as:

$$H_0 : E\left[1(y_t \leq y)\left\{ \pi_0^+(x_t) - 1(r_{t-1} \geq 0)\right\} \big| x_t = x \right] \leq 0$$

for all $(y, x) \in \mathcal{X}_y \times \mathcal{X}_x$, assuming $\pi_0^+(x) = 1 - \pi_0^-(x) > 0$ for all $x \in \mathcal{X}_x$.

The hypothesis H_0 can be equivalently stated using an unconditional moment inequality:

$$H_0 : E\left[1(y_t \leq y)g(x_t)\left\{ \pi_0^+(x_t) - 1(r_{t-1} \geq 0)\right\} \right] \leq 0 \qquad (4.5.1)$$

for all $(y, g) \in \mathcal{X}_y \times \mathcal{G}$, where g is an "instrument function" that depends on the conditioning variable x_t and $\mathcal{G}$ is the collection of instruments, e.g.,

$$\mathcal{G} = \left\{ g_{a,b} : g_{a,b}(x) = 1 \, (a < x \leq b) \text{ for some } a, b \in \mathcal{X}_x \right\};$$

see Section 4.3.4 for a general discussion about the unconditional moment representation approach.

In practice, the volatility σ_t^2 is unobserved and needs to be estimated using high frequency data. Let $\hat{y}_t$ and $\hat{x}_t$ be estimators of y_t and x_t, respectively, based on the estimated volatility $\hat{\sigma}_t^2$, e.g., realized variance:

$$\hat{\sigma}_t^2 = \sum_{j=1}^{n_t} r_{t_j}^2,$$

where r_{t_j} is the jth intraday log return on day t, n_t is the total number of intraday log return observations on day t.

Let $\hat{\pi}^+$ be a nonparametric kernel estimator of π_0^+, i.e.,

$$\hat{\pi}^+(x) = \frac{\sum_{t=2}^T 1(r_{t-1} \geq 0)K_h\left(x - \hat{x}_t\right)}{\sum_{t=2}^T K_h\left(x - \hat{x}_t\right)}.$$

The hypothesis can be tested based on the following statistic:

$$\hat{\tilde{m}}_T(y, g, \pi) = \frac{1}{T}\sum_{t=2}^T 1(\hat{y}_t \leq y)g\left(\hat{x}_t\right)\left\{\pi(\hat{x}_t) - 1(r_{t-1} \geq 0)\right\}.$$

$$(4.5.2)$$

LWY consider a supremum-type test statistic

$$S_T = \sup_{(y,g)\in\mathcal{Y}\times\mathcal{G}} \sqrt{T}\hat{\tilde{m}}_T(y, g, \hat{\pi}^+).$$

They also suggest a bias correction procedure that is designed to capture the leading consequence of estimating σ_t^2 from the high-frequency returns data.

The following theorem establishes the asymptotic distribution of S_T when the null hypothesis is true:

Theorem 4.5.1 *Under the null hypothesis H_0,*

$$S_T \Rightarrow \begin{cases} \sup_{(y,g) \in C_0} \left[v(y, g) \right] & \text{if } C_0 \neq \emptyset \\ -\infty & \text{if } C_0 = \emptyset \end{cases}, \tag{4.5.3}$$

where v is a mean-zero Gaussian process and

$$C_0 = \{(y, g) \\ \in \mathcal{Y} \times \mathcal{G} : E\left[1(y_t \leq y)g(x_t)\left\{ \pi_0^+(x_t) - 1(r_{t-1} \geq 0) \right\} \right] = 0 \}.$$

This theorem shows that S_T has a nondegenerate limiting distribution on the boundary of the null hypothesis, i.e., the case where the "contact set" C_0 is nonempty. Since the distribution depends on the true data generating process, one cannot tabulate it once and for all. LWY suggest estimating critical values by a subsampling procedure.

As an empirical application, LWY focus on testing whether there is a leverage effect between daily conditional variances and daily lagged returns in S&P500 (cash) index and individual stocks. The samples used for the test span from January 4, 1993 to December 31, 2009 (4,283 trading days). They use 5-minute intraday log return RV_t^{5min} on day t and the squared intraday range RG_t^2 to evaluate the realized variance $\hat{\sigma}_t^2$.

To practically evaluate the full sample statistic S_T, they apply the following procedures.

1. Set the instrument function $g\left(\hat{x}_t \right) = 1\left\{ \underline{\sigma} < \hat{x}_t \leq \overline{\sigma} \right\}$, where $\underline{\sigma}$ and $\overline{\sigma}$ are lower and upper bounds for $\hat{x}_t$ and the lower bound is fixed to be $\underline{\sigma} = \min_{t=2,...,T} \ln\left(0.9 \times \exp(\hat{x}_t) \right)$.

2. Find the combination of $(y, \overline{\sigma})$ that maximize the function $\hat{\tilde{m}}_T$, where:

$$y \in \left[\min_{t=2,...,T} \ln\left(0.9 \times \exp(\hat{y}_t) \right), \max_{t=2,...,T} \ln\left(1.1 \times \exp(\hat{y}_t) \right) \right],$$

$$\overline{\sigma} \in \left[\min_{t=2,...,T} \ln\left(0.9 \times \exp(\hat{x}_t) \right), \max_{t=2,...,T} \ln\left(1.1 \times \exp(\hat{x}_t) \right) \right].$$

3. Compute $\sqrt{T}$ times the maximum value of $\hat{\tilde{m}}_T$ as the evaluation of S_T.

Figure 4.2 shows a plot of $\hat{\tilde{m}}_T\left(y, g, \hat{\pi}^+ \right)$ (defined in Equation 4.5.2) against $(y, \overline{\sigma})$ to illustrate how the test statistic S_T behaves in the case of Microsoft (MSFT). It can be seen that the surface of $\hat{\tilde{m}}_T\left(y, g, \hat{\pi}^+ \right)$ is not negative

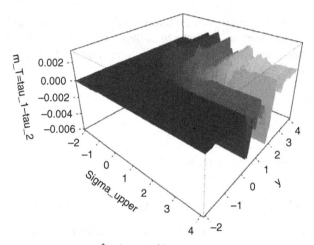

Figure 4.2 Plot of $\hat{\bar{m}}_T\left(y, g, \hat{\pi}^+\right)$ for MSFT
Note: Reprinted from Figure 2 of Linton, O., Whang, Y.-J., and Yen, Y.-M. (2016), "A nonparametric test of a strong leverage hypothesis," *Journal of Econometrics* 194(1), 153–186, with permission of Elsevier

everywhere. Searching for its maximum value, they find S_T is around 0.1782. To determine whether this value is significantly positive, subsample critical values and p-values are computed. The empirical p-values show decreasing trends as the subsample size b increases, which is consistent with the property that the approximated sample distribution becomes more concentrated as b approaches to the full sample size. Over different subsample sizes, the empirical p-value ranges from 0.8728 to 0.4974, which lends support to the claim that the leverage effect exists in MSFT.

Overall, LWY find that there is almost no evidence against the strong leverage effect in daily stock returns both at the individual stock level and the index level. Since the null hypothesis is quite strong, namely first-order distributional dominance, it is quite powerful that the data do not reject this hypothesis. The empirical evidence is shown to be robust along a number of directions; different time periods, different conditioning variables, more sophisticated volatility estimator, and alternative methods, etc.

5 Extensions of Stochastic Dominance

5.1 Multivariate Stochastic Dominance

The notion of stochastic dominance can be extended to comparing multivariate distributions. For example, in welfare analysis, there are many indicators of welfare and they may not easily be reduced to a single index. In this case, one may be interested in comparing those indicators simultaneously. Examples of the indicators include income and life expectancies; different forms of deprivations (such as low income, poor health, and bad housing); private consumption and access to publicly supplied goods; and income and leisure hours (Atkinson and Bourguignon, 1982). Multivariate stochastic dominance is also discussed extensively in portfolio theory (Levy and Paroush, 1974).

Atkinson and Bourguignon (1982) give sufficient conditions for *Multivariate Stochastic Dominance (MSD)*, focusing on the bivariate case. To discuss the conditions, consider the social welfare function

$$W = \int \int u(x)dF(x),$$

where F is a CDF defined over $x := (x_1, x_2) \in [0, a_1] \times [0, a_2] \subset \mathbb{R}^2$ and u is a utility function. The difference between social welfare functions for two populations F_A and F_B is given by

$$\Delta W = \int_0^{a_1} \int_0^{a_2} u_{12}(x_1, x_2)\Delta F(x_1, x_2)dx_2 dx_1$$
$$- \int_0^{a_1} u_1(x_1, a_2)\Delta F_1(x_1)dx_1$$
$$- \int_0^{a_2} u_2(a_1, x_2)\Delta F_2(x_2)dx_2, \qquad (5.1.1)$$

where u_{12}, u_1, and u_2 denote the (cross-) partial derivatives and $\Delta F(x_1, x_2) = F_A(x_1, x_2) - F_B(x_1, x_2)$, $\Delta F_1(x_1) = F_A(x_1, a_2) - F_B(x_1, a_2)$, and likewise for $\Delta F_2(x_2)$.

When $u \in \mathcal{U}^- := \{u : u_1, u_2 \geq 0, u_{12} \leq 0\}$, this implies that a sufficient condition for $\Delta W > 0$ is

$$\Delta F(x_1, x_2) \leq 0 \text{ for all } x_1, x_2.[1] \tag{5.1.2}$$

On the other hand, when $u \in \mathcal{U}^+ := \{u : u_1, u_2 \geq 0, u_{12} \geq 0\}$, a sufficient condition for $\Delta W > 0$ is

$$\Delta K(x_1, x_2) \leq 0 \text{ for all } x_1, x_2, \tag{5.1.3}$$

where $K(x_1, x_2) = F_1(x_1) - F_2(x_2) - F(x_1, x_2)$.

For second-order multivariate stochastic dominance, we need different sets of sufficient conditions. When $u \in \mathcal{U}^{--} := \{u : u_1, u_2 \geq 0, u_{11}, u_{22}, u_{12} \leq 0, u_{112}, u_{122} \geq 0, u_{1122} \leq 0\}$, $\Delta W > 0$ holds if

$$\Delta D(x_1, x_2) \leq 0, \quad \Delta D_1(x_1) \leq 0, \text{ and}$$
$$\Delta D_2(x_2) \leq 0 \text{ for all } x_1, x_2, \tag{5.1.4}$$

where $D(x_1, x_2) = \int_0^{x_1} \int_0^{x_2} F(s, t) dt ds$ and $D_k(x_k) = \int_0^{x_k} F_k(t) dt$ for $k = 1, 2$.[2] When $u \in \mathcal{U}^{++} := \{u : u_1, u_2 \geq 0, u_{12} \leq 0, u_{11}, u_{22} \leq 0, u_{112}, u_{122} \leq 0, u_{1122} \geq 0\}$, sufficient conditions for $\Delta W > 0$ are

$$\Delta L(x_1, x_2) \leq 0, \quad \Delta D_1(x_1) \leq 0, \text{ and}$$
$$\Delta D_2(x_2) \leq 0 \text{ for all } x_1, x_2, \tag{5.1.5}$$

where $L(x_1, x_2) = \int_0^{x_1} \int_0^{x_2} K(s, t) dt ds$. The above conditions can be readily extended to higher-order dominance and general K-dimensional distributions for $K \geq 1$.

The hypothesis of MSD (Equations 5.1.2–5.1.5) can be tested by extending the existing results for univariate stochastic dominance. For example, Crawford (2005) extends Anderson (1996)'s goodness-of-fit based method (Section 2.2.1) to K-dimensional contexts and applies it to UK data on household total expenditure and nonlabor market time. Duclos, Sahn, and Younger (2006) and Stengos and Thompson (2012) extend the Davidson and Duclos (2000) test (Section 2.2.1) to a multivariate context. Both procedures are based on multiple comparisons on a fixed set of grid points and critical values are obtained from the Studentized Maximum Modulus (SMM) type distribution or a bootstrap procedure (Stengos and Thompson, 2012). As we discussed earlier, they are not consistent against all alternatives and may be conservative. Stengos and Thompson (2012) apply their test to income and health

---

[1] The condition (5.1.2) implies, as a special case, the first-order stochastic dominance in the marginal distributions, i.e., $\Delta F_k(x) \leq 0$ for all x, $k = 1, 2$. Scarsini (1988) shows that first-order multivariate stochastic dominance between joint distributions is equivalent to univariate stochastic dominance between marginal distributions if and only if the two random vectors have the same dependence structure in the sense that they have the same unique copula.

[2] For second- and higher-order stochastic dominance, unlike first-order stochastic dominance, stochastic dominance in joint distributions does not necessarily imply dominance in marginal distributions, so they have to be tested jointly.

status data for two subgroups of the Canadian population and find that the joint distribution for foreign-born individuals dominates that of Canadian-born individuals stochastically in the first order. See also Yalonetzky (2013, 2014) for related results.

Anderson (2008) considers a supremum- (or Kolmogorov–Smirnov-) type test of MSD, which is designed to be consistent against all alternatives. To compute critical values, he suggests using the conservative bound of the distribution of the one-sample Kolmogorov–Smirnov statistic, using the results of Dvoretzky, Kiefer, and Wolfowitz (1956) and Kiefer (1961). He applies the test to a sample of 135 countries in the period 1987–99, where each country in the sample is represented by an agent characterized by per capita GNP, GNP growth rate, and average life expectancy of that country. (The data are weighted to adjust for different means.) The latter three variables are considered as instruments to evaluate the representative agent's lifetime welfare. He finds that the multidimensional comparison leads to substantially different conclusions from those drawn from traditional unidimensional comparisons.

On the other hand, McCaig and Yatchew (2007) propose an integral-type test of MSD by applying the general framework of Hall and Yatchew (2005) (Section 2.2.3). For example, the hypothesis (5.1.2) can be tested using the test statistic

$$MY_N = \int_0^{a_1} \int_0^{a_2} \max\{\bar{F}_A(x_1, x_2) - \bar{F}_B(x_1, x_2), 0\}^2 dx_1 dx_2,$$

where $\bar{F}_A$ and $\bar{F}_B$ are the empirical CDFs based on two independent random samples $\{X_{A,i}\}_{i=1}^{N_A}$ and $\{X_{B,i}\}_{i=1}^{N_A}$, respectively. McCaig and Yatchew (2007) suggest using bootstrap critical values computed from the pooled sample $\{X_{A,i}\}_{i=1}^{N_A} \cup \{X_{B,i}\}_{i=1}^{N_A}$. Although their test is consistent against all alternatives, it is conservative because the critical values are based on the least favorable case of the null hypothesis. They apply the test to data on income and leisure hours for individuals in Germany, the UK, and the USA, and find that no country first-order stochastically dominates the others in both dimensions for all years of comparison considered.

5.2 Analysis of Economic Inequality and Poverty

5.2.1 Lorenz Dominance

A *Lorenz curve* plots the percentage of total income earned by various portions of the population when the population is ordered by the size of their incomes, i.e., from the poorest to the richest. It is a fundamental tool for the analysis of economic inequality. It is well known that *Lorenz dominance* (see Equation 5.2.2) provides a partial ordering of income distributions based on minimal normative criteria and is closely related to stochastic dominance; see, e.g., Atkinson (1970).

There is a vast literature on Lorenz dominance. For example, Beach and Davidson (1983) consider Lorenz equality at fixed grid points. Shorrocks (1983) and Foster and Shorrocks (1988) discuss relationships among generalized Lorenz (GL) curves, poverty measurement, and welfare, and show that GL dominance is equivalent to the second-order stochastic dominance; see also Thistle (1989). Bishop, Chakraborti, and Thistle (1989) propose asymptotically distribution-free statistical inference for GL curves. Bishop, Formby, and Smith (1991) suggest a test of Lorenz dominance based on multiple pairwise comparisons. See also Davies, Green, and Paarsch (1998), Dardanoni and Forcina (1999), and Davidson and Duclos (2000) for tests of Lorenz dominance at fixed grid points. More recent examples include Barrett, Donald, and Bhattacharya (2014, BDB) who propose a bootstrap test of Lorenz dominance at all quantiles. We briefly discuss the results of BDB below.

Suppose that the population $k \in \{1, 2\}$ has a continuous distribution F_k with density f_k, assumed to be strictly positive on $[0, \infty)$. Let $Q_k(p) := F_k^{-1}(p)$ $= \inf\{x : F_k(x) \geq p\}$ denote the quantile function for F_k.

Definition 5.2.1 *The Lorenz Curve (LC) is defined to be*

$$L_k(p) := \frac{\int_0^{Q_k(p)} z f_k(z) dz}{\int_0^{\infty} z f_k(z) dz} = \frac{\int_0^p Q_k(t) dt}{\mu_k}, \tag{5.2.1}$$

for $p \in [0, 1]$, where μ_k denotes the mean of the distribution F_k for $k = 1, 2$.

The hypotheses of interest are given by

$$H_0 : L_2(p) \leq L_1(p) \text{ for all } p \in [0, 1], \tag{5.2.2}$$
$$H_1 : L_2(p) > L_1(p) \text{ for some } p \in [0, 1].$$

The null hypothesis corresponds to (weak) Lorenz dominance of L_1 over L_2. BDB consider two sampling schemes:

1. Independent Sampling (IS): $\mathcal{S}_k = \{X_{k,i}\}_{i=1}^{N_k}$ is a random sample from F_k for $k = 1, 2$, and $\mathcal{S}_1$ and $\mathcal{S}_2$ are independent with $N_1/(N_1+N_2) \to \lambda \in (0, 1)$ as $N_1, N_2 \to \infty$.

2. Matched Pair (MP) Sampling: $\mathcal{S}_{1,2} = \{(X_{1,i}, X_{2,i})\}_{i=1}^{N}$ is a random sample from the joint distribution F whose marginals are given by F_1 and F_2.

The Lorenz curve (5.2.1) can be estimated by

$$\hat{L}_k(p) = \frac{\int_0^p \hat{Q}_k(t) dt}{\hat{\mu}_k}, \ k = 1, 2,$$

where $\hat{\mu}_k = \bar{X}_k = N_k^{-1} \sum_{i=1}^{N_k} X_{k,i}$ denotes the sample mean, $\hat{Q}_k(p) = \inf\{x : \bar{F}_k(x) \geq p\}$ is the sample p quantile, and $\bar{F}_k(x) = N_k^{-1} \sum_{i=1}^{N_k} 1\left(X_{k,i} \leq x\right)$ is the empirical CDF.

Let

$$\hat{\phi}(p) = \hat{L}_2(p) - \hat{L}_1(p).$$

Both supremum- and integral-type test statistics are considered by BDB:

$$KS_N = r_N \sup_{p \in [0,1]} \left\{ \hat{\phi}(p) \right\},$$

$$CM_N = r_N \int_0^1 \left[\hat{\phi}(p) \right]_+ dp,$$

where $r_N = \left[N_1 N_2 / (N_1 + N_2) \right]^{1/2}$ under *IS* and $r_N = \sqrt{N}$ under *MP*.

The asymptotic properties of the test statistics depend on the following property of the empirical Lorenz process:

Theorem 5.2.1 *Under regularity conditions, for $k = 1, 2$,*

$$\sqrt{N_k} \left(\hat{L}_k(\cdot) - L_k(\cdot) \right) \Rightarrow \mathcal{L}_k(\cdot),$$

where

$$\mathcal{L}_k(p) = \frac{\mathcal{G}_k(p)}{\mu_k} - \frac{L_k(p)}{\mu_k} \mathcal{G}_k(1),$$

$$\mathcal{G}_k(p) = -\int_0^p \frac{\mathcal{B}_k(t)}{f_k(Q_k(t))} dt,$$

and $\mathcal{B}_k$ is a standard Brownian bridge.

Theorem 5.2.1 follows from the functional delta method and Hadamard differentiability of the Lorenz curve with respect to CDF (Goldie, 1977).

To compute critical values, bootstrap samples are generated differently under different sampling schemes:

1. Independent Sampling (IS): Take independent bootstrap samples $\mathcal{S}_1^* = \{X_{1,i}^*\}_{i=1}^{N_1}$ and $\mathcal{S}_2^* = \{X_{2,i}^*\}_{i=1}^{N_2}$ from $\mathcal{S}_1$ and $\mathcal{S}_2$, respectively.
2. Matched Pair (MP) Sampling: Take a bootstrap sample $\mathcal{S}_{1,2}^* = \{(X_{1,i}^*, X_{2,i}^*)\}_{i=1}^{N}$ from $\mathcal{S}_{1,2}$.

Using the bootstrap sample, compute the statistic

$$L_k^*(p) = \frac{\int_0^p \hat{Q}_k^*(t) dt}{\hat{\mu}_k^*}, \quad k = 1, 2,$$

$$\hat{\phi}^*(p) = \hat{L}_2^*(p) - \hat{L}_1^*(p),$$

where $\hat{\mu}_k^* = \bar{X}_k^* = N_k^{-1} \sum_{i=1}^{N_k} X_{k,i}^*$ denotes the mean of the bootstrap sample, $\hat{Q}_k^*(p) = \inf\{x : \bar{F}_k^*(x) \geq p\}$, and $\bar{F}_k^*(x) = N_k^{-1} \sum_{i=1}^{N_k} 1 \left(X_{k,i}^* \leq x \right)$. Next, compute the recentered bootstrap test statistics

$$K S_N^* = r_N \sup_{p \in [0,1]} \left\{ \hat{\phi}^*(p) - \hat{\phi}(p) \right\},$$

$$C M_N^* = r_N \int_0^1 \left[\hat{\phi}^*(p) - \hat{\phi}(p) \right]_+ dp.$$

One then rejects H_0 if the test statistic $K S_N$ ($C M_N$) is larger than the $(1 - \alpha)$ quantile of the bootstrap distribution of $K S_N^*$ ($C M_N^*$).

Compared to the other existing tests of Lorenz dominance based on fixed grid points, the BDB test is consistent against all alternatives, though it is conservative because of the recentering step, which imposes the LFC restriction of the null hypothesis.

5.2.2 Poverty Dominance

In poverty analysis, poverty gap profiles (defined in Equation 5.2.3) play a key role in poverty comparisons, analogous to the role of Lorenz curves in inequality measurements. Poverty comparisons based on poverty gap profiles are robust to normative properties of specific poverty indices and are closely related to stochastic dominance criteria.

Barrett, Donald, and Hsu (2016, BDH) propose a consistent test of *Poverty Gap Dominance* based on two estimated poverty gap profiles for two independent samples of individual income. Unlike standard stochastic dominance tests, the test allows the (possibly unknown) poverty lines to differ across distributions.

Let X denote an income with distribution function $F(x)$. Let

$$D(x, X) = [x - X]_+$$

denote the *poverty gap*, where x is a poverty line.

Definition 5.2.2 *The Poverty Gap Profile (PGP) is defined to be*

$$P(p, x) := E D(x, X) 1 (X \le Q(p)), \qquad (5.2.3)$$

where $Q(p)$ is the p quantile of the distribution F for $p \in [0, 1]$.

The PGP curve gives the average poverty gap for the poorest $100p\%$ of the population whenever p is a value below the "head-count ratio" $F(x)$ (i.e., the proportion of the population below the poverty line x).

Definition 5.2.3 *The Generalized Lorenz (GL) curve is defined to be*

$$GL(p) := E X 1 (X \le Q(p)) \qquad (5.2.4)$$

$$= \int_0^p Q(t) dt, \qquad (5.2.5)$$

where $Q(p)$ is the p quantile of the distribution F for $p \in [0, 1]$.

The PGP $P(p, x)$ is directly related to the GL curve via

$$P(p, x) = 1(Q(p) \leq x)(px - GL(p))$$
$$+ 1(Q(p) > x)(F(x)x - GL(F(x))).$$

Let F_1 and F_2 denote two income distributions with PGPs P_1 and P_2 and poverty lines x_1 and x_2, respectively. The null hypothesis of interest is (weak) PGP dominance of P_1 over P_2:

$$H_0 : P_2(p, x_2) \leq P_1(p, x_1) \text{ for all } p \in [0, 1],$$
$$H_1 : P_2(p, x_2) > P_1(p, x_1) \text{ for some } p \in [0, 1].$$

The null hypothesis implies that poverty is ranked as more severe in F_1 than in F_2 for a wide class of poverty indices.

To test the hypothesis, BDH consider an integral-type test based on the empirical analogue of (5.2.3), with poverty lines replaced by their estimates (e.g., sample mean or sample quantiles). To approximate critical values, they suggest a simulation method, combined with the recentering approach similar to Donald and Hsu (2014) and Andrews and Shi (2013).

5.2.3 Initial Dominance

The standard concept of stochastic dominance presupposes that a restriction on the difference between two CDFs holds over their entire supports or at least over a prespecified subset of the supports. However, in some contexts, it is useful to determine whether the restriction holds over some *unknown* subset of the supports.

For example, there is empirical evidence that the effects of Vietnam veteran status on earnings may be concentrated in lower tails of the earning distribution; see Section 3.4.1. Motivated by this finding, Bennett and Zitikis (2013, BZ) introduce the concept of *Initial Dominance* and propose a statistical inference procedure to test the hypothesis. Below we briefly summarize their results.

Let F_1 and F_2 denote two CDFs, both being continuous functions with supports on $[0, \infty)$.

Definition 5.2.4 F_1 *is said to initially dominate* F_2 *up to a point* x_1, *if* $F_1(x) \leq F_2(x)$ *for all* $x \in [0, x_1)$ *with strict inequality for some* $x \in (0, x_1)$. x_1 *is called the Maximal Point of Initial Dominance (MPID), if* F_1 *initially dominates* F_2 *up to* x_1, *and* $F_1(x) > F_2(x)$ *for all* $x \in (x_1, x_1 + \varepsilon)$ *for some* $\varepsilon > 0$ *sufficiently small.*

Definition 5.2.4 includes the standard first-order stochastic dominance as a special case by taking $x_1 = \infty$.

BZ consider the following hypotheses:

H_0 : F_1 does not initially dominate F_2,

H_1 : F_1 initially dominates F_2.

The alternative hypothesis of initial dominance has an interesting implication for poverty rankings. For example, consider the popular FGT poverty measure by Foster, Greer, and Thorbecke (1984, FGT):

$$\pi_{\alpha,x}(F) := E\left[g^\alpha(X, x)1(X \le x)\right], \qquad (5.2.6)$$

where X with CDF F denotes income, x is a poverty line, $g(y, x) = (x - y)/x$ is the normalized income shortfall, and $\alpha \ge 0$ is the poverty aversion indicator. If F_1 initially dominates F_2, then it implies that for every level of poverty aversion, the FGT poverty measure satisfies $\pi_{\alpha,x}(F_1) \le \pi_{\alpha,x}(F_2)$ for all poverty lines in $(0, x_1)$. Therefore, the initial dominance implies that every FGT poverty measure must record poverty greater in F_2 than in F_1 for any poverty line in the interval $(0, x_1)$.

Consider the population functional

$$d_{ID} := \int_0^{x_1} [F_2(x) - F_1(x)]_+ \, dx, \qquad (5.2.7)$$

where

$$x_1 = \lim_{t \downarrow 0} \inf\{y \ge 0 : H(y) \ge t\}, \qquad (5.2.8)$$

$$H(y) = \int_0^y [F_1(x) - F_2(x)]_+ \, dx. \qquad (5.2.9)$$

It can be seen that $d_{ID} = 0$ under the null hypothesis H_0, while $d_{ID} > 0$ under the alternative hypothesis H_1. This implies that a sample analog of d_{ID} can be used as a basis of a test statistic.

Suppose that $\{X_{1,i}\}_{i=1}^{N_1}$ and $\{X_{2,i}\}_{i=1}^{N_2}$ are two independent random samples from the distributions F_1 and F_2, respectively and $N = N_1 + N_2$. Assume that $N_1/N \to \lambda \in (0, 1)$ as $N_1, N_2 \to \infty$.

The test statistic considered by BZ is given by

$$BZ_N = r_N \int_0^{\hat{x}_1} \left[\bar{F}_2(x) - \bar{F}_1(x)\right]_+ \, dx, \qquad (5.2.10)$$

where $r_N = (N_1 N_2/N)^{1/2}$, $\bar{F}_k$ for $k = 1, 2$ denotes the empirical CDF, and

$$\hat{x}_1 = \inf\{y \ge 0 : H_N(y) \ge \delta_N\}, \qquad (5.2.11)$$

$$H_N(y) = \int_0^y \left[\bar{F}_1(x) - \bar{F}_2(x)\right]_+ \, dx. \qquad (5.2.12)$$

Here, $\delta_N > 0$ is a tuning parameter that satisfies $\delta_N \to 0$ and $r_N \delta_N \to \infty$.

BZ show that, under the least favorable case (LFC) of the null hypothesis $(F_1 = F_2)$, the test statistic converges weakly to a Gaussian process and it diverges to ∞ under the alternative hypothesis H_1. They suggest a bootstrap procedure based on the pooled sample to impose the LFC restriction and show that the test has an asymptotically correct size and is consistent against all alternatives (theorem 2.7 of BZ).

BZ apply their test to the veteran data (Section 3.4.1) and find that Vietnam veterans experienced poverty at least as severe as nonveterans for any poverty line up to $12,600, complementing the empirical results of Abadie (2002).

The test proposed by BZ can also be used in many applications other than the poverty analysis, where one suspects that stochastic dominance relation might hold over an unknown subset of supports of distributions and would like to figure out the range over which the dominance restriction is satisfied. It appears that the test can be adapted to higher-order dominance and dependent samples, as well as time series observations. Also, the power performance might be improved using, e.g., the tools discussed in Section 3.1. Confidence intervals for MPID (x_1) would be useful, but, as mentioned by BZ, it may be a technically challenging issue.

5.3 Analysis of Portfolio Choice Problems

5.3.1 Marginal Conditional Stochastic Dominance

Shalit and Yitzhaki (1994, SY) introduce the concept of *Marginal Conditional Stochastic Dominance* (MCSD), which states the conditions under which all risk-averse individuals, when presented with a given portfolio, prefer to increase the share of one risky asset over that of another. MCSD is a more confining concept than the second-order stochastic dominance because it considers only *marginal* changes in holding risky assets in a given portfolio.

Let $X = (X_1, \ldots, X_K)^{\mathsf{T}} \in \mathbb{R}^K$ be a vector of returns on a set of K risky assets. Consider a portfolio λ with return $X^{\mathsf{T}}\lambda$, where $\lambda = (\lambda_1, \ldots, \lambda_K)^{\mathsf{T}}$, $\Lambda = \{\lambda \in \mathbb{R}^K : e^{\mathsf{T}}\lambda = 1\}$, and $e = (1, \ldots, 1)^{\mathsf{T}}$. As before, let $\mathcal{U}_2$ denote the class of all increasing and concave utility functions. Let W_0 be an initial wealth and denote the final wealth W to be

$$W = W_0 \left(1 + X^{\mathsf{T}}\lambda\right).$$

We are interested in the following question: Given the portfolio λ, is there an asset $k \in \{1, \ldots, K\}$ such that increasing its amount, by giving up some asset $j \in \{1, \ldots, K\}$ for $j \neq k$, is preferred by all risk-averse individuals?

To answer the question, let $d\lambda_k$ be the marginal change in holding asset k, satisfying

$$d\lambda_k + d\lambda_j = 0, \quad j \neq k.$$

Then, the marginal change in the expected utility satisfies

$$\frac{dEu(W)}{d\lambda_k} = E\left[u'(W) \cdot W_0 \cdot (X_k - X_j)\right]. \tag{5.3.1}$$

If the right-hand side of (5.3.1) is nonnegative for all $u \in \mathcal{U}_2$, then the asset k is said to dominate the asset j in the sense of MCSD.

The necessary and sufficient condition for the MCSD can be characterized using *Absolute Concentration Curves* (ACCs). Let F_λ denote the CDF of the portfolio return $X^\mathsf{T}\lambda$. Let

$$\mu_k(p) = E\left(X_k | X^\mathsf{T}\lambda = p\right)$$

denote the conditional expectation of return on the asset k when the portfolio return equals p. The ACC of asset k is defined to be

$$ACC_{k,\lambda}(\tau) := \int_0^{F_\lambda^{-1}(\tau)} \mu_k(p) dF_\lambda(p) \tag{5.3.2}$$

$$= E\left[X_k \cdot 1\left(X^\mathsf{T}\lambda \le F_\lambda^{-1}(\tau)\right)\right]$$

for $\tau \in [0, 1]$. Notice that when $K = 1$ and $X^\mathsf{T}\lambda = X$, then the ACC is equivalent to the generalized Lorenz curve (Shorrocks (1983), see also Equation 5.2.5):

$$GL(\tau) := \int_0^\tau F_X^{-1}(t) dt = E\left[X \cdot 1(X \le F_X^{-1}(\tau))\right].$$

The necessary and sufficient condition for MCSD is given by the following theorem (theorem 2 of SY):

Theorem 5.3.1 *Given portfolio λ, asset k dominates asset j for all $u \in \mathcal{U}_2$ on W, if and only if*

$$ACC_{k,\lambda}(\tau) \ge ACC_{j,\lambda}(\tau) \text{ for all } \tau \in [0, 1], \tag{5.3.3}$$

with at least one strict inequality.

A nonparametric test of the hypothesis (5.3.3) is suggested by Schechtman, Shelef, Yitzhaki, and Zitikis (2008, SSYZ), who consider a supremum-type test based on the empirical analogue of the ACCs. We briefly discuss their result.

Let $\{X_i := (X_{1,i}, \dots, X_{K,i})^\mathsf{T} : i = 1, \dots, N\}$ denote an observed data set. SSYZ assume that the observations are serially independent but may be cross-sectionally dependent. For $k = 1, \dots, K$, define the estimator of ACC to be

$$\overline{ACC}_{k,\lambda}(\tau) := \frac{1}{N}\sum_{i=1}^N X_{k,i} \cdot 1\left(X_i^\mathsf{T}\lambda \le \bar{F}_\lambda^{-1}(\tau)\right), \tag{5.3.4}$$

where $\bar{F}_\lambda(x) = (1/N)\sum_{i=1}^N 1\left(X_i^\mathsf{T}\lambda \le x\right)$ is the empirical CDF and $\bar{F}_\lambda^{-1}(\tau) = \inf\{x : \bar{F}_\lambda(x) \ge \tau\}$ is the empirical quantile function.

Consider the null hypothesis of interest given by (5.3.3), with the alternative hypothesis being its negation. SSYZ suggest the following test statistic:

$$S_N = \sqrt{N} \sup_{\tau \in [0,1]} \left(\overline{ACC}_{j,\lambda}(\tau) - \overline{ACC}_{k,\lambda}(\tau) \right).^3 \qquad (5.3.5)$$

The asymptotic distribution of S_N under the least favorable case $(ACC_{k,\lambda}(\tau) = ACC_{j,\lambda}(\tau)$ for all τ) has been investigated by Rao and Zhao (1995) and Davydov and Egorov (2000); see also SSYZ (corollary 1).

Theorem 5.3.2 *Suppose that the distribution F_λ is continuous and other regularity conditions hold. Then, under the LFC of the null hypothesis,*

$$S_N \Rightarrow \sup_{\tau \in [0,1]} v(\tau), \qquad (5.3.6)$$

where

$$v(\tau) = -\int_0^\tau \mathcal{W}_1(u) d\mu_{(X_j - X_k | X^\mathsf{T}\lambda)} \left(F_\lambda^{-1}(u) \right)$$

$$+ \int_0^\tau \sigma^2_{(X_j - X_k | X^\mathsf{T}\lambda)} \left(F_\lambda^{-1}(u) \right) d\mathcal{W}_2(u),$$

$$\mu_{(X_j - X_k | X^\mathsf{T}\lambda)}(p) = E\left(X_j - X_k | X^\mathsf{T}\lambda = p\right),$$

$$\sigma^2_{(X_j - X_k | X^\mathsf{T}\lambda)}(p) = Var\left(X_j - X_k | X^\mathsf{T}\lambda = p\right),$$

and $\mathcal{W}_1$ and $\mathcal{W}_2$ are independent standard Brownian motion and Wiener process, respectively.

Since the limiting distribution (5.3.6) is not pivotal, one can compute the critical values by the (recentered) bootstrap (Barrett and Donald, 2003, section 2.2.2) or the subsampling (Linton, Maasoumi, and Whang, 2005, section 2.2.2) procedure.

5.3.2 Stochastic Dominance Efficiency

The portfolio choice problem is an important area for stochastic dominance because the latter requires less restrictive assumptions on investor preferences and asset return distributions than the traditional mean-variance approach does. However, practical implementation of the SD analysis is not straightforward because one has to compare infinitely many portfolios, while the traditional SD analysis relies on pairwise comparison of finite alternatives.

Post (2003) and Kuosmanen (2004) introduce the notion of *Stochastic Dominance Efficiency* (SDE) that allows full diversification of portfolios, and provide methods of inference based on the first-order optimality conditions of

---

[3] SSYZ also consider the null hypothesis of equal ACCs against non-equal alternatives, as well as the two-sided hypothesis, but here we focus on the one-sided hypothesis since the arguments are very similar.

the investor's expected utility maximization problem (see also Post and Versijp, 2007, and Post and Potí, 2017). They propose inference methods based on i.i.d. observations, suggesting novel computational procedures. On the other hand, Linton, Post, and Whang (2014, LPW) and Scaillet and Topaloglou (2010, ST) propose statistical tests of stochastic dominance efficiency of a given portfolio allowing for time-dependent observations.[4]

Let $X = (X_1, \ldots, X_K)^\mathsf{T}$ be a vector of returns on a set of K assets, and let Y be the return on the benchmark portfolio of X. The benchmark portfolio is taken as given, e.g., the market portfolio held by the representative investor or the actual portfolio held by a given individual investor.

Consider a portfolio with return $X^\mathsf{T}\lambda$, where $\lambda = (\lambda_1, \ldots, \lambda_K)^\mathsf{T}$, $\Lambda = \{\lambda \in \mathbb{R}_+^K : e^\mathsf{T}\lambda = 1\}$, and $e = (1, \ldots, 1)^\mathsf{T}$. Let Λ_0 be a subset of Λ reflecting whatever additional restrictions, if any, imposed on Λ. Let $\mathcal{U}_2$ denote the class of all increasing and concave utility functions.

Definition 5.3.1 (SSD Efficiency) *The asset Y is SSD efficient if for some $u \in \mathcal{U}_2$, $E[u(Y)] \geq E[u(X^\mathsf{T}\lambda)]$ for all $\lambda \in \Lambda_0$.*

In other words, Y is SSD efficient if there does not exist any portfolio in $\{X^\mathsf{T}\lambda : \lambda \in \Lambda_0\}$ that dominates Y. This definition can easily be extended to higher-order SD (Post, 2003, and Kuosmanen, 2004).

LPW consider testing the following null hypothesis:

$H_0 : Y$ is sth-order SD efficient.

The alternative hypothesis is the negation of H_0, i.e., there exists a portfolio with weight $\lambda_0 \in \Lambda_0$ that dominates Y.

Notice that when the set Λ_0 is a singleton, say λ_0, H_0 reduces to "the null hypothesis of no SD," i.e., $X^\mathsf{T}\lambda_0$ does not dominate Y, while H_1 becomes "the alternative hypothesis of SD." From the earlier discussions, we know that the null hypothesis of "no SD" can be tested only over a restricted subset of the supports; see Section 2.3. The problem becomes more complicated when the number of distributions compared is infinite.

Let $F_\lambda(\cdot)$ and $F_Y(\cdot)$ be the CDFs of $X^\mathsf{T}\lambda$ and Y, respectively. For a given integer $s \geq 2$, define the sth-order integrated CDF of $X^\mathsf{T}\lambda$ to be

$$F_\lambda^{(s)}(x) = \int_{-\infty}^{x} F_\lambda^{(s-1)}(y)dy,$$

where $F_\lambda^{(1)}(\cdot) = F_\lambda(\cdot)$, and likewise for $F_Y^{(s)}(x)$.

---

[4] Arvanitis and Topaloglou (2017) extend the result of Scaillet and Topaloglou (2010) to test *Prospect* (and *Markowitz*) *Stochastic Dominance Efficiency*. Post (2016b) proposes a test of *Stochastic Dominance Optimality* (Section 5.3.3), which is a stronger notion than stochastic dominance efficiency. On the other hand, Arvanitis et al. (2017) propose a test of *Stochastic Spanning*, which involves comparisons of two choice sets, with pairwise SD and SDE special cases that assume one or two of the choice sets to be a singleton.

Consider the population functional

$$d = \sup_{\lambda \in \Lambda_0} \inf_{x \in \mathcal{X}} \left[F_Y^{(s)}(x) - F_\lambda^{(s)}(x) \right].$$

This functional satisfies $d \leq 0$ under the null hypothesis, but there are some alternatives for which $d = 0$, so we cannot obtain a consistent test from this functional. For example, if $K = 1$, $Y \sim U[0, 1]$, and $X \sim U[0, 2]$, then X dominates Y, but $d = \inf_{x \in [0,2]} \left[F_Y^{(s)}(x) - F_X^{(s)}(x) \right] = 0$ because the two distributions coincide at the boundary $x = 0$.

LPW suggest considering a functional that is designed to prevent the inner infimum from ever being zero through equality on some part of $\mathcal{X}$:

$$d_*(\varepsilon, F) := \sup_{\lambda \in \Lambda_0} \inf_{x \in B_\lambda^\varepsilon} \left[F_Y^{(s)}(x) - F_\lambda^{(s)}(x) \right],$$

where B_λ^ε denotes the complement (in $\mathcal{X}$) of the ε – enlargement of the contact set $C_\lambda = \left\{ x : F_Y^{(s)}(x) = F_\lambda^{(s)}(x) \right\}$ for some $\varepsilon > 0$ when C_λ is a strict subset of $\mathcal{X}$. If $C_\lambda = \mathcal{X}$, define $B_\lambda^\varepsilon = \mathcal{X}$. We note that under the null hypothesis, $d_*(\varepsilon, F) \leq 0$ for each $\varepsilon \geq 0$, while under the alternative hypothesis, $d_*(\varepsilon, F) > 0$ for some $\varepsilon > 0$.

The test statistic of LPW is a sample analogue of $d_*(\varepsilon, F)$:

$$LPW_N = \sup_{\lambda \in \Lambda_0} \inf_{x \in \widehat{B}_\lambda^{\varepsilon_N}} \sqrt{N} \left[\bar{F}_Y^{(s)}(x) - \bar{F}_\lambda^{(s)}(x) \right], \tag{5.3.7}$$

where N is the sample size and $\widehat{B}_\lambda^{\varepsilon_N}$ is an estimator of the set B_λ^ε with ε_N being a sequence of positive constants that goes to zero at a rate not too fast (assumptions 4.2 and 4.4 of LPW).

Assuming that the observations are strictly stationary and α-mixing, LPW (theorems 4.1 and 4.2) show that LPW_N converges weakly to a functional of mean-zero Gaussian process and suggest a subsampling method to approximate critical values. They (theorems 4.3 and 4.4) also establish that the test is consistent against all alternatives satisfying certain tail conditions and has nontrivial asymptotic local power.

On the other hand, Scaillet and Topaloglou (2010, ST) suggest a consistent test of SDE by extending the pairwise SD test of Barrett and Donald (2003). As in LPW, ST assume stationary and α-mixing observations but suggest a block bootstrap method to compute critical values.[5]

---

[5] As explained in LMW (section 2.2.2), bootstrap is generally more efficient than subsampling because it uses full sample information. However, bootstrap requires imposing null restrictions and the standard nonparametric bootstrap based on the least favorable case can be less powerful than subsampling against some alternatives.

It is notable that ST consider a different notion of stochastic dominance efficiency as the null hypothesis.[6] Their null hypothesis is that Y is SD efficient in the sense that Y (weakly) dominates all the portfolios in $\{X^\top \lambda \; : \; \lambda \in \Lambda_0\}$, i.e.,

$$H_0^* : F_Y^{(s)}(x) \leq F_\lambda^{(s)}(x) \text{ for all } x \in \mathcal{X} \text{ and for all } \lambda \in \Lambda_0.$$

The alternative is the negation of H_0^*, i.e., there exists a portfolio with weight $\lambda_0 \in \Lambda_0$ that is not dominated by Y. Clearly, when the set $\Lambda_0 = \lambda_0$ is a singleton, H_0^* corresponds to "the null hypothesis of SD," i.e., Y dominates $X^\top \lambda_0$. Compared to the null hypothesis H_0 of LPW, H_0^* is a more restrictive hypothesis, excluding the cases where the distribution functions cross.[7]

ST propose the following supremum-type test statistic:

$$ST_N = \sup_{\lambda \in \Lambda_0} \sup_{x \in \mathcal{X}} \sqrt{N} q(x) \left[\bar{F}_Y^{(s)}(x) - \bar{F}_\lambda^{(s)}(x) \right],$$

where $q(x)$ is a positive weight function to allow for non-compact support $\mathcal{X}$ (Section 3.3.1). It is interesting to see that, in the special case of pairwise SD ($K = 1$), the test statistic ST_N reduces to that of Barrett and Donald (2003) with $q(x) = 1$.

ST (propositions 2.2 and 3.1) show that the test statistic ST_N converges weakly to a functional of a mean-zero Gaussian process and the test based on block bootstrap critical values is consistent against the fixed alternative.

ST also present mathematical programming formulations to compute the test statistic and apply them to evaluate efficiency of the Fama and French market portfolio with respect to the six benchmark portfolios formed on size and book-to-market equity ratio. They find that the hypothesis of efficient market portfolio is not rejected for $s = 1$ and 2. They emphasize that the efficiency of the market portfolio is of interest to investors, because, if it is not efficient, individual investors could diversify across diverse asset portfolios and outperform the market.

5.3.3 Convex Stochastic Dominance and Stochastic Dominance Optimality

In many applications, a decision-maker under uncertainty confronts a choice set that has more than one prospect. In this case, she can establish whether a given prospect is *SD admissible* (in the sense that it is not dominated by

---

[6] To avoid confusion, Arvanitis et al. (2017) later label the notion of SDE used by ST as *stochastic superefficiency*.

[7] For example, when $s = 1$ and $K = 1$, the null hypothesis "$H_0 : X$ is not dominated by Y" includes the case that F_Y crosses F_X. However, the case is not allowed under the hypothesis $H_0^* : Y$ dominates X. This implies that H_0^* is a stronger hypothesis than H_0.

any of the other alternatives) by making pairwise comparisons with all alternative prospects. However, some members of the SD admissible set may never be chosen by any individual with utility function in the hypothesized class. Instead, there may exist the *SD optimal* set, which is a subset of the SD admissible set that consists of the elements that *will* be chosen by some individual with a utility function in the hypothesized class. In other words, the SD nonoptimal alternatives will not be chosen by any individuals with a utility function in the class.

To identify the SD optimal set, Fishburn (1974) introduces the notion of *Convex Stochastic Dominance* (CSD), which is an extension of stochastic dominance to a mixture or a convex combination of distributions. He shows that the optimal set consists of the elements of the choice set that cannot be dominated by any convex combination of other elements of the choice set. This concept is useful because it can be used to eliminate alternatives that are SD admissible but not optimal from further considerations.

Bawa, Bodurtha, Rao, and Suri (1985) show how to compute SD optimal sets using linear programming algorithms. They show that, for example, for a choice set of 896 security returns, 454 and 25 distributions are in the first- and second-order CSD optimal sets, respectively, whereas 682 and 35 distributions are in the first- and second-order SD admissible sets, respectively.

Consider the set $\{X_1, \ldots, X_K\}$ of $K \geq 2$ distinct prospects, where $X_k \in \mathcal{X} := [a, b]$, $-\infty < a < b < \infty$, has distribution F_k, $k = 1, \ldots, K$. Let $\mathcal{F} = \{F_1, \ldots, F_K\}$. Suppose that we would like to evaluate a given prospect X_K. Let $\Lambda_{K-1} = \{\lambda \in \mathbb{R}_+^{K-1} : e^\mathsf{T}\lambda = 1\}$ and $e = (1, \ldots, 1)^\mathsf{T}$. Let $\mathcal{U}_2$ denote the class of all increasing and concave utility functions. (The results below can be easily adapted to stochastic dominance of orders other than 2.)

Fishburn (1974, theorem 2) (see also Bawa, Bodurtha, Rao, and Suri, 1985, theorem 5) establishes the following result:

Theorem 5.3.3 *Suppose $u \in \mathcal{U}_2$. Then,*

$$\sum_{j=1}^{K-1} \lambda_j F_j \succeq_2 F_K \text{ for some } \lambda \in \Lambda_{K-1} \tag{5.3.8}$$

if and only if

$$\int u(x) dF_j(x) \geq \int u(x) dF_K(x)$$

$$\text{for all } u \in \mathcal{U}_2 \text{ and for some } j \in \{1, \ldots, K-1\}. \tag{5.3.9}$$

This theorem implies that if a convex combination of the distributions in $\mathcal{F}_{-K} = \{F_k : k = 1, \ldots, K - 1\}$ (second-order) dominates F_K, then F_K is dominated by one of the distributions in $\mathcal{F}_{-K}$. This implies that if F_K is dominated by a mixture of distributions in $\mathcal{F}_{-K}$, then it is not optimal in the sense of CSD and can be eliminated from further consideration. This motivates the following definition of *SD optimality*:

Definition 5.3.2 *The distribution $F_K \in \mathcal{F}$ is SD optimal if it is the unique optimal solution for at least some utility function $u \in \mathcal{U}_2$, or equivalently*

$$\max_{u \in \mathcal{U}_2} \min_{F \in \mathcal{F}_{-K}} \left[\int u(x) dF_K(x) - \int u(x) dF(x) \right] > 0. \tag{5.3.10}$$

Otherwise, it is non-SD optimal.

On the other hand, SD admissibility based on pairwise comparisons is defined as follows:

Definition 5.3.3 *The distribution $F_K \in \mathcal{F}$ is SD admissible if it is non-dominated by all feasible alternatives in $\mathcal{F}_{-K}$, or equivalently*

$$\min_{F \in \mathcal{F}_{-K}} \max_{u \in \mathcal{U}_2} \left[\int u(x) dF_K(x) - \int u(x) dF(x) \right] > 0. \tag{5.3.11}$$

Otherwise, it is SD-inadmissible.

If $K = 2$, then SD-optimality and SD-admissibility are equivalent and they both reduce to pairwise non-SD dominance. However, in general, SD optimality is a stronger condition for utility maximization than SD admissibility. The SD optimality applies to discrete choice sets and is different from the SD efficiency (discussed in Section 5.3.2) that only applies to polyhedral choice sets.

Despite its importance, there are not many results available to test the hypothesis of SD optimality. Post (2016a) recently proposed an empirical likelihood (EL) test of SD optimality. He considers the null of optimality against the alternative of nonoptimality, i.e.,

$$H_0 : F_K \text{ is SD optimal vs. } H_1 : F_K \text{ is non-SD optimal.} \tag{5.3.12}$$

Let $\{X_i := (X_{1,i}, \ldots, X_{K,i}) : i = 1, \ldots, N\}$ be an observed data set. The observations are assumed to be serially independent but can be cross-sectionally dependent among the K prospects. Let $\Delta^N = \left\{ \mathbf{p} = (p_1, .., p_N) \in \mathbb{R}_+^N : \sum_{i=1}^N p_i = 1 \right\}$ denote a set of probability vectors.

Consider a constrained optimization problem

$$\max_{\mathbf{p}} \sum_{i=1}^N \ln p_i + N \ln(N) \text{ subject to } \mathbf{p} \in \Delta_0^N, \tag{5.3.13}$$

where $\Delta_0^N \subset \Delta^N$ satisfies the null hypothesis H_0. The optimal solution $\hat{\mathbf{p}} = (\hat{p}_1, .., \hat{p}_N)$ for the maximization problem gives the *implied probabilities* satisfying the null hypothesis. The empirical log likelihood ratio (ELR) statistic ELR_N is then defined to be

$$-\frac{1}{2}ELR_N = \sum_{i=1}^{N} \ln \hat{p}_i + N \ln(N). \tag{5.3.14}$$

Post (2016a) suggests approximating the distribution of ELR_N using the EL bootstrap (Brown and Newey, 2002), in which bootstrap samples are generated from the implied probabilities $\hat{\mathbf{p}} = (\hat{p}_1, .., \hat{p}_N)$, instead of the empirical distribution with weights $(1/N, \ldots, 1/N)$ (i.e., the standard nonparametric bootstrap). The EL bootstrap automatically imposes the null restriction from the optimization problem (5.3.13) and it is known that $\hat{\mathbf{p}}$ gives a more efficient estimator for the true distribution of X_i than the empirical CDF.

In practice, the optimization problem (5.3.13) requires a computational strategy. First, rank the observations $\{(X_{1,i}, \ldots, X_{K,i}) : i = 1, \ldots, N\}$ in the ascending order by the values of $X_K : X_{K,1} \leq \cdots \leq X_{K,N}$. Second, remove the prospects that take lower values than X_K from the choice set, so that $\min\{X_{k,1}, \ldots, X_{k,N}\} \geq X_{K,1}$, $k = 1, \ldots, K-1$. For a given probability vector $\mathbf{p} \in \Delta^N$, define the sample *lower partial moment (LPM)* (or the *expected shortfall*) of X_k, $k = 1, \ldots, K$ to be

$$LPK_k(\mathbf{p}, x) := \sum_{i=1}^{N} p_i(x - X_{k,i})\mathbf{1}\left(X_{k,i} \leq x\right). \tag{5.3.15}$$

Define the $N \times (K-1)$ matrices A_n, $n = 2, \ldots, N$ with elements

$$(A_n)_{i,k} := (X_{K,i} - X_{K,n})\mathbf{1}\left(X_{K,i} \leq X_{K,n}\right) - (X_{k,i} - X_{K,n})\mathbf{1}\left(X_{k,i} \leq X_{K,n}\right). \tag{5.3.16}$$

Then, for $k = 1, \ldots, K-1$, we have

$$\left(\mathbf{p}^\mathsf{T} A_n\right)_k = LPK_k(\mathbf{p}, X_{K,n}) - LPK_K(\mathbf{p}, X_{K,n}). \tag{5.3.17}$$

Notice that (5.3.17) approximates the difference between the integrated CDFs of X_k and X_K, i.e.,

$$\int_a^x F_k(y)dy - \int_a^x F_K(y)dy, \tag{5.3.18}$$

evaluated at $x = X_{K,n}$ using the probability vector $\mathbf{p}$.

Therefore, from Bawa, Bodurtha, Rao, and Suri (1985, p. 423) and Theorem 5.3.3, X_K is non-SD optimal if and only if the following system of linear equations has a feasible solution:

$$\left(\mathbf{p}^\mathsf{T} A_n\right) \gamma \leq 0, \ n = 2, \ldots, N, \tag{5.3.19}$$

$$\gamma \in \Delta^{K-1}.$$

That is, X_K is non-SD optimal if and only if some convex mixture of the (integrated) CDFs of the $(K-1)$ alternatives lies below that of F_K at all evaluation points. On the other hand, X_K is SD-optimal if the system (5.3.19) is not solvable.

For $k = 1, \ldots, K-1$, define the $N \times (N-1)$ matrix B_k with elements

$$(B)_{i,n} = (A_{n+1})_{i,k}.$$

Then, X_K is SD-optimal if and only if the following system is solvable:

$$\left(\mathbf{p}^\mathsf{T} B_k\right) \beta > 0, \ k = 1, \ldots, K-1,$$
$$\beta \in \Delta^{N-1}.$$

That is, X_K is SD-optimal if and only if the (integrated) F_K lies below all of the $(K-1)$ alternative (integrated) CDFs at some evaluation point.

Therefore, to compute the implied probability and the ELR statistic, Post (2016a) suggests solving the following optimization problem:

$$\max_\pi \sum_{i=1}^N \ln \pi_i + +N \ln(N) \tag{5.3.20}$$

subject to

$$\left(\pi^\mathsf{T} B_k\right) \beta > 0, \ k = 1, \ldots, K-1, \tag{5.3.21}$$
$$\beta \in \Delta^{N-1}, \tag{5.3.22}$$
$$\pi \in \Delta^N. \tag{5.3.23}$$

This model is not convex because (5.3.21) is a non-convex quadratic constraint. However, if K is not very large as is true in many applications, the system can be solved by solving a relatively small convex subproblem; see Post (2016a, section 5) for the details.

To sum up, the concepts of convex stochastic dominance and SD optimality based on CSD are useful in effectively eliminating the alternatives that will not be chosen by any individual with a utility function in a hypothesized class. There are not many statistical tests of SD optimality available in the literature yet. The ELR test of Post (2016a) is a natural approach to test the hypothesis, because it can easily impose the null restrictions and provide efficient estimates of distribution functions. The proposed computation strategy should work, unless the number of choice alternatives is large. However, the serial independence assumption to justify the empirical likelihood assumption might be restrictive in some financial applications and could be relaxed to weak dependence, e.g., by using the block empirical likelihood method (Kitamura, 1997).

5.4 Weaker Notions of Stochastic Dominance

5.4.1 Almost Stochastic Dominance

The stochastic dominance (SD) rule ranks distributions for *all* utility functions in a certain class. For example, the second-order stochastic dominance ranks distributions for all individuals with increasing and concave utility functions. This is an advantage of the SD rule in the sense that it gives a *uniform* ordering of prospects that does not depend on a specific utility function. However, this can be restrictive in practice, because a small violation of the SD rule can make the ranking invalid.

For example, consider two prospects X_1 and X_2, where X_1 provides either \$2 or \$3 with equal probability and X_2 provides \$1 or \$1,000,000 with equal probability. In this case, neither X_1 nor X_2 stochastically dominates the other. However, we expect that *almost all* reasonable investors would choose X_2 over X_1.

To circumvent the limitation of the SD rule, Leshno and Levy (2002) introduce the *Almost Stochastic Dominance (ASD)* rule that applies to *most* rather than *all* decision-makers, by eliminating economically pathological preferences. The ASD rule has been used in many areas; see e.g., Levy (2009, 2016) and Bali, Demirtas, Levy, and Wolf (2009).

Let X_1 and X_2 be two prospects supported on $\mathcal{X} = [a, b]$, $-\infty < a < b < \infty$ with distributions F_1 and F_2, respectively. For $s = 1, 2, \ldots$ and $0 < \varepsilon < 1/2$, define

$$
\mathcal{U}_s^*(\varepsilon) := \left\{ u \in \mathcal{U}_s : \sup_x \left\{ (-1)^{s+1} u^{(s)}(x) \right\} \right.
$$
$$
\left. \leq \inf_x \left\{ (-1)^{s+1} u^{(s)}(x) \right\} \left[\frac{1}{\varepsilon} - 1 \right] \right\}.
$$

For example, $\mathcal{U}_2^*(\varepsilon)$ denotes the class of all increasing and concave functions with second derivatives satisfying certain restrictions.

Let $F_k^{(2)}(x) = \int_{-\infty}^x F_k(t)dt$ denote the integrated CDF for $k = 1, 2$. The concept of (second-order) almost stochastic dominance is defined as follows:[8]

Definition 5.4.1 X_1 ε-*almost second-order stochastically dominates (or ε-ASSD) X_2, denoted $F_1 \succeq_2^{almost(\varepsilon)} F_2$ for $\varepsilon > 0$, if (a)*

$$
\int \left[F_1^{(2)}(x) - F_2^{(2)}(x) \right]_+ dx \leq \varepsilon \int \left| F_1^{(2)}(x) - F_2^{(2)}(x) \right| dx \quad (5.4.1)
$$

and $F_2^{(2)}(b) \geq F_1^{(2)}(b)$; or (b) $E[u(X_1)] \geq E[u(X_2)]$ for all $u \in \mathcal{U}_2^*(\varepsilon)$.

---

[8] This definition is due to Tzeng, Huang, and Shih (2013), who modified the original definition of ASD of Leshno and Levy (2002) to ensure the equivalence of (*a*) and (*b*). The definition can be straightforwardly extended to first- or higher-order ASD.

To understand this definition intuitively, define

$$I_2 := \frac{\int \left[F_1^{(2)}(x) - F_2^{(2)}(x) \right]_+ dx}{\int \left| F_1^{(2)}(x) - F_2^{(2)}(x) \right| dx}. \tag{5.4.2}$$

I_2 is the ratio of the area between the integrated CDFs $F_1^{(2)}$ and $F_2^{(2)}$ for which $F_1^{(2)}(x) \geq F_2^{(2)}(x)$ (i.e., the area that violates the condition of F_1 second-order stochastically dominating F_2) to the total area between $F_1^{(2)}$ and $F_2^{(2)}$. It takes values in $[0, 1]$ and can serve as a measure of disagreement with stochastic dominance, $I_2 = 0$ corresponding to the second-order stochastic dominance ($F_1 \succeq_2 F_2$). If $I_2 > 0$, then we no longer have SD but we still have ε- ASD as long as $I_2 \leq \varepsilon$. Therefore, ASD is certainly a weaker concept than SD.

The original notion of ASD is based on pairwise comparisons. However, if there are more than two prospects in the choice set, it may result in ASD-inadmissible prospects that may never be chosen by any individual having a utility function even in the class $\mathcal{U}_s^*(\varepsilon)$; see Section 5.3.3 for a related discussion. Therefore, an extension of ASD to allow multiple comparisons would be desirable. Also, despite the fact that ASD has been considered in many empirical and theoretical studies, there are not many results available for its statistical inference yet.

In view of this, Anderson, Post, and Whang (2018, APW) combine the notions of ASD and convex stochastic dominance (CSD) and propose the "*Utopia Index*," a measure of proximity to the (theoretically) optimal prospect, which corresponds to the lower envelope of the multiple integrated CDFs. The measure can be used to rank arbitrary number of prospects, which may be incomparable using the standard SD criterion.

Consider the finite set $\{X_1, \ldots, X_K\}$ of $K \geq 2$ distinct prospects, where $X_k \in \mathcal{X} := [a, b]$, $-\infty < a < b < \infty$, has distribution F_k, $k = 1, \ldots, K$. Let $\mathcal{F} = \{F_1, \ldots, F_K\}$, $\lambda = (\lambda_1, \ldots, \lambda_K)^{\mathsf{T}}$, $\Lambda = \{\lambda \in \mathbb{R}_+^K : e^{\mathsf{T}}\lambda = 1\}$, and $e = (1, \ldots, 1)^{\mathsf{T}}$. To get a decision rule that applies to multiple prospects, APW introduce the following definition:

Definition 5.4.2 *Prospect* X_k, $k = 1, \ldots, K$ *is second-degree utopian if it weakly second-order stochastically dominates all alternative mixture distributions:*

$$F_k^{(2)}(x) \leq \sum_{j=1}^{K} \lambda_j F_j^{(2)}(x) \text{ for all } x \in \mathbb{R} \text{ and all } \lambda \in \Lambda. \tag{5.4.3}$$

Recall that the prospect X_k is optimal if the inequality (5.4.3) holds for *some* $x \in \mathbb{R}$ and all $\lambda \in \Lambda$ (Section 5.3.3). Therefore, the optimal set is generally smaller than the utopian set, which enables further reduction of the choice set. However, in many cases, the utopian set may be empty. This motivates them to consider the following lower envelope as a surrogate benchmark in decision-making:

Definition 5.4.3 *The second-order lower envelope $\underline{\mathcal{F}}_2$ of $\mathcal{F}$ amounts to*

$$\underline{\mathcal{F}}_2(x) = \min\{F_1^{(2)}(x), \ldots, F_K^{(2)}(x)\}.$$

If one of the prospects is utopian, then its integrated CDF will coincide with the lower envelope. If the utopian set is empty, it seems tempting to view the lower envelope as the integrated CDF of an infeasible utopian prospect, or an order-theoretical "upper bound." However, this interpretation is not correct because the lower envelope is piecewise convex, rather than convex, and hence is not a (second-order) integrated CDF. Nevertheless, APW show that it can be interpreted as a locus of (normalized) maximal expected utility levels for elementary utility functions.

Given the interpretation, deviation of the prospect X_k from the lower envelope (or the optima for the elementary utility function) can be measured as

$$\mathcal{A}_{2,k} = \int_{\mathcal{X}} \left[F_k^{(2)}(x) - \underline{\mathcal{F}}_2(x)) \right] dx.$$

To normalize the violation area, consider the following second-order transvariation of $\mathcal{F}$:

$$\mathcal{T}_2 = \int_{\mathcal{X}} \left[\overline{\mathcal{F}}_2(x) - \underline{\mathcal{F}}_2(x) \right] dx.$$

The measure $\mathcal{T}_2$ extends the notions of bivariate transvariation (Gini, 1916, 1959) and multivariate transvariation (Dagnum, 1968) to a higher-order integration of distributions. By construction, $\mathcal{T}_2$ is an upper bound for the violation area: $\mathcal{A}_{2,k} \leq \mathcal{T}_2$ for any $k = 1, \ldots, K$.

Based on this result, APW suggest the following measure of utopianity:

Definition 5.4.4 *The second-degree Utopia Index for prospect X_k, $k = 1, \ldots, K$ amounts to*

$$\mathcal{I}_{2,k} := 1 - \frac{\mathcal{A}_{2,k}}{\mathcal{T}_2}. \tag{5.4.4}$$

The index $\mathcal{I}_{2,k}$ resembles the I_2 measure of ASD (defined in Equation 5.4.2), in the sense that it captures the normalized violation area of utopianity, just as I_2 captures the normalized violation area of pairwise dominance relations. In fact, when $K = 2$, it is easy to see that $I_2 = 1 - \mathcal{I}_{2,1}$.[9] Therefore, $\mathcal{I}_{2,k}$ can be regarded as an extension of ASD to the general case

---

[9] This follows from the elementary equalities $a - \min\{a, b\} = [a - b]_+$ and $\max\{a, b\} - \min\{a, b\} = |a - b|$.

$K \geq 2$, or the case where CSD applies. The index satisfies $0 \leq \mathcal{I}_{2,k} \leq 1$, with $\mathcal{I}_{2,k} = 0$ corresponding to utopianity. If $\mathcal{I}_{2,k} < 1$, then the utopian set is empty and there exist multiple optimal prospects. In this case, the prospect with highest utopia index comes closest to being a unique optimum.

In practice, the utopia index should be estimated. Let $\{X_i := (X_{1,i}, \ldots, X_{K,i}) : i = 1, \ldots, N\}$ be an observed data set. Then, the measure $\mathcal{I}_{2,k}$ can be estimated by

$$\hat{\mathcal{I}}_{2,k} = 1 - \frac{\hat{\mathcal{A}}_{2,k}}{\hat{\mathcal{T}}_2},$$

where $\hat{\mathcal{A}}_{2,k}$ and $\hat{\mathcal{T}}_2$ are defined with estimated integrated CDF

$$\bar{F}_k^{(2)}(x) = \frac{1}{N} \sum_{i=1}^{N} (x - X_{k,i}) 1 \left(X_{k,i} \leq x \right)$$

for $k = 1, \ldots, K$.

APW (proposition 6) show that, if the data are strictly stationary, α-mixing, and satisfies additional regularity conditions, then the asymptotic distribution of $\sqrt{N} \left(\hat{\mathcal{I}}_{2,k} - \mathcal{I}_{2,k} \right)$ is given by a functional of the mean zero Gaussian process. Since the asymptotic distribution depends on the true distributions in $\mathcal{F}$, APW (proposition 7) suggest approximating critical values by subsampling, and show that the subsample confidence interval has an asymptotically correct coverage.

5.4.2 Approximate Stochastic Dominance

The concept of stochastic dominance is often too strong if one tries to confirm it based on a sample. This leads to consider the idea of "restricted stochastic dominance," which essentially compares distributions over a fixed closed interval excluding the tails of the distributions; see Section 2.3. As an alternative way to overcome this difficulty, Álvarez-Esteban, del Barrio, Cuesta-Albertos, and Matrán (2016, ABCM) propose the concept of *Approximate Stochastic Dominance*, which is a weaker concept of the stochastic dominance relationship based on mixture (or contaminated) models.

For $\pi \in (0, 1)$, consider the model

$$\begin{cases} F_1 = (1 - \pi)G_1 + \pi F_1' \\ F_2 = (1 - \pi)G_2 + \pi F_2' \end{cases} \text{ for some } G_1, G_2 \text{ such that } G_2 \succeq_1 G_1,$$

$$(5.4.5)$$

where G_1, G_2, F_1', and F_2' are distribution functions. If the model (5.4.5) is true (for small π), then the stochastic dominance relation $F_2 \succeq_1 F_1$ holds except for a small fraction of observations coming from F_1 and F_2 and, in this sense, stochastic dominance of F_2 over F_1 holds only approximately.

Definition 5.4.5 *For distribution functions F_1 and F_2, we say that F_2 first-order stochastically dominates F_1 at level π, denoted $F_2 \succeq_1^\pi F_1$, if (5.4.5) holds.*

Note that the model (5.4.5) always holds by taking π large enough, e.g., $\pi = 1$. The smallest π for which the decomposition (5.4.5) is true measures the fraction of the population that violates the stochastic dominance relation. Therefore, it can serve as a measure of disagreement with the stochastic dominance relation $F_2 \succeq_1 F_1$. This measure can be identified by the following result (theorem 2.4 of ABCM):

Theorem 5.4.1 *For arbitrary distribution functions F_1, F_2 and $\pi \in (0, 1)$, (5.4.5) holds if and only if*

$$\pi \geq \pi(F_1, F_2),$$

where

$$\pi(F_1, F_2) := \sup_{x \in \mathbb{R}} (F_2(x) - F_1(x)). \tag{5.4.6}$$

ABCM also show that the approximate stochastic dominance model (5.4.5) holds if and only if there is stochastic dominance after trimming a π-fraction of the F_1 distribution at the right tail and a π-fraction of the F_2 distribution at the left tail. Furthermore, they show that $F_2 \succeq_1^\pi F_1$ if and only if

$$\int u(x) 1 \left(x \leq F_1^{-1}(1 - \pi) \right) dF_1(x) \leq \int u(x) 1 \left(x > F_2(\pi) \right) dF_2(x)$$

for all $u \in \mathcal{U}_1$.

In the context of the contamination model (5.4.5), $\pi(F_1, F_2)$ can be considered as a measure of disagreement with stochastic dominance; see Section 5.4.1 for an alternative measure. For example, suppose that $\pi(F_1, F_2) = 0$. Then, obviously, F_2 stochastically dominates F_1 at any level $\pi \geq 0$, i.e., there is no departure from stochastic dominance $F_2 \succeq_1 F_1$. On the other hand, suppose that $F_1(x) = x$, $x \in [0, 1]$ and $F_2(x) = \sqrt{x}$, $x \in [0, 1]$. Then, $F_1 \succeq_1 F_2$. However, since $\pi(F_1, F_2) = \sup_{x \in [0,1]} (\sqrt{x} - x) = 1/4$, we have $F_2 \succeq_1^\pi F_1$ if and only if $\pi \geq 1/4$. This implies that the dominance is reversed if one trims more than a $1/4$ fraction of the largest observations from F_1 and the smallest observations from F_2. In this case, the measure of departure from stochastic dominance $F_2 \succeq_1 F_1$ is $1/4$.[10]

---

[10] This example is from Álvarez-Esteban, del Barrio, Cuesta-Albertos, and Matrán (2016).

Based on this result, ABCM consider testing for *approximate stochastic dominance:*

$$H_0 : \pi(F_1, F_2) \geq \pi_0 \text{ vs. } H_1 : \pi(F_1, F_2) < \pi_0 \tag{5.4.7}$$

for a fixed $\pi_0 \in (0, 1)$. The rejection of the null hypothesis H_0 in (5.4.7) against H_1 implies that stochastic dominance of F_2 over F_1 holds, up to some small contamination level π_0.

Let $\{X_{1,i}\}_{i=1}^N$ and $\{X_{2,i}\}_{i=1}^N$ denote two random samples independently drawn from distributions F_1 and F_2, respectively. (For simplicity, we assume the equal sample size for the samples.) Let $\bar{F}_k$ be the empirical CDF for $k = 1, 2$. By the Glivenko–Cantelli theorem, $\pi(F_1, F_2)$ can be consistently estimated by

$$\pi(\bar{F}_1, \bar{F}_2) = \sup_{x \in \mathbb{R}} \left[\bar{D}_{2,1}(x) \right]. \tag{5.4.8}$$

It is straightforward to show that the asymptotic distribution of $\pi(\bar{F}_1, \bar{F}_2)$ is given by a functional of a Gaussian process:

Theorem 5.4.2 *Under regularity conditions,*

$$\sqrt{N} \left[\pi(\bar{F}_1, \bar{F}_2) - \pi(F_1, F_2) \right] \Rightarrow \nu(F_1, F_2), \tag{5.4.9}$$

where

$$\nu(F_1, F_2)$$
$$= \sup_{t \in T(F_1, F_2, \pi(F_1, F_2))} [\mathcal{B}_1(t) - \mathcal{B}_2(t - \pi(F_1, F_2))], \tag{5.4.10}$$
$$T(F_1, F_2, \pi)$$
$$= \left\{ t \in [\pi, 1] : F_2(x) = t, \ F_1(x) = t - \pi \text{ for some } x \in \bar{\mathbb{R}} \right\},$$

and $\mathcal{B}_1(t)$ and $\mathcal{B}_2(t)$ are independent standard Brownian bridges on $[0, 1]$.

Notice that the set $T(F_1, F_2, 0)$ corresponds to the image of the contact set introduced earlier (Section 3.1.1).

The asymptotic distribution $\nu(F_1, F_2)$ can be simulated by a bootstrap method. Instead, ABCM recommend approximating its upper and lower bounds by normal quantiles. That is, for $\alpha \in (0, 1/2)$, the α quantile $K_\alpha(F_1, F_2)$ of the asymptotic distribution $\nu(F_1, F_2)$ is bounded by

$$\sigma_{\pi(F_1, F_2)} \Phi^{-1}(\alpha) \leq K_\alpha(F_1, F_2),$$

where Φ denotes the standard normal CDF and

$$\sigma_{\pi(F_1, F_2)} = \min_{t \in T(F_1, F_2, \pi(F_1, F_2))} \sigma^2(t),$$
$$\sigma^2(t) = Var(\mathcal{B}_1(t) - \mathcal{B}_2(t - \pi(F_1, F_2))).$$

When $\pi \in (0, 1/2]$, ABCM show that rejecting the null H_0 in (5.4.7) when

$$\sqrt{N} \left[\pi(\bar{F}_1, \bar{F}_2) - \pi_0 \right] < \bar{\sigma}_{\pi_0} \Phi^{-1}(\alpha), \qquad (5.4.11)$$

provides a test of asymptotic size α which detects the fixed alternative with power exponentially close to one asymptotically, where $\bar{\sigma}_{\pi}^2 = (1 - \pi^2)/2$.

To improve the finite sample power performance, ABCM further suggest using a bias-corrected bootstrap critical value, i.e., reject H_0 when

$$\sqrt{N} \left[\hat{\pi}_{N,BOOT} - \pi_0 \right] < \hat{\sigma}_N \Phi^{-1}(\alpha), \qquad (5.4.12)$$

where

$$\hat{\sigma}_N^2 = \min_{t \in T(\bar{F}_1, \bar{F}_2, \pi(\bar{F}_1, \bar{F}_2))} \sigma^2(t),$$

$$\hat{\pi}_{N,BOOT} = \pi(\bar{F}_1, \bar{F}_2) - bias_{BOOT}\left(\pi(\bar{F}_1, \bar{F}_2)\right),$$

$$bias_{BOOT}\left(\pi(\bar{F}_1, \bar{F}_2)\right) = E^* \pi(\bar{F}_1^*, \bar{F}_2^*) - \pi(\bar{F}_1, \bar{F}_2).$$

Here, $\bar{F}_1^*$ and $\bar{F}_2^*$ are the bootstrap counterparts of $\bar{F}_1$ and $\bar{F}_2$, respectively, whose bootstrap samples are drawn independently from $\{X_{1,i} : i = 1, .., N\}$ and $\{X_{2,i} : i = 1, .., N\}$, respectively, and E^* denotes conditional expectation given the original samples.

Rather than testing for the approximate stochastic dominance hypothesis (5.4.7), one might prefer constructing confidence intervals for the measure $\pi(F_1, F_2)$ of disagreement with stochastic dominance. From (5.4.12), an upper bound for $\pi(F_1, F_2)$ with asymptotic level of at least $1 - \alpha$ for $\alpha \in (0, 1/2)$ is given by

$$\hat{\pi}_{N,BOOT} - N^{-1/2} \hat{\sigma}_N \Phi^{-1}(\alpha).$$

On the other hand, a lower bound $\pi(F_1, F_2)$ with asymptotic level of at least $1 - \alpha$ is given by

$$\pi(\bar{F}_1, \bar{F}_2) - N^{-1/2} K_{1-\alpha}\left(\pi(\bar{F}_1, \bar{F}_2)\right),$$

where $K_{1-\alpha}(\pi)$ denotes the $(1-\alpha)$ quantile of $\sup_{t \in [\pi, 1]} (\mathcal{B}_1(t) - \mathcal{B}_2(t - \pi))$. The quantiles $K_{1-\alpha}\left(\pi(\bar{F}_1, \bar{F}_2)\right)$ can be simulated numerically.

To sum up, the test suggested by ABCM is useful especially when distribution functions cross at the tails, but one wishes to infer (a weaker concept of) stochastic dominance by trimming away some fraction of the observations at the tails. The testing procedure is relatively easy to implement, because it is based on (scaled) standard normal critical values. However, since the critical values are based on the least favorable configuration of the null hypothesis, the test can be conservative in practice, though the bias-corrected bootstrap critical values might perform better. Also, the test and confidence interval are applicable only to *first-order* stochastic dominance and may not be directly generalized to higher-order stochastic dominance.

5.4.3 Infinite-Order Stochastic Dominance

Infinite-Order Stochastic Dominance (ISD), formally characterized by Thistle (1993), is the weakest notion of stochastic dominance. Since the SD efficient set or SD optimal sets are monotonically decreasing in the stochastic order s, the choice based on ISD yields the smallest SD efficient or optimal set, which is a useful property in the portfolio choice problem. From the duality of SD and expected utility, ISD also corresponds to a more restrictive class of utility functions, viz. completely monotone class, than any finite-order SD.

Let X_1 and X_2 be two prospects supported on $\mathcal{X} = [0, \infty)$, with distributions F_1 and F_2, respectively. ISD is defined by letting $s \to \infty$ in the definition of the s-th order SD. That is, $F_1 \succeq_\infty F_2$ holds if $Eu(X_1) \geq Eu(X_2)$ for all utility functions $u \in \mathcal{U}_\infty$.

The class $\mathcal{U}_\infty$ of utility functions has marginal utilities that are completely monotone.[11] It is argued that this class imposes reasonable restrictions on the utility functions (Scott and Horvath, 1980). Also, these utility functions are completely proper (Pratt and Zeckhauser, 1987), which implies that an undesirable risk cannot be made desirable by presence of additional risks. Furthermore, the class includes many popular utility functions such as logarithmic, exponential, and power utility functions.

It is well known that the SD relation is monotone in s, in the sense that if $F_1 \succeq_s F_2$ then $F_1 \succeq_r F_2$ for all $r > s$ but the converse is not true. Interestingly, however, a (partial) converse is true in the case of ISD. Specifically, Thistle (1993, proposition 1) establishes the following necessary and sufficient condition for ISD:

Theorem 5.4.3 $F_1 \succeq_\infty F_2$ *if and only if* $F_1 \succeq_s F_2$ *for some* $s < \infty$.

Therefore, the rejection of ISD is equivalent to the rejection of stochastic dominance of any finite order.

Assume that the utility functions are defined on $\mathbb{R}_+ = [0, \infty)$. To characterize the utility functions in $\mathcal{U}_\infty$, we need the following result (Bernstein's theorem):

Lemma 5.4.4 *A function f is completely monotone on $\mathbb{R}_+$ if and only if there exists a bounded nondecreasing function ψ such that*

$$f(x) = \int_0^\infty \exp(-tx) d\psi(t), \ \forall x \in \mathbb{R}_+.$$

---

[11] A function $f(x)$ is completely monotone if it is positive valued and has derivatives that alternate in sign with $f'(x) < 0$, $f''(x) > 0$, and so on.

Since the utility function $u \in \mathcal{U}_\infty$ has a completely monotone marginal utility u', we have that $u \in \mathcal{U}_\infty$ if and only if

$$
\begin{aligned}
u(x) &= \int_0^x u'(z)dz \\
&= \int_0^x \int_0^\infty \exp(-tz)d\psi(t)dz \\
&= \int_0^\infty t^{-1}(1 - \exp(-tx))\, d\psi(t)
\end{aligned}
$$

for some bounded and nondecreasing ψ. Therefore,

$$
Eu(X_1) > Eu(X_2) \text{ for all } u \in \mathcal{U}_\infty,
$$

if and only if

$$
\begin{aligned}
&\int_0^\infty \int_0^\infty t^{-1}(1 - \exp(-tx))\, d\psi(t)dF_1(x) \\
&> \int_0^\infty \int_0^\infty t^{-1}(1 - \exp(-tx))\, d\psi(t)dF_2(x)
\end{aligned}
$$

or, equivalently, if and only if

$$
\int_0^\infty t^{-1}\left[M_{F_1}(-t) - M_{F_2}(-t)\right] d\psi(t) < 0,
$$

for all bounded and nondecreasing function ψ, where

$$
M_F(t) := E_F \exp(tX)
$$

denotes the Laplace transform (or the moment-generation function) associated with X that has CDF F. This leads to the following main result of Thistle (1993, Proposition 4):[12]

Theorem 5.4.5 $F_1 \succeq_\infty F_2$ *if and only if* $M_{F_1}(-t) < M_{F_2}(-t)$ *for all* $t \in \mathbb{R}_+$.

In particular, Theorem 5.4.5 suggests that one can test the hypothesis of ISD based on the difference between empirical Laplace transforms of distribution functions of the prospects.

Knight and Satchell (2008) suggest a multiple comparison-based testing procedure for the ISD hypothesis. The test is an extension of Anderson (1996, Section 2.2.1)'s test for the standard SD hypothesis. Knight and Satchell (2008) consider the null hypothesis of equal Laplace transform functions at *finite* grid points.

---

[12] The one-sided Laplace tranformation $M_F(-t) = E_F \exp(-tX)$ is always well-defined, because $E_F |\exp(-tX)| < \infty$ for all nonnegative random variables X and all $t \in \mathbb{R}_+$.

Define

$$\Delta_{1,2}(t) := M_{F_1}(-t) - M_{F_2}(-t).$$

The hypotheses of interest considered are given by

$$H_0 : \Delta_{1,2}(t) = 0 \text{ for all } t \in \mathcal{T}_0,$$
$$H_1 : \Delta_{1,2}(t) > 0 \text{ for some } t \in \mathcal{T}_0,$$

where $\mathcal{T}_0 = \{t_1, \ldots, t_J\} \subset \mathbb{R}_+$ denotes a set of grid points chosen by an investigator for $J < \infty$.

Let $\{X_{1,i} : i = 1, \ldots, N\}$ and $\{X_{2,i} : i = 1, \ldots, N\}$ be random samples from F_1 and F_2, respectively. Let

$$\hat{\Delta}_{1,2}(t) = \hat{M}_{F_1}(-t) - \hat{M}_{F_2}(-t),$$

where

$$\hat{M}_{F_k}(-t) = \frac{1}{N} \sum_{i=1}^{N} \exp(-t X_{k,i})$$

denotes the empirical Laplace transform for F_k for $k = 1, 2$.

Under the null hypothesis H_0, by a CLT for i.i.d. observations,

$$\sqrt{N} \left[\hat{\Delta}_{1,2}(t_1), \ldots, \hat{\Delta}_{1,2}(t_J) \right]^{\mathsf{T}} \Rightarrow N(0, \Sigma),$$

where $\Sigma = (\Sigma_{j,l})$ with

$$\Sigma_{j,l} = 2M_{F_1}(-t_j - t_l) - M_{F_1, F_2}(-t_j, -t_l) - M_{F_1, F_2}(-t_l, -t_j),$$
$$M_{F_1, F_2}(t, s) = E \exp(t X_1 + s X_2).$$

Let $\hat{\Sigma} = (\hat{\Sigma}_{j,l})$ denote the sample analogue of $\Sigma = (\Sigma_{j,l})$. Consider the maximum t-statistic

$$MaxT_N = \max_{j=1,\ldots,J} \frac{\hat{\Delta}_{1,2}(t_j)}{\sqrt{\hat{\Sigma}_{j,j}}}.$$

We can compute the critical values associated with $MaxT_N$ using

$$\lim_{N \to \infty} P(MaxT_N \le x)$$
$$= \int_{-\infty}^{x} \cdots \int_{-\infty}^{x} \left(\frac{1}{2\pi} \right)^{N/2} |\Omega|^{-1/2} \exp\left(-\frac{1}{2} z^{\mathsf{T}} \Omega z \right) dz,$$

where $\Omega = (\Omega_{j,l})$ and

$$\Omega_{j,l} = \frac{\Sigma_{j,l}}{\sqrt{\Sigma_{j,j}} \sqrt{\Sigma_{l,l}}}.$$

Provided J is not large, the critical values can be simulated by computing the multivariate integral with Ω replaced by $\hat{\Omega}$. One then may reject the null hypothesis H_0 if $MaxT_N$ takes values larger than the critical value.

The testing procedure of Knight and Satchell (2008) is attractive in the sense that it is relatively easy to implement in practice. However, as we discussed earlier (Section 2.2.1), the choice of grid points $T_0 = \{t_1, \ldots, t_J\}$ can be arbitrary and may affect the power performance of the test. A more practical problem is that computation of the critical values is difficult even when J is moderately large, say $J > 5$.

In a subsequent work, Bennett (2007) considers the following hypotheses

$$H_0 : \Delta_{1,2}(t) \leq 0 \text{ for all } t \in \mathbb{R}_+,$$
$$H_1 : \Delta_{1,2}(t) > 0 \text{ for some } t \in \mathbb{R}_+.$$

He considers a supremum-type test

$$BNT_N = \sup_{t \in \mathbb{R}_+} \sqrt{N} \hat{\Delta}_{1,2}(t)$$

which takes maximum over the *entire* domain. Under the least favorable case of the null hypothesis (i.e., $\Delta_{1,2}(t) = 0$ for all $t \in \mathbb{R}_+$), the test statistic BNT_N converges weakly to a Gaussian process. The critical values based on a multiplier method are suggested.

In contrast to the Knight and Satchell (2008)'s test, Bennett (2007)'s test does not require a choice of grid points and is designed to be consistent against all alternatives H_1. More recently, Tabri (2010) extends the result of Bennett (2007) and suggests an integral-type test and a simulation procedure to compute critical values. A caveat is that all of the aforementioned tests assume independent samples and are not directly applicable to dynamic settings, e.g., financial data.

5.5 Related Concepts of Stochastic Dominance

5.5.1 Density Ratio Dominance

Let F_1 and F_2 be two CDFs on $\mathbb{R}$ with common support $\mathcal{X}$. If the density ratio dF_2/dF_1 is nonincreasing, then we say that F_1 *density ratio (or likelihood ratio) dominates* F_2. Density ratio dominance is a stronger property than first-order stochastic dominance: If F_1 density ratio dominates F_2, then F_1 first-order stochastically dominates F_2.

The concept of density ratio dominance (or density ratio ordering) is frequently used in economics, finance, and other fields. See Roosen and Hennessy (2012) for a discussion of its applications to portfolio choice, insurance, mechanism design, and auction theory. See also Beare (2011) and Beare and Schmidt (2015) for recent applications to the pricing-kernel puzzle in finance.

In the literature, there are some, though not many, results on testing density ratio ordering. Examples include Dykstra, Kochar, and Robertson (1995) and Roosen and Hennessy (2012) who are the first to consider inference on density ratio ordering for discrete distributions. Carolan and Tebbs (2005, CT) allow continuous distributions and propose testing concavity of ordinal dominance curves (defined in Equation 5.5.3) based on the L_1 and sup-norm distances between the empirical ordinary dominance curve and its least concave majorant. They derive the asymptotic null distributions of the test statistics when $F_1 = F_2$. Beare and Moon (2015, BM) generalize the approach of CT to L_p-norm distance for $p \geq 1$ and show that the case $F_1 = F_2$ is not the least favorable case for $p \in (2, \infty]$. They recommend using the CT statistic for $p \in [1, 2]$. More recently, Beare and Shi (2015) show how to improve powers of the CT and BM tests by employing the contact set approach (Section 3.1.1).

Let X_1 and X_2 be random variables with absolute continuous distributions F_1 and F_2 with densities f_1 and f_2, respectively.

Definition 5.5.1 X_1 *density ratio dominates* X_2 *if*

$$\frac{f_2(t)}{f_1(t)} \text{ is nonincreasing over } t \qquad (5.5.1)$$

or, equivalently,

$$f_1(s)f_2(t) \leq f_1(t)f_2(s) \text{ for all } s \leq t, \qquad (5.5.2)$$

or, equivalently, the Ordinal Dominance Curve (ODC)

$$R(t) := F_2\left(F_1^{-1}(t)\right) \text{ is concave.} \qquad (5.5.3)$$

Density ratio dominance is related to first-order dominance (Shaked and Shanthikumar, 1994, p. 29):

Theorem 5.5.1 X_1 *density ratio dominates* X_2 *if and only if*

$X_1 | (a \leq X_2 \leq b)$ *first-order stochastically dominates* $X_2 | (a \leq X_1 \leq b)$

whenever $a \leq b$, *where* $X|A$ *denotes the conditional distribution of* X *given* A.

Also, the integrated area of the ODC satisfies

$$\int_0^1 R(t)dt = \int_0^1 F_2(F_1^{-1}(t))dt = \int_{-\infty}^{\infty} F_2(t)dF_1(t). \qquad (5.5.4)$$

Therefore, if $F_1 = F_2$, then $\int_0^1 R(t)dt = 1/2$ and this property is the basis of the *Mann–Whitney–Wilcoxon-type test* of equality of two distributions.[13]

Let Θ denote the collection of strictly increasing, continuously differentiable maps $\theta : [0, 1] \to [0, 1]$ with $\theta(0) = 0$ and $\theta(1) = 1$. Let $\Theta_0 = \{\theta \in \Theta : \theta \text{ is concave}\}$. Then, the hypotheses of interest are

$$H_0 : R \in \Theta_0 \text{ vs. } H_1 : R \in \Theta \backslash \Theta_0.$$

---

[13] See Section 2.4 for the test.

Let $\{X_{1,i}\}_{i=1}^{N_1}$ and $\{X_{2,i}\}_{i=1}^{N_2}$ denote two independent random samples from the distributions F_1 and F_2, respectively. Assume that $N_1/(N_1 + N_2) \to \lambda \in (0, 1)$ as $N_1, N_2 \to \infty$. Let the *empirical ODC* be given by

$$\bar{R} = \bar{F}_2 \circ \bar{F}_1^{-1}, \text{ where}$$

$$\bar{F}_k(x) = \frac{1}{N_k} \sum_{i=1}^{N_k} 1(X_{k,i} \le x), \ k = 1, 2.$$

Consider the test statistic

$$CT_N = r_N \left\| T\bar{R} - \bar{R} \right\|,$$

where T is the least concave majorant operator,[14] $r_N = (N_1 N_2/(N_1 + N_2))^{1/2}$, $\|\cdot\|$ is the L^p-norm with respect to Lebesgue measure on $[0, 1]$, and $p \in [1, \infty]$.

The following weak convergence result of the empirical ODC is well known (Hsieh and Turnbull, 1996, theorem 2.2, and Beare and Moon, 2015, lemma 3.1):

Theorem 5.5.2 *Suppose $R \in \Theta$. Then,*

$$r_N \left(\bar{R} - R \right) \Rightarrow v_R,$$

where

$$v_R(u) = \lambda^{1/2} \mathcal{B}_1 \left(R(u) \right) + (1 - \lambda)^{1/2} R'(u) \mathcal{B}_2(u), \ u \in [0, 1],$$

and $\mathcal{B}_1$ and $\mathcal{B}_2$ are independent standard Brownian bridges on $[0, 1]$.

To characterize the asymptotic properties of the test statistic CT_N, we also need the following concepts of differentiation:

Definition 5.5.2 *Let X and Y be real Banach spaces. A map $\phi : X \to Y$ is said to be Hadamard directionally differentiable at $x \in X$ tangentially to a linear space $X_0 \subset X$, if there exists a map $\phi'_x : X_0 \to Y$ such that*

$$\phi'_x (z) = \lim_{n \to \infty} \frac{\phi(x + t_n z_n) - \phi(x)}{t_n}$$

for any sequences $z_n \in X$ and $t_n \in (0, 1]$ with $z_n \to z \in X_0$ and $t_n \downarrow 0$. We call $\phi'_x (z)$ as the Hadamard directional derivative at x in direction z. If ϕ'_x is linear, then we say that ϕ is Hadamard differentiable at x tangentially to X_0.

Let $\mathcal{A} : l^\infty[0, 1] \to \mathbb{R}$ be an operator such that

$$\mathcal{A}f = \|Tf - f\|, \ f \in l^\infty[0, 1].$$

---

[14] See Section 4.3.2 for the definition.

When $R \in \Theta_0$, the test statistic can be written as

$$CT_N = r_N \left(A\bar{R} - AR \right).$$

The operator $\mathcal{A}$ is shown to be Hadamard directionally differentiable at $R \in \Theta_0$ tangentially to $C([0, 1])$, with directional derivative

$$\mathcal{A}'_R h = \left\| T'_R h - h \right\|, \quad h \in C([0, 1]).$$

From the functional delta method applicable to Hadamard directional differentiable operators (Shapiro, 1991; Fang and Santos, 2016) and the continuous mapping theorem, BM obtain the following asymptotic null distribution of the test statistic:

Theorem 5.5.3 *Suppose $R \in \Theta_0$. Then,*

$$CT_N \Rightarrow \mathcal{A}'_R \nu_R.$$

BM further show that, for $p \in [1, 2]$, $\mathcal{A}'_R \nu_R$ is stochastically dominated by $\mathcal{A}'_I \nu_I = \|T\mathcal{B} - \mathcal{B}\|$, where I is the identity map on $[0, 1]$ and $\mathcal{B}$ is a standard Brownian bridge. This implies that the case $R = I$ corresponds to the least favorable case of the null hypothesis. The distribution $\|T\mathcal{B} - \mathcal{B}\|$ can be simulated to yield conservative critical values, as suggested by CT. However, when $p \in (2, \infty]$, the case $R = I$ is no longer least favorable and there is no finite critical value that will control for asymptotic size everywhere in Θ_0. Therefore, CT_N should not be used for testing Θ_0 against $\Theta \backslash \Theta_0$ when $p > 2$.

When R is strictly concave, $\mathcal{A}'_R \nu_R = 0$ so that CT_N degenerates to zero. If R is concave, but not strictly concave, then the limiting distribution of CT_N is nondegenerate. This case corresponds to the boundary of the null hypothesis, in the spirit of Linton, Song, and Whang (2010) (Section 3.1.1).

By estimating the "contact set" over which CT_N is asymptotically nondegenerate, Beare and Shi (2015) propose a bootstrap procedure that significantly improves the power performance of BM.

5.5.2 Uniform Stochastic Ordering

Let X_1 and X_2 be nonnegative random variables with distribution functions F_1 and F_2, respectively.

Definition 5.5.3 X_1 *is uniformly stochastically larger than* X_2, *or* $X_1 \succeq_{usd} X_2$, *if*

$$\frac{1 - F_2(t)}{1 - F_1(t)} \text{ is nonincreasing in } t \in [0, b_{F_2}), \tag{5.5.5}$$

where $1 - F_k$ *denotes the survival function for* $k = 1, 2$, *and* $b_{F_2} = \inf\{x : F_2(x) = 1\}$.

Equivalently, (5.5.5) can be written as

$$[1 - F_1(s)][1 - F_2(t)] \le [1 - F_1(t)][1 - F_2(s)], \text{ for all } s \le t. \quad (5.5.6)$$

Also, if F_1 and F_2 are absolutely continuous with densities f_1 and f_2, respectively, then (5.5.5) is equivalent to their hazard rate functions being ordered, i.e.,

$$r_1(t) \le r_2(t), \; \forall t \in \mathbb{R}_+, \quad (5.5.7)$$

where

$$r_k(t) := \lim_{\Delta t \to 0} \frac{P(t < X_k \le t + \Delta t \mid X > t)}{\Delta t} = \frac{f_k(t)}{1 - F_k(t)} \quad (5.5.8)$$

denotes the hazard rate function of X_k, $k = 1, 2$. This is again equivalent to

$$
\begin{aligned}
P(X_2 &> t + s \mid X_2 > t) \\
&\le P(X_1 > t + s \mid X_1 > t), \; \forall t, s \in \mathbb{R}_+. \quad (5.5.9)
\end{aligned}
$$

If X_k denotes the lifetime (say, hours) of some object k, then (5.5.9) implies that the probability that object 1 will survive for an additional s hours, given that it has survived for t hours, is larger than that corresponding to object 2.

Uniform stochastic ordering is useful in many applications in which risks change dynamically over time. For example, in choosing medical treatments, the survival time of "treatment A" might stochastically dominate that of "treatment B" at the initial stage, but this may not be true when patients are examined at later stages. Uniform stochastic ordering can also be used to compare distributions in upper tails of financial returns.

Uniform stochastic ordering is a stronger concept than first-order stochastic dominance: If X_1 is uniformly stochastically larger than X_2, then X_1 first-order stochastically dominates X_2. This can be easily verified by taking $s = -\infty$ in (5.5.6), so that

$$1 - F_2(t) \le 1 - F_1(t), \text{ for all } t.$$

On the other hand, uniform stochastic ordering is a weaker concept than density ratio (or likelihood ratio) ordering. To see this, suppose that X_1 density ratio dominates X_2, that is,

$$f_1(t)f_2(x) \le f_1(x)f_2(t) \text{ for all } t \le x.$$

Then, X_1 is uniformly stochastically larger than X_2 because

$$
\begin{aligned}
r_1(t) &= \frac{f_1(t)}{\int_t^\infty f_1(x)\,dx} \\
&\le \frac{f_1(t)}{\int_t^\infty [f_2(x)f_1(t)/f_2(t)]\,dx}
\end{aligned}
$$

$$= \frac{f_2(t)}{\int_t^\infty \left[f_2(x) \right] dx}$$
$$= r_2(t).$$

There are some, though not many, statistical tests of uniform stochastic ordering in the literature. For example, Dykstra, Kochar, and Robertson (1991) propose nonparametric maximum likelihood estimators of uniformly stochastically ordered distribution functions and suggest a likelihood ratio test for the null of *equal* distributions against uniformly stochastically ordered alternatives. The test focuses on multinomial distributions and hence is parametric. El Barmi and McKeague (2016, hereafter EM), on the other hand, suggest a nonparametric empirical likelihood based test based on K (≥ 2) independent random samples.[15] See EM for more references of existing inference procedures of uniform stochastic ordering.

Suppose that we are given independent random samples $\{X_{k,i} : i = 1, \ldots, N_k\}$ from the distribution F_k for $k = 1, \ldots, K$, where $K \geq 2$. Assume that the proportion $\gamma_k = N_k/N$ is fixed as the total sample size $N = \sum_{k=1}^K N_k$ changes.

Let $\theta_k(s, t) = [1 - F_k(t)] / [1 - F_k(s)]$ for $k = 1, \ldots, K$. EM consider the following hypotheses:

$$H_0 : \theta_1(s, t) = \cdots = \theta_K(s, t) \text{ for all } s < t, \tag{5.5.10}$$
$$H_1 : \theta_1(s, t) \leq \cdots \leq \theta_K(s, t) \text{ for all } s < t,$$

where at least one of the inequalities under H_1 is strict.

For a given (s, t), the localized empirical likelihood ratio (ELR) is given by

$$\mathcal{R}(s, t) = \frac{\sup \left\{ \prod_{k=1}^K L(F_k) : \theta_1(s, t) = \cdots = \theta_K(s, t) \right\}}{\sup \left\{ \prod_{k=1}^K L(F_k) : \theta_1(s, t) \leq \cdots \leq \theta_K(s, t) \right\}}, \tag{5.5.11}$$

where $L(F_k)$ denotes the nonparametric likelihood function. To compute $\mathcal{R}(s, t)$ at a given (s, t), it suffices to maximize

$$\prod_{k=1}^K [\theta_k(s, t)]^{N_k(1 - \bar{F}_k(t))} [1 - \theta_k(s, t)]^{N_k(\bar{F}_k(t) - \bar{F}_k(s))}$$

subject to the constraints $0 < \theta_1(s, t) = \cdots = \theta_K(s, t) < 1$ or $0 < \theta_1(s, t) \leq \cdots \leq \theta_K(s, t) < 1$, depending on whether it is the numerator or the denominator of (5.5.11), respectively.

---

[15] El Barmi and McKeague (2013) use a similar method to study an empirical likelihood-based test for the standard stochastic dominance.

It can be shown that

$$\mathcal{R}(s, t) = \prod_{k=1}^{K} \left[\frac{\hat{\theta}(s, t)}{\tilde{\theta}_k(s, t)} \right]^{N_k(1 - \bar{F}_k(t))} \left[\frac{1 - \hat{\theta}(s, t)}{1 - \tilde{\theta}_k(s, t)} \right]^{N_k(\bar{F}_k(t) - \bar{F}_k(s))},$$

where $\hat{\theta}(s, t) = \left[1 - \bar{F}(t) \right] / \left[1 - \bar{F}(s) \right]$, $\bar{F}(t) = \sum_{k=1}^{K} \gamma_k \bar{F}_k(t)$, and

$$\tilde{\theta}_k(s, t) = \left[E_{\mathbf{w}} \left(\hat{\theta}(s, t) | \mathcal{I} \right) \right]_k.$$

Here, $E_{\mathbf{w}} \left(\hat{\theta}(s, t) | \mathcal{I} \right)$ is the *isotonic regression*, i.e., the weighted least squares projection of $\hat{\theta}(s, t) = \left(\hat{\theta}_1(s, t), \ldots, \hat{\theta}_K(s, t) \right)^{\mathsf{T}}$ onto $\mathcal{I} = \{ \mathbf{z} \in \mathbb{R}^K :$ $z_1 \leq \cdots \leq z_K \}$, with random weights $w_k(t) = \gamma_k \left[1 - \bar{F}_k(t) \right]$, where $\hat{\theta}_k(s, t) = \left[1 - \bar{F}_k(t) \right] / \left[1 - \bar{F}_k(s) \right]$ is the unconstrained estimator; see Robertson, Wright, and Dykstra (1988) for an algorithm to compute the projection.

To test (5.5.10), EM suggest the following integrated empirical likelihood statistic:

$$EM_N = -2 \int_0^\infty \int_s^\infty \log \mathcal{R}(s, t) d\bar{F}(t) d\bar{F}(s)$$

$$= -\frac{2}{N^2} \sum_{Z_i < Z_k} \log \mathcal{R}(Z_i, Z_k),$$

where $\{ Z_i : i = 1, \ldots, N \}$ is the pooled sample.

EM (theorem 2) show that the asymptotic null distribution of the test statistic is a functional of Gaussian processes:

Theorem 5.5.4 *Under H_0 and assuming that the common distribution function F is continuous,*

$$EM_N \Rightarrow \sum_{k=1}^{K} \gamma_k \int_0^1 \int_s^1 \frac{\left\{ \left[E_\gamma \left(\mathbf{Z} \left(f(s, t) \right) | I \right) \right]_k - \bar{Z} \left(f(s, t) \right) \right\}^2}{f(s, t)} dt ds,$$

where $\mathbf{Z} = \left(\mathcal{B}_1 / \sqrt{\gamma_1}, \ldots, \mathcal{B}_K / \sqrt{\gamma_K} \right)^{\mathsf{T}}$, $\{ \mathcal{B}_k \}_{k=1}^{K}$ are independent standard Brownian motions, $\bar{Z} = \gamma^{\mathsf{T}} \mathbf{Z}$, $\gamma = (\gamma_1, \ldots, \gamma_K)^{\mathsf{T}}$, and $f(s, t) = (t - s) / \left[(1 - s)(1 - t) \right]$.

Theorem 5.5.4 shows that the asymptotic distribution is pivotal and hence does not depend on the underlying true distributions $\{ F_k \}$. The critical values are tabulated by EM (p. 963). For example, at the 5% significance level, the critical values are 0.777, 1.112, 1.373, and 1.490 for $K = 2, 3, 4$, and 5, respectively.

The testing procedure of EM is attractive in that it does not require bootstrap or Monte Carlo simulations. However, the assumption of independent random sampling can be restrictive in some applications and it is an open question how to extend the results to the case of paired samples or time series observations. Also, since the null of the equal distributions is not the negation of the ordered alternatives, it is possible that both the null and alternative hypotheses might be false. Therefore, sometimes it is not straightforward interpreting the testing results; see Section 2.4 for a discussion.

5.5.3 Positive Quadrant Dependence

Let X and Y be two random variables with CDFs F and G, respectively.

Definition 5.5.4 X *is Positive Quadrant Dependent on* Y, *or* $PQD(X|Y)$, *if*

$$P\left(X \leq x, Y \leq y\right) \geq P\left(X \leq x\right) P\left(Y \leq y\right) \text{ for all } (x, y) \in \mathbb{R}^2.$$
(5.5.12)

The definition is symmetric with respect to X and Y, so that $PQD(X|Y)$ is equivalent to $PQD(Y|X)$. Also, $PQD(X|Y)$ holds if and only if $PQD(a(X)|b(Y))$ for any strictly increasing functions a and b. From the property of conditional probability, PQD is the same as saying that "$F(\cdot)$ first-order stochastically dominates $F(\cdot|Y \leq y)$ for all $y \in \mathbb{R}$." PQD implies that the probability that two random variables are simultaneously large (or small) is at least as great as it would be were they independent.

The concept of positive quadrant dependence has been used extensively in finance, insurance, and risk management. For its applications, see Dhaene and Goovaerts (1996), Denuit, Dhaene, and Ribas (2001), Embrechts, McNeil, and Straumann (2002), Denuit and Scaillet (2004), Levy (1992), Shaked and Shanthikumar (1994), Drouet, Mari, and Kotz (2001), and Scaillet (2005), among others.

For a stochastic inference of PQD, Denuit and Scaillet (2004, DS) consider pairwise comparisons at fixed grid points. Scaillet (2005), on the other hand, proposes a consistent test based on the entire support. The latter test suggests bootstrap critical values under the LFC. Other inference methods include Scaillet (2005), Gijbels, Omelka, and Sznajder (2010), Gijbels and Sznajder (2013), and Ledwina and Wyłupek (2014). Below we sketch the main idea of DS.

Let $C(\cdot, \cdot)$ denote the *copula function* (Sklar, 1959):

$$P\left(X \leq x, Y \leq y\right) = C\left\{P\left(X \leq x\right), P\left(Y \leq y\right)\right\}.$$

The hypotheses of interest can be stated using the copula function:

$$H_0 : C(u, v) \geq uv \text{ for all } (u, v) \in [0, 1]^2,$$

$$H_1 : C(u, v) < uv \text{ for some } (u, v) \in [0, 1]^2.$$

Let $\{(X_i, Y_i)\}_{i=1}^{N}$ be a random sample taking values in $\mathbb{R}^2$. For $(u, v) \in [0, 1]^2$, define the empirical copula function to be

$$C_N(u, v) = \frac{1}{N} \sum_{i=1}^{N} 1\left\{\bar{F}(X_i) \leq u, \bar{G}(Y_i) \leq v\right\},$$

where $\bar{F}$ and $\bar{G}$ denote the empirical CDFs of $\{X_i\}_{i=1}^{N}$ and $\{Y_i\}_{i=1}^{N}$, respectively.

Let $D(u, v) = uv - C(u, v)$ and $D_N(u, v) = uv - C_N(u, v)$. DS consider a supremum-type test statistic

$$S_N = \sqrt{N} \sup_{u, v \in [0, 1]} D_N(u, v).$$

The asymptotic null distribution of S_N follows from the weak convergence result of the empirical copula process (Scaillet, 2005, lemma 1):

Theorem 5.5.5 *Suppose that the copula function C has continuous partial derivatives $\partial C(u, v)/\partial u = C_1(u, v)$ and $\partial C(u, v)/\partial v = C_2(u, v)$. Then,*

$$\sqrt{N} D_N(\cdot, \cdot) \Rightarrow \nu_C(\cdot, \cdot),$$

where

$$\nu_C(u, v) = \mathcal{B}_C(u, v) - C_1(u, v)\mathcal{B}_C(u, 1) - C_2(u, v)\mathcal{B}_C(1, v)$$

and $\mathcal{B}_C$ is a tight Brownian bridge on $[0, 1]^2$ with covariance function

$$\Omega(u, v, u', v') = E\left[\mathcal{B}_C(u, v)\mathcal{B}_C(u', v')\right]$$
$$= C\left(u \wedge u', v \wedge v'\right) - C(u, v)C(u', v')$$

for each $u, v, u', v' \in [0, 1]$.

Let

$$S_\infty := \sup_{u, v \in [0, 1]} \nu_C(u, v)$$

and c_α be the $(1 - \alpha)$ quantile of S_∞.

Theorem 5.5.6 *(a) If H_0 is true, then*

$$\lim_{N \to \infty} P(S_N > c_\alpha) \leq P(S_\infty > c_\alpha) = \alpha,$$

with equality when $C(u, v) = uv$ for all $(u, v) \in [0, 1]^2$. (b) Under H_1,

$$\lim_{N \to \infty} P(S_N > c_\alpha) = 1.$$

DS suggest two (conservative) methods to simulate the p-values, similar to those of Barrett and Donald (2003). A multiplier method requires generating the process ν_C from

$$\tilde{v}_C(u, v) = \frac{1}{\sqrt{N}} \sum_{i=1}^{N} V_i \left[1 \left\{ \bar{F}(X_i) \le u, \bar{G}(Y_i) \le v \right\} - C_N(u, v) \right]$$

$$- C_{1,N}(u, v) \frac{1}{\sqrt{N}} \sum_{i=1}^{N} V_i \left[1 \left\{ \bar{F}(X_i) \le u \right\} - u \right]$$

$$- C_{2,N}(u, v) \frac{1}{\sqrt{N}} \sum_{i=1}^{N} V_i \left[1 \left\{ \bar{G}(Y_i) \le v \right\} - v \right],$$

where $\{V_i\}_{i=1}^{N}$ are i.i.d. $N(0, 1)$ random variables independent of the original sample and $C_{k,N}(u, v)$ is a consistent estimator of $C_k(u, v)$ for $k = 1, 2$. Examples of $C_{k,N}(u, v)$ include partial derivatives of a smoothed version of the empirical copula process (Fermanian and Scaillet, 2003):

$$C_{1,N}(u, v) = \frac{\partial}{\partial x} \hat{H} \left\{ \bar{F}^{-1}(u), \bar{G}^{-1}(v) \right\} / \hat{f}(\bar{F}^{-1}(u)),$$

$$C_{2,N}(u, v) = \frac{\partial}{\partial y} \hat{H} \left\{ \bar{F}^{-1}(u), \bar{G}^{-1}(v) \right\} / \hat{g}(\bar{G}^{-1}(v)),$$

where $\hat{H}$, $\hat{f}$, and $\hat{g}$ are the kernel estimators of the joint distribution H and marginal densities f and g, respectively. Multiplier p-values can then be estimated from

$$p_N^M = P_U \left(\sup_{u, v \in [0,1]} \tilde{v}_C(u, v) > S_N \right).$$

DS also suggest a bootstrap procedure. First, generate bootstrap samples $\{(X_i^*, Y_i^*)\}_{i=1}^{N}$ from $\{(X_i, Y_i)\}_{i=1}^{N}$ and compute the statistic C_N^* using the bootstrap sample. Then, calculate the recentered bootstrap test statistic

$$S_N^* = \sqrt{N} \sup_{u, v \in [0,1]} \left\{ C_N^*(u, v) - C_N(u, v) \right\}$$

and estimate bootstrap p-values from

$$p_N^B = P^* \left(S_N^* > S_N \right).$$

5.5.4 Expectation Dependence Dominance

Expectation dominance, originally proposed by Wright (1987), is a measure of dependence between random variables. Let X and Y be two random variables with CDFs F_X and F_Y, respectively.

Definition 5.5.5 Y *is Positive Expectation Dependent on X, or $PED(Y|X)$, if*

$$E(Y) - E(Y|X \le x) \ge 0 \text{ for all } x, \tag{5.5.13}$$

with strict dependence if the inequality is strict for a set of x with positive probability.

The negative expectation dependence of Y on X (or $NED(Y|X)$) is defined as in (5.5.13) with the inequality reversed.

If Y is positive (negative) expectation dependent on X, then we expect Y to be smaller (larger) when X is small (in the sense that $X \leq x$) than when there is no restriction on X.[16]

Expectation dependence is a weaker concept than quadrant dependence (Section 5.5.3) but is a stronger concept than correlation. The concept plays a pivotal role in portfolio theory. For example, consider the classical portfolio choice problem with two risky assets Y, X and risk-averse preferences expressed through a utility function $u \in \mathcal{U}_2$. That is, maximize $Eu(\lambda Y + (1 - \lambda)X)$ with respect to $\lambda \in [0, 1]$. When $EY = EX$, it is shown (Wright, 1987, theorem 4.2) that the necessary and sufficient condition for the optimal $\lambda^* \in (0, 1)$ (diversification) is

$$E(Y - X|X \leq x) \geq 0 \quad \text{and} \quad E(X - Y|Y \leq y) \geq 0 \qquad (5.5.14)$$

for all x, y with strict inequality on a set of (x, y) that occurs with probability one. The conditions (5.5.14) are equivalent to the negative expectation dependence of $Y - X$ on X and $X - Y$ on Y, respectively. See, e.g., Hong, Lew, MacMinn, and Brockett (2011) and Guo and Li (2016) and the references therein for further applications of the expectation dependence.

Zhu, Guo, Lin, and Zhu (2016, hereafter ZGLZ) propose a statistical test of the positive expectation dependence hypothesis. Their null hypothesis is (5.5.13) and the alternative hypothesis is its negation. (ZGLZ also consider higher-order expectation dependence, but for simplicity we shall focus on the first-order case.) They note that (5.5.13) is equivalent to

$$\text{Cov}\,(Y, 1\,(X > x)) \geq 0 \text{ for all } x. \qquad (5.5.15)$$

This follows from the elementary equality

$$P\,(X > x)\,[E\,(Y|X > x) - E\,(Y)] \qquad (5.5.16)$$
$$= P\,(X \leq x)\,[E\,(Y) - E\,(Y|X \leq x)],$$

so that (5.5.13) holds if and only if the left-hand side of (5.5.16) is nonnegative or, equivalently, (5.5.15) holds.

To test the hypothesis (5.5.15), ZGLZ consider a supremum-type test statistic. Let $\{(X_i, Y_i) : i = 1, \ldots, N\}$ be i.i.d. copies of (X, Y). Let

$$D_N(x) = -\frac{1}{N} \sum_{i=1}^{N} \left(Y_i - \bar{Y}\right) 1(X_i > x), \; x \in \mathbb{R},$$

---

[16] Li (2011) extends the concept to higher-order expectation dependence.

where $\bar{Y} = (1/N) \sum_{i=1}^{N} Y_i$. The test statistic is given by

$$ZZ_N = \sqrt{N} \sup_{x \in \mathbb{R}} (D_N(x)).$$

By the functional CLT (using the fact that $\{Y1(X > x) : x \in \mathbb{R}\}$ is a VC class of functions[17]), the test statistic ZZ_N converges weakly to the supremum of a mean zero Gaussian process with the covariance function given by

$$C(x_1, x_2) = \text{Cov}\,(Y1\,(X > x_1)\,, Y1\,(X > x_2))\,.$$

Critical values can be computed by a bootstrap or simulation method. ZGLZ suggest a multiplier method. Specifically, let

$$D_N^*(x) = -\frac{1}{N} \sum_{i=1}^{N} V_i \left(Y_i - \bar{Y}\right) 1(X_i > x),$$

where $\{V_i\}_{i=1}^{N}$ are random draws from $N(0, 1)$, independent of the original sample. Then, by simulating the values of

$$ZZ_N^* = \sqrt{N} \sup_{x \in \mathbb{R}} \left(D_N^*(x)\right),$$

one can compute simulated critical values and p-values. Conditional on the original sample $\{(X_i, Y_i)\}_{i=1}^{N}$, the test based on the simulated critical values has an asymptotically correct size and is consistent against the fixed alternative.

The independence assumption might be restrictive in most financial applications and the test cannot be directly applied to multiple hypotheses (e.g., (5.5.14)). In view of this, Linton, Whang, and Yen (2016) recently extended the result to a multivariate expectation dependence hypothesis, which allows for time series observations, so that portfolio choice and asset allocation problems can be handled.

5.5.5 Central Dominance

Gollier (1995) considers conditions under which a change in distribution increases the optimal value of a decision variable for all risk-averse agents and introduces the concept of *Central Dominance*. Compared with stochastic dominance that provides a preference ordering of distributions, central dominance implies a deterministic change in optimal decision variables such as demand for risky assets or a social welfare policy when the distribution changes. It is shown that (second-order) stochastic dominance is neither sufficient nor necessary for central dominance.

For example, if one income distribution F_1 centrally dominates the other distribution F_2, then this implies that any government with an increasing and

---

[17] See Section A.2.1 in Appendix A for the concept.

concave social welfare function trying to maximize its expected welfare should have lower optimal income tax rate for the distribution F_1 than the one for F_2. Also, if the return distribution F_1 of a risky asset centrally dominates the return distribution F_2, then any risk-averse investor should have a higher proportion of the risky asset in his portfolio for the distribution F_1 than F_2.

Consider a representative agent who tries to maximize his expected payoff, assuming an increasing and concave von Neumann–Morgenstern utility function $u \in \mathcal{U}_2$. Let $z(x, \alpha)$ denote the payoff function which depends on the decision variable α and the realization x of random variable X. The optimal decision problem can be written as

$$\alpha(u, F) := \arg\max_{\alpha \in \mathcal{A}} H(\alpha, u, F), \qquad (5.5.17)$$

where

$$H(\alpha, u, F) := E_F u\left(z(X, \alpha)\right)$$
$$= \int_a^b u(z(x, \alpha)) dF(x),$$

$\mathcal{A} = [0, 1]$ is the range of α, and F is the distribution of X whose support is $[a, b]$. It is assumed that $z_\alpha(x, \alpha) := (\partial/\partial\alpha) z(x, \alpha) > 0$ and $z_{\alpha\alpha}(x, \alpha) := (\partial^2/\partial\alpha^2) z(x, \alpha) \leq 0$, which makes H concave in α.

The first-order condition of (5.5.17) is given by

$$H_\alpha\left(\alpha(u, F), u, F\right)$$
$$= \int_a^b u'(z(x, \alpha(u, F))) z_\alpha\left(x, \alpha(u, F)\right) dF(x) = 0, \quad (5.5.18)$$

where $H_\alpha\left(\alpha, u, F\right) = (\partial/\partial\alpha) H\left(\alpha, u, F\right)$. Integration by parts of (5.5.18) yields

$$H_\alpha\left(\alpha, u, F\right) = u'\left(z(b, \alpha)\right) T\left(b, \alpha, F\right)$$
$$- \int_a^b u''(z(x, \alpha)) z_\alpha(x, \alpha) T(x, \alpha, F) dx, \qquad (5.5.19)$$

where

$$T(x, \alpha, F) := \int_a^x z_\alpha(t, \alpha) dF(t) \qquad (5.5.20)$$

denotes the "location-weighted probability mass function."

Gollier (1995, proposition 1) establishes the following main result:

Theorem 5.5.7 *All risk-averse individuals selecting α under F_1 and F_2 reduce their optimal level of α after change in CDF from F_1 to F_2 (or, equivalently, $\alpha(u, F_2) \leq \alpha(u, F_1) \, \forall u \in \mathcal{U}_2$), if and only if there exists $\gamma \in \mathbb{R}$ such that*

$$T(x, \alpha, F_2) \leq \gamma T(x, \alpha, F_1) \text{ for all } x \in [a, b]. \qquad (5.5.21)$$

The sufficient condition in Theorem 5.5.7 can be established immediately from the optimization problem (5.5.17). To see this, suppose that (5.5.21) holds. Then, from (5.5.19), we have

$$
\begin{aligned}
H_\alpha\left(\alpha, u, F_2\right) &= u'\left(z(b, \alpha)\right) T\left(b, \alpha, F_2\right) \\
&\quad - \int_a^b u''(z(x, \alpha)) z_\alpha(x, \alpha) T(x, \alpha, F_2) dx \\
&\le u'\left(z(b, \alpha)\right) \gamma T\left(b, \alpha, F_1\right) \\
&\quad - \int_a^b u''(z(x, \alpha)) z_\alpha(x, \alpha) \gamma T(x, \alpha, F_1) dx \\
&= \gamma H_\alpha\left(\alpha, u, F_1\right),
\end{aligned}
\tag{5.5.22}
$$

where the inequality occurs because $u' > 0$ and $u'' \le 0$ for $u \in \mathcal{U}_2$, and $z_\alpha > 0$ and (5.5.21) hold by assumption. From the first-order condition (5.5.18), the last expression of (5.5.22) is 0 for $\alpha = \alpha(u, F_1)$. Therefore, we have

$$
H_\alpha\left(\alpha(u, F_1), u, F_2\right) \le 0 = H_\alpha\left(\alpha(u, F_2), u, F_2\right),
\tag{5.5.23}
$$

where the equality holds by the first-order condition (5.5.18) with $F = F_2$. The result (5.5.23) then implies that we must have $\alpha(u, F_2) \le \alpha(u, F_1)$ by the concavity of H with respect to α. The latter result holds for all $u \in \mathcal{U}_2$, thereby establishing the sufficient condition. For the necessary condition of Theorem 5.5.7, see Gollier (1995).

Theorem 5.5.7 gives the necessary and sufficient condition for central dominance, so that we may define:[18]

Definition 5.5.6 F_1 *centrally dominates* F_2, *denoted* $F_1 \succeq_{CD} F_2$ *(or F_1 CD F_2), if (5.5.21) holds for some $\gamma \in \mathbb{R}$.*

Despite its importance in economics, there have not been many testing procedures available for the central dominance hypothesis. Recently, Chuang, Kuan, and Tzeng (2017, CKT) proposed an integral-type test statistic and suggested a bootstrap procedure to compute critical values. We briefly discuss their result below.

The null of hypothesis of interest is that $F_1 \succeq_{CD} F_2$ and the alternative hypothesis is its negation. In other words,

$$
H_0 : T(x, \alpha, F_2) \le \gamma T(x, \alpha, F_1) \text{ for all } x \in [a, b], \text{ for some } \gamma \in \Gamma,
$$
$$
H_1 : T(x, \alpha, F_2) > \gamma T(x, \alpha, F_1) \text{ for some } x \in [a, b], \text{ for all } \gamma \in \Gamma,
$$

where Γ is a compact subset of $\mathbb{R}$ specified by a researcher.

---

[18] Gollier (1995) refers to this relation as "F_2 *is centrally riskier than* F_1" and denotes it as "F_1 CR F_2."

To test the hypothesis, CKT consider a linear payoff function

$$z(x, \alpha) = \alpha x + z_0, \tag{5.5.24}$$

where z_0 is an exogenous parameter. This formulation entails the standard portfolio problem, the production problem faced by a competitive firm with constant marginal costs, and the insurance problem. In the standard portfolio problem, variable x is the excess return of a risky asset over the risk-free rate and variable α is the demand for the risky asset; see section 3 of Gollier (1995). It is further assumed that $EX > 0$.

Under the above assumptions, the weighted probability mass function T is simplified to

$$T(x, \alpha, F) = T(x, F) := \int_a^x t dF(t) = E_F[X 1(X \le x)]. \tag{5.5.25}$$

Let

$$\Delta(\gamma, x) = \gamma T(x, F_1) - T(x, F_2), \tag{5.5.26}$$

$$Q(\gamma) = \int_a^b [\Delta(\gamma, x)]_- dx, \tag{5.5.27}$$

$$d_{CD} = \max_{\gamma \in \Gamma} Q(\gamma), \tag{5.5.28}$$

where $[x]_- = \min\{x, 0\}$. It is easy to see that $Q(\gamma) \le 0$ for all $\gamma \in \mathbb{R}$ and $Q(\gamma_0) = 0$ if and only if $\Delta(\gamma_0, x) \ge 0$ for all $x \in [a, b]$. Therefore, under the null hypothesis, $d_{CD} = 0$, while under the alternative hypothesis $d_{CD} < 0$. CKT consider an empirical analog of d_{CD} as the basis of their test statistic.

Suppose that $\{X_{1,i}\}_{i=1}^{N_1}$ and $\{X_{2,i}\}_{i=1}^{N_2}$ are two independent random samples from the distributions F_1 and F_2, respectively. Assume that $N_1/(N_1 + N_2) \to \lambda \in (0, 1)$ as $N_1, N_2 \to \infty$.

Let

$$T(x, \bar{F}_k) = \frac{1}{N_k} \sum_{i=1}^{N_k} X_{k,i} 1(X_{k,i} \le x) \text{ for } k = 1, 2$$

$$\hat{\Delta}(\gamma, x) = \gamma T(x, \bar{F}_1) - T(x, \bar{F}_2)$$

$$\hat{Q}(\gamma) = \int_a^b [\hat{\Delta}(\gamma, x)]_- dx.$$

CKT consider the following test statistic:

$$CKT_N = \max_{\gamma \in \Gamma} r_N \hat{Q}(\gamma), \tag{5.5.29}$$

where $r_N = (N_1 N_2/(N_1 + N_2))^{1/2}$.

By the functional CLT and continuous mapping theorem, it is straightforward to show that, for each $\gamma \in \Gamma$,

$$r_N \left[\hat{\Delta}(\gamma, x) - \Delta(\gamma, x) \right]$$
$$\Rightarrow \sqrt{1 - \lambda} T(x, \mathcal{B}_1) - \sqrt{\lambda} T(x, \mathcal{B}_2) := \nu_F(x),$$

where $\mathcal{B}_1$ and $\mathcal{B}_2$ are two independent standard Brownian bridges.

Let

$$\mathcal{C}(\gamma) = \{x \in [a, b] : \Delta(\gamma, x) = 0\}$$

denote the contact set for $\gamma \in \Gamma$. Under the null hypothesis H_0, the set

$$\Gamma_0 := \{\gamma \in \Gamma : Q(\gamma) = 0\}$$

is nonempty. If $\Gamma_0 = \{\gamma^0\}$ is a singleton, then we have

$$0 \geq CKT_N \geq r_N \hat{Q}(\gamma^0) = r_N \int_a^b \left[\hat{\Delta}(\gamma^0, x) \right]_- dx$$

$$\Rightarrow \int_{\mathcal{C}(\gamma^0)} [\nu_F(x)]_- dx, \tag{5.5.30}$$

where the weak convergence follows from an argument similar to that of Linton, Song, and Whang (2010); see Equation 3.1.6 of Section 3.1.1. If Γ_0 is an interval, on the other hand, it can be shown that CKT_N degenerates to zero (theorem 3.4 of CKT). Therefore, the limit distribution (5.5.30) is the asymptotic lower bound of CKT_N under the null hypothesis. Under the alternative hypothesis H_1, Γ_0 is an empty set and $CKT_N \to -\infty$.

CKT suggest the following bootstrap procedure to test the hypothesis H_0:

1. When $\max_{\gamma \in \Gamma} \hat{Q}(\gamma) \neq 0$, let

    $$\hat{\gamma}^0 = \arg\max_{\gamma \in \Gamma} \hat{Q}(\gamma).$$

    Otherwise, accept the null hypothesis H_0.
2. Take a sequence $c_N \to 0$ and $r_N c_N \to \infty$, and compute the estimated contact set

    $$\hat{\mathcal{C}}(\hat{\gamma}^0) = \left\{ x \in [a, b] : \left| \hat{\Delta}(\hat{\gamma}^0, x) \right| \leq c_N \right\}.$$

3. For $b = 1, \ldots, B$, draw bootstrap samples $\{X_{k,i,b}^*\}_{i=1}^{N_k}$ from $\{X_{k,i}\}_{i=1}^{N_k}$ for $k = 1, 2$. Compute the bootstrap statistic

    $$CKT_{N,b}^* = r_N \int_{\hat{\mathcal{C}}(\hat{\gamma}^0)} \left[\hat{\Delta}_b^*(\hat{\gamma}^0, x) - \hat{\Delta}(\hat{\gamma}^0, x) \right]_- dx,$$

where

$$\hat{\Delta}_b^*(\gamma, x) = \gamma T(x, \bar{F}_{1,b}^*) - T(x, \bar{F}_{2,b}^*)$$

$$T(x, \bar{F}_{k,b}^*) = \frac{1}{N_k} \sum_{i=1}^{N_k} X_{k,i,b}^* 1\left(X_{k,i,b}^* \leq x\right), k = 1, 2.$$

4. Compute the α-level bootstrap critical value

$$c_{\alpha,N,B}^* = \sup\left\{t : \frac{1}{B}\Sigma_{b=1}^B 1\{CKT_{N,b}^* > t\} \geq 1 - \alpha\right\}$$

   for $\alpha \in (0, 1/2]$.
5. Reject the null hypothesis H_0 if

$$CKT_N < c_{\alpha,N,B}^* - \eta := c_{\alpha,N,B,\eta}^*,$$

   where $\eta > 0$ is an arbitrary small constant, say $\eta = 10^{-3}$.

The introduction of η in the last step is to ensure that the test has asymptotically correct size even when Γ_0 is an interval, in which case both the test statistic and the bootstrap critical values degenerate to zero.

It can be shown that the test based on the above procedure has an asymptotically correct size and is consistent against H_1, in the sense that

$$\limsup_{N\to\infty} P\left(CKT_N < c_{\alpha,N,B,\eta}^*\right) \leq \alpha \text{ under } H_0, \qquad (5.5.31)$$

$$\lim_{N\to\infty} P\left(CKT_N < c_{\alpha,N,B,\eta}^*\right) = 1 \text{ under } H_1.$$

CKT apply their test to the daily return distributions of the S&P500 index from 2001 to 2013. They find, for example, that the return distribution in 2003 centrally dominates that in 2004. This finding implies that the optimal investment for the index in 2004 should be lower than what they were in 2003.

To summarize, the concept of central dominance is useful because it implies a comparative static of a change in optimal decision when the distribution of a prospect changes, while stochastic dominance does not have such an implication. The test of CKT is a valuable extension of the SD and moment inequality literature. A caveat is that its application can be somewhat limited, because it applies only to linear payoff functions. Also, the test can be conservative because the critical values are based on the lower bound of the asymptotic null distribution. Furthermore, the asymptotic theory is based on pointwise (not uniform) asymptotics and does not explicitly take into account the effect of the estimation of $\hat{\gamma}^0$.

5.5.6 Spatial Dominance

Park (2005) introduces the notion of *Spatial Dominance*, which is a general-ization of stochastic dominance to compare performances of two assets over a given time interval. It is useful because optimal investment strategies might be horizon dependent (Goyal and Welch, 2008; Cochrane, 2005).

To define the concept, let $\{X_t : t \in [0, T]\}$ be a (possibly nonstationary) time series (e.g., cumulative stock returns). The *local time* of the time series X_t is defined to be

$$l(T, x) = \lim_{\varepsilon \to 0} \frac{1}{2\varepsilon} \int_0^T 1\{|X_t - x| < \varepsilon\} dt,$$

which is the frequency at which the process visits the spatial point x up to time T. It may be interpreted as a "density" function over a given interval $[0, T]$. The discounted spatial distribution function of X_t is defined to be

$$\Lambda(T, x) := \int_{-\infty}^x \int_0^T e^{-rt} El(dt, x) = \int_0^T e^{-rt} P\{X_t \le x\} dt,$$

where $r > 0$ denotes a discount rate.

Now suppose we have two nonstationary stochastic processes X_t and Y_t with spatial distribution functions $\Lambda^X(T, x)$ and $\Lambda^Y(T, x)$.

Definition 5.5.7 *X_t first-order spatially dominates Y_t if*

$$\Lambda^X(T, x) \le \Lambda^Y(T, x) \text{ for all } x \in \mathbb{R} \tag{5.5.32}$$

or, equivalently,

$$\int_0^T e^{-rt} Eu(X_t) dt \le \int_0^T e^{-rt} Eu(Y_t) dt$$

for all $u \in \mathcal{U}_1$.

This concept can be easily extended to higher-order spatial dominance.

Park (2005) suggests a supremum-type test of the hypothesis (5.5.32) based on estimators of the spatial distributions (using discrete time series data) and derives its asymptotic null distribution (via infill asymptotics). He suggests a subsampling procedure to compute critical values.

Recent applications of the method include Ibarra (2013), who tests for spa-tial dominance between the cumulative return series for stocks and bonds at different investment horizons, from 1 to 15 years, using the US daily data from the year 1962 to the year 2012. He finds that bonds second-order spatially dom-inate stocks for the horizons from 1 to 4 years, but stocks spatially dominate bonds for the horizons of 6 years and longer.

6 Some Further Topics

6.1 Distributional Overlap Measure

Anderson, Linton, and Whang (2012, ALW) consider the question of estimation and inference about the scalar parameter

$$\theta := \int_{\mathbb{R}^d} \min\{f_1(x), f_2(x)\}dx, \tag{6.1.1}$$

where f_1 and f_2 are the PDFs of d-dimensional random vectors X_1 and X_2, respectively. This is a number between zero and one, with zero corresponding to the distributions having supports with no intersection and one to the perfect matching of two distributions, i.e., $f_1(x) = f_2(x)$ almost everywhere. It follows that θ is a measure of the extent to which the distributions overlap.

Note that θ is a unit-free measure, invariant to a common smooth monotonic transformation. This quantity has received a lot of attention in various areas including medical statistics and ecology, where it is known as the *overlap coefficient* or the *coefficient of community*. In economics, this measure has recently been proposed as a measure of the polarization between two well-defined groups, defined by race, occupation, gender, or location of dwelling; see Anderson (2004b) and Anderson, Ge, and Leo (2010). The quantity is also related to stochastic dominance and in fact it can be regarded as a measure of disagreement with stochastic dominance, because θ will take smaller values as the degree of FSD of one distribution over the other distribution increases; see Sections 5.4.1 and 5.4.2 for alternative measures.

Suppose that there is a random sample $\{(X_{1,i}, X_{2,i}) : i = 1, \ldots, N\}$ of size N from the population. ALW propose to estimate θ by

$$\widehat{\theta} = \int_C \min\{f_{1,N}(x), f_{2,N}(x)\}dx = \int_C \min\left\{1, \frac{f_{2,N}(x)}{f_{1,N}(x)}\right\} f_{1,N}(x)dx, \tag{6.1.2}$$

where

$$f_{k,N}(x) = \frac{1}{N} \sum_{i=1}^{N} K_h \left(x - X_{k,i} \right), k = 1, 2,$$

$C \subseteq \mathbb{R}^d$ is the union of the supports or some subset of interest, while K is a multivariate kernel, $K_h(\cdot) = K(\cdot/h)/h^d$, and h is a bandwidth sequence. In practice, one may consider an unsmoothed estimator which has the same (first-order) asymptotic properties as $\widehat{\theta}$:

$$\widehat{\theta}_E = \frac{1}{N} \sum_{i=1}^{N} \min \left\{ 1, \frac{f_{2,N}(X_{1,i})}{f_{1,N}(X_{1,i})} \right\} = \int_C \min \left\{ 1, \frac{f_{2,N}(x)}{f_{1,N}(x)} \right\} d\bar{F}_1(x),$$

(6.1.3)

where $\bar{F}_1$ denotes the empirical CDF of $\{X_{1,i}\}_{i=1}^{N}$.

Define the contact set

$$\mathcal{C}_{1,2} = \left\{ x \in \mathbb{R}^d : f_1(x) = f_2(x) > 0 \right\}.$$

(6.1.4)

This set can be either empty, contain a countable number of isolated points, or a union of intervals. In the first case, the asymptotics for $\widehat{\theta}$ are trivial because this implies that one density always lies strictly below the other, and is not very interesting. The second case yields standard normal type asymptotics as in between the contact points one density estimate always prevails. The third case is a sort of 'boundary value case.' It is of interest because it corresponds to the case where distributions overlap perfectly over some range. This is an important case because, in some applications, the hypothesis of interest can be that the two distributions are identical (or identical over a range).

In the last case, there are binding inequality restrictions, which may be expected to induce non-normal asymptotics. ALW show the distribution theory for this latter case using the Poissonization method due to Beirlant and Mason (1995) and Giné, Mason, and Zaitsev (2003); see Section A.3 for the basic idea. It turns out that the limiting distribution of $\widehat{\theta}$ is normal after a bias correction (ALW, theorem 1), i.e.,

$$\sqrt{N} \left(\widehat{\theta} - \theta \right) - b_N \Rightarrow N(0, v),$$

where the bias b_N and asymptotic variance v depend on the contact set (6.1.4). They suggest a bias-corrected estimator along with an asymptotic variance estimator and propose an inference method for θ.

ALW apply the method to study the polarization within China in recent years, which has been an important policy issue, using a household survey data. Their multidimensional examination of urban household well-being in an internal (Shaanxi) and a coastal (Guangdong) province in China over the period of economic reforms demonstrates that the two groups of agents have bi-polarized significantly.

6.2 Generalized Functional Inequalities

Lee, Song, and Whang (2017, LSW2) propose a general method for testing inequality restrictions on general nonparametric functions such as conditional mean, quantile, hazard, and distribution functions and their derivatives. They propose a one-sided L_p-type test statistic based on nonparametric estimators of the functions. They provide a general asymptotic theory for the test statistic and suggest a bootstrap procedure to compute the critical values. They show that the test has a correct uniform asymptotic size and is not conservative when the contact set is estimated over which the inequalities are binding.

To describe their testing problem, let $v_{\tau,1}, \ldots, v_{\tau,J}$ denote nonparametric real-valued functions on $\mathbb{R}^d$ for each index $\tau \in \mathcal{T}$, where $\mathcal{T}$ is a subset of a finite dimensional space. The hypotheses of interest are

$$H_0 : v_{\tau,j}(x) \leq 0 \text{ for all } (x, \tau, j) \in \mathcal{X} \times \mathcal{T} \times \mathbb{N}_J$$
$$H_1 : v_{\tau,j}(x) > 0 \text{ for some } (x, \tau, j) \in \mathcal{X} \times \mathcal{T} \times \mathbb{N}_J,$$

where $\mathcal{X} \times \mathcal{T}$ is the domain of interest and $\mathbb{N}_J = \{1, \cdots, J\}$.

The null hypothesis is very general and encompasses many interesting restrictions. For example, it includes the *conditional stochastic dominance* hypothesis (discussed in Chapter 4) as a special case, by taking $J = 1$ and

$$v_{\tau,1}(x) := v_\tau(x) = Q_2(\tau|x) - Q_1(\tau|x),$$

where $Q_k(\tau|x) := \inf\{y : F_k(y|x) \geq \tau\}$ denotes the τ-th conditional quantile of Y_k given $X = x \in \mathbb{R}^d$ for $k = 1, 2$ and $\tau \in (0, 1) = \mathcal{T}$.

Let $\hat{Q}_k(\tau|x)$, $k = 1, 2$ be a kernel-type (local polynomial) estimator of $Q_k(\tau|x)$ and define

$$\hat{v}_\tau(x) = \hat{Q}_2(\tau|x) - \hat{Q}_1(\tau|x).$$

The test statistic of LSW2 is given by

$$\hat{\theta} = \int_{\mathcal{X} \times \mathcal{T}} \left[r_N \hat{v}_\tau(x) \right]_+^p d\mu(x, \tau), \tag{6.2.1}$$

where $p \geq 1$, $[x]_+ = \max\{x, 0\}$, $r_N = N^{1/2} h^{d/2} \to \infty$ is a normalizing sequence, and μ is a measure on $\mathcal{X} \times \mathcal{T}$ (e.g., Lebesgue measure). It turns out that the limiting distribution of $\hat{\theta}$ depends on the property of the true function $v_\tau(x)$ under the null hypothesis. In particular, it depends on the contact set over which the inequality in H_0 holds with equality.

To improve the power performance, LSW2 suggest estimating the contact set by

$$\hat{B}(c_N) := \left\{ (x, \tau) \in \mathcal{X} \times \mathcal{T} : \left| r_N \hat{v}_\tau(x) \right| \leq c_N \right\},$$

where c_N is a sequence such that $\sqrt{\log N}/c_N + c_N/r_N \to 0$. The critical values are based on the bootstrap test statistic

$$\hat{\theta}^* = \int_{\hat{B}(c_N)} \left[r_N(\hat{v}_\tau^*(x) - \hat{v}_\tau(x)) \right]_+^p d\mu(x, \tau),$$

where $\hat{v}_\tau^*(x)$ is the bootstrap counterpart of $\hat{v}_\tau(x)$. To adjust for the bias term of test statistic, one also needs to compute

$$\hat{a}^* = \int_{\hat{B}(c_N)} E^* \left[r_N(\hat{v}_\tau^*(x) - \hat{v}_\tau(x)) \right]_+^p d\mu(x, \tau),$$

where E^* denotes the expectation under the bootstrap distribution. Let c_α^* be the $(1 - \alpha)$ quantile from the bootstrap distribution of $\hat{\theta}^*$ and take

$$c_{\alpha,\eta}^* = \max\{c_\alpha^*, h^{d/2}\eta + \hat{a}^*\}$$

as the critical value, where $\eta := 10^{-3}$ is a small fixed number. Then, LSW2 suggest

Reject H_0 if $\hat{\theta} > c_{\alpha,\eta}^*$.

The following theorem shows that the test has a uniformly correct size under the null hypothesis:

Theorem 6.2.1 *Under Assumptions A1–A6 and B1–B4 of LSW2,*

$$\limsup_{N \to \infty} \ \sup_{P \in \mathcal{P}_0} \ P\left(\hat{\theta} > c_{\alpha,\eta}^* \right) \le \alpha.$$

It also shows that the test has an asymptotically exact size α under a subset of distributions satisfying the null hypothesis. They show that the test is consistent against the fixed alternative hypothesis H_1 in the sense

$$P\left(\hat{\theta} > c_{\alpha,\eta}^* \right) \to 1.$$

We now discuss the results of LSW2 in the context of testing for conditional SD hypothesis (Chapter 4). The asymptotic theory uses the Poissonization method also used by Lee and Whang (2009) (see Section 4.3.1), but is different from the latter in that LSW2 consider bootstrap critical values and establish uniform size validity of the test for a general class of nonparametric functions. Therefore, critical values of LSW2 are computationally more demanding but the LSW2 test may have better finite sample performance both in terms of size and power. Also, compared to Delgado and Escanciano (2013) and Gonzalo and Olmo (2014), who suggest critical values based on the LFC of the null hypothesis, the LSW2 test is expected to be more powerful because the critical values depend only on the binding restrictions of the null hypothesis. Finally, both LSW2 and Andrews and Shi (2017) use information on "contact sets" and hence their tests, if applicable, are more powerful than tests based on the

LFC. However, the unconditional moment representation of the conditional moments may not be directly applicable to conditional quantile functions to test conditional stochastic dominance.

As an empirical example, LSW2 apply the test to verify implications from auction models. In particular, in first-price auctions, Guerre, Perrigne, and Vuong (2009, GPV) show that the quantiles of the observed equilibrium bid distributions with different numbers of bidders should satisfy a set of inequality restrictions (equation (5) of GPV). If the auctions are heterogeneous so that the private values are affected by observed characteristics, one may consider conditionally exogenous participation with a conditional version of the restrictions.

Specifically, suppose that the number of bidders (I) can take two values, 2 and 3 (that is, $I \in \{2, 3\}$). For each τ such that $0 < \tau < 1$, let $Q_k(\tau|x)$ denote the τth conditional quantile (given $X = x$) of the observed equilibrium bid distribution when the number of bidders is $I = k$, where $k = 2, 3$. A conditional version of equation (5) of GPV (with $I_1 = 2$ and $I_2 = 3$ in their notation) provides the following testable restrictions (see also Equation 1.2.2 of Section 1.2.3):

$$
\begin{aligned}
v_{\tau,1}(x) &:= \quad Q_2(\tau|x) - Q_3(\tau|x) \leq 0, \\
v_{\tau,2}(x) &:= \underline{b} - 2Q_2(\tau|x) + Q_3(\tau|x) \leq 0,
\end{aligned}
\tag{6.2.2}
$$

for any $\tau \in (0, 1]$ and for any $x \in \mathcal{X}$, where $\mathcal{X}$ is the (common) support of X, and $\underline{b}$ is the left endpoint of the support of the observed bids. The first hypothesis for $v_{\tau,1}$ can be interpreted as the conditional stochastic dominance of the observed bid distribution with 3 bidders over that with 2 bidders, conditional on the observed auction characteristics X.

Using the timber auction data of Lu and Perrigne (2008), LSW2 test the hypotheses (6.2.2), with the appraisal value as the covariate X. Summary statistics show that average bids become higher as the number of bidders increases from 2 to 3.

A plot of estimated curves of $v_{\tau,1}(x)$, each representing a particular conditional quantile, ranging from the tenth percentile to the 90th percentile, shows that there are strictly positive values of $v_{\tau,1}(x)$ at the lower end of appraisal values. The test based on (6.2.1) can formally tell whether positive values of $v_{\tau,1}(x)$ at the lower end of appraisal values can be viewed as evidence against economic restrictions imposed by (6.2.2).

LSW2 find that, in all cases considered, the bootstrap p-values are close to 1, suggesting that positive values of $v_{\tau,1}(x)$ at the lower end of appraisal values cannot be interpreted as evidence against the null hypothesis beyond random sampling errors.[1] This implies that there are no significant empirical evidence against the economic implications imposed by (6.2.2).

---

[1] In fact, LSW2 consider test statistics to test whether the restrictions for $v_{\tau,1}$ and $v_{\tau,2}$ in (6.2.2) hold jointly.

6.3 Distributions with Measurement Errors

Measurement errors are quite common in economic and statistical data. Bound, Brown, and Mathiowetz (2001) point out that income data or household surveys such as the CPS data are inherently affected by various sources of measurement errors such as imprecise memory, difference in identities of recorders and earners, and incentives to evade taxes, etc. Chesher and Schluter (2002) study how measurement errors of various degrees can lead to bias in the estimation of poverty indexes and Gini coefficients and apply their results to regional poverty and inequality comparisons in India. See, e.g., Chen, Hong, and Nekipelov (2011) for an excellent survey of recent methods for identifying and estimating models with classical and nonclassical measurement errors.

Many of the existing empirical studies often assume away the existence of measurement errors in their data and proceed as if there were no measurement errors, or at least they were not substantial. However, sometimes this practice might lead to misleading conclusions on the underlying true distributions and hence on the main research questions.

Adusumilli, Otsu, and Whang (2017, AOW) develop a *deconvolution method* to make inferences on the latent true CDFs, with stochastic dominance hypothesis as one of their applications. To explain their main idea, suppose that we observe an i.i.d. sample $\{X_i, Y_i\}_{i=1}^{N}$ of (X, Y), generated from

$$X = X^* + \epsilon,$$
$$Y = Y^* + \delta, \tag{6.3.1}$$

where (X^*, Y^*) are unobservable variables of interest and (ϵ, δ) are measurement errors assumed to be independent of (X^*, Y^*) (i.e., they are the *classical* measurement errors). For simplicity, we shall assume that the densities (f_ϵ, f_δ) of the errors are known.[2] Let F_{X^*} and F_{Y^*} be the CDFs of X^* and Y^*, respectively. The null hypothesis of interest is given by:

$$H_0 : F_{X^*}(t) \leq F_{Y^*}(t) \quad \text{for all } t \in \mathcal{T}, \tag{6.3.2}$$

where $\mathcal{T}$ is a compact interval of interest specified by the researcher. The alternative hypothesis is the negation of H_0.

If one neglects the presence of measurement errors and tries to test H_0 using the observed data on (X, Y), then the standard SD test results can be misleading. To illustrate this point, consider the following simulation experiment: generate the model (6.3.1) with $X^* \sim N(0, 3.5)$, $Y^* \sim N(0, 3.5)$, $\epsilon \sim$ Laplace$(0, \sigma_\epsilon^2)$, and $\delta \sim$ Laplace$(0, 0.5)$. Under this design, the distributions of X^* and Y^* are equal and hence should satisfy H_0 in (6.3.2). However, as can be seen from Table 6.1, the standard BD test based on the contaminated

---

[2] When they are unknown, it is still possible to construct a valid testing procedure if repeated measurements are available; see AOW (section 3) for details.

Table 6.1 *Rejection probabilities of the BD test*
under measurement errors

n	$\sigma_\epsilon^2 = 0.5$	$\sigma_\epsilon^2 = 1.0$	$\sigma_\epsilon^2 = 2.0$	$\sigma_\epsilon^2 = 3.0$
100	0.072	0.050	0.078	0.088
250	0.049	0.054	0.082	0.148
500	0.053	0.055	0.152	0.334
1000	0.051	0.098	0.275	0.667

data (X, Y) has substantial size distortions. This motivates AOW to consider a
SD test that takes into account measurement errors explicitly.

Let $i = \sqrt{-1}$ and f^{ft} be the Fourier transform of a function f. If the
PDF f_ϵ of ϵ is known, the PDF f_{X^*} of X^* can be estimated by the so-called
deconvolution kernel density estimator (see, e.g., Stefanski and Carroll, 1990)

$$\hat{f}_{X^*}(t) = \frac{1}{Nh} \sum_{i=1}^{N} \mathbb{K}\left(\frac{t - X_i}{h}\right), \quad \text{where} \tag{6.3.3}$$

$$\mathbb{K}(u) = \frac{1}{2\pi} \int_{-1}^{1} e^{-i\omega u} \frac{K^{\text{ft}}(\omega)}{f_\epsilon^{\text{ft}}(\omega/h)} d\omega,$$

h is a bandwidth, and K is a kernel function with K^{ft} supported on $[-1, 1]$.
The asymptotic properties of $\hat{f}_{X^*}$ are well known: It is consistent under mild
assumptions, but its convergence rate depends heavily on the shape of f_ϵ,
especially the decay rate of $f_\epsilon^{\text{ft}}(t)$ as $t \to \pm\infty$.

Definition 6.3.1

(i) *A density is the Ordinary Smooth (OS) type if its Fourier transform*
satisfies: for some $\beta > 0$ and $C_2 > C_1 > 0$,

$$C_1 (1 + |t|)^{-\beta} \leq |f_\epsilon^{\text{ft}}(t)| \leq C_2 (1 + |t|)^{-\beta} \text{ for all } t \in \mathbb{R}.$$

(ii) *A density is the Super Smooth (SS) type if its Fourier transform*
satisfies, for some $\lambda > 0$, $C_2 > C_1 > 0$, and $d_1 > d_2 > 0$,

$$C_1 |\omega|^{\lambda_0} \exp(-d_1 |t|^\lambda) \leq |f_\epsilon^{\text{ft}}(t)| \leq C_2 |\omega|^{\lambda_0} \exp(-d_2 |t|^\lambda)$$

for all $t \in \mathbb{R}$.

Examples of the OS type include Laplace and gamma distributions, while
normal and Cauchy distributions are examples of the SS type. Under the OS
errors, $\hat{f}_{X^*}$ typically converges at a polynomial rate. However, under the SS
errors, $\hat{f}_{X^*}$ typically converges at a log rate, which is much slower.

If f_ϵ is symmetric, then integration of $\hat{f}_{X^*}$ yields the following estimator
for the CDF F_{X^*} of X^*.

$$\hat{F}_{X^*}(t) = \frac{1}{2} + \frac{1}{N} \sum_{i=1}^{N} \mathbb{L}\left(\frac{t - X_i}{h}\right), \quad \text{where} \tag{6.3.4}$$

$$\mathbb{L}(u) = \frac{1}{2\pi} \int_{-1}^{1} \frac{\sin(\omega u)}{\omega} \frac{K^{\text{ft}}(\omega)}{f_\epsilon^{\text{ft}}(\omega/h)} d\omega,$$

and likewise for F_{Y^*} of Y^* (Hall and Lahiri (2008)).

To test (6.3.2), consider a supremum-type test based on the deconvolution CDF estimators:

$$D_N = \sup_{t \in \mathcal{T}} \left[\hat{F}_{X^*}(t) - \hat{F}_{Y^*}(t)\right],$$

where $\hat{F}_{X^*}$ and $\hat{F}_{Y^*}$ are defined as in (6.3.4) using observations $\{X_i\}_{i=1}^{N_1}$ and $\{Y_i\}_{i=1}^{N_2}$ on X and Y, respectively, and $N = N_1 + N_2$. (It is assumed that the two samples are independently drawn, but this assumption can be easily extended to the case of paired samples.) In practice, the bandwidth h needs to be chosen. AOW suggest a bandwidth selection method based on the method of Bissantz, Dümbgen, Holzmann, and Munk (2007, section 5.2).

To approximate the critical values, AOW suggest considering the recentered bootstrap test statistic:

$$D_N^\# = \sup_{t \in \mathcal{T}} \left[\hat{F}_{X^*}^\#(t) - \hat{F}_{Y^*}^\#(t) - \{\hat{F}_{X^*}(t) - \hat{F}_{Y^*}(t)\}\right],$$

where $\hat{F}_{X^*}^\#$ and $\hat{F}_{Y^*}^\#$ are computed as in (6.3.4) using nonparametric bootstrap resamples $\{X_i^\#\}_{i=1}^{N_1}$ and $\{Y_i^\#\}_{i=1}^{N_2}$ from $\{X_i\}_{i=1}^{N_1}$ and $\{Y_i\}_{i=1}^{N_2}$, respectively.

Let $\hat{c}_\alpha^D$ denote the $(1 - \alpha)$ quantile of the bootstrap statistic $D_N^\#$. Then, the bootstrap test is asymptotically valid in the sense that, under H_0,

$$P\left(D_N > \hat{c}_\alpha^D\right) \le \alpha + \varrho_N, \tag{6.3.5}$$

for some positive sequence $\varrho_N = O(N^{-c})$ (under OS errors) or $\varrho_N = O((\log N)^{-c})$ (under SS errors) with $c > 0$, provided $N_1/(N_1 + N_2) \to \lambda \in (0, 1)$ as $N_1, N_2 \to \infty$. On the other hand, under the alternative H_1 (i.e., H_0 is false), the test is consistent in the sense that

$$P\left(D_N > \hat{c}_\alpha^D\right) \to 1.$$

AOW apply the deconvolution-based SD test to compare the income distributions of Korea between 2006 and 2012 across various age groups. They consider the null hypotheses of SD for five different age groups. Their findings are as follows: for age groups 25–45 and 45–65, the 2012 income (first- and second-order) dominates the 2006 income. However, for age group 70 and over, the 2006 income (first- and second-order) dominates the 2012 income. This is consistent with the recent empirical findings that the welfare status of the retirement age group is worsening. The results of the standard BD test and the AOW test are significantly different in the case of FSD (for age group 60 and over) and SSD (for age group 65 and over). This implies that one may need to explicitly consider the presence of measurement errors to draw sensible conclusions on true latent income distributions.

6.4 Stochastic Dominance Tests with Many Covariates

In a variety of applications, there are many covariates (whose dimension may grow to infinity as the sample size diverges) that are potentially related to the distribution of a variable of interest. In this case, it is not practical to apply the conditional stochastic dominance tests discussed in Section 4.3 with all of the covariates, due to the well-known curse of dimensionality problem in fully nonparametric methods.

For example, in comparing the distributions of the US sectoral portfolios distributions, Gonzalo and Olmo (2014, Section 4.3.3) apply their test to US sectoral portfolios conditional on the dynamics of market portfolio. They assume that the information set at a given time contains only the excess return on the market portfolio. However, in practice, the sectoral portfolios could be potentially well predicted by many factors other than the market portfolio and we are often not sure about the identity of the relevant factors. In this case, it is reasonable to select the relevant factors first based on the sample information and proceed to the conditional stochastic dominance test using the (low-dimensional) selected factors (or covariates).

Linton, Seo, and Whang (2017, LSW3) propose a test of conditional stochastic dominance hypothesis with *many* covariates using the tools for high-dimensional sparse models. Below we briefly introduce the main idea of LSW3.

Let $\{(Y_{1,i}, Y_{2,i}, Q_i) \in \mathbb{R}^{d+2} : i \geq 1\}$ denote a strictly stationary and β-mixing $(d+2)$-dimensional time series process, where the dimension d of Q_i may be potentially large. The null hypothesis of interest is given by[3]

$$H_0 : P\left(Y_{1,i} \leq y | \mathcal{F}_{i-1}\right) \leq P\left(Y_{2,i} \leq y | \mathcal{F}_{i-1}\right) \text{ for all } y \in \mathbb{R}, \quad (6.4.1)$$

where $\mathcal{F}_{i-1}$ is the information set observed at time $i - 1$. The alternative hypothesis is the negation of H_0. The dimension of the available information $\mathcal{F}_{i-1}$ is allowed to be large, but it can be reduced to the most essential components, whose dimension, nevertheless, is allowed to grow with the sample size.

The approach of LSW3 is based on the following model (for each $k = 1, 2$):

$$Y_{k,i} = g^k(Q_i) + \sigma^k(Q_i)\varepsilon_{k,i}, \ i = 1, \ldots, N, \quad (6.4.2)$$

---

[3] Extension to higher-order stochastic dominance is straightforward.

where $g^k(\cdot)$ and $\sigma^k(\cdot)$ are unknown real-valued functions and the innovation $\{\varepsilon_{k,i} : i \geq 1\}$ is a strictly stationary sequence with the common distribution F^k, which is continuously differentiable with bounded derivative f^k and whose first moment is zero. The function σ^k is assumed to be bounded away from zero. Assume that $\{\varepsilon_{k,i}\}$ and $\{Q_i\}$ are mutually independent. Then, the conditional distribution of $Y_{k,i}$ given Q_i is characterized by the distribution of $\varepsilon_{k,i}$, that is,

$$F^k(y|q) := P\left(Y_{k,i} \leq y | Q_i = q\right) = F^k\left(\frac{y - g^k(q)}{\sigma^k(q)}\right) \tag{6.4.3}$$

for all $y \in \mathbb{R}$ and $q \in \mathbb{R}^d$.

Let

$$X_i := \left(X_{i,1}, \ldots, X_{i,p}\right)^\mathsf{T} := \left(X_{i,1}(Q_i), \ldots, X_{i,p}(Q_i)\right)^\mathsf{T}$$

denote a $p = p_N$ dimensional vector that contains transformations of Q_i, including a constant. For example, the vector X_i can be composed of various interactions, their dummies, polynomials, B-splines, and even interactions of the basic series transformations. The dimension p of X_i is potentially huge because the dimension d of Q_i itself may be high or the number of the basis transformations that are employed may be big. Let $|a|_0$ denote the number of nonzero components of a vector a.

One of the key assumptions to deal with the high dimensional model is that the function g^k satisfies the approximate sparsity assumption, which demands that the true regression function $g^k(\cdot)$ can be well approximated by at most s^k series terms up to approximation error $r_{Y,i}^k = g^k(Q_i) - X_i^\mathsf{T}\beta_0^k$, whose size is bounded by $o_p\left(N^{-1/2}\right)$. However, the identity of those terms is unknown and may not be unique. Also, the variance function $\sigma^k(Q_i)$ is assumed to satisfy an analogous approximate sparsity assumption. For brevity, we shall discuss below only the homoskedastic case $\sigma^k(q) = 1$.

To estimate the true conditional CDF (6.4.3), the unknown functions F^k and g^k should be estimated first. Let $\hat{g}^k$ be an estimator of g^k (to be defined below). Then, the distribution function F^k of $\varepsilon_{k,i}$ can be estimated by the empirical CDF of the estimated residuals $\hat{\varepsilon}_{k,i} = Y_{k,i} - \hat{g}^k(Q_i), i = 1, \ldots, N$.

To estimate g^k under the sparsity assumption, the Lasso estimator (Tibshirani, 1996) can be used. Specifically, the coefficient vector β_0^k is estimated by minimizing the ℓ_1-penalized least squares, with penalty varying for each element in β:

$$\hat{\beta}_{Lasso}^k := \arg\min_\beta \frac{1}{N} \sum_{i=1}^{N} \left|Y_{k,i} - X_i^\mathsf{T}\beta\right|_2^2 + \lambda^k |D\beta|_1, \tag{6.4.4}$$

where D is a weighting matrix and $\lambda^k \to 0$ is a tuning parameter.

To prevent overfitting of the model, LSW3 suggest using a post-Lasso procedure, in particular the Thresholded Lasso (Tasso) with refitting. Let

$$\hat{S}^k = \left\{ l : \left| \hat{\beta}^k_{Lasso,l} \right| > \lambda^k_{thr}, \ l = 1, \ldots, p \right\}, \tag{6.4.5}$$

where the threshold λ^k_{thr} satisfies the lower bound $\lambda^k s^k = o\left(\lambda_{thr}\right)$. Since a deviation bound for $\left| \hat{\beta}^k_{Lasso} - \beta^k_0 \right|_\infty$ is $O_p\left(\lambda s\right)$, the thresholding makes $\hat{S}^k$ select only the relatively significant variables. After the selection, re-estimate β^k_0 by the OLS. That is, the thresholded Lasso estimator is defined to be

$$\hat{\beta}^k_{Tasso} = \arg \min_{\beta : \beta_l = 0, l \notin \hat{S}^k} \sum_{i=1}^N \left(Y_{k,i} - X_i^\top \beta \right)^2.$$

The final estimator $\hat{g}^k$ of the unknown function g^k is now given by

$$\hat{g}^k\left(Q_i\right) = X_i^\top \hat{\beta}^k_{Tasso} = \left(\hat{X}_i^k \right)^\top \hat{\beta}^k, \tag{6.4.6}$$

where $\hat{X}_i^k = X_{i,\hat{S}^k}$.

Under the model (6.4.2) (with $\sigma^k(\cdot) = 1$), the hypothesis (6.4.1) can be equivalently stated as

$$H_0 : F^1\left(y - g^1\left(q\right) \right) \le F^2\left(y - g^2\left(q\right) \right) \text{ for all } (y,q). \tag{6.4.7}$$

LSW3 suggest a supremum-type test statistic. It can be constructed using the following steps:

1. Let $\hat{S}^k$ denote the support of $\hat{\beta}^k_{Tasso}$ defined in (6.4.5) and let $\tilde{S} = \hat{S}^1 \cup \hat{S}^2$. Define $\tilde{X}_i = X_{i,\tilde{S}}$, i.e., the collection of selected elements of X_i in at least one of the two regressions. Likewise, let S denote the collection of indices for the relevant variables in at least one of the two regressions and $X_i := X_{i,S}$.

2. Let $\tilde{\beta}^k$ denote the OLS estimate in the regression of $Y_{k,i}$ on $\tilde{X}_i$ and compute the residual $\tilde{\varepsilon}_{k,i} = Y_{k,i} - \left(\tilde{X}_i \right)^\top \tilde{\beta}^k$, and its empirical distribution function

$$\hat{F}^k\left(\tau\right) = \frac{1}{N} \sum_{i=1}^N \mathbf{1}\left(\tilde{\varepsilon}_{k,i} \le \tau \right).$$

3. Construct the test statistic

$$T_N = \sqrt{N} \sup_{y,q} \left\{ \hat{F}^1\left(y - \tilde{X}\left(q\right)^\top \tilde{\beta}^1 \right) - \hat{F}^2\left(y - \tilde{X}\left(q\right)^\top \tilde{\beta}^2 \right) \right\},$$

$$\tag{6.4.8}$$

where $\tilde{X}\left(q\right) = X_{\tilde{S}}\left(q\right)$.

LSW3 (theorem 6) show that, under the least favorable case of the null hypothesis, T_N converges weakly to a Gaussian process. However, the distribution is not pivotal and the critical values cannot be tabulated. They suggest a smoothed stationary bootstrap procedure by combining the ideas of Politis and Romano (1994b) and Neumeyer (2009). They show that the test based on the smoothed bootstrap critical values has an asymptotically correct size and is consistent against the fixed alternative.

LSW3 apply the method to compare the US and the Global equity returns, in order to investigate the home bias puzzle in a conditional context. They find that the conditional dominance of the US series over the global series is rejected at the 5% level of significance, except for the periods of 1992–4, 2004–6, and 2008–12.

6.5 Robust Forecasting Comparisons

The standard forecast comparison based on forecast errors depends on the choice of loss functions, which are usually defined in terms of *moments* of forecast error, e.g., mean squared forecast error or mean absolute forecast error.

Jin, Corradi, and Swanson (2016, JCS) suggest a forecast comparison method that compares the *entire distributions* of forecast errors. In particular, they introduced the notion of *general-loss (GL) forecast superiority* and *convex-loss (CL) forecast superiority*, which are essentially generalizations of first-order and second-order stochastic dominance, respectively. Their method is an out-of-sample generalization of the tests introduced by Linton, Maasoumi, and Whang (2005) (Section 2.2.2).[4]

Let $\mathcal{L}_C$ be the class of nonnegative loss functions L with $L(e) = 0$ if $e = 0$ and $L'(e)sgn(e) \geq 0$ for all $e \in \mathbb{R}$, where $sgn(x) = 1$ if $x \geq 0$ and $sgn(x) = -1$ if $x < 0$. Then, we say e_1 Generalized-Loss (GL) outperforms e_2 if

$$EL(e_1) \leq EL(e_2) \; \forall L \in \mathcal{L}_C.$$

This condition is equivalent to the bi-directional stochastic dominance:

$$G_{2,1}(x) = (F_2(x) - F_1(x))\,sgn(x) \leq 0 \; \forall x \in \mathcal{X},$$

where F_1 and F_2 denote the distributions of e_1 and e_2, respectively. This definition can be straightforwardly extended to convex-loss forecast superiority by further restricting L to be a convex function.

Now, suppose that there are l sets of forecasts to be ranked with corresponding sequences of forecast errors $\{e_{1t}\}, \ldots, \{e_{lt}\}$. Then, the null hypothesis of interest is that e_1 GL outperforms e_k for $k = 2, \ldots, l$, i.e.,

---

[4] See also Pinar, Stengos, and Yazgan (2012) for another approach of using the concept of stochastic dominance efficiency in optimal forecast problems, and Corradi and Swanson (2013) for a survey of the related literature.

$$H_0 : \max_{k=2,\ldots,l} \sup_{x \in \mathcal{X}^+} G_{k,1}(x) \leq 0 \text{ and } \max_{k=2,\ldots,l} \sup_{x \in \mathcal{X}^-} G_{k,1}(x) \leq 0.$$

The alterative hypothesis is the negation of H_0.

JCS propose a Kolmogorov–Smirnov test of H_0 based on the empirical CDFs of estimated forecast errors. They suggest a stationary bootstrap procedure to compute critical values and apply it to evaluate forecast errors from two sets of forecast models for spot exchange rates among six industrialized countries.

7 Conclusions

This book discusses econometric methods for stochastic dominance and related concepts. Since the early work of McFadden (1989), the related literature has been expanding quite rapidly over the past decades. One of the main reasons is that stochastic dominance is a fundamental concept in decision theory under uncertainty. Also, it often yields interesting testable implications from economic theory in many different contexts and is closely linked to the structural interpretation of econometric models, whose importance has been well recognized in economics. Another reason is that there have been important technical advances in statistical inference methods, which can be directly applied to stochastic dominance. Stochastic dominance is a set of inequality relations that may hold between distribution functions. Since a distribution function may take different values over an interval, the number of inequalities to be compared is large (usually infinite), and hence the inference method can be complicated. It turns out that the inference problem is closely related to the partial identification/moment inequality literature, which also has been very popular in econometrics in recent years. Therefore, the newly developed methods for the latter can be readily extended to do inference on stochastic dominance (of course, after some modifications).

What would be the future directions for econometric research on stochastic dominance? The answer will be inevitably subjective and let me mention a few topics that might be worth considering.

1. **Choice of Test Statistics**: There are many alternative tests available for a given stochastic dominance hypothesis, but not enough practical guidance is provided to the researchers regarding the choice of the testing procedure. There are many different notions of efficiency for nonparametric tests and it is unlikely that there exists one test that has an absolute advantage over the other tests. However, it would be useful if one can suggest reasonable criteria to choose a testing procedure; see Armstrong (2018) for a related study in the context of finite dimensional parameters.

2. **Power Improvements**: Many of the existing SD tests are based on the least favorable cases of the null hypotheses to compute critical values. However, as we discussed before, those tests can be too conservative in practice. It would be possible to improve power performances by adopting the approaches of Section 3.1 or by suggesting a better approach.

3. **Choice of Tuning Parameters**: Some of the nonparametric tests discussed in this book require a choice of tuning parameters, such as the bandwidth or the parameters needed to estimate the contact set, etc. It is a challenging issue how to choose the parameters "optimally" in some sense, because they typically do not affect the first-order asymptotic distribution. However, it might be possible to consider higher-order asymptotic approximations to find a reasonable way of choosing the parameters; see Gao and Gijbels (2008) for a related study in the context of a nonparametric goodness-of-fit test problem.

4. **General Sampling Schemes**: Many of the existing SD tests assume i.i.d. observations. This assumption can be restrictive, for example in financial applications. It would be useful to relax the assumption to cover various types of data, such as time series, panel, network, or continuous time data, etc.

5. **High-Dimensional Distributional Relations**: Economic variables are often thought to be determined jointly by a system of interdependent relations. In practice, however, there are too many potential variables, and it is not easy to exactly identify the relevant ones. Also, there is a lot of uncertainty about the form of dependency among variables. In view of this, some of the recently developed methods for high-dimensional models and machine learning appear to be promising to study the distributional relations among economic variables; see Section 6.4 for a pilot study.

This book intends to give an overview of statistical inference methods for stochastic dominance and related concepts in a unified framework. However, there is an extensive amount of research in this area, and there must be many important topics left uncovered. I hope that I can address them in a future revision of this book.

Appendix A Basic Technical Tools

In this appendix, we summarize some of the basic tools and concepts of the empirical process methods used in the main text. More details can be found from van der Vaart and Wellner (1996, VW), van der Vaart (1998), Andrews (1994), and Davidson (1994). We also explain the main idea of the Poissonization method.

A.1 A Probability Background

Definition A.1.1 *A class $\mathcal{A}$ of subsets of Ω is a σ-field if (i) $\Omega \in \mathcal{A}$; (ii) if $A \in \mathcal{A}$, then $A^c \in \mathcal{A}$; (iii) if $A_n \in \mathcal{A}$ for each $n = 1, 2, \ldots$, then $\cup_{n=1}^{\infty} A_n \in \mathcal{A}$.*

Definition A.1.2 *Let $(\Omega, \mathcal{A})$ be a measurable space. A real valued function $\mathbb{P}$ on $\mathcal{A}$ is a probability measure if (i) $\mathbb{P}(A) \geq 0$ for each $A \in \mathcal{A}$; (ii) $\mathbb{P}(\Omega) = 1$; (iii) $\mathbb{P}\left(\cup_{n=1}^{\infty} A_n\right) = \sum_{n=1}^{\infty} \mathbb{P}(A_n)$ for any disjoint sequence $\{A_n\}_{n=1}^{\infty}$ in $\mathcal{A}$.*

The collection $(\Omega, \mathcal{A}, \mathbb{P})$ is called a *probability space*. The Borel σ-field on $\mathbb{R}$ is the smallest collection of sets (called the *Borel sets*) generated by all the open (or closed) intervals of $\mathbb{R}$.

Definition A.1.3 *Let $(\Omega, \mathcal{A})$ be a measurable space. A function $X : \Omega \to \mathbb{R}$ is a random variable if it is an $\mathcal{A}$-measurable function, that is for any Borel set B, $\{\omega \in \Omega : X(\omega) \in B\} \in \mathcal{A}$.*

Definition A.1.4 *A collection of random variables $\{X_t : t \in \mathbb{T}\}$ defined on the same probability space $(\Omega, \mathcal{A}, \mathbb{P})$ is called a stochastic process indexed by $\mathbb{T}$.*

Letting $X = \{X_t : t \in \mathbb{T}\}$, we may think of X as a mapping

$$X : \Omega \times \mathbb{T} \to \mathbb{R}.$$

If we fix $t \in \mathbb{T}$, $X(\cdot, t) = X_t$ is a random variable, i.e., an $\mathcal{A}$-measurable function from $\Omega \mapsto \mathbb{R}$. If we fix $\omega \in \Omega$, then $X(\omega, \cdot)$ defines a function from

$\mathbb{T} \mapsto \mathbb{R}$, which is called the *sample path* of the process X at ω. So we can think of a stochastic process X as a random function whose realizations are the sample paths, i.e., a random variable taking values in the space of functions from $\mathbb{T} \mapsto \mathbb{R}$.

Definition A.1.5 *Let* $(\Omega, \mathcal{A})$ *and* $(S, \mathcal{S})$ *be measurable spaces. An S-valued random variable is an $\mathcal{A}/\mathcal{S}$-measurable function from Ω into S.*

Definition A.1.6 *A function* $d : S \times S \to \mathbb{R}_+$ *is a metric on S if for all* $x, y, z \in S$, *(i)* $d(x, y) = d(y, x)$; *(ii)* $d(x, z) \leq d(x, y) + d(y, z)$; *(iii)* $d(x, y) = 0$ *if and only if* $x = y$.

We call the pair (S, d) a *metric space*. *Pseudo-metric* is the one with properties (i) and (ii) but not necessarily (iii).

Example A.1 Take $S = \mathbb{R}^q$ for some $q \geq 1$. An S-valued random variable is a q-dimensional random vector. We usually take d to be the *Euclidean metric*:

$$d(x, y) = \left(\sum_{i=1}^{q} (x_i - y_i)^2 \right)^{1/2}.$$

Let $\mathbb{T}$ be an index set and denote $\mathcal{G}$ to be the collection of functions from $\mathbb{T}$ into $\mathbb{R}$. Take

$$S = l^\infty (\mathbb{T}) := \{ f \in \mathcal{G} : \sup_{t \in \mathbb{T}} |f(t)| < \infty \},$$

i.e., the collection of real-valued functions on $\mathbb{T}$ with bounded sample paths. We can take d to be the *uniform metric*:

$$d(f, g) = \sup_{t \in \mathbb{T}} |f(t) - g(t)| := \| f - g \|_\infty \text{ for } f, g \in l^\infty (\mathbb{T}).$$

Example A.2 (*Uniform Empirical Process*) Suppose that $W_1, W_2, \ldots, W_N$ are i.i.d. $U(0, 1)$. Define

$$X_N(\omega, t) := X_N(t) := \frac{1}{\sqrt{N}} \sum_{i=1}^{N} [1(W_i(\omega) \leq t) - t], \text{ for } t \in \mathbb{T} = [0, 1].$$

For each $t \in \mathbb{T}$, $X_N(t)$ is distributed as $N^{-1/2}[B(N, t) - Nt]$, where $B(n, p)$ denotes the binary distribution with parameters n and p. The sample path is piecewise linear with jump discontinuities at N points $(W_1(\omega), \ldots, W_N(\omega))$. X_N is a random element of the space $D[0, 1]$ of all real-valued *cadlag* (continue à droite, limites à gauche) functions on $[0, 1]$. Note that

$$E(X_N(t)) = 0,$$
$$Var(X_N(t)) = t(1 - t),$$
$$Cov(X_N(t), X_N(s)) = min\{t, s\} - ts.$$

How does X_N behave as $N \to \infty$? By a central limit theorem (CLT), for each $t \in \mathbb{T}$, $X_N(t) \Rightarrow N(0, t(1-t))$. Also, for $t < s$,

$$\begin{pmatrix} X_N(t) \\ X_N(s) \end{pmatrix} \Rightarrow N \left(\begin{pmatrix} 0 \\ 0 \end{pmatrix}, \begin{pmatrix} t(1-t) & t(1-s) \\ t(1-s) & s(1-s) \end{pmatrix} \right).$$

Generally, the finite-dimensional distribution of $(X_N(t_1), \dots, X_N(t_k))^\mathsf{T}$ converges in distribution to that of a *Brownian bridge*. However, there are many properties of a random function that are not determined by its finite dimensional distributions, so we need a more general definition of convergence in distribution for random functions. In fact, we can show that the distribution of X_N *converges weakly* to a Brownian bridge.

Definition A.1.7 *We call a stochastic process $\mathcal{B}$ a Brownian bridge if (i) $\mathcal{B}(0) = \mathcal{B}(1) = 0$ and $\mathcal{B}$ has continuous sample paths; (ii) for any k and any $(t_1, \dots, t_k)$, $(\mathcal{B}(t_1) \dots \mathcal{B}(t_k))^\mathsf{T}$ follows a multivariate normal distribution with mean zero and covariance $Cov(\mathcal{B}(t_i), \mathcal{B}(t_j)) = min\{t_i, t_j\} - t_i t_j, \forall i, j$.*

The Brownian bridge $\mathcal{B}$ is a special version of a Gaussian process.

Definition A.1.8 *A stochastic process $\{X_t : t \in \mathbb{T}\}$ is called Gaussian if for each $k \in \mathbb{N} := \{1, 2, 3, \dots\}$ and $\{t_1, \dots, t_k\} \subseteq \mathbb{T}$, the random vector $(X_{t_1}, \dots, X_{t_k})^\mathsf{T}$ has a multivariate normal distribution.*

Let $(X_N)_{N=1}^\infty$ and X be S-valued random variables taking values in a metric space (S, d).

Definition A.1.9 *We say X_N converges weakly (or in distribution, or in law) to X, written as $X_N \Rightarrow X$ (or $X_N \rightsquigarrow X$), if for every bounded continuous function $f : S \mapsto \mathbb{R}$, $Ef(X_N) \to Ef(X)$.*

There are many equivalent ways to define the weak convergence (Portmanteau theorem; see van der Vaart, 1998, lemma 2.2). One equivalent definition only requires the function f to be bounded and Lipschitz.[1]

Definition A.1.10 *A metric space (S, d) is separable if it has a countable dense subset.*

Theorem A.1.1 *(Almost Sure Representation): Suppose that (S, d) is a separable metric space. Let $(X_N)_{N=1}^\infty$ and X be S-valued random variables. Then, $X_N \Rightarrow X$ if there exist random variables $(\tilde{X}_N)_{N=1}^\infty$ and $\tilde{X}$, possibly defined on a different probability space, such that $\tilde{X}_N \sim X_N$, $\tilde{X} \sim X$, and $\tilde{X}_N \to_{a.s.} \tilde{X}$. (Here "$\sim$" denotes "has the same distribution as.")*

---

[1] A function $f : S \longmapsto \mathbb{R}$ is *Lipschitz* if there exists some $K > 0$ such that $|f(x) - f(y)| \leq K d(x, y)$ for all $x, y \in S$.

Example A.3 Let $U \sim U(0, 1)$ be a uniform random variable defined on a probability space $(\tilde{\Omega}, \mathcal{A}, \tilde{P})$, where $\tilde{\Omega} = [0, 1]$. Define $\tilde{X}_N(\omega) = F_N^{-1}(U(\omega))$ and $\tilde{X}(\omega) = F^{-1}(U(\omega))$ $\forall \omega \in \tilde{\Omega}$, where F_N and F denote the CDF of X_N and X, respectively, and

$$G^{-1}(u) = \inf\{x \in \mathbb{R} : G(x) \geq u\} \text{ for } u \in (0, 1)$$

denotes the inverse function for G $(= F_N$ or $F)$. By construction, $\tilde{X}_N$ is defined on a probability space different from that of X_N, but $\tilde{X}_N$ has the same distribution as X_N because for each $x \in \mathbb{R}$

$$
\begin{aligned}
P\left(\tilde{X}_N \leq x\right) &= P\left(F_N^{-1}(U) \leq x\right) \\
&= P\left(U \leq F_N(x)\right) \\
&= F_N(x) \\
&= P\left(X_N \leq x\right).
\end{aligned}
$$

Similarly, $\tilde{X}$ has the same distribution as X. If $F_N(x)$ converges to $F(x)$ at each continuity point x of F, then its inverse function $F_N^{-1}(u)$ also converges to $F^{-1}(u)$ at each continuity point u of F^{-1}. Since F^{-1} is nondecreasing on $(0, 1)$, it has at most countably many discontinuities. This implies that $\tilde{X}_N$ converges to $\tilde{X}$ almost surely; see Billingsley (1995, proof of theorem 25.6) for a rigorous proof.

Theorem A.1.2 *(Continuous Mapping Theorem, CMT): Let (S, d) and (T, ρ) be separable metric spaces. Let X_N and X be S-valued random variables. Let $f : S \mapsto T$ be a function such that $\mathbb{P}\{\omega \in \Omega : f \text{ is discontinuous at } X(\omega)\} = 0$. If $X_N \Rightarrow X$, then $f(X_N) \Rightarrow f(X)$.*

A.2 Empirical Processes

A.2.1 Independent Observations

Let $\{X_i\}_{i=1}^N$ be a real valued random sample. Let P and F denote the distribution and CDF of X_i, respectively, i.e.,

$$F(x) = \mathbb{P}(-\infty, x] = P(X_i \leq x).$$

Definition A.2.1 *A dirac measure is a measure δ_z on a set $\mathcal{Z}$ (with any σ-field of subsets of $\mathcal{Z}$) such that, for a given $z \in \mathcal{Z}$ and any (measurable) set $A \subseteq \mathcal{Z}$,*

$$\delta_z(A) := \mathbf{1}_A(z) = \begin{cases} 0 & z \notin A \\ 1 & z \in A \end{cases}.$$

Definition A.2.2 *The empirical CDF of the sample* $\{X_i\}_{i=1}^{N}$ *is defined by*

$$\bar{F}_N(x) := \frac{1}{N} \sum_{i=1}^{N} 1(X_i \leq x)$$

$$= \frac{1}{N} \sum_{i=1}^{N} \delta_{X_i}((-\infty, x]) = \mathbb{P}_N(-\infty, x],$$

where $\mathbb{P}_N = \frac{1}{N} \sum_{i=1}^{N} \delta_{X_i}$ *denotes the empirical measure.*

Theorem A.2.1 *(Glivenko–Cantelli): We have*

$$\sup_{x \in \mathbb{R}} \left| \bar{F}_N(x) - F(x) \right| \rightarrow_{a.s.} 0.$$

This theorem can be equivalently stated as

$$\sup_{f \in \mathcal{F}} |\mathbb{P}_N f - P f| \rightarrow_{a.s.} 0, \qquad (A.2.1)$$

where $\mathcal{F} = \left\{ \mathbf{1}_{(-\infty, x]} : x \in \mathbb{R} \right\}$, i.e., $\mathbb{P}_N$ converges to P uniformly over the family $\mathcal{F}$ of indicator functions of half real lines. In fact, this property holds for more general classes of functions. Whenever Equation A.2.1 holds for a class of functions $\mathcal{F}$, we call $\mathcal{F}$ a *Glivenko–Cantelli class*.

By a CLT for i.i.d. random variables, if $Ef(X_i)^2 < \infty$, we have

$$\mathbb{G}_N f \Rightarrow N\left(0, Pf^2 - (Pf)^2\right),$$

where

$$\mathbb{G}_N = \sqrt{N}\left(\mathbb{P}_N - P\right). \qquad (A.2.2)$$

We call $\{\mathbb{G}_N f : f \in \mathcal{F}\}$ an *empirical process indexed by* $\mathcal{F}$. We can think of $\mathbb{G}_N$ as an abstract random variable taking values in the space of functions defined on $\mathcal{F}$. Let

$$l^\infty(\mathcal{F}) = \left\{ L : \mathcal{F} \to \mathbb{R} : \sup_{f \in \mathcal{F}} |L(f)| < \infty \right\}$$

denote the space of bounded functions defined on $\mathcal{F}$. We equip the space $l^\infty(\mathcal{F})$ with the uniform metric $\|\cdot\|_\infty$. Now, $\mathbb{G}_N$ can be considered as an $l^\infty(\mathcal{F})$-valued random variable. If $\mathbb{G}_N$ converges weakly (to a tight limit process) in this abstract space $l^\infty(\mathcal{F})$, then the class $\mathcal{F}$ is called a *Donsker Class*.[2]

---

[2] When $\mathcal{F}$ is uncountable, the empirical process $\mathbb{G}_N$ may not be Borel measurable in $(l^\infty(F), \|\cdot\|_\infty)$. Therefore, in this case, Definition A.1.9 may not be directly applicable. One way to resolve the measurability issue is to introduce outer-expectations; see VW for details. For simplicity, however, we do not stress measurability issues in this appendix.

All Donsker classes are Glivenko–Cantelli classes, but the converse is not true. Examples of the Donsker class include the class of indicator functions

$$\mathcal{F} = \{\mathbf{1}_{(-\infty, \, x]} : x \in \mathbb{R}\}.$$

Theorem A.2.2 *(Classical Donsker): The process* $N^{1/2} \left(\bar{F}_N(\cdot) - F(\cdot) \right)$ *converges weakly to a mean zero Gaussian process* v *with* $Ev(t)v(s) = F (\min\{t, s\}) - F(t)F(s)$.

The limiting Gaussian process in the above theorem is called an *F-Brownian bridge* (denoted as $\mathcal{B}(F)$). In the special case when F is the CDF of $U[0, 1]$, it is called a *standard Brownian bridge* (denoted as $\mathcal{B}$).

The Glivenko–Cantelli theorem (functional or uniform LLN) and the Donsker theorem (functional CLT) are concerned with a family of functions $\mathcal{F}$. If $\mathcal{F}$ contains only finitely many elements, then it is both Glivenko–Cantelli (by SLLN) and Donsker (by CLT). But as $\mathcal{F}$ becomes more complex, then it is more difficult to show the functional limit theorems.

The complexity of $\mathcal{F}$ can be quantified with a concept called *entropy*. Let $\|\cdot\|$ be a norm on $\mathcal{F}$ and $\varepsilon > 0$.

Definition A.2.3 *The covering number* $N(\varepsilon, \mathcal{F}, \|\cdot\|)$ *is defined to be the smallest number of* ε-*balls to cover* $\mathcal{F}$. *The entropy is* $\log N(\varepsilon, \mathcal{F}, \|\cdot\|)$.

Definition A.2.4 *Given two functions* l *and* u, *the bracket* $[l, u]$ *is the set of all functions* f *with* $l \leq f \leq u$. *An* ε-*bracket is a bracket* $[l, u]$ *with* $\|u - l\| < \varepsilon$. *The bracketing number* $N_{[]}(\varepsilon, \mathcal{F}, \|\cdot\|)$ *is the minimum number of* ε-*brackets needed to cover* $\mathcal{F}$. *The entropy with bracketing is* $\log N_{[]}(\varepsilon, \mathcal{F}, \|\cdot\|)$.

Roughly speaking, $\mathcal{F}$ is Glivenko–Cantelli if the entropy is finite for each $\varepsilon > 0$. However, the Donsker property requires more: When ε decreases to 0, the entropy should not increase too fast.

Definition A.2.5 *Let* $\mathbb{T}$ *be an arbitrary index set and* $\{Y_N\}_{N>1}$ *be a sequence of* $l^\infty (\mathbb{T})$-*valued random variables. We say that* $\{Y_N\}_{N \geq 1}$ *is asymptotically tight if for all* $\varepsilon > 0$, *there exists some compact* $K \subseteq l^\infty (\mathbb{T})$ *such that for all* $\delta > 0$

$$\liminf_{N \to \infty} \mathbb{P} \left(Y_N \in K^\delta \right) \geq 1 - \varepsilon,$$

where $K^\delta = \{y \in l^\infty (\mathbb{T}) : d(y, K) < \delta\}$ *and* d *is the uniform metric.*

Definition A.2.6 *A metric space* $(\mathbb{T}, d)$ *is totally bounded if for all* $\varepsilon > 0$, *there exists* $m \in \mathbb{N}$ *and* $\{t_i : i = 1, \ldots, m\} \subseteq \mathbb{T}$ *such that* $\mathbb{T}$ *is covered by the* ε-*balls centered at* t_i, $1 \leq i \leq m$.

The following theorem gives sufficient conditions for asymptotic tightness (theorem 1.5.7 of VW):

Theorem A.2.3 *A sequence* $\{Y_N\}_{N\geq 1}$ *of* l^∞ *($\mathbb{T}$)-valued random variables is asymptotically tight if there exists a pseudometric ρ on $\mathbb{T}$ such that ($\mathbb{T}, \rho$) is totally bounded and $\{Y_N : N \geq 1\}$ is stochastically equicontinuous, i.e., for all $\eta > 0$ and $\varepsilon > 0$, there exists $\delta > 0$ such that*

$$\limsup_{N\to\infty} \mathbb{P}\left(\sup_{s,t\in\mathbb{T}:\rho(s,t)<\delta} |Y_N(s) - Y_N(t)| > \eta\right) < \varepsilon.$$

The next theorem shows that asymptotic tightness and finite dimensional (fidi) convergence yield weak convergence (theorem 1.5.4 of VW).

Theorem A.2.4 *If $\{Y_N\}_{N\geq 1}$ is asymptotically tight and the marginals of Y_N converge in distribution to the marginals of some random variable Y, then $Y_N \Rightarrow Y$.*

To see the plausibility of the stochastic equicontinuity condition in Theorem A.2.3, suppose that Y_N denotes an empirical process based on an i.i.d. sample $\{X_i\}_{i=1}^N$. Suppose $\mathcal{F}$ contains only the linear functions, i.e., $\mathcal{F} = \{f_t : t \in \mathbb{R}^k\}$ for $f_t(x) = x^\mathsf{T} t$, ρ is the Euclidean metric, and $Y_N(t) = \mathbb{G}_N f_t$ denotes the empirical process. Then,

$$\limsup_{N\to\infty} \mathbb{P}\left(\sup_{s,t\in\mathbb{R}^k:\rho(s,t)<\delta} |Y_N(s) - Y_N(t)| > \eta\right)$$

$$= \limsup_{N\to\infty} \mathbb{P}\left(\sup_{s,t\in\mathbb{R}^k:\|s-t\|<\delta} \left|\frac{1}{\sqrt{N}}\sum_{i=1}^N (X_i - EX_i)^\mathsf{T}(s-t)\right| > \eta\right)$$

$$\leq \limsup_{N\to\infty} \mathbb{P}\left(\left|\frac{1}{\sqrt{N}}\sum_{i=1}^N (X_i - EX_i)\right| > \frac{\eta}{\delta}\right) < \varepsilon,$$

where the last inequality holds for δ sufficiently small, provided

$$\frac{1}{\sqrt{N}}\sum_{i=1}^N (X_i - EX_i) = O_p(1).$$

Thus, $\{Y_N\}_{N\geq 1}$ is stochastically equicontinuous if the random variables $\{X_i\}_{i\geq 1}$ satisfy an ordinary CLT.

However, for classes of nonlinear functions, it is substantially more difficult to verify the stochastic equicontinuity property than for linear functions. Indeed, it can be shown that *it does not hold for all classes of functions* (Andrews, 1994, pp. 2252–3). Some restrictions on $\mathcal{F}$ are necessary, i.e., $\mathcal{F}$ cannot be too large. We need to place restrictions on the complexity/size of the class of functions $\mathcal{F}$, so that the stochastic equicontinuity holds. Such restrictions can often be expressed in terms of conditions on the entropy of $\mathcal{F}$.

Theorems A.2.3 and A.2.4 show that if (i) total boundedness, (ii) stochastic equicontinuity, and (iii) the finite dimensional convergence hold, then we have a weak convergence. The finite dimensional distributional convergence is usually verified by a CLT and total boundedness and stochastic equicontinuity are verified using an entropy condition.

The following theorem (theorem 2.5.2 of VW) shows that the Donsker property holds under an entropy condition and a moment condition:

Theorem A.2.5 *(Donsker Theorem): Let $\mathcal{F}$ be a class of measurable functions with square integrable envelope function $\bar{M}$ (meaning $\sup_{f \in \mathcal{F}} |f(\cdot)| \leq \bar{M}(\cdot)$ with $P\bar{M}^2 < \infty$) combined with the uniform entropy condition*

$$\int_0^1 \sup_{Q \in \mathcal{Q}} \sqrt{\log N\left(\varepsilon \left\|\bar{M}\right\|_{Q,2}, \mathcal{F}, \|\cdot\|_{Q,2}\right)} d\varepsilon < \infty, \tag{A.2.3}$$

where $\|\cdot\|_{Q,2}$ is the $L_2(Q)$ norm (meaning $\left\|\bar{M}\right\|_{Q,2}^2 = \int \bar{M}^2 dQ$) and $\mathcal{Q}$ is the set of all distributions with finite support. Then, $\mathcal{F}$ is Donsker.

The class of functions that satisfy the uniform entropy condition in Theorem A.2.5 includes a collection of indicator functions of VC class of sets, i.e., $\mathcal{F} = \{1_C : C \in \mathcal{C}\}$, where $\mathcal{C}$ is a VC class of sets (e.g., the class of half intervals $\{(-\infty, x] : x \in \mathbb{R}\}$; see VW (section 2.6, pp. 134–149) for the definition).

The Donsker property can also be established under the bracketing entropy condition (VW, theorem 2.5.6):

$$\int_0^1 \sqrt{\log N_{[]}\left(\varepsilon, \mathcal{F}, \|\cdot\|_{P,2}\right)} d\varepsilon < \infty. \tag{A.2.4}$$

The bracketing entropy condition holds, for example, for $\mathcal{F} = \left\{1_{(-\infty,t]} : t \in \mathbb{R}\right\}$. To see this, note that

$$\left\|1_{(-\infty,t]} - 1_{(-\infty,s]}\right\|_{P,2} = \left(\int \left[1_{(-\infty,t]}(x) - 1_{(-\infty,t]}(x)\right]^2 dP(x)\right)^{1/2}$$

$$= (F(t) - F(s))^{1/2}.$$

We can choose points $-\infty = t_0 < t_1 < \cdots < t_k = \infty$ such that $k \leq 2/\varepsilon$ and $F(t_{j+1}-) - F(t_j) < \varepsilon$. Consider the ε-bracket $[1_{(-\infty,t_j]}, 1_{(-\infty,t_{j+1})}]$. Then, $N_{[]}\left(\varepsilon^{1/2}, \mathcal{F}, \|\cdot\|_{P,2}\right) \leq (2/\varepsilon)$, or, equivalently, $N_{[]}\left(\varepsilon, \mathcal{F}, \|\cdot\|_{P,2}\right) = O\left(\varepsilon^{-2}\right)$, which in turn satisfies (A.2.4).

For more examples of the classes of functions that satisfy the uniform and bracketing entropy conditions and their stability properties, see VW (sections 2.6 and 2.7) and Andrews (1994).

A.2.2 Dependent Observations

Let $\mathbb{N}$ and $\mathbb{I}$ denote the set of all positive integers and integers, respectively.

Definition A.2.7 *A sequence of random vectors $\{X_i\}_{i \in \mathbb{I}}$ defined on the same probability space $(\Omega, \mathcal{A}, \mathbb{P})$ is strictly stationary if for each $k \in \mathbb{N}$ and $\{i_1, \ldots, i_k\} \subseteq \mathbb{I}$ and for each $h \in \mathbb{I}$, the joint distributions of $(X_{i_1}, \ldots, X_{i_k})^\mathsf{T}$ and $(X_{i_1+h}, \ldots, X_{i_k+h})^\mathsf{T}$ are the same.*

In other words, a random sequence is strictly stationary if the *joint* distribution of the variables in the sequence is identical, regardless of the date (or the time index) of the first observation. If a sequence is just identically distributed, then it is not necessarily strictly stationary, because it is possible to construct different joint distributions that have identical marginal distributions. On the other hand, strict stationarity is weaker than the i.i.d. assumption, because i.i.d. sequences are stationary, but strictly stationary sequences do not have to be independent.

Definition A.2.8 *A one-to-one transformation $T : \Omega \mapsto \Omega$ defined on $(\Omega, \mathcal{A}, \mathbb{P})$ is measurable if $T^{-1}(\mathcal{A}) \subset \mathcal{A}$.*

Definition A.2.9 *A transformation $T : \Omega \mapsto \Omega$ is measure preserving if it is measurable and if $\mathbb{P}\left(T^{-1}A\right) = \mathbb{P}(A)$ for all $A \in \mathcal{A}$.*

If $\{X_i\}_{i \in \mathbb{I}}$ is a stationary sequence, then there exists a measure-preserving transformation T defined on $(\Omega, \mathcal{A}, \mathbb{P})$ such that $X_1(\omega) = X_1(\omega)$, $X_2(\omega) = X_1(T\omega), \ldots, X_N(\omega) = X_1(T^{N-1}\omega)$ for all $\omega \in \Omega$.

Definition A.2.10 *Let T be a measure-preserving transformation. A strictly stationary sequence $\{X_i\}_{i \in \mathbb{I}}$ is ergodic if $\lim_{N \to \infty} N^{-1} \sum_{n=1}^{N} \mathbb{P}(A \cap T^n B) = \mathbb{P}(A)\mathbb{P}(B)$ for all $A, B \in \mathcal{A}$. It is called mixing if $\lim_{n \to \infty} \mathbb{P}(A \cap T^n B) = \mathbb{P}(A)\mathbb{P}(B)$ for all $A, B \in \mathcal{A}$.*

If A and B were independent, then $\mathbb{P}(A \cap B) = \mathbb{P}(A)\mathbb{P}(B)$. We may think of $T^i B$ as the event B shifted i periods into the future. By strict stationarity, we have $\mathbb{P}\left(T^i B\right) = \mathbb{P}(B)$. Hence, the definition of ergodicity implies that, for any events A and B, the two events A and $T^i B$ are independent on average in the limit. That is, ergodicity can be thought of as a form of "average asymptotic independence" of a random sequence. On the other hand, mixing is a more direct measure of weak dependence. It is straightforward to see that mixing is a stronger concept than ergodicity; see Doob (1954), White (1983, p. 41), and Davidson (1994, pp. 191–208) for details.

There are different notions of mixing and we introduce the concepts that have been most commonly exploited in asymptotic theory.

Definition A.2.11 *Let $(\Omega, \mathcal{A}, \mathbb{P})$ be a probability space and let $\mathcal{G}$ and $\mathcal{H}$ be σ-subfields of $\mathcal{A}$. Define*

$$\alpha(\mathcal{G}, \mathcal{H}) = \sup_{G \in \mathcal{G}, H \in \mathcal{H}} |\mathbb{P}(G \cap H) - \mathbb{P}(G)\mathbb{P}(H)| \tag{A.2.5}$$

$$\beta(\mathcal{G}, \mathcal{H}) = \sup \frac{1}{2} \sum_{(i,j) \in I \times J} |\mathbb{P}(G_i \cap H_j) - \mathbb{P}(G_i)\mathbb{P}(H_j)| \tag{A.2.6}$$

$$\phi(\mathcal{G}, \mathcal{H}) = \sup_{G \in \mathcal{G}, H \in \mathcal{H}; \mathbb{P}(G) > 0} |\mathbb{P}(H|G) - \mathbb{P}(H)|, \tag{A.2.7}$$

where the supremum in (A.2.6) is taken over all the finite partitions $(G_i)_{i \in I}$ and $(H_j)_{j \in J}$ of Ω with $G_i \in \mathcal{G}$ and $H_j \in \mathcal{H}$. We call $\alpha(\mathcal{G}, \mathcal{H})$, $\beta(\mathcal{G}, \mathcal{H})$, and $\phi(\mathcal{G}, \mathcal{H})$ as the strong mixing (or α-mixing) coefficient, the absolutely regular mixing (or β-mixing) coefficient, and the uniform mixing (or ϕ-mixing) coefficient, respectively.

Definition A.2.12 *For a sequence $\{X_i\}_{i \in \mathbb{I}}$, let $\mathcal{A}^n_{-\infty} = \sigma(\{X_i\}_{i \leq n})$ and $\mathcal{A}^\infty_{n+m} = \sigma(\{X_i\}_{i \geq n+m})$ denote the σ-fields generated by $\{X_i(\omega)\}^n_{i=-\infty}$ and $\{X_i(\omega)\}^\infty_{i=n+m}$, respectively. For $\gamma = \alpha, \beta,$ and ϕ, define the mixing coefficient $\gamma(m) = \sup_{n \in \mathbb{I}} \gamma\left(\mathcal{A}^n_{-\infty}, \mathcal{A}^\infty_{n+m}\right)$ and we call $\{X_i\}_{i \in \mathbb{I}}$ γ-mixing if $\gamma(m) \to 0$ as $m \to \infty$. We say that $\gamma(m)$ is of size $-\lambda$ if $\gamma(m) = O(m^{-\lambda-\delta})$ for some $\delta > 0$.*

The mixing coefficients $\alpha(m)$, $\beta(m)$, and $\phi(m)$ measure how much dependence exists between two events separated by at least m time periods. By allowing them to approach zero as $m \to \infty$, we consider the situations in which the two events are asymptotically independent. It can be shown that the following relation holds among the coefficients: for each $m \in \mathbb{N}$,

$$2\alpha(m) \leq \beta(m) \leq \phi(m) \leq 1.$$

Therefore, α-mixing is the weakest notion among them and is implied by β-mixing and ϕ-mixing. For example, if $\{X_i\}_{i \in \mathbb{I}}$ is an *m-dependent* sequence (meaning that X_i is independent of $X_{i-\tau}$ for all $\tau > m$), then $\alpha(s) = \beta(s) = \phi(s) = 0$ for all $s > m$. On the other hand, a Gaussian AR(1) process is α-mixing, but not ϕ-mixing; see Doukhan (1994) for more examples.

The next results are central limit theorems (CLTs) for strictly stationary sequences. Define

$$S_N = N^{-1/2} \sum_{i=1}^N (X_i - EX_i).$$

Theorem A.2.6 *(CLT for m-dependent sequences) Let $\{X_i\}_{i \in \mathbb{I}}$ be a strictly stationary m-dependent sequence for some integer $m \geq 0$. If $EX_1^2 < \infty$ and $Var(X_1) + 2 \sum_{k=1}^m Cov(X_1, X_{1+k}) = \sigma_m^2 > 0$, then $S_N \Rightarrow N(0, \sigma_m^2)$.*

Theorem A.2.7 *(Hall and Heyde, 1980, corollary 5.1) Let $0 < \delta \leq \infty$ be fixed. Suppose that a sequence $\{X_i\}_{i \in \mathbb{I}}$ is strictly stationary and α-mixing* *with $E |X_1|^{2+\delta} < \infty$, in case $0 < \delta < \infty$; or $|X_1| \leq c < \infty$ if $\delta = \infty$; while $\sum_{m=1}^{\infty} [\alpha(m)]^{\delta/(2+\delta)} < \infty$. Then, $\lim_{N\to\infty} Var(S_N) = \sigma^2 < \infty$. If, in addition, $\sigma^2 > 0$, then $S_N \Rightarrow N(0, \sigma^2)$.*

The next result extends the results to heterogenous sequences:

Theorem A.2.8 *(Herrndorf, 1984, corollary 1) Let $\{X_i\}_{i \in \mathbb{I}}$ be an α-mixing sequence with $\sup_{i \in \mathbb{I}} E |X_i|^{2+\delta} < \infty$ for some $\delta > 0$ and $\sum_{m=1}^{\infty} [\alpha(m)]^{\delta/(2+\delta)} < \infty$. If $\lim_{N\to\infty} Var(S_N) = \sigma^2 > 0$ for some $\sigma^2 > 0$, then $S_N \Rightarrow N(0, \sigma^2)$.*

The following result establishes the Donsker property of the empirical process $\{\mathbb{G}_N f : f \in \mathcal{F}\}$ (defined in Equation A.2.2) for bounded α-mixing sequences.

Theorem A.2.9 *(Andrews and Pollard, 1994, theorem 2.2)*[3] *Let $\{X_i\}_{i \in \mathbb{I}}$ be a strictly stationary and α-mixing sequence with common marginal distribution P. Assume that the mixing coefficients satisfy $\sum_{m=1}^{\infty} m^{q-2} [\alpha(m)]^{\delta/(q+\delta)} < \infty$ for some even integer $q > 2$ and some $\delta > 0$. Let $\mathcal{F}$ be a uniformly bounded class of real-valued functions whose bracketing numbers satisfy*

$$\int_0^1 \varepsilon^{-\delta/(2+\delta)} \left[N_{[]} \left(\varepsilon, \mathcal{F}, \|\cdot\|_{P,2}\right)\right]^{1/q} d\varepsilon < \infty \tag{A.2.8}$$

for the same q and δ. Then, for each $\eta > 0$, there exists $\gamma > 0$ such that

$$\limsup_{N\to\infty} \left\| \sup_{f,g \in \mathcal{F}: \rho(f,g) < \gamma} |\mathbb{G}_N f - \mathbb{G}_N g| \right\|_{P,q} < \eta,$$

where $\rho(f) = \|f(X_i)\|_{P,2}$ is the $L_2(P)$-norm. If, in addition, $(\mathbb{G}_N f_1, \ldots, \mathbb{G}_N f_k)$ has an asymptotically normal distribution for all choices of $(f_1, \ldots, f_k)$ from $\mathcal{F}$, then $\{\mathbb{G}_N f : f \in \mathcal{F}\}$ converges weakly to a Gaussian process with continuous sample paths.

To establish the finite-dimensional convergence in distribution in the above theorem, one may use the CLTs for mixing sequences introduced earlier (i.e., Theorems A.2.6, A.2.7, and A.2.8). On the other hand, the mixing condition and the bracketing condition (A.2.8) hold if, for example, $N_{[]} \left(\varepsilon, \mathcal{F}, \|\cdot\|_{P,2}\right) = O(\varepsilon^{-B})$ and $\alpha(m) = O(m^{-A})$ for some $B > 0$ and $A > (q-1)(1+q/2)$ with q equal to the smallest even integer greater than $2B$ and $\delta = 2$. For example, if $\mathcal{F}$ is a parametric family $\mathcal{F} = \{f(\cdot, \theta) : \theta \in \Theta\}$ with Θ being a bounded subset of some Euclidean space $\mathbb{R}^d$ and the functions satisfy the $L_2(P)$-*continuity condition*, i.e., for some $C > 0$ and $\lambda > 0$ and for all r small enough,

---

[3] In fact, the results of Andrews and Pollard (1994) are more general and allow for heterogeneous strong mixing arrays.

$$P \sup_{B(\theta,r)} |f(X_i, \theta') - f(X_i, \theta)|^2 \leq C^2 r^{2\lambda} \text{ for all } \theta,$$

where $B(\theta, r)$ is the ball of radius r around θ, then it can be shown that the bracketing numbers are of order $O(\varepsilon^{-d/\lambda})$.

On the other hand, Doukhan, Massart, and Rio (1995) establish the Donsker property for possibly *unbounded* β-mixing sequences. Let $\mathcal{L}_q(P)$ be the class of real-valued functions such that $\|f(X_i)\|_{P,q} < \infty$ for $q \geq 1$. For any $f \in \mathcal{L}_1(P)$, let Q_f denote the quantile function of $|f(X_1)|$.

Theorem A.2.10 *(Doukhan, Massart, and Rio, 1995, theorem 1) Let $\{X_i\}_{i \in \mathbb{I}}$ be a strictly stationary and β-mixing sequence with common marginal distribution P. Assume that the mixing coefficients satisfy $\sum_{m=1}^{\infty} \beta(m) < \infty$. Let*

$$\mathcal{F} \subset \mathcal{L}_{2,\beta}(P) := \{f : \|f\|_{2,\beta} := \sqrt{\int_0^1 \beta^{-1}(u) [Q_f(u)]^2 du} < \infty\} \text{ be a class}$$

of functions. Assume that the entropy with bracketing with respect to $\|\cdot\|_{2,\beta}$ satisfies the integrability condition

$$\int_0^1 \sqrt{\log N_{[]} (\varepsilon, \mathcal{F}, \|\cdot\|_{2,\beta})} d\varepsilon < \infty. \tag{A.2.9}$$

Then, $\{\mathbb{G}_N f : f \in \mathcal{F}\}$ converges weakly to a Gaussian process with continuous sample paths.

The conditions in the above theorem hold if, for example, either (a) for some $r \in (1, \infty)$, the mixing coefficients satisfy $\sum_{m=1}^{\infty} m^{1/(r-1)} \beta(m) < \infty$ and the class $\mathcal{F} \subset \mathcal{L}_{2r}(P)$ satisfies the entropy condition $\int_0^1 \sqrt{\log N_{[]} (\varepsilon, \mathcal{F}, \|\cdot\|_{P,2r})} d\varepsilon < \infty$; or (b) the mixing coefficients satisfy $\beta(m) = O(m^{-b})$, the envelope function of $\mathcal{F}$ is in $\mathcal{L}_{2r}(P)$ for $r > 1$, and the class $\mathcal{F} \subset \mathcal{L}_2(P)$ satisfies the entropy condition $\int_0^1 \varepsilon^{-r/(b(r-1))} \sqrt{\log N_{[]} (\varepsilon, \mathcal{F}, \|\cdot\|_{P,2})} d\varepsilon < \infty$ with $b > r/(r-1)$.

For more sufficient conditions for the Donsker property of dependent sequences, the reader is referred to Doukhan, Massart, and Rio (1995, pp. 403–405) and Andrews (1993, 1994).

A.3 Poissonization Methods

This section explains the main idea of the Poissonization method using a nonparametric PDF estimator (The nonparametric conditional CDF estimator has similar asymptotic properties as the nonparametric PDF estimator.)

Consider the nonparametric kernel density estimator of the true density f

$$f_N(x) = \frac{1}{Nh} \sum_{i=1}^{N} K\left(\frac{x - X_i}{h}\right).$$

It is well known that, under suitable regularity conditions, f_N is consistent for f and $\sqrt{Nh}\,(f_N(x) - Ef_N(x))$ is asymptotically normal at each x; see, e.g., Parzen (1962).

However, proving a weak convergence of the random process

$$v_N(\cdot) = \sqrt{Nh}\,(f_N(\cdot) - Ef_N(\cdot)) \tag{A.3.1}$$

in a function space is known to be a difficult problem. In fact, Nishiyama (2011) proves the impossibility of weak convergence of $v_N(\cdot)$ to a nondegenerate law in the Hilbert space; see also Ruymgaart (1998) and Stupfler (2014) for related results. The lack of weak convergence makes the asymptotic analysis of the statistic based on the process $v_N(\cdot)$ complicated, because the standard technique based on the functional CLT and continuous mapping theorem may not be directly applicable in these cases. In particular, it is not straightforward to obtain the limit distribution of a (nonlinear) functional of f_N, e.g., the L_1-distance between f_N and f.[4]

Giné, Mason, and Zaitsev (2003, GMZ) show that the L_1-distance, when suitably normalized, is asymptotically normal using a *Poissonization* technique. The idea of Poissonization is to randomize the sample size by a Poisson random variable, so that the additional randomness allows the application of the techniques that exploit the independence of the increments and the behaviors of moments. In general, the Poissonization method requires weaker assumptions on the underlying nonparametric functions than the alternative methods such as the *strong Gaussian approximation*.

Specifically, GMZ consider the following L_1-distance of the kernel density estimator from its mean

$$T_N = \sqrt{N} \int_{\mathbb{R}} |f_N(x) - Ef_N(x)|\,dx. \tag{A.3.2}$$

They show that the statistic converges in distribution to a normal distribution under very weak assumptions.

Theorem A.3.1 *(GMZ, theorem 1.1) Suppose that $K(\cdot)$ satisfies $K(u) = 0$ for $|u| > 1/2$ and $\kappa := \int K^2(u)du < \infty$. If $h \to 0$ and $N^{1/2}h \to \infty$, then*

$$T_N - ET_N \Rightarrow N(0, \sigma^2),$$

where

$$\sigma^2 = \kappa \int_{-1}^{1} Cov\left(\left|\sqrt{1 - \rho^2(t)}\mathbb{Z}_1 + \rho(t)\mathbb{Z}_2\right|, |\mathbb{Z}_2|\right) dt,$$

$$\rho(t) = \frac{\int_{\mathbb{R}} K(u)K(u + t)du}{\kappa},$$

and $\mathbb{Z}_1$ and $\mathbb{Z}_2$ are mutually independent standard normal random variables.

---

[4] For L_∞ and L_2-distances between f_N and f, Bickel and Rosenblatt (1973, theorems 3.1 and 4.1) obtain limit theorems using a Skorohod-type embedding.

This result is interesting because the norming constant in (A.3.2) is a parametric rate ($\sqrt{N}$) and the asymptotic variance depends only on the kernel function K, but not on the true density f.

It is informative to understand the main steps of the proof of Theorem A.3.1. Let $\mathcal{N}$ be a Poisson random variable (with mean N) independent of the i.i.d. sequence $\{X_i : i \geq 1\}$. Consider a Poissonization version of T_N (restricted to $C \subset \mathbb{R}$):

$$T_{\mathcal{N}}(C) = \sqrt{N} \int_C |f_{\mathcal{N}}(x) - Ef_N(x)| \, dx,$$

where

$$f_{\mathcal{N}}(x) := \frac{1}{Nh} \sum_{i=1}^{\mathcal{N}} K\left(\frac{x - X_i}{h}\right).$$

Poissonization of the statistic T_N by $T_{\mathcal{N}}(C)$ brings great convenience in the asymptotic analysis. In particular, it is well known that if $\mathcal{N}$ is a Poisson random variable independent of the i.i.d. sequence $\{X_i : i \geq 1\}$ and $\{A_k : k \geq 1\}$ are disjoint measurable sets, then the processes $\sum_{i=0}^{\mathcal{N}} 1(X_i \in A_k)\delta_{X_i}, k = 1, 2, \ldots$, are independent, where δ_{X_i} denotes the dirac measure at X_i. Therefore, if the kernel function K has a compact support (say, $[-1/2, 1/2]$), the Poissonized kernel densities $f_{\mathcal{N}}(x)$ and $f_{\mathcal{N}}(y)$ are mutually independent if the distance between x and y is greater than a certain threshold (say, $2h$). This facilitates the computation of the asymptotic variance of $T_{\mathcal{N}}(C)$. Also, since a Poisson process is infinitely divisible, we may write $\sum_{i=0}^{\mathcal{N}} X_i \overset{d}{=} \sum_{i=0}^{N} Z_i$, where $\{Z_i : i \geq 1\}$ are i.i.d. with $Z \overset{d}{=} \sum_{i=0}^{\eta_1} X_i$ and η_1 is a Poisson random variable with mean 1 and independent of $\{X_i : i \geq 1\}$.[5] These results allow us to derive the asymptotic distribution of $T_{\mathcal{N}}(C)$, using standard machineries such as the CLTs for independent observations.

To get the limit distribution of the original statistic T_N, we have to remove the influence of the extra randomness introduced by the Poissonization step. For this purpose, the following *de-Poissonization lemma* is useful:

Theorem A.3.2 *(GMZ, lemma 2.4) Let $\mathcal{N}_{1,N}$ and $\mathcal{N}_{2,N}$ be independent Poisson random variables with $\mathcal{N}_{1,N}$ being $Poisson(N(1 - \alpha))$ and $\mathcal{N}_{2,N}$ being $Poisson(N\alpha)$, where $\alpha \in (0, 1/2)$. Denote $\mathcal{N}_N = \mathcal{N}_{1,N} + \mathcal{N}_{2,N}$ and set*

$$U_N = \frac{\mathcal{N}_{1,N} - N(1 - \alpha)}{\sqrt{N}} \text{ and } V_N = \frac{\mathcal{N}_{2,N} - N\alpha}{\sqrt{N}}.$$

Let $\{S_{\mathcal{N}_N} : N \geq 1\}$ be a sequence of random variables such that (i) for each $N \geq 1$, the random vector $(S_{\mathcal{N}_N}, U_N)$ is independent of V_N; and (ii) for some $\sigma^2 > 0$ and ξ such that $(1 - \alpha)\sigma^2 - \xi^2 > 0$,

---

[5] The notation $X \overset{d}{=} Y$ denotes that X and Y have the same distribution.

$$(S_{\mathcal{N}_N}, U_N)^{\mathsf{T}} \Rightarrow N(0, \Sigma),$$

where

$$\Sigma = \begin{pmatrix} \sigma^2 & \xi \\ \xi & 1-\alpha \end{pmatrix}.$$

Then, for all x, we have

$$P\left(S_{\mathcal{N}_N} \leq x \mid \mathcal{N}_N = N\right) \to P\left(\sqrt{\sigma^2 - \xi^2}\, \mathbb{Z} \leq x\right),$$

as $N \to \infty$, where $\mathbb{Z}$ denotes the standard normal random variable.

To illustrate Theorem A.3.2 in a simple context, consider a statistic $\Lambda_N = N^{-1/2} \sum_{i=1}^{N} [1(X_i \in B) - P(X \in B)]$, where $B \subset \mathbb{R}$ is a Borel set. By a CLT, $\Lambda_N \Rightarrow N(0, p_B(1 - p_B))$, where $p_B = P(X \in B)$. Now, consider the Poissonized statistic $S_N = N^{-1/2} \sum_{i=1}^{\mathcal{N}} 1(X_i \in B) - N^{1/2} P(X \in B)$. The asymptotic distribution of S_N is given by $N(0, p_B)$, which is different from that of Λ_N. However, letting $U_N = N^{-1/2} \sum_{i=1}^{\mathcal{N}} 1(X_i \in C) - N^{1/2} P(X \in C)$ and $V_N = N^{-1/2} \sum_{i=1}^{\mathcal{N}} 1(X_i \in \mathbb{R} \backslash C) - N^{1/2} P(X \in \mathbb{R} \backslash C)$, where $B \subset C \subset \mathbb{R}$ is a Borel set, and applying the de-Poissonization lemma, we see that the conditional distribution of S_N given $\mathcal{N} = N$ coincides with the distribution of Λ_N asymptotically.

More specifically, the main steps of the proof of Theorem A.3.1 are as follows:

1. Show

$$\sigma_N^2(C) := Var\left(T_{\mathcal{N}}(C)\right) \to \sigma_C^2 := p_C \cdot \sigma^2.$$

2. Let

$$S_{\mathcal{N}} = \frac{[T_{\mathcal{N}}(C) - ET_{\mathcal{N}}(C)]}{\sigma_N(C)},$$

$$U_N = N^{-1/2} \left[\sum_{j=1}^{\mathcal{N}} 1\left(X_j \in [-M, M]\right) \right.$$

$$\left. - N \cdot P\left(X \in [-M, M]\right) \right],$$

$$V_N = N^{-1/2} \left[\sum_{j=1}^{\mathcal{N}} 1\left(X_j \notin [-M, M]\right) \right.$$

$$\left. - N \cdot P\left(X \notin [-M, M]\right) \right].$$

Then show, by a CLT for 1-dependent random variables,

$$(S_{\mathcal{N}}, U_N) \Rightarrow (\mathbb{Z}_1, \sqrt{1 - \alpha}\mathbb{Z}_2).$$

3. Apply the *de-Poissonization lemma (Theorem A.3.2)* to show

$$(S_{\mathcal{N}} \mid \mathcal{N} = N) \stackrel{d}{=} \frac{[T_N(C) - ET_{\mathcal{N}}(C)]}{\sigma_N(C)} \Rightarrow \mathbb{Z}.$$

4. Show

$$ET_{\mathcal{N}}(C) - ET_N(C) \to 0$$

so that, using steps 1 and 3,

$$\frac{T_N(C) - ET_N(C)}{\sigma_C} \Rightarrow \mathbb{Z}. \tag{A.3.3}$$

5. Since (A.3.3) holds for any increasing set $\{C_k : k \geq 1\}$, apply theorem 4.2 of Billingsley (1968) to get

$$\frac{T_N - ET_N}{\sigma} \Rightarrow \mathbb{Z}.$$

Appendix B Computer Code for Stochastic Dominance Tests

B.1 Introduction

This section provides MATLAB code for some of the SD tests discussed in this book. Most code consists of three parts: *Input, Subroutine,* and *Output*. A user can execute each SD test program by just feeding the "parameters" and "data" into the *Input* part of the program, without having to read the *Subroutine* part. Even if you are not familiar with the MATLAB programming language, you should be able to perform the test. All you need to know is where you should put the parameters and data into the code you are using.

We first introduce the definitions of the variables which frequently appear in the *Input* part. The number of parameters you should feed varies depending on the test.

- sample1: A column of numeric data whose distribution stochastically dominates that of the other, sample2, under the null hypothesis.
- sample2: A column of numeric data whose distribution is stochastically dominated by that of sample1, under the null hypothesis.
- bootstrap method: A string-type variable indicating the type of the bootstrap method, whose value is one of 'Multiplier', 'Pooled', or 'Recentered'.
- B: A positive integer indicating the number of bootstrap repetitions.
- SDorder: A positive integer variable representing the order of stochastic dominance in the null hypothesis.
- ngrid: A nonnegative integer variable determining the number of points in a grid. The grid is used to approximate the suprema featured in the test statistic. If ngrid equals 0, all observations in the combined sample are set to be the grid points. Otherwise, ngrid determines the number of equally spaced points (between the maximum and the minimum of the combined sample) to be used as a grid.

Once you enter the parameter values and data and execute the SD test program, a p-value of the test will be printed out on your screen.

To help the user's understanding, we shall not only explain the program code in detail, but also report testing results from simple simulation experiments.[1]

Specifically, we consider the following data-generating processes:

Design 1: $X = V + \mu_x$ where $\mu_x = 0$ and $Y = U$
Design 2: $X = V + \mu_x$ where $\mu_x = -0.1$ and $Y = U$
Design 3: $X = V + \mu_x$ where $\mu_x = 0.5$ and $Y = U$
Design 4: $X = \sigma_x V$ where $\sigma_x = 0.5$ and $Y = U$,

where U and V are independent standard normal random variables. The first two designs conform to the null hypothesis that "Y FSD X," whereas the last two designs correspond to the alternative hypothesis that "Y does not FSD X." Figure B.1 presents the CDFs of these designs.

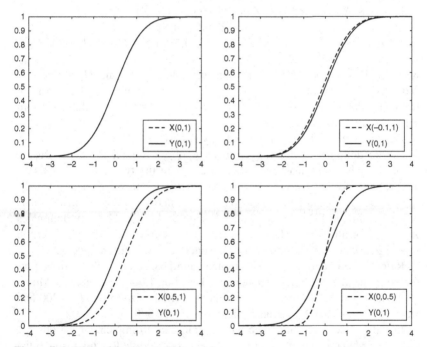

Figure B.1 CDFs of Designs 1, 2, 3, and 4

---

[1] It must be noted that the purpose of the simulations is to check the code and to help the user's practical implementation, but not to compare the performance of different tests. For the latter, an extensive simulation study is required, which is certainly beyond the scope of this book.

For the Linton–Maasoumi–Whang test, we consider designs for which two random variables are serially correlated and mutually dependent. Specifically, the following designs are considered.

Design 5: $X_i = 0.9 \cdot (1 + 9 \cdot (\sqrt{0.1}Z_{0i} + \sqrt{0.9}Z_{Xi})) + 0.1 \cdot X_{i-1}$,
$Y_i = 0.9 \cdot 9 \cdot (\sqrt{0.1}Z_{0i} + \sqrt{0.9}Z_{Yi}) + 0.1 \cdot Y_{i-1}$
Design 6: $X_i = 0.9 \cdot (-1 + 4 \cdot (\sqrt{0.1}Z_{0i} + \sqrt{0.9}Z_{Xi})) + 0.1 \cdot X_{i-1}$,
$Y_i = 0.9 \cdot 1 \cdot (\sqrt{0.1}Z_{0i} + \sqrt{0.9}Z_{Yi}) + 0.1 \cdot Y_{i-1}$,

where (Z_{0i}, Z_{Xi}, Z_{Yi}) are i.i.d. standard normal random variables, mutually independent. Design 5 conforms to the null hypothesis, while Design 6 corresponds to the alternative hypothesis.

In the case of a SD test with covariates, we consider different data-generating processes. Specifically, for the Lee–Whang test, we consider the following four designs:

Design 7: $X = V$ and $Y = Z \cdot U_1 + (1 - Z) \cdot U_0$
Design 8: $X = V$ and $Y = Z \cdot (X + U_1) + (1 - Z) \cdot U_0$
Design 9: $X = V$ and $Y = Z \cdot (-X + U_1) + (1 - Z) \cdot U_0$
Design 10: $X = V$ and $Y = Z \cdot ((-X + 0.5) \cdot 1.5 + U_1) + (1 - Z) \cdot U_0$,

where V is a uniform $U(0, 1)$ random variable and U_0 and U_1 are normal $N(0, 0.1)$ random variables. Z (treatment indicator) is a random variable following the Bernoulli distribution with parameter 0.5. All these random variables are drawn independently.

Designs 7 and 8 belong to the null hypothesis, i.e., the (weak) first-order stochastic dominance of $F_{Y|X,Z=1}$ over $F_{Y|X,Z=0}$ for all $X = x$. Design 7 corresponds to the least favorable case, where the two conditional CDFs are the same. Under Design 8, $F_{Y|X,Z=1}$ strictly dominates $F_{Y|X,Z=0}$ for all $X = x$. Designs 9 and 10 correspond to the alternative hypothesis, i.e., no first-order conditional SD relation. Under Design 9, $F_{Y|X,Z=0}$ strictly dominates $F_{Y|X,Z=1}$ for all $X = x$. Under Design 10, the two conditional CDFs cross. Figure B.2 depicts the conditional CDFs under the four different designs.

Rejection probabilities (at 5% nominal significance level) that will be presented in the later sections are calculated based on 1,000 repetitions of Monte Carlo simulations. In most cases, we fix the sample size to be $N = 200$ and we set the number of bootstrap replications B to be 500.

In the following sections, we will explain how to implement various SD tests with MATLAB and present the relevant code. While looking through the code, notice that a line starting with the percentage mark % is annotation. It is intended to help the user; the computer does not execute lines with the percent mark.

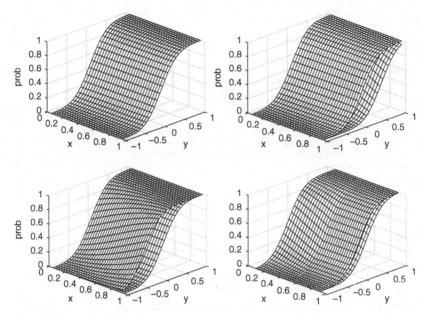

Figure B.2 CDFs of Designs 7, 8, 9, and 10

B.2 Supremum-Type Tests

B.2.1 McFadden Test

In this subsection, we provide MATLAB code for the McFadden (1989, Section 2.2.2) test of the FSD hypothesis. This requires entering four input variables introduced above. This code is composed of three parts: *Input, Subroutine,* and *Output.* Each part is separated with a dash line. In *Subroutine* part, it measures the size of the data, builds a grid which will be used as a support, and computes the test statistic. The computed test statistic (defined in Equation 2.2.23 with $s = 1$) is stored as stat. A p-value is presented as an output.

```
%------------------------- Input -------------------------%

sample1=randn(200,1);
sample2=randn(200,1);
ngrid=10;
SDorder=1;


%----------------------- Subroutine ----------------------%

% Measure the size of data
N1=size(sample1,1);
N2=size(sample2,1);
```

```
% Construct a Support
pooled=sort([sample1; sample2]);
if ngrid==0
   grid=sort(pooled);
else
   grid=linspace(min(pooled),max(pooled),ngrid)';
end

% Compute the Test Statistic
operator=@(X,z)(X<= z).*(z-X).^(SDorder-1)/factorial(SDorder-1);
rawcdf1=mean(bsxfun(operator, sample1, reshape(grid,[1,1,ngrid])),1);
rawcdf2=mean(bsxfun(operator, sample2, reshape(grid,[1,1,ngrid])),1);
cdf1=squeeze(rawcdf1);
cdf2=squeeze(rawcdf2);
stat=sqrt(N1*N2/(N1+N2))*max(cdf1-cdf2);

%-------------------------- Output --------------------------%

pvalue=exp(-2*stat^2)
```

Table B.1 *Rejection probabilities of the McFadden test*

Design	1	2	3	4
Rejection Probabilities	0.025	0.001	0.982	0.903

The table above shows the simulated rejection probabilities at 5% significance level under different designs. Under Designs 1 and 2, the probabilities are less than the nominal level, which implies that the size of the McFadden test is well controlled. The rejection probabilities under the alternative hypothesis (Designs 3 and 4) are close to 1, which implies that the McFadden test has good powers against the alternatives.

B.2.2 Barrett–Donald Test

This subsection presents MATLAB code for the Barrett and Donald (2003, Section 2.2.2, BD) test. The code implements the test based on three different methods: the multiplier method ($KS2^*$ in Equation 2.2.38), the pooled sample bootstrap ($KSB2^*$ in Equation 2.2.39), and the recentered bootstrap ($KSB3^*$ in Equation 2.2.40). BD test has five different input variables: sample1, sample2, bmethod, B, ngrid, and SDorder. Definitions of the inputs are given at the outset of this section.

Following Barrett and Donald, we use a grid to approximate the suprema featured in the test statistic. If ngrid is a positive integer, we take equally spaced `ngrid` points between the minimum and maximum of the pooled sample for the grid. Otherwise, we use the pooled sample for the grid. Since this is under the control of the user, one can approximate the value of the test statistic as accurately as possible by increasing `ngrid`, given the time and computational constraints. In their simulation study, Barrett and Donald set `ngrid` to be 100. `operator` corresponds to the empirical integrated CDF $\bar{F}_k^{(s)}$, and `cdf1` and `cdf2` are the empirical CDFs. The value of the test statistic is stored as `ksstat`. Bootstrap statistics are stored as `bksstat`. Note that the way to compute the bootstrap statistics differs depending on the function input `bmethod`. A calculated p-value is stored as `pvalue`, which will be printed out on the screen after the execution.

```
%------------------------- Input -------------------------%

sample1=randn(200,1);
sample2=randn(200,1);
bmethod='Multiplier';
B=500;
SDorder=1;
ngrid=100;


%--------------------- Subroutine ----------------------%

% Measure the size of data
N1=size(sample1,1);
N2=size(sample2,1);

% Construct a Support
pooled=sort([sample1; sample2]);
if ngrid==0
grid=pooled;
else
grid=linspace(min(pooled), max(pooled), ngrid);
end

% Compute the Test Statistic
operator=@(X,z)(X<= z).*(z-X).^(SDorder-1)/factorial(SDorder-1);
rawcdf1=mean(bsxfun(operator,sample1,reshape(grid, [1,1,ngrid])),1)
    ;
rawcdf2=mean(bsxfun(operator,sample2,reshape(grid, [1,1,ngrid])),1)
    ;
cdf1=squeeze(rawcdf1); % ECDF
cdf2=squeeze(rawcdf2); % ECDF
stat=sqrt(N1*N2/(N1+N2))*max(cdf1-cdf2); % test statistic

% Multiplier method
if strcmp(bmethod,'Multiplier')==1
temp1=bsxfun(operator,sample1,reshape(grid,[1,1,ngrid]))-repmat(
    rawcdf1, [N1,1,1]);
temp2=bsxfun(operator,sample2,reshape(grid,[1,1,ngrid]))-repmat(
    rawcdf2, [N2,1,1]);
bcdf1=sqrt(N1)*mean(repmat(temp1,[1,B,1]).*randn(N1,B,ngrid), 1);
```

```
bcdf2=sqrt(N2)*mean(repmat(temp2,[1,B,1]).*randn(N2,B,ngrid), 1);
lambda=N2/(N1+N2);
bksstat=max(sqrt(lambda)*bcdf1 - sqrt(1-lambda)*bcdf2,[],3);

% Recentered bootstrap
elseif strcmp(bmethod,'Recentered')==1
  index1=randi(N1,N1,B);
  index2=randi(N2,N2,B);
bsample1=sample1(index1); % bootstrap sample
bsample2=sample2(index2); % bootstrap sample
bcdf1=mean(bsxfun(operator,bsample1,reshape(grid,[1,1,ngrid])),1) -
    repmat(rawcdf1,[1,B,1]);
bcdf2=mean(bsxfun(operator,bsample2,reshape(grid,[1,1,ngrid])),1) -
    repmat(rawcdf2,[1,B,1]);
bksstat=sqrt(N1*N2/(N1+N2))*max(bcdf1 - bcdf2,[],3);

% Pooled sample bootstrap
elseif strcmp(bmethod,'Pooled')==1
index=randi(N2+N1,B);
index1=index(1:N1,:);
index2=index(N1+1:N2+N1,:);
bsample1=pooled(index1); % bootstrap sample
bsample2=pooled(index2); % bootstrap sample
bcdf1=mean(bsxfun(operator,bsample1,reshape(grid,[1,1,ngrid])),1);
bcdf2=mean(bsxfun(operator,bsample2,reshape(grid,[1,1,ngrid])),1);
bksstat=sqrt(N1*N2/(N1+N2))*max(bcdf1 - bcdf2,[],3);
end

%------------------------- Output -------------------------%

pvalue=sum(bksstat>stat)/B
```

Table B.2 *Rejection probabilities of the Barrett–Donald test*

Design	1	2	3	4
Multiplier Method	0.041	0.008	0.992	0.980
Pooled Sample Bootstrap	0.066	0.016	0.998	0.990
Recentered Bootstrap	0.066	0.014	0.998	0.989

The number of grid points `ngrid` is 20. It appears that the simulation results are consistent with the theoretical prediction. Rejection probabilities are close to the nominal level (5%) under the least favorable case (the first design). Rejection probabilities under the Design 2 (an "interior" case) are close to zero, as expected, while they are close to 1 under the alternative hypotheses (Designs 3 and 4).

B.2.3 Linton–Maasoumi–Whang Test

We present MATLAB code for the Linton, Maasoumi, and Whang (2005, Section 2.2.2, LMW) test. The code has seven different input variables sample1, sample2, SDorder, ngrid, b, timeseries, and centering. The first four variables are the same as those for BD test. The other input variables are defined as follows:

- b: a natural number indicating subsample size
- timeseries: a string type variable determining a subsampling method, whose value is either 'Yes' or 'No'. If timeseries equals to 'Yes', then it implements a block subsampling method (suited for time series observations). Otherwise, subsamples of size b are generated from the original sample (suited for independent observations).
- centering: a string type variable whose value is either 'Yes' or 'No'. If centering equals to 'Yes', then the code implements recentered subsampling. Otherwise, it implements subsampling without recentering.

The code is similar to that of the BD test, and hence we skip explaining repetitive parts and focus on the subsampling. To implement a subsampling, a user may choose a subsampling method. If timeseries is set to be 'Yes', then it generates N-b+1 block subsamples. A block subsample contains b consecutive observations. If a user set timeseries to be 'No', then it generates B subsamples. Each subsample contains b observations randomly selected from the original sample without replacement. The number of cases of selecting b observations out of N observations can be huge. For example, the number of cases to draw 20 observations from 100 observations is about 5.4 $\times 10^{20}$. Thus we only consider B($<< N$) subsamples. The code automatically chooses B as N-b+1, but a user can change this value. The subsamples are stored as the variable subsample1 and subsample2. Computed N-b+1 or B subsample test statistics are stored as subksstat. A calculated p-value is stored as pvalue.

As this code is intended to be used with a paired sample, the size of two samples must be the same. Moreover, note that this code does not choose the subsample size automatically. A user needs to repeat the test with multiple subsample sizes to choose the best subsample size or to modify the code to implement an automatic choice procedure, as suggested by LMW.

```
%------------------------- Input -------------------------%

sample1=randn(200,1);
sample2=randn(200,1);
SDorder=1;
ngrid=20;
b=10;
timeseries='Yes';
centering='No';

%---------------------- Sub-routine ----------------------%

% Measure the size of data
N=size(sample1,1);
B=N-b+1;
if size(sample2, 1)~=N
error('Two sample sizes must be the same.');
end

% Construct a Support
pooled=sort([sample1; sample2]);
if ngrid==0
grid=pooled;
else
grid=linspace(min(pooled), max(pooled), ngrid);
end

% Compute the Test Statistic
operator=@(X,z)(X<= z).*(z-X).^(SDorder-1)/factorial(SDorder
    -1);
rawcdf1=mean(bsxfun(operator,sample1,reshape(grid, [1,1,ngrid
    ])),1);
rawcdf2=mean(bsxfun(operator,sample2,reshape(grid, [1,1,ngrid
    ])),1);
cdf1=squeeze(rawcdf1);
cdf2=squeeze(rawcdf2);
stat=sqrt(N)*max(cdf1-cdf2);

% Block Subsampling
if strcmp(timeseries,'Yes')==1
    subindex=transpose(1:1:b);
    for i=2:N-b+1
        temp=transpose(i:1:(i+b-1));
        subindex=[subindex temp];
    end

% Random Subsampling
  elseif strcmp(timeseries,'No')==1
    subindex=zeros(1,b);
    while size(unique(subindex,'rows'),1)<B+1
        subindex=[subindex; randperm(N,b)];
    end
    subindex(1,:)=[];
    subindex=transpose(subindex);
  end
```

```
% Subsamples
subsample1=sample1(subindex);
subsample2=sample2(subindex);
subcdf1=mean(bsxfun(operator,subsample1,reshape(grid,[1,1,
    ngrid])) ,1);
subcdf2=mean(bsxfun(operator,subsample2,reshape(grid,[1,1,
    ngrid])) ,1);

% Subsampling statistics
if strcmp(centering,'Yes')==1
subksstat=sqrt(b)*max(subcdf1-subcdf2-repmat(rawcdf1-
    rawcdf2,[1,B,1]),[],3);

% Centred subsampling statistics
elseif strcmp(centering,'No')==1
    subksstat=sqrt(b)*max(subcdf1-subcdf2,[],3); % un-centred
        subsample statistics
    end

%------------------------- Output -----------------------%

pvalue=sum(subksstat>ksstat)/B
```

Table B.3 *Rejection probabilities of the Linton–Maasoumi–Whang test*

Design	1	2	3	4	5	6
Subsampling	0.048	0.004	0.988	0.989	0.001	0.454
Centered Subsampling	0.066	0.010	0.997	0.985	0.012	0.811

The above table shows the rejection probabilities of the LMW test under the six different designs. We took different subsample sizes for non-centered/recentered subsampling tests. For the non-centered subsampling test, we took 10 for the subsample size for Designs 1 to 4, and we took 30 for Designs 5 and 6. We used 15 for the recentered subsampling for Designs 1 to 4, and we used 30 for Designs 5 and 6. For Designs from 1 to 4, since the data are independently and identically distributed, a random subsampling is implemented, while a block subsampling was performed for the last two designs.

B.2.4 Donald–Hsu Test

The Donald and Hsu (2014, Section 3.1.2, DH) test has eight different input variables, sample1, sample2, bmethod, B, SDorder, ngrid, alpha, and a. The first six input variables have already been introduced. The definitions of the last two variables are as follows:

- alpha: A real number between 0 and 0.5. This corresponds to the significance level.
- a: A real number determining the tuning parameter, the coefficient for the sequence seq_a featured in the sequence a_N in the recentering function $\hat{\mu}_N$.

As DH suggest, we set $a_N = -a\sqrt{\log\log(N1 + N2)}$ where $N1$ and $N2$ denote two sample sizes. They use $a = 0.1$, but we recommend performing the test with various coefficient values a, so as to obtain a robust result. Unlike other tests returning p-values as the test result, the DH test returns a binary result, indicating whether the test rejects the null hypothesis or not at a prespecified significance level.

The code consists of three parts. Each part is separated by a dashed line. The code is very similar to that of the BD test. At the beginning of the *Subroutine* part, it defines the other tuning parameter eta (η). Following the authors, we set eta to be 10^{-6}. In the bootstrap part, the recentering function is stored into the variable recenter. In the *Output* part, the variable reject takes the value 1 if it rejects the null hypothesis and 0 otherwise.

```
%------------------------- Input ------------------------%

sample1=randn(200,1);
sample2=randn(200,1);
bmethod='Multiplier';
B=500;
SDorder=1;
ngrid=100;
alpha=0.05;
a=0.1;

%----------------------- Subroutine ---------------------%

% Measure the size of data
N1=size(sample1,1);
N2=size(sample2,1);

% Construct a support
pooled=sort([sample1; sample2]);
if ngrid==0
grid=pooled;
else
grid=linspace(min(pooled), max(pooled), ngrid);
end

% Define tuning parameters
seq_a=-a*sqrt(log(log(N1+N2)));
eta=10^(-6);
```

```
% Compute the Test Statistic
operator=@(X,z)(X<= z).*(z-X).^(SDorder-1)/factorial(SDorder
    -1);
rawcdf1=mean(bsxfun(operator, sample1, reshape(grid, [1,1,
    ngrid])),1);
rawcdf2=mean(bsxfun(operator, sample2, reshape(grid, [1,1,
    ngrid])),1);
cdf1=squeeze(rawcdf1); % ECDF
cdf2=squeeze(rawcdf2); % ECDF
stat=sqrt(N1*N2/(N1+N2))*max(cdf1-cdf2);

% Multiplier method
if strcmp(bmethod,'Multiplier')==1
    temp1=bsxfun(operator, sample1, reshape(grid,[1,1,ngrid]))
        -repmat(rawcdf1,[N1,1,1]);
    temp2=bsxfun(operator, sample2, reshape(grid,[1,1,ngrid]))
        -repmat(rawcdf2,[N2,1,1]);
    bcdf1=mean(repmat(temp1,[1,B,1]).*randn(N1,B,ngrid),1);
    bcdf2=mean(repmat(temp2,[1,B,1]).*randn(N2,B,ngrid),1);

% Recentered Bootstrap
elseif strcmp(bmethod,'Recentered')==1
    index1=randi(N1,N1,B);
    index2=randi(N2,N2,B);
    bsample1=sample1(index1); % bootstrap samples
    bsample2=sample2(index2); % bootstrap samples
    bcdf1=mean(bsxfun(operator,bsample1,reshape(grid,[1,1,
        ngrid])),1) - repmat(rawcdf1,[1,B,1]);
    bcdf2=mean(bsxfun(operator,bsample2,reshape(grid,[1,1,
        ngrid])),1) - repmat(rawcdf2,[1,B,1]);

% Pooled Sample Bootstrap
elseif strcmp(bmethod,'Pooled')==1
    index=randi(N2+N1,B);
    index1=index(1:N1,:);
    index2=index(N1+1:N2+N1,:);
    bsample1=pooled(index1); % bootstrap sample
    bsample2=pooled(index2); % bootstrap sample
    bcdf1=mean(bsxfun(operator,bsample1,reshape(grid,[1,1,
        ngrid])),1);
    bcdf2=mean(bsxfun(operator,bsample2,reshape(grid,[1,1,
        ngrid])),1);
end

% Recentering function
recenter=reshape((cdf1-cdf2).*(sqrt(N1)*(cdf1-cdf2)<seq_a)
    ,[1,1,ngrid]);

% Bootstrap test statistics
bksstat=sqrt(N1*N2/(N1+N2))*max(bcdf1 - bcdf2 + repmat(
    recenter,[1, B, 1]),[],3);

%------------------------ Output ------------------------%

reject=max(quantile(bksstat,1-alpha),eta)<stat
```

Table B.4 *Rejection probabilities of the Donald–Hsu test*

Design	1	2	3	4
Multiplier Method	0.044	0.002	0.995	0.998
Pooled Sample Bootstrap	0.060	0.007	0.998	0.999
Recentered Bootstrap	0.057	0.007	0.996	0.999

The above table shows the rejection probabilities of the DH test under the four designs. The tuning parameter a is 0.1, and we took 0.05 for the significance level. Under Design 1, rejection probabilities are close to the nominal level, while they are close to zero under Design 2. The powers under Designs 3 and 4 are close to 1.

B.3 Integral-Type Test

B.3.1 Hall–Yatchew Test

The test of Hall and Yatchew (2005, Section 2.2.3, HY) requires five different input variables: `sample1`, `sample2`, `bmethod`, `B`, and `SDorder`. Definitions of the input variables are the same as before, except that `bmethod` must have a string value of either `'Recentered'` or `'Pooled'`.

Like the other tests, the code consists of three parts. Three variables `summand`, `integrand`, and `stat` contain the difference between the two empirical CDFs, the integrand, and the test statistic, respectively. Bootstrap statistics are computed and stored as `stat_b`. Note that the way to compute the bootstrap statistics differs depending on the function input `bmethod`. A calculated p-value is stored as `pvalue`.

To perform the test, we need an additional function file, `step`. The function `step` requires three input variables: `cdf_sample`, `eval_sample`, and `SDorder`. It computes the empirical integrated CDF at order `SDorder`, evaluated at the points `eval_sample` based on the data `cdf_sample`. The function code is attached to the main code.

```
%-------------------------- Input --------------------------%
sample1=randn(100,1);
sample2=randn(100,1);
bmethod='Pooled';
B=300;
SDorder=1;
```

```
%---------------------- Subroutine ----------------------%

% Measure the size of data
N1=size(sample1,1);
N2=size(sample2,1);
N=N1+N2;

% Generate the pooled sample
pooled=sort([sample1; sample2]);

% Compute the test statistic
summand=step(sample1,pooled,SDorder)-step(sample2,pooled,
    SDorder);
summand(end)=[];
integrand=summand.*(summand>0).*(pooled(2:end)-pooled(1:end-1));
stat=(N1*N2)/N * sum(integrand);

% Pooled Sample Bootstrap
stat_b=zeros(B,1);
if strcmp(bmethod,'Pooled')==1
    index=randi(N,N,B);
    pooled_t=pooled(index);
    sample1_b=pooled_t(1:N1,:);
    sample2_b=pooled_t(N1+1:N,:);
    for b=1:B
        pooled_b=sort(pooled_t(:,b));
        summand_b=step(sample1_b(:,b),pooled_b,SDorder)-step(
            sample2_b(:,b), pooled_b,SDorder);
        summand_b(end)=[];
        summand_b=summand_b .*(summand_b>0).*(pooled_b(2:end)-
            pooled_b(1:end-1));
        stat_b(b)=(N1*N2)/N * sum(summand_b);
    end

% Recentered Bootstrap
elseif strcmp(bmethod,'Recentered')==1
    sample1_b=sample1(randi(N1,N1,B));
    sample2_b=sample2(randi(N2,N2,B));
    pooled_t=[sample1_b; sample2_b];
    for b=1:B
        pooled_b=sort(pooled_t(:,b));
        becdf1=step(sample1_b(:,b),pooled_b,SDorder)-step(sample1
            , pooled_b,SDorder);
        becdf2=step(sample2_b(:,b),pooled_b,SDorder)-step(sample2
            , pooled_b,SDorder);
        summand_b=becdf1-becdf2;
        summand_b(end)=[];
        summand_b=summand_b .*(summand_b>0).*(pooled_b(2:end)-
            pooled_b(1:end-1));
        stat_b(b)=(N1*N2)/N * sum(summand_b);
    end
end

%---------------------- Output ----------------------%

pvalue=mean(stat_b>stat);
```

Table B.5 *Rejection probabilities of the Hall–Yatchew test*

Design	1	2	3	4
Pooled Sample Bootstrap	0.057	0.013	1.000	0.934
Recentered Bootstrap	0.053	0.012	1.000	0.932

Below, we present the function code. You should make an additional function file containing the following code. Put the function file in the current directory with the main script file so that the computer is allowed to access this function file while processing the main code.

```
function output = step(cdf_sample, eval_sample, SDorder)

% ECDF of cdf_sample
operator=@(X,z)(X<=z).*(z-X).^(SDorder-1)/factorial(SDorder-1);
leq=@(x,y)(x<=y);
cdf_sample=reshape(sort(cdf_sample),[length(cdf_sample),1]);
distfun=[0; transpose(mean(bsxfun(operator, cdf_sample,
    transpose(cdf_sample)), 1))];

% Evaluate ECDF at eval_sample points
eval_sample=reshape(eval_sample,[1,length(eval_sample)]);
arg=sum(bsxfun(leq,cdf_sample,eval_sample),1)+1;
output=reshape(distfun(arg),[length(arg),1]);
end
```

The above table presents the simulated rejection probabilities of the HY test under the four different designs. Similar to the other tests, the rejection rates under Design 1 with $\mu_x = 0$ are close to the nominal significance level 0.05, and they are close to zero under Design 2 with $\mu_x = -0.03$. Under the two alternative hypotheses (Designs 3 and 4), the rejection probabilities are close to one.

B.3.2 Bennett Test

The code for the Bennett (2008, Section 2.2.3) test has six different input variables sample1, sample2, bmethod, B, SDorder, and q. bmethod must have a string value either 'Recentered' or 'Pooled'. Definition of q is as follows:

- q: A real number between 0 and 2, determining the exponent of the denominator in the integrand of the test statistic.

This code is very similar to that of the HY test, and thus we skip explaining the repetitive parts. To prevent the numerical error that occurs when the denominator of the integrand in the test statistic goes close to zero, the function is coded to set the integrand to zero when the value of the denominator is smaller than 10^{-6}. When q equals either zero or one and SDorder is chosen to be one, the test computes the p-value from the pivotal distribution instead of bootstrapping. Like the HY test, the sub-function stepfun is necessary to run the test, so a user needs to attach the sub-function code to the main code to perform the test.

```
%------------------------- Input -------------------------%

sample1=randn(200,1);
sample2=randn(200,1);
bmethod='Recentered';
B=500;
SDorder=1;
q=0;

%----------------------- Subroutine ----------------------%

% Measure the size of data
N1=size(sample1,1);
N2=size(sample2,1);
N=N1+N2;

% Generate the pooled sample
pooled=sort([sample1; sample2]);

% Compute the Test Statistic
summand=step(sample1,pooled,SDorder)-step(sample2,pooled,SDorder
    );
integrand=summand.^2.*(summand>0);
if q==0
    stat=(N1*N2)/N * sum(integrand) /N;
elseif q<=2
    p_ecdf=stepfun(pooled,pooled,1);
    denom=(p_ecdf.*(1-p_ecdf)).^q;
    temp=abs(denom)<10^(-6);
    denom(temp)=0.5;
    integrand=integrand.*(1-temp);
    stat=(N1*N2)/N * sum(integrand./denom) /N;
end

% Asymptotic distribution in the case q=0 and SDorder=1
if q==0 & SDorder==1
    T = 1; Nsimu = 1000; dt = T/Nsimu; Rsimu=1000;
    dWiener = sqrt(dt)*randn(Nsimu,Rsimu);
    Wiener = cumsum(dWiener,1);
    tgrid=transpose(dt:dt:T);
    Brown = Wiener-repmat(tgrid,[1,Rsimu]).*repmat(Wiener(end,:)
        ,[Nsimu,1]); % Brownian bridge
    bstat=sum(Brown.^2,1)*dt;

    % Asymptotic distribution in the case q=1 and SDorder=1
elseif q==1 & SDorder==1
```

```
    T = 1; Nsimu = 1000; dt = T/Nsimu; Rsimu=1000;
    dWiener = sqrt(dt)*randn(Nsimu-1,Rsimu);
    Wiener = cumsum(dWiener,1);
    tgrid=transpose(dt:dt:T-dt);
    Brown = Wiener-repmat(tgrid,[1,Rsimu]).*repmat(Wiener(end,:)
        ,[Nsimu-1,1]); % Brownian bridge
    bstat=sum(Brown.^2./ repmat(tgrid.*(1-tgrid),[1,Rsimu]),1)*
        dt;

% Pooled Sample Bootstrap
elseif strcmp(bmethod,'Pooled')==1
    index=randi(N,N,B);
    bpooled=pooled(index);
    bsample1=bpooled(1:N1,:); % bootstrap sample
    bsample2=bpooled(N1+1:N,:); % bootstrap sample
    bstat=zeros(B,1);
    for b=1:B
        bsummand=step(bsample1(:,b),bpooled(:,b),SDorder)-step(
            bsample2(:,b), bpooled(:,b), SDorder);
        bsummand=bsummand.^2 .*(bsummand>0);
        if q==0
            bstat(b)=(N1*N2)/N * sum(bsummand) /N;
        elseif q<=2
            bpooledecdf=step(bpooled(:,b),bpooled(:,b),1);
            bdenom=(bpooledecdf.*(1-bpooledecdf)).^q;
            temp=abs(bdenom)<10^(-6);
            bdenom(temp)=0.5;
            bsummand=bsummand.*(1-temp);
            bstat(b)=(N1*N2)/N * sum(bsummand./bdenom) /N; %
                bootstrap statistics
        end
    end

% Recentered Bootstrap
elseif strcmp(bmethod,'Recentered')==1
    bsample1=sample1(randi(N1,N1,B)); % bootstrap sample
    bsample2=sample2(randi(N2,N2,B)); % bootstrap sample
    bpooled=sort([bsample1; bsample2]);
    bstat=zeros(B,1);
        for b=1:B
        becdf1=step(bsample1(:,b),bpooled(:,b),SDorder)-step(
            sample1,bpooled(:,b),SDorder);
        becdf2=step(bsample2(:,b),bpooled(:,b),SDorder)-step(
            sample2,bpooled(:,b),SDorder);
        bsummand=becdf1-becdf2;
        bsummand=bsummand.^2 .*(bsummand>0);
        if q==0
            bstat(b)=(N1*N2)/N * sum(bsummand) /N;
        elseif q<=2
            bpooledecdf=step(bpooled(:,b),bpooled(:,b),1);
            bdenom=(bpooledecdf.*(1-bpooledecdf)).^q;
            temp=abs(bdenom)<10^(-6);
            bdenom(temp)=0.5;
            bsummand=bsummand.*(1-temp);
            bstat(b)=(N1*N2)/N * sum(bsummand./bdenom) /N; %
                bootstrap statistics
        end
    end
```

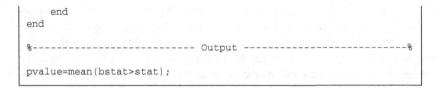

```
         end
  end

  %------------------------- Output -------------------------%

  pvalue=mean(bstat>stat);
```

Table B.6 *Rejection probabilities of the Bennett test*

Design	1	2	3	4
q=0	0.028	0.003	0.999	0.770
q=0.5	0.054	0.008	0.999	0.965
q=1	0.022	0.002	1.000	0.957

The above table shows the rejection probabilities of the Bennett test. We provide the results with various q values: 0, 0.5, and 1. Recall that the critical values are tabulated in the case q equals to 0 or 1. In the other cases, we compute the bootstrap p-values. For the table, we implemented a recentered bootstrap. Under Design 1, the rejection probability with q=0.5 is close to the nominal level 0.05, while the probabilities with q=0 or q=1 are less than the nominal level. The rejection probabilities in Design 2 are close to zero. The rejection probabilities, which correspond to the powers under Designs 3 and 4, are close to 1.

B.3.3 Linton–Song–Whang Test

The code for the Linton, Song, and Whang (2010, Section 3.1.1, LSW) test has six different arguments: sample1, sample2, B, SDorder, ngrid, and c. The definition of c is given by:

- c: A real number determining the coefficient for *seq_c* where *seq_c* is the threshold c_N used to estimate the contact set.

Sample sizes of sample1 and sample2 must be equal, otherwise an error message will pop up.

The code consists of three parts: *Input, Subroutine,* and *Output*. At the beginning of the *Subroutine* part, we define the sequence c_N, which is used to estimate the contact set. We set $c_N = c \log(\log(N))$, as suggested by the authors, where N is the sample size. For the coefficient, they use $c \in \{3.0, 3.2, \cdots, 4.0\}$ in their simulation study. We use a trapezoidal rule to approximate integrals. The estimated CDFs are stored as cdf1 and cdf2, and `cmstat` is the test statistic. In the bootstrap part, a recentered bootstrap based on two separate samples is implemented. Bootstrap samples are stored as `bsample1` and `bsample2`. The empirical CDFs obtained from the bootstrap samples are `bcdf1` and `bcdf2`, and bootstrap test statistics are stored as `bcmstat`. `contact` contains the information on the contact set. If the estimated contact set `contact` is not empty, the bootstrap statistic is integrated over the contact set. Otherwise, it is integrated over the whole support. As an output, the p-value is reported as `pvalue`.

```
%------------------------- Input -------------------------%

sample1=randn(200,1);
sample2=randn(200,1);
B=300;
SDorder=1;
ngrid=20;
c=3.0;

%--------------------- Subroutine ---------------------%

% Measure the size of data
N1=size(sample1,1);
N2=size(sample2,1);
N=N1+N2;

% Construct a Support
pooled=sort([sample1; sample2]);
grid=linspace(min(pooled),max(pooled),ngrid)';

% Setting up the tuning parameter
seq_c=c*log(log(N))/sqrt(N);

% Compute the Test Statistic
    operator=@(X,z)(X<= z).*(z-X).^(SDorder-1)/factorial(
        SDorder-1);
    rawcdf1=mean(bsxfun(operator, sample1, reshape(grid,[1,1,
        ngrid])),1);
    rawcdf2=mean(bsxfun(operator, sample2, reshape(grid,[1,1,
        ngrid])),1);
    cdf1=squeeze(rawcdf1);
    cdf2=squeeze(rawcdf2);
    base=(max(pooled)-min(pooled))/ngrid;
    cmstat=N*trapz( ((cdf1-cdf2)>0).*(cdf1-cdf2).^ 2)*base;

% Bootstrap
    index1=randi(N1,N1,B);
    index2=randi(N2,N2,B);
    bsample1=sample1(index1);  % bootstrap sample
    bsample2=sample2(index2);  % bootstrap sample
    bcdf1=mean(bsxfun(operator, bsample1, reshape(grid, [1, 1,
        ngrid])), 1) - repmat(rawcdf1, [1, B, 1]);
    bcdf2=mean(bsxfun(operator, bsample2, reshape(grid, [1, 1,
        ngrid])), 1) - repmat(rawcdf2, [1, B, 1]);
```

```
contact=(abs(cdf1-cdf2)<seq_ c); % contact set
   if sum(contact)==0
bcmstat=N*trapz( ((bcdf1 - bcdf2)>0).*(bcdf1 - bcdf2).^ 2, 3)
   *base;
   else
ct_rep=repmat(contact,[1,B]);
ct_num=size(ct_rep,1);
bcdf1=transpose(squeeze(bcdf1));
bcdf2=transpose(squeeze(bcdf2));
bcdf1=reshape(bcdf1(ct_ rep==1),[ct_ num, B]);
bcdf2=reshape(bcdf2(ct_ rep==1),[ct_ num, B]);
bcmstat=N*trapz( ((bcdf1-bcdf2)>0).*(bcdf1-bcdf2).^ 2)*base;
   end

%------------------------- Output -------------------------%

pvalue= sum(bcmstat>cmstat)/B;
```

Table B.7 *Rejection probabilities of the Linton–Song–Whang test*

Design	1	2	3	4
Rejection Probabilities	0.040	0.003	1.000	0.9840

The above table shows the rejection probabilities of the Linton–Song–Whang test. The tuning parameter c is set to 3. Under Design 1, the rejection probability is close to the nominal level, implying that the size is well controlled. The rejection probabilities in Design are close to zero, as expected. The powers under Designs 3 and 4 are very close to 1.

B.4 Stochastic Dominance with Covariates: Lee–Whang Test

We provide code for the test of Lee and Whang (2009, LW) and Chang, Lee, and Whang (2015) that evaluates conditional distributional treatment effects; see Section 4.3.1. The code is based on the Gauss code written by LW.

The code has seven different input variables. A user should input the covariate data into x, output data into y, and the treatment indicator data into treatment. This code allows only one covariate, and thus x must be a vector. The sizes of x, y, and treatment must be conformative, and treatment must contain either 1 or 0, which indicates the treatment status. Also a user needs to set new parameter values: kx, ky, kt, and c. Among them, kx, ky, and kt denote the numbers of grid points. c is a bandwidth constant.

The *Subroutine* section starts with preliminary steps: obtaining a bandwidth, checking whether sizes of the data are conformative, defining functions, and computing the grid points. The bandwidth is determined by the rule

$$h = c * (\text{standard deviation of covariate}) * (\text{sample size})^{\wedge}(-2/7).$$

LW consider a set of values $\{4.0, 4.5, \cdots, 6.5\}$ for c in their empirical study. Estimated $\hat{\tau}(y, x)$ is stored as tau, and the weight function $\hat{w}(y, x)$ is saved as wft. The code computes two types of the test statistic T_N (defined in Equation 4.3.3), one with a uniform weight function tn and the other with an inverse-standard-error weight function tn_w. The estimated contact set, $F(\rho)$, asymptotic bias ($\hat{a}_N$), and $\hat{\sigma}$ are saved as cutoff, F_rho, an_cse, and bn_cse, respectively. If the estimated contact set is empty, it returns the test statistic based on the least favorable case. In the end, two types of p-values are stored as test_lw and test_lw_w: one based on the uniform weight function and the other based on the inverse-standard-error weight function.

```
%--------------------------- Input --------------------------%

x=randn(200,1);
y=randn(200,1);
treatment=floor(rand(200,1));
kx=20;
ky=20;
kt=20;
c=4.0;

%------------------------- Subroutine -----------------------%

% Measure the sample size
   [N,d]=size(x);

% Bandwidth
   h=c*std(x,1)'*N^(-2/7); % d * 1

% Functions
   kl=@(x,rv)(3/2)*(1-(2*(x-rv)).^2).*(abs(x-rv)*4<=0.5);  %
      kernel function
   kls=@(u)(6/5)*((1-abs(u)).^3).*((u.^2)+3*abs(u)+1).*(abs(u)<=1)
      ;    % convolution kernel
   cmp=@(x, rv)(rv<=x); % function for computing ECDF

% Construct grids
   xgrid=linspace(min(x),max(x), kx)';
   xgridl=abs(xgrid(1)-xgrid(2));
   ygrid=linspace(min(y),max(y),ky)';
   ygridl=abs(ygrid(1)-ygrid(2));
   tgrid=linspace(-0.9, 0.9, kt)';
   tgridl=abs(tgrid(1)-tgrid(2));

% Estimation of tau
   gy=bsxfun(cmp, ygrid, reshape(y,[1 1 N])); % ECDF for y
   kerx=ones(kx,N);
   for i=1:d
   tmp=bsxfun(kl, xgrid(:,i)/h(i), x(:,i)'/h(i))/h(i) ;
   kerx=kerx.*(tmp);
```

```
    end
    p1=mean(kerx.*repmat(treatment', [kx 1]),2)';
    p0=mean(kerx.*repmat((1-treatment)', [kx 1]),2)';
    %finite sample adjustment
    p1=p1+1e-8*(p1==0);
    p0=p0+1e-8*(p0==0);
    kerx=reshape(kerx, [1 kx N]);
    phi1=bsxfun(@times,(p1.^(-1)),reshape(treatment  ,[1 1 N])));
    phi0=bsxfun(@times,(p0.^(-1)),reshape(1-treatment, [1 1 N])));
    tau=mean(repmat(gy, [1 kx 1]).* repmat(kerx.*(phi1-phi0), [ky 1
        1]) ,3);

% Estimation of the weight function
    mu1=mean(repmat(gy.^2, [1 kx 1]).* repmat(kerx.*(phi1), [ky 1
        1]) ,3) ./ repmat(p1, [ky 1]) + mean(repmat(gy.^2, [1 kx
        1]).* repmat(kerx.*(phi0), [ky 1 1]),3) ./ repmat(p0, [ky
        1]);
    mu2=mean(repmat(gy, [1 kx 1]).* repmat(kerx.*(phi1), [ky 1 1])
        ,3).^2 ./ repmat(p1, [ky 1]) + mean(repmat(gy, [1 kx 1]).*
        repmat(kerx.*(phi0), [ky 1 1]),3).^ 2 ./ repmat(p0, [ky 1])
        ;
    rho2=(6/5)* (mu1-mu2);
    %finite sample adjustment
    rho2 = rho2 + 1e-8*(rho2<=0);
    wft=(rho2).^(-1/2);
    tn=sqrt(N)*trapz(ygrid, trapz(xgrid, tau.*(tau>0),2),1);
    tn_w=sqrt(N)*trapz(ygrid, trapz(xgrid, tau.*(tau>0).*wft,2),1)
        ;

% Contact set estimation
    eta_n=h * N^(2/7) * N^(-11/56);
    cutoff = (abs(tau) <= eta_n);

% Estimation of F(rho)
    r1kerx=reshape(kerx, [1 1 kx N]);
    r1phi1=reshape(phi1, [1 1 kx N]);
    r1phi0=reshape(phi0, [1 1 kx N]);
    r1gy=reshape(gy,[1 ky N]);
    r1gy=reshape(repmat(gy,[1 ky 1]) .* repmat(r1gy,[ky 1 1]), [ky
        ky 1 N]);
    r1= mean(repmat(r1kerx.*(r1phi1.^2 + r1phi0.^2),[ky ky 1 1]) .*
        repmat(r1gy, [1 1 kx 1]) ,4);
    r21=mean(repmat(gy, [1 kx 1]).* repmat(kerx.*phi1, [ky 1 1]) ,3)
        ;
    r20=mean(repmat(gy, [1 kx 1]).* repmat(kerx.*phi0, [ky 1 1]) ,3)
        ;
    r2j1=repmat(reshape(r21, [ky 1 kx]),[1 ky 1]) .* repmat(reshape(
        r21, [1 ky kx]),[ky 1 1]);
    r2j0=repmat(reshape(r20, [ky 1 kx]),[1 ky 1]) .* repmat(reshape(
        r20, [1 ky kx]),[ky 1 1]);
    r2= r2j1.*repmat(reshape(p1.^(-1),[1 1 kx]),[ky ky 1]) + r2j0.*
        repmat(reshape(p0.^(-1),[1 1 kx]),[ky ky 1]);
    denom=repmat(reshape(rho2,[ky 1 kx]),[1 ky 1]) .* repmat(reshape
        (rho2,[1 ky kx]),[ky 1 1]);
    denom = denom + 1e-8*(denom<=0);
    rho_bar=(r1-r2)./sqrt(denom);
```

```
rho=repmat((rho_bar),[1 1 1 kt]).* repmat(reshape(kls(tgrid), [1
    1 1 kt]),[ky ky kx 1]);

% Finite sample adjustment
rho=rho+(-rho+1-1e-4).*(rho>=1);
rho=rho+(-rho-1+1e-4).*(rho<=-1);
temp1=exp(-0.5*(rho.^2) ./ (1-rho.^2)).*sqrt(1-rho.^2);
temp2=(pi*rho).*cdf('normal', rho./sqrt(1-rho.^2), 0,1);
F_rho=(temp1+temp2-1)/(2*pi);

% Estimation of the asymptotic bias and variance
    an=prod(h)^(-1/2) * trapz(ygrid,trapz(xgrid,ones(size(tau)),2)
        ,1) / sqrt(2*pi);
    bn=sqrt(trapz(xgrid, trapz(ygrid,trapz(ygrid, trapz(tgrid,
        F_rho, 4),1),2),3));
    if sum(sum(cutoff))==0
        an_cse=an;
        bn_cse=bn;
    else
        an_cse=prod(h)^(-1/2) * trapz(ygrid,trapz(xgrid,cutoff,2)
            ,1) / sqrt(2*pi);
        bn_cse=trapz(tgrid, F_rho, 4);
        for b=1:kx
            for a=1:ky
                if cutoff(a,b)==0
                    bn_cse(a,:,b)=0;
                    bn_cse(:,a,b)=0;
                end
            end
        end
        bn_cse=sqrt(trapz(xgrid, trapz(ygrid,trapz(ygrid, bn_cse,1)
            ,2),3));
    end

% Test statistics
    stat_lw=(tn-an_cse)/bn_cse;
    stat_lw_w=(tn_w-an_cse)/bn_cse;

%------------------------- Output -------------------------%

test_lw=1-cdf('normal',stat_lw, 0, 1)
test_lw_w=1-cdf('normal',stat_lw_w, 0, 1)
```

Table B.8 *Rejection probabilities of the Lee–Whang test*

Design	7	8	9	10
Uniform Weight	0.002	0.000	1.000	0.7540
Inverse Standard Error Weight	0.035	0.000	1.000	0.9640

The above table shows the rejection probabilities of the Lee–Whang test. We set the number of grid points to 20 and took $c = 4.0$. Under the null hypothesis, the test tends to under-reject. Under the alternative hypotheses, however, the test appears to perform satisfactorily.

Bibliography

Abadie, A. (2002). "Bootstrap tests for distributional treatment effects in instrumental variable models," *Journal of the American Statistical Association* **97**(457), 284–292.

Abhyankar, A., Ho, K.-Y., and Zhao, H. (2009). "International value versus growth: Evidence from stochastic dominance analysis," *International Journal of Finance & Economics* **14**(3), 222–232.

Abrevaya, J. (2006). "Estimating the effect of smoking on birth outcomes using a matched panel data approach," *Journal of Applied Econometrics* **21**(4), 489–519.

Adusumilli, K., Otsu, T., and Whang, Y.-J. (2017). "Inference on distribution functions under measurement error," Working paper, London School of Economics.

Agliardi, E., Agliardi, R., Pinar, M., Stengos, T., and Topaloglou, N. (2012). "A new country risk index for emerging markets: A stochastic dominance approach," *Journal of Empirical Finance* **19**(5), 741–761.

Agliardi, E., Pinar, M., and Stengos, T. (2014). "A sovereign risk index for the Eurozone based on stochastic dominance," *Finance Research Letters* **11**(4), 375–384.

Álvarez-Esteban, P., del Barrio, E., Cuesta-Albertos, J., and Matrán, C. (2016). "A contamination model for the stochastic order," *Test* **25**(4), 751–774.

Amin, S., Rai, A. S., and Topa, G. (2003). "Does microcredit reach the poor and vulnerable? Evidence from Northern Bangladesh," *Journal of Development Economics* **70**(1), 59–82.

Anderson, G. (1996). "Nonparametric tests of stochastic dominance in income distributions," *Econometrica* **65**(5), 1183–1193.

Anderson, G. (2003). "Poverty in America 1970–1990: Who did gain ground? An application of stochastic dominance criteria employing simultaneous inequality tests in a partial panel," *Journal of Applied Econometrics* **18**(6), 621–640.

Anderson, G. (2004*a*). "Making inferences about the polarization, welfare and poverty of nations: A study of 101 countries 1970–1995," *Journal of Applied Econometrics* **19**(5), 537–550.

Anderson, G. (2004*b*). "Toward an empirical analysis of polarization," *Journal of Econometrics* **122**(1), 1–26.

Anderson, G. (2008). "The empirical assessment of multidimensional welfare, inequality and poverty: Sample weighted multivariate generalizations of the

Kolmogorov–Smirnov two sample tests for stochastic dominance," *The Journal of Economic Inequality* **6**(1), 73–87.

Anderson, G., Ge, Y., and Leo, T. W. (2010). "Distributional overlap: Simple, multivariate, parametric, and nonparametric tests for alienation, convergence, and general distributional difference issues," *Econometric Reviews* **29**(3), 247–275.

Anderson, G. and Leo, T. W. (2009). "Child poverty, investment in children and generational mobility: The short and long term wellbeing of children in urban China after the one child policy," *Review of Income and Wealth* **55**(s1), 607–629.

Anderson, G., Linton, O. B., and Whang, Y.-J. (2012). "Nonparametric estimation and inference about the overlap of two distributions," *Journal of Econometrics* **171**(1), 1–23.

Anderson, G., Post, T., and Whang, Y.-J. (2018). "Somewhere between utopia and dystopia: Choosing from multiple incomparable prospects," Working paper, University of Toronto.

Andrews, D. W. K. (1993). "An introduction to econometric applications of empirical process theory for dependent random variables," *Econometric Reviews* **12**(2), 183–216.

Andrews, D. W. K. and Pollard, D. (1994). "An introduction to functional central limit theorems for dependent stochastic processes," *International Statistical Review* **62**(1), 119–132.

Andrews, D. W. K. (1994). "Empirical process methods in econometrics," in *Handbook of Econometrics*, edited by R. F. Engle and D. L. McFadden, Vol. 4, Chapter 37, pp. 2247–2294, Elsevier.

Andrews, D. W. K. and Guggenberger, P. (2009). "Validity of subsampling and 'plug-in asymptotic' inference for parameters defined by moment inequalities," *Econometric Theory* **25**(3), 669–709.

Andrews, D. W. K. and Shi, X. (2013). "Inference based on conditional moment inequalities," *Econometrica* **81**(2), 609–666.

Andrews, D. W. K. and Shi, X. (2017). "Inference based on many conditional moment inequalities," *Journal of Econometrics* **196**(2), 275–287.

Angrist, J. D. and Keueger, A. B. (1991). "Does compulsory school attendance affect schooling and earnings?" *The Quarterly Journal of Economics* **106**(4), 979–1014.

Arellano, M. and Bonhomme, S. (2012). "Identifying distributional characteristics in random coefficients panel data models," *The Review of Economic Studies* **79**(3), 987–1020.

Armstrong, T. B. (2018). "On the choice of test statistic for conditional moment inequalities," forthcoming in *Journal of Econometrics*.

Arnold, J. M. and Hussinger, K. (2010). "Exports versus FDI in German manufacturing: Firm performance and participation in international markets," *Review of International Economics* **18**(4), 595–606.

Arvanitis, S., Hallam, M., Post, T., and Topaloglou, N. (2017). "Stochastic spanning," forthcoming in *Journal of Business & Economics Statistics*.

Arvanitis, S. and Topaloglou, N. (2017). "Testing for prospect and Markowitz stochastic dominance efficiency," *Journal of Econometrics* **198**(2), 253–270.

Aryal, G. and Gabrielli, M. F. (2013). "Testing for collusion in asymmetric first-price auctions," *International Journal of Industrial Organization* **31**(1), 26–35.

Athey, S. and Imbens, G. W. (2017). "The econometrics of randomized experiments," in *Handbook of Economic Field Experiments*, edited by A. V. Banerjee and E. Duflo, Vol. 1, Chapter 3, pp. 73–140, Elsevier.

Atkinson, A. B. (1970). "On the measurement of inequality," *Journal of Economic Theory* **2**(3), 244–263.

Atkinson, A. B. and Bourguignon, F. (1982). "The comparison of multi-dimensioned distributions of economic status," *The Review of Economic Studies* **49**(2), 183–201.

Bali, T. G., Demirtas, K. O., Levy, H., and Wolf, A. (2009). "Bonds versus stocks: Investors' age and risk taking," *Journal of Monetary Economics* **56**(6), 817–830.

Barrett, G. F. and Donald, S. G. (2003). "Consistent tests for stochastic dominance," *Econometrica* **71**(1), 71–104.

Barrett, G. F., Donald, S. G., and Bhattacharya, D. (2014). "Consistent nonparametric tests for Lorenz dominance," *Journal of Business & Economic Statistics* **32**(1), 1–13.

Barrett, G. F., Donald, S. G., and Hsu, Y.-C. (2016). "Consistent tests for poverty dominance relations," *Journal of Econometrics* **191**(2), 360–373.

Bawa, V. S., Bodurtha, J. N., Rao, M., and Suri, H. L. (1985). "On determination of stochastic dominance optimal sets," *The Journal of Finance* **40**(2), 417–431.

Beach, C. M. and Davidson, R. (1983). "Distribution-free statistical inference with Lorenz curves and income shares," *The Review of Economic Studies* **50**(4), 723–735.

Beare, B. K. (2011). "Measure preserving derivatives and the pricing kernel puzzle," *Journal of Mathematical Economics* **47**(6), 689–697.

Beare, B. K. and Moon, J.-M. (2015). "Nonparametric tests of density ratio ordering," *Econometric Theory* **31**(03), 471–492.

Beare, B. K. and Shi, X. (2015). "An improved bootstrap test of density ratio ordering," Working paper, University of California, San Diego.

Beare, B. K. and Schmidt, L. (2015). "Empirical implications of the pricing kernel puzzle for the return on contingent claims," Working paper, University of California, San Diego.

Beirlant, J. and Mason, D. (1995). "On the asymptotic normality of L_p-norms of empirical functionals," *Mathematical Methods of Statistics* **4**(1), 1–19.

Bekele, W. (2005). "Stochastic dominance analysis of soil and water conservation in subsistence crop production in the Eastern Ethiopian highlands: The case of the Hunde-Lafto area," *Environmental and Resource Economics* **32**(4), 533–550.

Bennett, C. J. (2013). "Inference for dominance relations," *International Economic Review* **54**(4), 1309–1328.

Bennett, C. J. (2007). "A bootstrap test for infinite-degree stochastic dominance with applications to finance," Working paper, Vanderbilt University.

Bennett, C. J. (2008). "New consistent integral-type tests for stochastic dominance," Working paper, Vanderbilt University.

Bennett, C. J. and Zitikis, R. (2013). "Examining the distributional effects of military service on earnings: A test of initial dominance," *Journal of Business & Economic Statistics* **31**(1), 1–15.

Berger, R. L. (1988). "A nonparametric, intersection-union test for stochastic order," in *Statistical Decision Theory and Related Topics IV*, edited by S. S. Gupta and J. O. Berger, Vol. 2, Springer-Verlag, New York.

Bickel, P. J. and Rosenblatt, M. (1973). "On some global measures of the deviations of density function estimates," *The Annals of Statistics* **1**(6), 1071–1095.

Billingsley, P. (1968). *Convergence of Probability Measures*, John Wiley & Sons, New York.

Billingsley, P. (1995). *Probability and Measure*, John Wiley, New York.

Bishop, J. A., Chakraborti, S., and Thistle, P. D. (1989). "Asymptotically distribution-free statistical inference for generalized Lorenz curves," *The Review of Economics and Statistics* **71**(4), 725–727.

Bishop, J. A., Formby, J. P., and Smith, W. J. (1991). "International comparisons of income inequality: Tests for Lorenz dominance across nine countries," *Economica* **58**(232), 461–477.

Bishop, J. A., Formby, J. P., and Thistle, P. D. (1989). "Statistical inference, income distributions, and social welfare," *Research on Economic Inequality* **1**, 49–82.

Bishop, J. A., Formby, J. P., and Zeager, L. A. (2000). "The effect of food stamp cashout on undernutrition," *Economics Letters* **67**(1), 75–85.

Bissantz, N., Dümbgen, L., Holzmann, H., and Munk, A. (2007). "Non-parametric confidence bands in deconvolution density estimation," *Journal of the Royal Statistical Society* **69**(3), 483–506.

Bitler, M. P., Gelbach, J. B., and Hoynes, H. W. (2006). "What mean impacts miss: Distributional effects of welfare reform experiments," *The American Economic Review* **96**(4), 988–1012.

Black, F. (1976). "Studies of stock price volatility changes," *Proceedings for the 1976 Meetings of the American Statistical Association*.

Blundell, R., Gosling, A., Ichimura, H., and Meghir, C. (2007). "Changes in the distribution of male and female wages accounting for employment composition using bounds," *Econometrica* **75**(2), 323–363.

Bound, J., Brown, C., and Mathiowetz, N. (2001). "Measurement error in survey data," in *Handbook of Econometrics*, edited by J. J. Heckman and E. Leamer, Vol. 5, Chapter 59, pp. 3705–3843, Elsevier.

Brown, B. W. and Newey, W. K. (2002). "Generalized method of moments, efficient bootstrapping, and improved inference," *Journal of Business & Economic Statistics* **20**(4), 507–517.

Carolan, C. A. and Tebbs, J. M. (2005). "Nonparametric tests for and against likelihood ratio ordering in the two-sample problem," *Biometrika* **92**(1), 159–171.

Carrington, A. (2006). "Regional convergence in the European Union: A stochastic dominance approach," *International Regional Science Review* **29**(1), 64–80.

Chan, C.-Y., de Peretti, C., Qiao, Z., and Wong, W.-K. (2012). "Empirical test of the efficiency of the UK covered warrants market: Stochastic dominance and likelihood ratio test approach," *Journal of Empirical Finance* **19**(1), 162–174.

Chang, M., Lee, S., and Whang, Y.-J. (2015). "Nonparametric tests of conditional treatment effects with an application to single-sex schooling on academic achievements," *The Econometrics Journal* **18**(3), 307–346.

Chen, W.-H. (2008). "Comparing low income of Canada's regions: A stochastic dominance approach," Working paper, Statistics Canada, OECD.

Chen, X., Hong, H., and Nekipelov, D. (2011). "Nonlinear models of measurement errors," *Journal of Economic Literature* **49**(4), 901–937.

Chernozhukov, V. and Fernández-Val, I. (2005). "Subsampling inference on quantile regression processes," *Sankhya: The Indian Journal of Statistics* **67**(2), 253–276.

Chernozhukov, V., Fernández-Val, I., and Galichon, A. (2010). "Quantile and probability curves without crossing," *Econometrica* **78**(3), 1093–1125.

Chernozhukov, V., Fernández-Val, I., and Melly, B. (2013). "Inference on counterfactual distributions," *Econometrica* **81**(6), 2205–2268.

Chernozhukov, V. and Hansen, C. (2005). "An IV model of quantile treatment effects," *Econometrica* **73**(1), 245–261.

Chernozhukov, V. and Hansen, C. (2006). "Instrumental quantile regression inference for structural and treatment effect models," *Journal of Econometrics* **132**(2), 491–525.

Chernozhukov, V., Hong, H., and Tamer, E. (2007). "Estimation and confidence regions for parameter sets in econometric models," *Econometrica* **75**(5), 1243–1284.

Chernozhukov, V., Lee, S., and Rosen, A. M. (2013). "Intersection bounds: Estimation and inference," *Econometrica* **81**(2), 667–737.

Chesher, A. and Schluter, C. (2002). "Welfare measurement and measurement error," *The Review of Economic Studies* **69**(2), 357–378.

Cho, Y.-H., Linton, O. B., and Whang, Y.-J. (2007). "Are there monday effects in stock returns: A stochastic dominance approach," *Journal of Empirical Finance* **14**(5), 736–755.

Christie, A. A. (1982). "The stochastic behavior of common stock variances: Value, leverage and interest rate effects," *Journal of Financial Economics* **10**(4), 407–432.

Chuang, O.-C., Kuan, C.-M., and Tzeng, L. Y. (2017). "Testing for central dominance: Method and application," *Journal of Econometrics* **196**(2), 368–378.

Cochrane, J. H. (2005). *Asset Pricing*, Princeton University Press, New Jersey.

Contreras, D. (2001). "Economic growth and poverty reduction by region: Chile 1990–96," *Development Policy Review* **19**(3), 291–302.

Corradi, V. and Swanson, N. R. (2013). "A survey of recent advances in forecast accuracy comparison testing, with an extension to stochastic dominance," in *Recent Advances and Future Directions in Causality, Prediction, and Specification Analysis: Essays in Honor of Halbert L. White Jr*, edited by X. Chen and N. R. Swanson, Chapter 5, pp. 121–143, Springer, New York.

Cowell, F. A. and Flachaire, E. (2015). "Statistical methods for distributional analysis," in *Handbook of Income Distribution*, edited by A. B. Atkins and F. Bourguignon, Vol. 2A, Chapter 6, pp. 359–465, Elsevier.

Crawford, I. (2005). "A nonparametric test of stochastic dominance in multivariate distributions," Working paper, University of Surrey.

Dagum, C. (1968). *Multivariate Transvariation Theory among Several Distributions and Its Economic Applications*, Princeton University Press, New Jersey.

Dalton, H. (1920). "The measurement of the inequality of incomes," *The Economic Journal* **30**(119), 348–361.

Dardanoni, V., Fiorini, M., and Forcina, A. (2012). "Stochastic monotonicity in intergenerational mobility tables," *Journal of Applied Econometrics* **27**(1), 85–107.

Dardanoni, V. and Forcina, A. (1998). "A unified approach to likelihood inference on stochastic orderings in a nonparametric context," *Journal of the American Statistical Association* **93**(443), 1112–1123.

Dardanoni, V. and Forcina, A. (1999). "Inference for Lorenz curve orderings," *The Econometrics Journal* **2**(1), 49–75.

Davidson, J. (1994). *Stochastic Limit Theory*, Oxford University Press, Oxford.

Davidson, R. (2009). "Testing for restricted stochastic dominance: Some further results," *Review of Economic Analysis* **1**, 34–59.

Davidson, R. (2010). "Innis lecture: Inference on income distributions," *Canadian Journal of Economics* **43**(4), 1122–1148.

Davidson, R. and Duclos, J.-Y. (2000). "Statistical inference for stochastic dominance and for the measurement of poverty and inequality," *Econometrica* **68**(6), 1435–1464.

Davidson, R. and Duclos, J.-Y. (2013). "Testing for restricted stochastic dominance," *Econometric Reviews* **32**(1), 84–125.

Davies, J. B., Green, D. A., and Paarsch, H. J. (1998). "Economic statistics and social welfare comparisons: A review," in *Handbook of Applied Economic Statistics*, edited by A. Ullah and D. E. A. Giles, Vol. 155, Chapter 1, pp. 1–38, Marcel Dekker, New York.

Davydov, Y. and Egorov, V. (2000). "Functional limit theorems for induced order statistics," *Mathematical Methods of Statistics* **9**(3), 297–313.

De Silva, D. G., Dunne, T., and Kosmopoulou, G. (2003). "An empirical analysis of entrant and incumbent bidding in road construction auctions," *The Journal of Industrial Economics* **51**(3), 295–316.

Delgado, M. A. and Escanciano, J. C. (2012). "Distribution-free tests of stochastic monotonicity," *Journal of Econometrics* **170**(1), 68–75.

Delgado, M. A. and Escanciano, J. C. (2013). "Conditional stochastic dominance testing," *Journal of Business & Economic Statistics* **31**(1), 16–28.

Delgado, M. A., Farinas, J. C., and Ruano, S. (2002). "Firm productivity and export markets: A non-parametric approach," *Journal of International Economics* **57**(2), 397–422.

Denuit, M., Dhaene, J., and Ribas, C. (2001). "Does positive dependence between individual risks increase stop-loss premiums?" *Insurance: Mathematics and Economics* **28**(3), 305–308.

Denuit, M. and Scaillet, O. (2004). "Nonparametric tests for positive quadrant dependence," *Journal of Financial Econometrics* **2**(3), 422–450.

Deshpande, J. V. and Singh, H. (1985). "Testing for second order stochastic dominance," *Communications in Statistics-Theory and Methods* **14**(4), 887–893.

Dhaene, J. and Goovaerts, M. J. (1996). "Dependency of risks and stop-loss order," *Astin Bulletin* **26**(02), 201–212.

DiNardo, J., Fortin, N. M., and Lemieux, T. (1996). "Labor market institutions and the distribution of wages, 1973–1992: A semiparametric approach," *Econometrica* **64**(5), 1001–1044.

Donald, S. G. and Hsu, Y.-C. (2014). "Estimation and inference for distribution functions and quantile functions in treatment effect models," *Journal of Econometrics* **178**(3), 383–397.

Donald, S. G. and Hsu, Y.-C. (2016). "Improving the power of tests of stochastic dominance," *Econometric Reviews* **35**(4), 553–585.

Doob, J. (1954). *Stochastic Processes*, Wiley, New York.

Doukhan, P. (1994). *Mixing: Properties and Examples*, Springer-Verlag, New York.

Doukhan, P., Massart, P., and Rio, E. (1995). "Invariance principles for absolutely regular empirical processes," *Annales de Institut Henri Poincare* **31**(2), 393–427.

Duclos, J.-Y., Sahn, D. E., and Younger, S. D. (2006). "Robust multidimensional poverty comparisons," *The Economic Journal* **116**(514), 943–968.

Dvoretzky, A., Kiefer, J., and Wolfowitz, J. (1956). "Asymptotic minimax character of the sample distribution function and of the classical multinomial estimator," *The Annals of Mathematical Statistics* **27**(3), 642–669.

Dykstara, R. L., Madsen, R. W., and Fairbanks, K. (1983). "A nonparametric likelihood ratio test," *Journal of Statistical Computation and Simulation* **18**(4), 247–264.

Dykstra, R., Kochar, S., and Robertson, T. (1991). "Statistical inference for uniform stochastic ordering in several populations," *The Annals of Statistics* **19**(2), 870–888.

Dykstra, R., Kochar, S., and Robertson, T. (1995). "Inference for likelihood ratio ordering in the two-sample problem," *Journal of the American Statistical Association* **90**(431), 1034–1040.

El Barmi, H. and McKeague, I. W. (2013). "Empirical likelihood-based tests for stochastic ordering," *Bernoulli* **19**(1), 295.

El Barmi, H. and McKeague, I. W. (2016). "Testing for uniform stochastic ordering via empirical likelihood," *Annals of the Institute of Statistical Mathematics* **68**(5), 955–976.

Elliott, R. and Zhou, Y. (2013). "State-owned enterprises, exporting and productivity in China: A stochastic dominance approach," *The World Economy* **36**(8), 1000–1028.

Embrechts, P., McNeil, A., and Straumann, D. (2002). "Correlation and dependence in risk management: Properties and pitfalls," in *Risk management: Value at Risk and Beyond*, edited by M. A. H. Dempster, pp. 176–223, Cambridge University Press.

Eren, O. and Henderson, D. J. (2008). "The impact of homework on student achievement," *The Econometrics Journal* **11**(2), 326–348.

Eren, O. and Millimet, D. L. (2008). "Time to learn? The organizational structure of schools and student achievement," in *The Economics of Education and Training*, edited by C. Dustmann, B. Fitzenberger, and S. Machin, Chapter 4, pp. 47–78, Physica-Verlag, Springer.

Eubank, R., Schechtman, E., and Yitzhaki, S. (1993). "A test for second order stochastic dominance," *Communications in Statistics-Theory and Methods* **22**(7), 1893–1905.

Fama, E. (1970). "Efficient capital markets: A review of theory and empirical work," *The Journal of Finance* **25**(2), 383–417.

Fan, J. and Gijbels, I. (1996). *Local Polynomial Modelling and Its Applications*, CRC Press.

Fang, Z. and Santos, A. (2016). "Inference on directionally differentiable functions," Working paper, UCSD, available at *https://arxiv.org/abs/1404.3763*.

Feng, Y. and Wang, J. (2007). "Likelihood ratio test against simple stochastic ordering among several multinomial populations," *Journal of Statistical Planning and Inference* **137**(4), 1362–1374.

Fermanian, J.-d. and Scaillet, O. (2003). "Nonparametric estimation of copulas for time series," *Journal of Risk* **5**(4), 25–54.

Fishburn, P. C. (1974). "Convex stochastic dominance with continuous distribution functions," *Journal of Economic Theory* **7**(2), 143–158.

Fleurbaey, M. (2009). "Beyond GDP: The quest for a measure of social welfare," *Journal of Economic Literature* **47**(4), 1029–1075.

Fong, W. M. (2010). "A stochastic dominance analysis of Yen Carry Trades," *Journal of Banking & Finance* **34**(6), 1237–1246.

Fong, W. M., Wong, W. K., and Lean, H. H. (2005). "International momentum strategies: A stochastic dominance approach," *Journal of Financial Markets* **8**(1), 89–109.

Fortin, N., Lemieux, T., and Firpo, S. (2011). "Decomposition methods in economics," in *Handbook of Labor Economics*, edited by O. Ashenfelter and D. Card, Vol. 4A, Chapter 1, pp. 1–102, Elsevier, Amsterdam.

Foster, J. E. and Shorrocks, A. F. (1988). "Poverty orderings and welfare dominance," in *Distributive Justice and Inequality*, edited by W. Gaertner and P. K. Pattanaik, Chapter 6, pp. 91–110, Springer-Verlag, Berlin.

Gao, J. and Gijbels, I. (2008). "Bandwidth selection in nonparametric kernel testing," *Journal of the American Statistical Association* **103**(484), 1584–1594.

Ghosal, S., Sen, A., and van der Vaart, A. W. (2000). "Testing monotonicity of regression," *The Annals of Statistics* **28**(4), 1054–1082.

Gijbels, I., Omelka, M., and Sznajder, D. (2010). "Positive quadrant dependence tests for copulas," *Canadian Journal of Statistics* **38**(4), 555–581.

Gijbels, I. and Sznajder, D. (2013). "Positive quadrant dependence testing and constrained copula estimation," *Canadian Journal of Statistics* **41**(1), 36–64.

Giné, E., Mason, D. M., and Zaitsev, A. Y. (2003). "The L_1-norm density estimator process," *Annals of Probability* **31**(2), 719–768.

Gini, C. (1916). "Il concetto di 'transvariazione' e le sue prime applicazioni," *Giornale degli Economisti e Rivista di Statistica* **52**(1), 13–43.

Gini, C. (1959). *Transvariazione*, Libreria Goliardica, Roma.

Girma, S., Görg, H., and Strobl, E. (2004). "Exports, international investment, and plant performance: Evidence from a non-parametric test," *Economics Letters* **83**(3), 317–324.

Girma, S., Kneller, R., and Pisu, M. (2005). "Exports versus FDI: An empirical test," *Review of World Economics* **141**(2), 193–218.

Goldie, C. M. (1977). "Convergence theorems for empirical Lorenz curves and their inverses," *Advances in Applied Probability* **9**(4), 765–791.

Gollier, C. (1995). "The comparative statics of changes in risk revisited," *Journal of Economic Theory* **66**(2), 522–535.

Gonzalo, J. and Olmo, J. (2014). "Conditional stochastic dominance tests in dynamic settings," *International Economic Review* **55**(3), 819–838.

Goodman, A. (1967). *Modern Calculus with Analytic Geometry*, MacMillan, New York.

Green, J. R., Lau, L. J., and Polemarchakis, H. M. (1978). "A theorem on the identifiability of the von Neumann–Morgenstern utility function from asset demands," *Economics Letters* **1**(3), 217–220.

Green, R. C. and Srivastava, S. (1986). "Expected utility maximization and demand behavior," *Journal of Economic Theory* **38**(2), 313–323.

Greene, W. (2012). *Econometric Analysis*, Seventh Edition, Prentice Hall, New Jersey.

Guerre, E., Perrigne, I., and Vuong, Q. (2009). "Nonparametric identification of risk aversion in first-price auctions under exclusion restrictions," *Econometrica* **77**(4), 1193–1227.

Guo, X. and Li, J. (2016). "Confidence band for expectation dependence with applications," *Insurance: Mathematics and Economics* **68**, 141–149.

Guo, Z. (2013). "A survey on stochastic dominance rules, tests, and applications in risk management and portfolio selection," in *Two Essays on Stochastic Dominance and One Essay on Correlation Stress Tests*, Doctoral dissertation, Chapter 1, University of Konstanz.

Hadar, J. and Russell, W. R. (1969). "Rules for ordering uncertain prospects," *The American Economic Review* **59**(1), 25–34.

Hall, P. and Heyde, C. (1980). *Martingale Limit Theory and Its Applications*, Academic Press, San Diego.

Hall, P. and Lahiri, S. N. (2008). "Estimation of distributions, moments and quantiles in deconvolution problems," *The Annals of Statistics* **36**(5), 2110–2134.

Hall, P. and Yatchew, A. (2005). "Unified approach to testing functional hypotheses in semiparametric contexts," *Journal of Econometrics* **127**(2), 225–252.

Hampel, F. R. (1974). "The influence curve and its role in robust estimation," *Journal of the American Statistical Association* **69**(346), 383–393.

Hanoch, G. and Levy, H. (1969). "The efficiency analysis of choices involving risk," *The Review of Economic Studies* **36**(3), 335–346.

Hansen, P. R. (2005). "A test for superior predictive ability," *Journal of Business & Economic Statistics* **23**(4), 365–380.

Hayashi, F. (2000). *Econometrics*, Princeton University Press, New Jersey.

Herrndorf, N. (1984). "A functional central limit theorem for weakly dependent sequences of random variables," *Annals of Probability* **12**(1), 141–153.

Heshmati, A. and Rudolf, R. (2014). "Income versus consumption inequality in Korea: Evaluating stochastic dominance rankings by various household attributes," *Asian Economic Journal* **28**(4), 413–436.

Hirano, K., Imbens, G. W., and Ridder, G. (2003). "Efficient estimation of average treatment effects using the estimated propensity score," *Econometrica* **71**(4), 1161–1189.

Hong, S. K., Lew, K. O., MacMinn, R., and Brockett, P. (2011). "Mossin's theorem given random initial wealth," *Journal of Risk and Insurance* **78**(2), 309–324.

Hopenhayn, H. A. and Prescott, E. C. (1992). "Stochastic monotonicity and stationary distributions for dynamic economies," *Econometrica* **60**(6), 1387–1406.

Horváth, L., Kokoszka, P., and Zitikis, R. (2006). "Testing for stochastic dominance using the weighted McFadden-type statistic," *Journal of Econometrics* **133**(1), 191–205.

Hsieh, F., Turnbull, B. W. (1996). "Nonparametric and semiparametric estimation of the receiver operating characteristic curve," *The Annals of Statistics* **24**(1), 25–40.

Ibarra, R. (2013). "A spatial dominance approach to evaluate the performance of stocks and bonds: Does the investment horizon matter?" *The Quarterly Review of Economics and Finance* **53**(4), 429–439.

Imbens, G. W. and Wooldridge, J. M. (2009). "Recent developments in the econometrics of program evaluation," *Journal of Economic Literature* **47**(1), 5–86.

Jin, S., Corradi, V., and Swanson, N. R. (2016). "Robust forecast comparison," *Econometric Theory* **32**(5), 1–46.

Jun, S. J., Lee, Y., and Shin, Y. (2016). "Treatment effects with unobserved heterogeneity: A set identification approach," *Journal of Business & Economic Statistics* **34**(2), 302–311.

Kahneman, D. and Tversky, A. (1979). "Prospect theory: An analysis of decision under risk," *Econometrica* **47**(2), 263–291.

Kassie, M., Pender, J., Yesuf, M., Kohlin, G., Bluffstone, R., and Mulugeta, E. (2008). "Estimating returns to soil conservation adoption in the Northern Ethiopian highlands," *Agricultural Economics* **38**(2), 213–232.

Kassie, M., Zikhali, P., Manjur, K., and Edwards, S. (2009). "Adoption of sustainable agriculture practices: Evidence from a semi-arid region of Ethiopia," *A United Nations Sustainable Development Journal* **33**(3), 189–198.

Kaur, A., Rao, B. P., and Singh, H. (1994). "Testing for second-order stochastic dominance of two distributions," *Econometric Theory* **10**(5), 849–866.

Kiefer, J. (1961). "On large deviations of the empiric d.f. of vector chance variables and a law of the iterated logarithm," *Pacific Journal of Mathematics* **11**(2), 649–660.

Kitamura, Y. (1997). "Empirical likelihood methods with weakly dependent processes," *The Annals of Statistics* **25**(5), 2084–2102.

Klecan, L., McFadden, R., and McFadden, D. (1991). "A robust test for stochastic dominance," Working paper, MIT.

Knight, J. and Satchell, S. (2008). "Testing for infinite order stochastic dominance with applications to finance, risk and income inequality," *Journal of Economics and Finance* **32**(1), 35–46.

Kodde, D. A. and Palm, F. C. (1986). "Wald criteria for jointly testing equality and inequality restrictions," *Econometrica* **54**(5), 1243–1248.

Koenker, R. (2005). *Quantile Regression*, Cambridge University Press, Cambridge.

Koenker, R. and Bassett Jr, G. (1978). "Regression quantiles," *Econometrica* **46**(1), 33–50.

Koenker, R. and Xiao, Z. (2002). "Inference on the quantile regression process," *Econometrica* **70**(4), 1583–1612.

Kudo, A. (1963). "A multivariate analogue of the one-sided test," *Biometrika* **50**(3/4), 403–418.

Kuosmanen, T. (2004). "Efficient diversification according to stochastic dominance criteria," *Management Science* **50**(10), 1390–1406.

Langyintuo, A. S., Yiridoe, E. K., Dogbe, W., and Lowenberg-Deboer, J. (2005). "Yield and income risk-efficiency analysis of alternative systems for rice production in the Guinea Savannah of Northern Ghana," *Agricultural Economics* **32**(2), 141–150.

Ledwina, T. (1994). "Data-driven version of Neyman's smooth test of fit," *Journal of the American Statistical Association* **89**(427), 1000–1005.

Ledwina, T. and Wyłupek, G. (2012*a*). "Nonparametric tests for stochastic ordering," *Test* **21**(4), 730–756.

Ledwina, T. and Wyłupek, G. (2012*b*). "Two-sample test against one-sided alternatives," *Scandinavian Journal of Statistics* **39**(2), 358–381.

Ledwina, T. and Wyłupek, G. (2013). "Tests for first-order stochastic dominance," Working paper, University of Wroclaw.

Ledwina, T. and Wyłupek, G. (2014). "Validation of positive quadrant dependence," *Insurance: Mathematics and Economics* **56**, 38–47.

Lee, S., Linton, O. B., and Whang, Y.-J. (2009). "Testing for stochastic monotonicity," *Econometrica* **77**(2), 585–602.

Lee, S., Song, K., and Whang, Y.-J. (2017). "Testing for a general class of functional inequalities," forthcoming in *Econometric Theory*, available at *https://arxiv.org/abs/1311.1595*.

Lee, S. and Whang, Y.-J. (2009). "Nonparametric tests of conditional treatment effects," Cowles Foundation Discussion Paper No. 1740, Yale University.

Lee, Y. J. and Wolfe, D. A. (1976). "A distribution-free test for stochastic ordering," *Journal of the American Statistical Association* **71**(355), 722–727.

Lefranc, A., Pistolesi, N., and Trannoy, A. (2008). "Inequality of opportunities vs. inequality of outcomes: Are Western societies all alike?" *Review of Income and Wealth* **54**(4), 513–546.

Lefranc, A., Pistolesi, N., and Trannoy, A. (2009). "Equality of opportunity and luck: Definitions and testable conditions, with an application to income in France," *Journal of Public Economics* **93**(11), 1189–1207.

Lehmann, E. and Romano, J. P. (2005). *Testing Statistical Hypotheses*, Third Edition, Springer.

Leshno, M. and Levy, H. (2002). "Preferred by "all" and preferred by "most" decision makers: Almost stochastic dominance," *Management Science* **48**(8), 1074–1085.

Levy, H. (1992). "Stochastic dominance and expected utility: Survey and analysis," *Management Science* **38**(4), 555–593.

Levy, H. (2016). *Stochastic Dominance: Investment Decision Making under Uncertainty*, Third Edition, Springer.

Levy, H. and Paroush, J. (1974). "Multi-period stochastic dominance," *Management Science* **21**(4), 428–435.

Levy, M. (2009). "Almost stochastic dominance and stocks for the long run," *European Journal of Operational Research* **194**(1), 250–257.

Levy, M. and Levy, H. (2002). "Prospect theory: Much ado about nothing?" *Management Science* **48**(10), 1334–1349.

Li, J. (2011). "The demand for a risky asset in the presence of a background risk," *Journal of Economic Theory* **146**(1), 372–391.

Li, S. and Linton, O. B. (2010). "Evaluating hedge fund performance: A stochastic dominance approach," in *Handbook of Portfolio Construction*, edited by J. B. G. Jr., Chapter 21, pp. 551–564, Springer.

Lien, G., Flaten, O., Korsaeth, A., Schumann, K. D., Richardson, J. W., Eltun, R., and Hardaker, B. J. (2006). "Comparison of risk in organic, integrated and conventional cropping systems in Eastern Norway," *Journal of Farm Management* **12**(7), 385–401.

Linton, O. B. (2005). "Nonparametric inference for unbalanced time series data," *Econometric Theory* **21**(1), 143–157.

Linton, O. B., Maasoumi, E., and Whang, Y.-J. (2005). "Consistent testing for stochastic dominance under general sampling schemes," *The Review of Economic Studies* **72**(3), 735–765.

Linton, O. B., Post, T., and Whang, Y.-J. (2014). "Testing for the stochastic dominance efficiency of a given portfolio," *The Econometrics Journal* **17**(2), S59–S74.

Linton, O. B., Seo, M., and Whang, Y.-J. (2017). "Testing stochastic dominance with many conditioning variables," Working paper, University of Cambridge.

Linton, O. B., Song, K., and Whang, Y.-J. (2010). "An improved bootstrap test of stochastic dominance," *Journal of Econometrics* **154**(2), 186–202.

Linton, O. B., Whang, Y.-J., and Yen, Y.-M. (2016). "A nonparametric test of a strong leverage hypothesis," *Journal of Econometrics* **194**(1), 153–186.

Linton, O. B. and Xiao, Z. (2017). "Quantile regression applications in finance," in *Handbook of Quantile Regression*, edited by R. Koenker, V. Chernozhukov, X. He, and L. Peng, Chapman & Hall.

Liontakis, A., Papadas, C. T., and Tzouramani, I. (2010). "Regional economic convergence in Greece: A stochastic dominance approach," Working paper, Agricultural University of Athens.

Lok, T. M. and Tabri, R. V. (2015). "An improved bootstrap test for restricted stochastic dominance," Working paper, University of Sydney.

Lu, J. and Perrigne, I. (2008). "Estimating risk aversion from ascending and sealed-bid auctions: The case of timber auction data," *Journal of Applied Econometrics* **23**(7), 871–896.

Maasoumi, E. (1999). "Multidimensional approaches to welfare analysis," in *Handbook of Income Inequality Measurement*, edited by J. Silber, Chapter 15, pp. 437–484, Kluwer Academic Publishers, Dordrecht and New York.

Maasoumi, E. (2001). "Parametric and nonparametric tests of limited domain and ordered hypotheses in economics," in *A Companion to Econometric Theory*, edited by B. H. Baltagi, Chapter 25, Wiley Blackwell Publisher, New Jersey.

Maasoumi, E. and Heshmati, A. (2000). "Stochastic dominance amongst Swedish income distributions," *Econometric Reviews* **19**(3), 287–320.

Maasoumi, E., Millimet, D. L., and Rangaprasad, V. (2005). "Class size and educational policy: Who benefits from smaller classes?" *Econometric Reviews* **24**(4), 333–368.

Maasoumi, E., Millimet, D. and Sarkar, D. (2009). "Who benefits from marriage?" *Oxford Bulletin of Economics and Statistics* **71**(1), 1–33.

Maasoumi, E., Su, B., and Heshmati, A. (2013). "Analysis of stochastic dominance ranking of Chinese income distributions by household attributes," Working paper, Korea University.

Maasoumi, E. and Wang, L. (2018). "The gender gap between earnings distributions," forthcoming in *Journal of Political Economy*.

Madden, D. (2012). "A profile of obesity in Ireland, 2002–2007," *Journal of the Royal Statistical Society* **175**(4), 893–914.

Mahoney, P. R., Olson, K. D., Porter, P. M., Huggins, D. R., Perillo, C. A., and Crookston, R. K. (2004). "Profitability of organic cropping systems in Southwestern Minnesota," *Renewable Agriculture and Food Systems* **19**(1), 35–46.

Maier, M. (2011). "Tests for distributional treatment effects under unconfoundedness," *Economics Letters* **110**(1), 49–51.

Mari, D. D. and Kotz, S. (2001). *Correlation and Dependence*, World Scientific.

McCaig, B. and Yatchew, A. (2007). "International welfare comparisons and non-parametric testing of multivariate stochastic dominance," *Journal of Applied Econometrics* **22**(5), 951–969.

McFadden, D. (1989). "Testing for stochastic dominance," in *Studies in the Economics of Uncertainty*, edited by T. B. Fomby and T. K. Seo, Chapter 7, pp. 113–134, Springer.

Melitz, M., Helpman, E., and Yeaple, S. (2004). "Export versus FDI with heterogeneous firms," *The American Economic Review* **94**, 300–316.

Millimet, D. L. and Wang, L. (2006). "A distributional analysis of the gender earnings gap in urban China," *The BE Journal of Economic Analysis & Policy* **5**(1), 1–50.

Minicozzi, A. L. (2003). "Estimation of sons' intergenerational earnings mobility in the presence of censoring," *Journal of Applied Econometrics* **18**(3), 291–314.

Moon, H. R. and Schorfheide, F. (2012). "Bayesian and frequentist inference in partially identified models," *Econometrica* **80**(2), 755–782.

Mosler, K. and Scarsini, M. (1993). *Stochastic Orders and Applications: A Classified Bibliography*, Springer-Verlag.

Nayak, T. K. and Gastwirth, J. L. (1989). "The use of diversity analysis to assess the relative influence of factors affecting the income distribution," *Journal of Business & Economic Statistics* **7**(4), 453–460.

Neumann, M. H. (1998). "Strong approximation of density estimators from weakly dependent observations by density estimators from independent observations," *The Annals of Statistics* **26**(5), 2014–2048.

Neumeyer, N. (2009). "Smooth residual bootstrap for empirical processes of non-parametric regression residuals," *Scandinavian Journal of Statistics* **36**(2), 204–228.

Newey, W. K. and West, K. (1987). "A simple positive definite, heteroscedasticity and autocorrelation consistent covariance matrix estimator," *Econometrica* **55**, 703–708.

Neyman, J. (1937). "Smooth test for goodness of fit," *Scandinavian Actuarial Journal* **1937**(3–4), 149–199.

Ng, P., Wong, W.-K., and Xiao, Z. (2017). "Stochastic dominance via quantile regression with applications to investigate arbitrage opportunity and market efficiency," *European Journal of Operational Research* **261**(2), 666–678.

Nishiyama, Y. (2011). "Impossibility of weak convergence of kernel density estimators to a non-degenerate law in $L_2(\mathbb{R}^d)$," *Journal of Nonparametric Statistics* **23**(1), 129–135.

Owen, A. B. (1988). "Empirical likelihood ratio confidence intervals for a single functional," *Biometrika* **75**(2), 237–249.

Pak, T.-Y., Ferreira, S., and Colson, G. (2016). "Measuring and tracking obesity inequality in the United States: Evidence from NHANES, 1971–2014," *Population Health Metrics* **14**(1), 12.

Pakes, A. (1986). "Patents as options: Some estimates of the value of holding European patent stocks," *Econometrica* **54**(4), 755–784.

Park, J. Y. (2005). "The spatial analysis of time series," Working paper, Rice University.

Parker, T. (2015). "Inference for stochastic dominance using large deviations asymptotics," Working paper, University of Waterloo.

Parzen, E. (1962). "On estimation of a probability density function and mode," *The Annals of Mathematical Statistics* **33**(3), 1065–1076.

Perlman, M. D. (1969). "One-sided testing problems in multivariate analysis," *The Annals of Mathematical Statistics* **40**(2), 549–567.

Pesendorfer, M. (2000). "A study of collusion in first-price auctions," *The Review of Economic Studies* **67**(3), 381–411.

Pinar, M., Stengos, T., and Topaloglou, N. (2013). "Measuring human development: A stochastic dominance approach," *Journal of Economic Growth* **18**(1), 69–108.

Pinar, M., Stengos, T., and Yazgan, M. E. (2012). "Is there an optimal forecast combination? A stochastic dominance approach to the forecasting combination puzzle," Working paper, University of Guelph and Fondazione Eni Enrico Mattei.

Politis, D. N. and Romano, J. P. (1994*a*). "Large sample confidence regions based on subsamples under minimal assumptions," *The Annals of Statistics* **22**(4), 2031–2050.

Politis, D. N. and Romano, J. P. (1994*b*). "The stationary bootstrap," *Journal of the American Statistical Association* **89**(428), 1303–1313.

Politis, D. N., Romano, J. P., and Wolf, M. (1999). *Subsampling*, Springer, New York.

Post, T. (2003). "Empirical tests for stochastic dominance efficiency," *The Journal of Finance* **58**(5), 1905–1932.

Post, T. (2016*a*). "Empirical tests for stochastic dominance optimality," *Review of Finance* **21**(2), 793–810.

Post, T. (2016*b*). "Standard stochastic dominance," *European Journal of Operational Research* **248**(3), 1009–1020.

Post, T. and Potí, V. (2017). "Portfolio analysis using stochastic dominance, relative entropy and empirical likelihood," *Management Science* **63**(1), 153–165.

Post, T. and van Vliet, P. (2006). "Downside risk and asset pricing," *Journal of Banking & Finance* **30**(3), 823–849.

Post, T. and Versijp, P. (2007). "Multivariate tests for stochastic dominance efficiency of a given portfolio," *Journal of Financial and Quantitative Analysis* **42**(2), 489–515.

Powell, J. L. (1984). "Least absolute deviations estimation for the censored regression model," *Journal of Econometrics* **25**(3), 303–325.

Powell, J. L. (1986). "Censored regression quantiles," *Journal of Econometrics* **32**(1), 143–155.

Pratt, J. W. and Zeckhauser, R. J. (1987). "Proper risk aversion," *Econometrica* **55**(1), 143–154.

Qu, Z. and Yoon, J. (2015). "Nonparametric estimation and inference on conditional quantile processes," *Journal of Econometrics* **185**(1), 1–19.

Rao, C. and Zhao, L. (1995). "Convergence theorems for empirical cumulative quantile regression functions," *Mathematical Methods of Statistics* **4**(3), 359–359.

Rao, R. C. (1973). *Linear Statistical Inference and Its Applications*, Wiley, New York.

Ribera, L. A., Hons, F., and Richardson, J. W. (2004). "An economic comparison between conventional and no-tillage farming systems in Burleson County, Texas," *Agronomy Journal* **96**(2), 415–424.

Robertson, T. and Wright, F. (1981). "Likelihood ratio tests for and against a stochastic ordering between multinomial populations," *The Annals of Statistics* **9**(6), 1248–1257.

Robertson, T., Wright, F., and Dykstra, R. (1988). *Order Restricted Statistical Inference*, Wiley, New York.

Roosen, J. and Hennessy, D. A. (2012). "Testing for the monotone likelihood ratio assumption," *Journal of Business & Economic Statistics* **22**(3), 358–366.

Ross, S. (1996). *Stochastic Processes*, Wiley, New York.

Rothe, C. (2010). "Nonparametric estimation of distributional policy effects," *Journal of Econometrics* **155**(1), 56–70.

Rothe, C. (2012). "Partial distributional policy effects," *Econometrica* **80**(5), 2269–2301.

Rothschild, M. and Stiglitz, J. E. (1970). "Increasing risk: I. A definition," *Journal of Economic Theory* **2**(3), 225–243.

Ruymgaart, F. H. (1998). "A note on weak convergence of density estimators in Hilbert spaces," *Statistics* **30**(4), 331–343.

Sahn, D. E. (2009). "Weights on the rise: Where and for whom?" *Journal of Economic Inequality* **7**(4), 351–370.

Scaillet, O. (2005). "A Kolmogorov–Smirnov-type test for positive quadrant dependence," *Canadian Journal of Statistics* **33**(3), 415–427.

Scaillet, O. and Topaloglou, N. (2010). "Testing for stochastic dominance efficiency," *Journal of Business & Economic Statistics* **28**(1), 169–180.

Scarsini, M. (1988). "Multivariate stochastic dominance with fixed dependence structure," *Operations Research Letters* **7**(5), 237–240.

Schechtman, E., Shelef, A., Yitzhaki, S., and Zitikis, R. (2008). "Testing hypotheses about absolute concentration curves and marginal conditional stochastic dominance," *Econometric Theory* **24**(4), 1044–1062.

Schmid, F. and Trede, M. (1996). "Testing for first-order stochastic dominance: A new distribution-free test," *The Statistician* **45**(3), 371–380.

Schmid, F. and Trede, M. (1998). "A Kolmogorov-type test for second-order stochastic dominance," *Statistics & Probability Letters* **37**(2), 183–193.

Schwarz, G. (1978). "Estimating the dimension of a model," *The Annals of Statistics* **6**(2), 461–464.

Scott, R. C. and Horvath, P. A. (1980). "On the direction of preference for moments of higher order than the variance," *The Journal of Finance* **35**(4), 915–919.

Seo, J. (2016). "Tests of stochastic monotonicity with improved size and power properties," Working paper, National University of Singapore.

Seyhun, H. N. (1993). "Can omitted risk factors explain the january effect? A stochastic dominance approach," *Journal of Financial and Quantitative Analysis* **28**(02), 195–212.

Shaked, M. and Shanthikumar, J. G. (1994). *Stochastic Orders and Their Applications*, Academic Press.

Shalit, H. and Yitzhaki, S. (1994). "Marginal conditional stochastic dominance," *Management Science* **40**(5), 670–684.

Shapiro, A. (1991). "Asymptotic analysis of stochastic programs," *Annals of Operations Research* **30**(1), 169–186.

Sharpe, W. F. (1992). "Asset allocation: Management style and performance measurement," *The Journal of Portfolio Management* **18**(2), 7–19.

Shen, S. (2017). "Estimation and inference of distributional partial effects: Theory and application," forthcoming in *Journal of Business & Economic Statistics*.

Shorrocks, A. F. (1983). "Ranking income distributions," *Economica* **50**(197), 3–17.

Shorrocks, A. F. and Foster, J. E. (1987). "Transfer sensitive inequality measures," *The Review of Economic Studies* **54**(3), 485–497.

Sklar, M. (1959). "Fonctions de repartition an dimensions et leurs marges," *Publications de l'Institut de statistique de l'Université de Paris* **8**, 229–231.

Skoufias, E. and Di Maro, V. (2008). "Conditional cash transfers, adult work incentives, and poverty," *The Journal of Development Studies* **44**(7), 935–960.

Smith, E. G., Clapperton, M. J., and Blackshaw, R. E. (2004). "Profitability and risk of organic production systems in the Northern Great Plains," *Renewable Agriculture and Food Systems* **19**(3), 152–158.

Solon, G. (1992). "Intergenerational income mobility in the United States," *The American Economic Review* **82**(3), 393–408.

Sriboonchita, S., Wong, W. -K., Dhompongsa, S., and Hung, T. N. (2010). *Stochastic Dominance and Applications to Finance, Risk and Economics*, CRC Press.

Stengos, T. and Thompson, B. S. (2012). "Testing for bivariate stochastic dominance using inequality restrictions," *Economics Letters* **115**(1), 60–62.

Stock, J. H. (1991). "Nonparametric policy analysis: An application to estimating hazardous waste cleanup benefits," in *Nonparametric and Semiparametric Methods in Econometrics and Statistics*, edited by J. P. William, A. Barnett, and G. Tauchen, Chapter 3, pp. 77–98, Cambridge University Press.

Stokey, N. L. (1989). *Recursive Methods in Economic Dynamics*, Harvard University Press.

Stoline, M. R. and Ury, H. K. (1979). "Tables of the studentized maximum modulus distribution and an application to multiple comparisons among means," *Technometrics* **21**(1), 87–93.

Stupfler, G. (2014). "On the weak convergence of kernel density estimators in L^p spaces," *Journal of Nonparametric Statistics* **26**(4), 721–735.

Tabri, T. V. (2010). "A consistent test for infinite order stochastic dominance," Working paper, University of Sydney.

Tesfatsion, L. (1976). "Stochastic dominance and the maximization of expected utility," *The Review of Economic Studies* **43**(2), 301–315.

Thistle, P. D. (1989). "Ranking distributions with generalized Lorenz curves," *Southern Economic Journal* **56**(1), 1–12.

Thistle, P. D. (1993). "Negative moments, risk aversion, and stochastic dominance," *Journal of Financial and Quantitative Analysis* **28**(2), 301–311.

Tibshirani, R. (1996). "Regression shrinkage and selection via the lasso," *Journal of the Royal Statistical Society* **58**(1), 267–288.

Tong, Y. (1990). *The Multivariate Normal Distribution*, Springer-Verlag.

Tzeng, L. Y., Huang, R. J., and Shih, P.-T. (2013). "Revisiting almost second-degree stochastic dominance," *Management Science* **59**(5), 1250–1254.

Valenzuela, M., Lean, H. H., and Athanasopoulos, G. (2014). "Economic inequality in Australia between 1983 and 2010: A stochastic dominance analysis," *Economic Record* **90**(288), 49–62.

van der Vaart, A. W. (1998). *Asymptotic Statistics*, Cambridge University Press.

van der Vaart, A. W. and Wellner, J. A. (1996). *Weak Convergence and Empirical Processes*, Springer, New York.

Varian, H. R. (1983). "Non-parametric tests of consumer behaviour," *The Review of Economic Studies* **50**(1), 99–110.

Wagner, J. (2006). "Exports, foreign direct investment, and productivity: Evidence from German firm level data," *Applied Economics Letters* **13**(6), 347–349.

Wang, Y. (1996). "A likelihood ratio test against stochastic ordering in several populations," *Journal of the American Statistical Association* **91**(436), 1676–1683.

Welch, I. and Goyal, A. (2008). "A comprehensive look at the empirical performance of equity premium prediction," *Review of Financial Studies* **21**(4), 1455–1508.

White, H. (1983). *Asymptotic Theory for Econometricians*, Academic Press, Orlando.

Whitmore, G. A. (1970). "Third-degree stochastic dominance," *The American Economic Review* **60**(3), 457–459.

Whitmore, G. A. and Findlay, M. C. (1978). *Stochastic Dominance: An Approach to Decision-Making under Risk*, Lexington Books.

Wolak, F. A. (1987). "An exact test for multiple inequality and equality constraints in the linear regression model," *Journal of the American Statistical Association* **82**(399), 782–793.

Wolak, F. A. (1989). "Local and global testing of linear and nonlinear inequality constraints in nonlinear econometric models," *Econometric Theory* **5**(01), 1–35.

Wolak, F. A. (1991). "The local nature of hypothesis tests involving inequality constraints in nonlinear models," *Econometrica* **59**(4), 981–995.

Wolfstetter, E. (1999). *Topics in Microeconomics: Industrial Organization, Auctions, and Incentives*, Cambridge University Press.

Wooldridge, J. M. (2005). "Fixed-effects and related estimators for correlated random-coefficient and treatment-effect panel data models," *The Review of Economics and Statistics* **87**(2), 385–390.

Wright, R. (1987). "Expectation dependence of random variables, with an application in portfolio theory," *Theory and Decision* **22**(2), 111–124.

Yalonetzky, G. (2013). "Stochastic dominance with ordinal variables: Conditions and a test," *Econometric Reviews* **32**(1), 126–163.

Yalonetzky, G. (2014). "Conditions for the most robust multidimensional poverty comparisons using counting measures and ordinal variables," *Social Choice and Welfare* **43**(4), 773–807.

Zarco, I. A., Pérez, C. G., and Alaiz, M. P. (2007). "Convergence among the Spanish regions: An inference-based stochastic dominance approach," Working paper, Instituto Nacional de Estadística.

Zheng, B., Formby, J. P., Smith, W. J., and Chow, V. K. (2000). "Inequality orderings, normalized stochastic dominance, and statistical inference," *Journal of Business & Economic Statistics* **18**(4), 479–488.

Zhu, X., Guo, X., Lin, L., and Zhu, L. (2016). "Testing for positive expectation dependence," *Annals of the Institute of Statistical Mathematics* **68**(1), 135–153.

Index

Printed in the United States
by Baker & Taylor Publisher Services